The Feminist Reference Desk

This book is number eight in the Series on Gender and Sexuality in Information Studies, Emily Drabinski, series editor.

Also in the series:

Queer Library Alliance: Global Reflections and Imaginings
edited by Rae-Anne Montague and Lucas McKeever

Queers Online: LGBT Digital Practices in Libraries, Archives, and Museums
edited by Rachel Wexelbaum

Ephemeral Material: Queering the Archive
by Alana Kumbier

Feminist and Queer Information Studies Reader
edited by Rebecca Dean and Patrick Keilty

Feminist Pedagogy for Library Instruction
by Maria Accardi

Make Your Own History: Documenting Feminist and Queer Activism in the 21st Century
edited by Lyz Bly and Kelly Wooten

Out Behind the Desk: Workplace Issues for LGBTQ Librarians
edited by Tracy Nectoux

The Feminist Reference Desk:

Concepts, Critiques, and Conversations

Edited by
Maria T. Accardi

Library Juice Press
Sacramento, California

Copyright respective authors, 2017

Published by Library Juice Press in 2017

Library Juice Press
PO Box 188784
Sacramento, CA 95818

http://libraryjuicepress.com

This book is printed on acid-free, sustainably-sourced paper.

Library of Congress Cataloging-in-Publication Data

Names: Accardi, Maria T., editor.
Title: The feminist reference desk : concepts, critiques, and conversations / edited by Maria T. Accardi.
Description: Sacramento, California : Library Juice Press, 2017. | Series: Gender and sexuality in information studies ; number 8 | Includes bibliographical references and index.
Identifiers: LCCN 2017030856 | ISBN 9781634000185 (acid-free paper)
Subjects: LCSH: Reference services (Libraries)--Philosophy. | Academic libraries--Reference services--Philosophy. | Research--Methodology--Study and teaching. | Information literacy--Study and teaching. | Librarians--Professional ethics. | Feminist ethics. | Critical pedagogy. | Feminism and higher education.
Classification: LCC Z711 .F46 2017 | DDC 025.5/2--dc23
LC record available at https://lccn.loc.gov/2017030856

This book is dedicated to Constance
and to the memory of Mama

Grinstead Girls Forever

Table of Contents

Acknowledgements ix

Introduction 1

Prelude

Female Articulation and the Librarian (*Or, So Hard to Say*)
Michelle Reale 15

Part I – Emotional Work and Ethics of Care

Behavioral Expectations for the Mommy Librarian:
The Successful Reference Transaction as Emotional Labor
Celia Emmelhainz, Erin Pappas, and Maura Seale 27

"Nothing More than a Gear in your Car:"
Neutrality and Feminist Reference in the Academic Library
Nina Clements 47

Purposeful and Productive Care: The Feminist Ethic of Care
and the Reference Desk
Sara Howard 61

Feminist Reference Services: Transforming Relationships
through an Ethic of Care
Sharon Ladenson 73

A Woman's Work is Never Done: Reference outside the Library
Kelly McElroy 85

Part II – Ways of Doing and Rethinking the Work

Seeing Writing Center Practices through a Feminist Lens &
Applying the Lessons Learned to Reference Desk Practice
Dory Cochran 105

Margaret Fuller's Legacy Interpreted for the Postmodern Library
Mellissa J. Hinton 119

Proceed With Care: Reviewing Reference Services Through The Feminist Lens
Elizabeth Hoppe and Karen Jung 137

Feminist Pedagogy and Special Collections Reference: Shifting the Balance
Melanie J. Meyers 161

Filling in the Gaps: Using Zines to Amplify the Voices
of People Who Are Silenced in Academic Research
Dawn Stahura 175

Information of My Own: Peer Reference and Feminist Pedagogy
Lauren Wallis 189

Social Justice in the Stacks: Opening the Borders of Feminism in Libraries
Gina Watts 205

PART III: INTERSECTIONAL AND COLLABORATIVE WORK

Intersectionality at the Reference Desk: Lived Experiences of
Women of Color Librarians
Rose L. Chou and Annie Pho 225

Reference and Beyond: Aspiring Librarians and Intersectional
Feminist Strategies
*Nicole A. Cooke, Jennifer Margolis Jacobs, Katrina Spencer,
Chloe Collins, and Rebekah Loyd* 253

Feminist Pedagogy and the Critical Catalog
Katherine Crowe and Erin Elzi 269

Feminist LibGuides: Towards Inclusive Practices in Guide Creation,
Use, and Reference Interactions
Amanda Meeks 293

Exploring a Feminist Disability Studies Reference Desk
Brian A. Sullivan and Malia Willey 313

LIS Graduate Student Workers, Feminist Pedagogy,
and the Reference Desk: Praxis and a Narrative
Raina Bloom 321

Feminist Pedagogy and the Reference Desk: A Conversation
Jeremy McGinniss and Angela Pashia 343

POSTLUDE

The Creature Questions its Reflection: Lyrical Feminist Explorations of
Reference Desk Interactions
Corinne Gilroy and Alexandrina Hanam 367

Contributor Biographies 385

Index 394

Acknowledgements

I have so many people to thank for making this book possible. The prevailing theme here is my good fortune, which humbles me immensely.

First, I have to thank the contributors to this volume for sharing their words and ideas with the world. There would be no book without you. Your voices are vital to the continuing conversation about feminism and the academic library. I am also very grateful for your patience with me during my many delays with this project. I am thankful and honored that I got to work with all of you.

Emily Drabinski remains the best editor ever and I am so lucky to get to work with her. I had no idea that staring at the back of her head in our shared office at Sarah Lawrence College in 2006 would turn into such a rich, fruitful, and meaningful friendship and collaboration. Thanks to Emily for her kindness, wisdom, patience, humor, and for encouraging me to respond to a certain match.com message when we were ALA roomies in Anaheim in the summer of 2008.

Thank you to Rory Litwin for creating a space where a book like this can exist. Working with Library Juice Press has been perhaps one of the greatest strokes of luck of my career.

Tessa Withorn played an important role in the life of this book. She served as an editorial assistant during her library instruction practicum with me in the summer of 2016, and her keen insights helped usher this book through the early editing stages. I am so lucky to have had the chance to work with her.

I am grateful to Marty Rosen for giving me the time and space to pursue this project. Thank you for showing me how it is possible to be a real person who works, and how that work can sustain life outside of work, and how that life outside of work is really the most important thing.

Thanks to Matt Gilbert for empowering me to ask for what I need, to accept help when offered, and to trust my own wisdom and insights. These were crucial ingredients that enabled me to not just finish this book, but also prioritize my mental health during the process. This is the real work.

Thanks to Erin Kate Ryan, whose continued presence in my life sustains and feeds me, and who serves as an example of and inspiration for how to successfully pursue a life of meaning and purpose through creativity, art, and social justice.

Thanks to Amanda Folk, my library school bestie, who has enriched my life in innumerable ways through her friendship, encouragement, and support.

I am thankful for Emily Stenberg, whose writing companionship helped me complete my first book, and whose continued friendship is perhaps the best thing I got out of ALA Emerging Leaders 2009.

My poetry club friends—Laura Cullinane, Glenn Roosevelt, and Terry Schuhmann—help me remember that both art and friendship are essential to the creative process. I am so grateful for their camaraderie and support. It is always better to travel with friends.

Thanks to Donna Witek for helping me to see the intersections of spirituality and pedagogy, and for the exciting possibilities of our future collaborations.

Thank you to Tony Mick, whose friendship formed the backbone of an intellectually formative time in my life, and who remains a source of cerebral sustenance and soul-enriching laughter.

My father, Phil Accardi, inspires me to be early for everything, to attack the problem, and to make a joke while doing it. I am grateful to be his daughter.

Constance Merritt is my beloved, my always and everything, my *sine qua non*, whose unwaveringly sweet and loving presence in my life is a gift I never expected or dreamed possible but I have the good fortune to experience nonetheless. I have always said she is as constant and persistent and resolute as her name, and these qualities nurture and support me in ways I can't even begin to name. We definitely have the best life ever. Look around, look around at how lucky we are to be alive right now.

I will always be grateful to my late mother-in-law and mother-in-love, Addie B. Merritt, for the unexpected joy we brought to each other, as well as the endless supply of Werther's Originals, which somehow keep appearing throughout our house months after her death. Her absence is palpable and incomprehensible, and I am grateful that I got to be a part of her life and to care for her as she transitioned from this world to the next. Mama always said, "Maria has a *good* job." She was right.

Finally, thanks to all of you for reading *Feminist Pedagogy for Library Instruction*, for engaging so thoughtfully and critically with my work, for helping me believe that this new book was worth pursuing and midwifing into the world, and for writing me beautiful and heartfelt messages that astonish me with their generosity. I can't believe how lucky I am.

Maria T. Accardi
Louisville, Kentucky
May 8, 2017

Introduction

I find myself finishing the manuscript of this book in a strange, stomach-churning time: the months following the inauguration of President Donald Trump. Each day since January 20, 2017 has produced a new horror that prompts disbelief, resistance, despair, or drives me to stick my head in the sand like some kind of freaked out ostrich in denial. As I write this, I see librarians entering the fray, pushing for a place in the conversation fighting the scourge of "fake news" and "alternative facts." I am one of those librarians. I am a librarian who has spent much of her career teaching students how to evaluate information, so I understand the impulse to connect our work to current events, provide a solution to a dangerous problem, and, in so doing, legitimize the entire premise of our pedagogy and practice.

But I am also a librarian who feels strongly that simple solutions, checklists, and teaching strategies are not enough to eradicate "fake news," because everything is much more complicated than that. I am a librarian who believes that the intersections of feminist pedagogy and the reference desk matter a whole lot, and that these intersections are a way of complicating the superficial and overly simplistic approaches our profession sometimes seems to embrace. As a feminist librarian, I fully understand and wholeheartedly value the power of consciousness-raising and what Paulo Freire called *unveiling of reality*: "Whereas banking education anesthetizes and inhibits creative power, problem-posing education involves a constant unveiling of reality. The former attempts to maintain the *submersion* of consciousness; the latter strives for the *emergence* of consciousness and *critical intervention* in reality."[1]

---

1 Paulo Freire, *Pedagogy of the Oppressed* (New York: Continuum, 2000), 81.

I believe that librarians have the power to help unveil reality. I have personally experienced and witnessed this happening in interactions with students at the reference desk, such as the time when a student searching for books about the Incas was surprised and disturbed to learn that Library of Congress Subject Headings centered the colonizer rather than the colonized. I'm also reminded of a time when I helped a student find primary sources related to Japanese internment camps during World War II. We were both horrified to find a 1942 *New York Times* article that claimed that the detainees *liked* the internment camp. But I don't believe these kinds of unveiling of reality moments are moments that one can reasonably expect to enact in every single one-shot instruction session or in a single reference desk encounter. At best, we can plant seeds.

I'm reminded of a song from *Hamilton*, another cultural reference from the time I'm writing this. In the scene in which Alexander Hamilton is killed in a duel, he contemplates his imminent demise before the bullet strikes: "Legacy. What is a legacy? It's planting trees in a garden you never get to see."[2] Having listened to the soundtrack roughly a thousand times, I was surprised to be struck anew by these lines when hearing them performed live in Chicago in January 2017. For the librarian who engages with students primarily through one-shot classes and one-shot[3] encounters, we don't always get to see the impact of our work. We're planting seeds in the hope they will sprout into a garden that we will more than likely never see, at least not face-to-face, but we have to believe that this garden matters, that those seeds will sprout, and that we can also find ways, whenever possible, to witness the garden flourish.

Garden metaphors have been making their way into my writing over the past few years, and I've learned that it's better to embrace the metaphors that want to be made known rather than fight them. Growth, life, green things, flowers, tomatoes, and even weeds give me new language to understand and describe how I try to approach the work I do at the reference desk from an intersectional feminist

---

2 Lin-Manuel Miranda and Jeremy McCarter, *Hamilton: The Revolution: Being the Complete Libretto of the Broadway Musical, with a True Account of Its Creation, and Concise Remarks on Hip-Hop, the Power of Stories, and the New America*. (New York: Grand Central Publishing, 2016), 273.

3 Please note that I am exercising major restraint in not turning this into another *Hamilton* reference.

point of view. This means that when I think about this book, I think of companion planting. My wife, who was once a certified Master Gardener, tells me that companion planting is an approach to gardening that understands that some plants have mutually beneficial relationships, so it makes sense to plant them next to each other. Marigolds and tomatoes, for example, are companion plants, because marigolds have some sort of quality that repels the pests that want to destroy the tomatoes. When I conceived of the idea of *The Feminist Reference Desk*, I thought of it as an extension of my 2013 book *Feminist Pedagogy for Library Instruction*, a companion volume that expands upon the ideas in my book and opens the conversation for other people to participate. Like the tomatoes and marigolds planted in the same bed, these books are helping the other exist, providing mutual support, helping the other to grow and take on new life. Companion planting also strikes me as a parallel to feminist pedagogy, in that it values collaboration, mutual respect and support, and sees each entity as valuable and necessary to the survival and thriving of others.

The story of this book contains two important intertwining tendrils that shaped how it came into existence and supported its growth and flourishing.

I

In January of 2015, my wife Constance and I bought a house in order to move her mother Addie in with us. In December 2015, Addie was diagnosed with cancer, and in the summer of 2016, while I was in the midst of reading and editing the first drafts of this book, she began in-home hospice care. It soon became clear that I could not pay attention to the hard work of the wonderful contributors to this volume while also navigating the heartbreak of caring for a dying family member. When I found myself weeping while listening to Willie Nelson in a coffee shop where I was trying to read chapters from this book, I knew that I was going to have to take leave from work at some point, and take a break from this book, while my wife Constance and I made the most of Addie's last months on earth. She died on September 1, 2016, in a hospital bed in our family room, where usually we watched *General Hospital* together, but instead now we watched her. Constance and I were with her when she died, as was our little cat, Gertie, who was best friends with her Grandma.

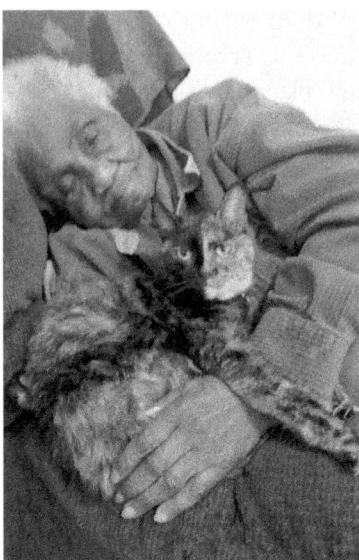

Gertie and Grandma, three days after her admission to hospice

Playing cards on Addie's 84th birthday, January 9, 2016

Caring for Addie, and witnessing her death, transformed me in ways that I barely understand now, eight months later as of this writing, and I will probably never completely untangle. One of the many, many important and challenging insights that emerges from the haze of grief is that work is work, and life is life, and sometimes those things overlap, and that's fine, but other times these things need distinct and definitive boundaries, and that's not just fine; it's necessary. In retrospect, insisting on those distinct and definitive boundaries between work-life and life-life feels like a feminist act to me, although I certainly didn't have the presence of mind to think that way at the time. I prioritized self-care, and caring for my family, and made use of the option of paid leave from my job instead of struggling to negotiate work-life and life-life in pursuit of the fictional impossibility of "work-life balance."

II

Also in the summer of 2016, I had the great pleasure and privilege of supervising an MLS practicum student at Indiana University, Tessa

Withorn[4]. She lived in Bloomington, a two-hour drive from my IU regional campus in New Albany, Indiana, and once a week she made the four-hour round trip to spend the day on campus with me, while completing the rest of her tasks remotely. I know Tessa says she learned valuable things during our summer together, but I contend that the experience was just as valuable and educational for me.

When we met for the first time to envision what she wanted her practicum experience to be like, I consciously employed feminist pedagogical strategies to collaboratively develop the goals while privileging her voice, desires, and needs. Based on my previous interactions with Tessa, I knew that she was interested in critical and feminist pedagogies, so planning her practicum seemed like an ideal way of modeling and enacting feminist approaches. There were requirements she needed to fulfill in order to earn academic credit, but I knew that these requirements didn't need to be limiting. There was plenty of room to shape this opportunity to meet her own needs and desires and goals. I tried from the start to use language that would empower her, not subordinate her. While filling out the necessary paperwork, Tessa asked what her title should be. Neither of us liked the word "intern," and instead we settled on "library instruction assistant," which accurately represented her role in supporting the library instruction program without the exploitative connotation that is often associated with "intern." While we brainstormed goals and projects and plans, I encouraged her to write the goals in terms of what *she* wanted to do, what *she* wanted to accomplish. I wanted her to know that she was not a source of cheap labor; she was a *person*, a talented individual full of potential, and I wanted to help facilitate her growth working alongside her. Technically, I had to be her supervisor and sign off on her timesheets and official academic paperwork. But in actual practical application, I tried to be the guide on the side, rather than the sage on the stage, that reference and instruction librarians often talk about and strive to be.

I also wanted Tessa to know that I didn't necessarily prioritize or privilege the traditional markers of what makes a "good" practicum. Yes, she had projects, and yes, there were going to be tangible deliverables, but the intangible was just as important to me as the facilitator of her summer experience. The affective dimension of learning was just as important, as was her intellectual growth, observations, and lived experience.

---

4 Tessa read this introduction and consented to my writing about her.

By the end of the summer, Tessa accomplished amazing, impressive work that made a substantial impact on the library instruction program I coordinate. For example, she designed and created high-quality information literacy modules in Canvas completely on her own, based on program outcomes and infused with critical pedagogical concepts. These modules address a previously unmet need for library instruction for students in 100% online courses. Tessa also served as an editorial assistant for this book. She read early drafts of a number of chapters and helped me provide editorial feedback, and her astute and insightful perspectives helped me see things in fresh and different ways. But in addition to her measurable accomplishments, the things that I put on her official evaluation and she can put on her CV, she also made a substantial impact on me as a librarian and a person. Beyond the actual literal work of her practicum, my work with Tessa was a real-life illustration of this work-life and life-life tension I was grappling with last summer. As Tessa noted on her reflective blog that summer, "The highlight of this weekend was definitely witnessing Maria snag tickets during her reference shift to *Hamilton* in Chicago. A feat to be admired, for sure. 'We're real people at the reference desk, right?' she joked."[5] It was a joke that was almost painful in how true it was. I was *such* a real person at the desk that summer, and it was fortunate for me that summer reference desk shifts are not that busy, because I was being undone by my home life. I had very little to give to the people who approached the desk, needing things from me. Public-facing work felt excruciating at times because my bandwidth was so low.

Due to Addie's rapidly declining condition, my presence at work during that summer was spotty at best. I was crushed to be absent on Tessa's last day of her practicum, where she presented the results of her work over the summer to the library faculty and staff. As Tessa noted on her blog, "On my final day at IUS, I'm sad to be spending it without Maria. She wasn't able to come in today for personal reasons, but that's okay. My time with Maria this summer has been personal. A feminist instructor strives to understand the student as a whole person, with autonomy and feelings about a million other things

---

5 Tessa Withorn, "Burnout and the Information Spectrum," Accessed May 5, 2017, https://acriticalsummer.wordpress.com/2016/06/24/burnout-the-information-spectrum/

going on in their head that affect how and what they learn."⁶ It is very interesting now, in retrospect, to see how my emphasis and insistence on seeing the whole lives of students when we encounter them in the classroom and at the reference desk suddenly felt very real when I applied that same logic to my own self. I am a whole person, with autonomy and feelings about a million other things going on in my head that affect how and what I learn, and did, and how I worked. Feminist pedagogy insists on seeing and honoring the full humanity of learners, and this includes the reference and instruction librarian as well. Valuing my own humanity, my own worth and value as a person who deserves to be in the world, seems to be something that I have to keep learning and re-learning. It is not a thing you learn and then you're done—hooray, you're a Whole Person, welcome to the rest of your life. No, it's more iterative, something you keep seeing anew in different eyes and from different perspectives.

ABOUT THE BOOK:

New eyes and different perspectives form the backbone of this book. The essays in this book provide exciting and diverse visions of feminist work at the reference desk. Feminist methodologies see and affirm that there are multiple ways of knowing and seeing the world outside of the realm and rigors of blind peer review, or IRB-approved studies, or numbers crunched in SPSS. This is not to suggest that those methods are *in*valid—in fact, some pieces in this book do make use of these important and useful and valuable methods, such as Rose Chou and Annie Pho's study of intersectionality and women of color librarians. But creating and disseminating and legitimizing knowledge does not need to be restricted to those methods, and creative writing and personal narrative are just as important to the story of this book as well. Thus, I deliberately tried to invite a variety of approaches and voices in this book in order to be consistent with feminist methodologies. The value of lived experience and personal narrative is reflected in multiple chapters in this book, such as Kelly McElroy's essay about the gendered nature of public-facing reference work.

---

6 Tessa Withorn, "Final Reflection," Accessed May 5, 2017,
    https://acriticalsummer.wordpress.com/2016/08/16/final-reflection/

And in the editorial process of shepherding this book from proposals and abstracts to the fully realized chapters you're about to read, I was very mindful of and intentional about using a feminist approach to working with the authors of these chapters. I tried to balance my role as editor in a way that also honored and respected the voices of the contributors. I wanted this process to be as collaborative as possible, while still acknowledging that I still had responsibilities as an editor. I wanted the writers to feel comfortable with my suggestions, and I was genuinely glad when both they responded positively to my suggestions, and equally as genuinely glad when they told me that they weren't comfortable with a particular suggestion. This kind of negotiation felt similar to the kind of negotiation that happens at the reference desk, where I strive to flatten the hierarchy that confers power and authority to me and subordinates the student.

When it was time to think about how all of the chapters fit together and should be organized, I struggled at first, because I saw interrelationships between everything. How could I possibly impose some sort of order on all of this? But I realized that I needed to step back and tried to see the how the tomatoes and marigolds fit together instead of seeing individual plants, and then a design made itself known to me. I saw how the chapters could be divided into three groups: 1) Emotional Work and Ethics of Care, 2) Ways of Doing and Rethinking the Work, and 3) Intersections and Collaborative Work.

The Emotional Work and Ethics of Care section contains chapters that examine, describe, and illustrate how a feminist ethic of care operates in and affects reference work, as well as how the gendered nature of emotional labor makes feminist work more complicated and fraught. The Ways of Doing and Rethinking the Work section contains chapters that outline feminist approaches to rethinking reference desk staffing and training, the accessibility of collections, and cataloging. Finally, Intersectional and Collaborative Work focuses on intersectionality, the interconnections of collaborative relationships, and how these intersections and collaborations might inform the education of future library professionals. Bookending these three sections are two creative works: a poem by Michelle Reale, and a work of lyric scholarship by Corinne Gilroy and Alexandrina Hanam. Both works are quite different in form but are equally innovative in the creative expression of how feminist pedagogy informs the interactions and relationships that happen at the reference desk.

This book is a tangible object that represents the intangible tensions between work-life and life-life that existed alongside my work in midwifing it into the world. I read and reread chapters and wrote emails and read and reread revisions. I watched eggplants ripen in my backyard, which I picked and cooked and ate, and I watched the okra plant climb to impossible heights, which I abandoned, because Addie loved okra but no longer had any appetite. I watched Tessa thrive. I watched Addie die. This book is the companion plant that gave me hope, something to look forward to, and enabled me to connect to work I love when everything else seemed bleak and hopeless.

Another thread that has been emerging in my work in recent years explores burnout in academic instruction and reference librarians—what it is, what it looks like, its origins, its ramifications. As I contemplate burnout, I find myself pulled away from the language of problems and solutions, just as I resist the simplistic checklists that seek to thwart "fake news," and instead I'm finding myself repeatedly drawn to this passage in the New Zealand version of the Anglican Daily Office: "Let us be filled with the presence of the great compassion towards ourselves and towards all living beings." I have this written on the back of an old catalog card and it's taped just below my computer monitor in my office. Our students deserve this great compassion. We, the librarians who teach them and learn alongside them, deserve this great compassion, the compassionate companion plant that enables us to thrive and empowers us to enact a vision for peace and social justice in our libraries, in our classrooms, and at our reference desks.

During this rich and difficult and generative time that provided the fertile soil that informed this book, I happened upon this passage from Wendell Berry's *Standing by Words*: "It may be that when we no longer know what to do we have come to our real work and that when we no longer know which way to go we have begun our real journey. The mind that is not baffled is not employed. The impeded stream is the one that sings."[7] The message of these words, for me, is that the stuck places can actually be productive places, places of growth and transformation, and when the path seems hazy or obscured by weeds and I'm not sure what to do or where to go next or even how I'm supposed to feel, this is an opportunity to embrace the uncertainty and growth that this stuck place promises. The intersection of feminist

---

7 Berry, Wendell, *Standing by Words: Essays* (San Francisco: North Point Press, 1983), 97.

work at the reference desk is one such stuck place, a place where we can grapple with approaching our work with a vision that ultimately wants to change the world, while knowing that we're doing this work in a culture and context that wants to see librarian-student interaction as a sterile transaction, a dehumanizing exchange of information. In the end, a brook cannot babble if there are no stones in it. The music, the beauty, the richness of our lives cannot happen if there are no obstacles, nothing to provide friction. Attempting to be explicit, overt, and visible about feminist work in the academic library in a culture that is hostile to feminism and social justice is a kind of friction that is simultaneously heartbreaking and life-giving. This babbling brook is a place for work-life and life-life to co-exist. Let's navigate this impeded stream together.

Bibliography

Berry, Wendell. *Standing by Words: Essays*. San Francisco: North Point Press, 1983.

Freire, Paulo. *Pedagogy of the Oppressed*. New York: Continuum, 2000.

Miranda, Lin-Manuel, and Jeremy McCarter. *Hamilton: The Revolution: Being the Complete Libretto of the Broadway Musical, with a True Account of Its Creation, and Concise Remarks on Hip-Hop, the Power of Stories, and the New America*. New York: Grand Central Publishing, 2016.

Withorn, Tessa. "A Critical Summer with Maria Accardi at IU Southeast Library." Accessed May 05, 2017. https://acriticalsummer.wordpress.com/.

Prelude

Female Articulation and the Librarian
(Or, So Hard to Say)

Michelle Reale

Tentative:
- Provisional or experimental
- Hesitant, uncertain, cautious.

Disarticulation:
- In medical terminology, disarticulation is the separation of two bones at their joint, either naturally by way of injury or by a surgeon during amputations.

Articulation:
- The act of putting into words an idea or feeling of a specific type.
- The state of being *join*ted (*italics mine*)

How it often begins:

Um, sorry, ah, I think, I'm not sure, I might have misunderstood, I know I should know this, I didn't look it up yet, I didn't know where to… I didn't understand.
    This will only take a minute, so sorry to bother you…

Tentative
    Anxious
Feeling at odds with

                     the need
          to only
articulate

as though getting ones information needs is as easy as a mechanism that trusts itself, like the elbow that can be counted on to bend itself to bring the glass to the mouth when thirsty, like the door that opens and shuts in just the right way at the appropriate time. But there has been a cut off, a severance—something is severed and the voice goes unheard beneath the
clamor of the brain loop that
persistently whispers:
you should know this.

Symmetrical:
- Balance is achieved by making all elements visual or equal on all sides

And behind the reference desk, I push my tortoise-shell glasses further up the bridge of what is perceived as my long and all- important nose. I am partially concealed behind my computer as a barricade to all reasonable approachability, but in a moment

I
    am
on
        my
    feet,

bridging the literal and figurative space between us.

***"Empowerment is only possible when there is a sense of mutuality."*[1]**

I roll a chair behind the desk, the great barrier between me and the one who "needs to find out." Sitting side by side, she pulls out numerous papers from a backpack laden with small political pins, and "plushies" on key chains. Her cheeks are a mottled red, forming a floral pattern.

---

1 Carolyn M. Shrewsbury, "What Is Feminist Pedagogy?" *Women's Studies Quarterly* 21, no. 3/4 (1993): 8–16.

I feel energy in her breathlessness, but I want to slow things down a bit, allow her to take her time to articulate her question.

Eventually...

But I don't even know enough to ask... and her voice trails off.

I modulate my tone, take off my glasses, place them beside me.
She begins to tell me what she doesn't know which, in her own words is
nearly everything.

I remind her to breathe. She does so, visibly. I do the same.

"...Change does not take place magically, but by the active exercise of agency, whether directed at ourselves or at structures"[2]

How easy it would be to grab the syllabus, interpret the assignment, and throw out a
few ideas to her,
like seed thrown to a
yard chicken....see what she grabs up
what she thinks she might be able
to handle, with the least amount of work
because she does not feel equal to the task.
And we sit. Until she figures it out.

"By focusing on empowerment, feminist pedagogy embodies a concept of power as energy, capacity and potential rather than as domination."

I keep quiet, I lean in a bit, wait for her to speak.

The shuffling of papers does not bother me, but she seems to feel she is giving herself away:
    the sloppy student;
    the slacker
the female soft-speaker—if she could even find the words.

---

2 Shrewsbury, 14.

Adrienne Rich urged us to 'claim an education'[3]
and I watch
as she attempts to begin,
pushing some power behind the effort.

Not knowing is a great way to begin, I tell her and that is where we start. We begin a conversation. No probing. No interrogation. No impatience as if I need to be anywhere but where I am at that very moment.

She had no one to talk to.
I feel like everyone 'gets' it—that I am the only one who doesn't have a clue. I tell her she definitely has a clue. She does not respond. Merely winces. But that reassurance rings hollow in my own ears. How can I convince her? We dance around the conversation and make an almost imperceptible transition
into the assignment that
       she has the merest,
most tenuous
       hold on.

"...change does not take place magically, but by the exercise of agency, whether directed at ourselves or at structures."[4]

Disarticulation—something disconnected becomes articulation
by leaving a
       space
    open
           being receptive.

She begins to write down some ideas and
her face is making the micro contortions that
signal thought(s) in process

She is not angry that I am not providing the "answers"
though she has, of yet, no questions.
She knows that I stand right by her

---

3 Adrienne Rich, "Claiming an Education," *Open Questions*, ed. Chris Anderson and Lex Runciman (New York: Bedford/St. Martin's, 2005), 608-611.

4 Shrewsbury, 14.

feeling not unlike a midwife standing watch at a long
and difficult birth.
But in fact (and more importantly)
      she is more than competent
                       in many ways
and she is about to find out.

Ideas are about to be born.

If proximity lends support
then that is the role I will play.
    I am beside her, waiting without expectation or hurry.

"By focusing on empowerment, feminist pedagogy embodies a concept of power as energy, capacity and potential rather than domination."[5]

A few databases into the process and a short trip to the
stacks, she nets a book ("the one I wanted was checked out")
a writes a few notes while I offer my two cents minus one.

"Empowering strategies allow students to find their own voices, to discover the power of authenticity"[6]

        Tell me what you found; what you are
writing
    down...

She opens her mouth, then closes it again.
Begins: *I have no idea if this is even right...*

I interject: *don't even worry about that now—-*
what you have here is a departure point!

And she begins to explain the connections she's made,
    how to continue
since she has already begun, she now proceeds
      in waves,
    in   choppy   waters
in a shaky boat but,

---

5 Ibid., 10.

6 Ibid., 11.

nonetheless...

If feminist pedagogy is based on communities, then the reference desk is our classroom, where we welcome learners from all communities to both
inquire and contribute,
       where the balance of power become those
                of the community
                in question.

"Theories of power are implicitly theories of community." [7]

Because thinking is hard and we often, in our excitement, desperately need to extricate ourselves from our breakthroughs,
she announces the
need
for food
    coffee.

"How long will you be here?" she asked.

Are you coming back?

Yeah, she says with a restrained curling of the corners of her mouth.

Her community of learners, a membership she simply does not understand (yet) that she fully belongs to, carries on around her.

"To be empowered is to be able to engage in significant learning." [8]

When we get out of the way, *but stay within reach*, offer suggestions rather than definitive proclamations, we can begin to see where our own thoughts take us.

    After a time, she returns, large coffee in hand.
I motion to the chair beside me. Turn the computer screen
      her way and
        slide
    the keyboard over to her.
              She will drive this car!

---

7 Ibid., 11.

8 Ibid., 10.

> *I don't want to think about getting articles yet.*
> *I need to process this out loud.*
> (articulates her needs, her process)

Go right ahead, I encourage her. (*Push, push!*)
You might want to write that down. (*Relax, now breathe…*)
Oh, good thought! I interject.

Okay. Finally! she says, slapping both hands on the knees of her skinny jeans. Exhaling like a weight has been lifted off her frail form.

I hear words that make me remember why I am a librarian:

" Okay. I think I got this.

I really do."

Reflection

In aligning critical and feminist pedagogical precepts with librarianship, I am able to work within my articulated value system—a value system that seeks not only to empower myself, but others as well. I see the teaching aspect of librarianship as one of both *witness* and *care*. It seems imperative to witness—to fully see and engage with each student and not only their informational needs, but who they are as people, researchers, and students. What might be holding them back? What narrative have they told themselves, or worse, been told about their ability to seek and learn, to ask questions? The care comes in when we allow the student a safe space for full articulation—an articulation that often struggles and is, paradoxically, at least not at first one that is not always "articulate." But in fact, we make the road by walking. On the part of the librarian it entails true listening, which in and of itself has the ability to empower. To be heard is to be empowered.

I have learned patience at the reference desk—to leave an open space and not rush to fill that space with all of *my* thoughts *or* "helpful" suggestions has not always been easy. This means not pushing the student before they are ready, but rather *facilitating* learning by leaving enough room for them to find their own way.

In a time when we have been pressured to "teach" all of the (proprietary) tools we have purchased at costs quite alarming, sacrificing thought and communicating in the formation of ideas first, before we put our anxious hands on the keyboard, enacting feminism at the reference desk can guide students into the (correct) thinking that all knowledge is process and it is okay not to know what, in fact, you do not know!

The empty space, as in a vessel meant to carry water, is perhaps the most valuable of all. What might be perceived as "lack" in another context, in fact, holds potential for great things. Hope and confidence in ourselves and who we are and what we can be, holds great promise. As librarians we are incredibly fortunate to be in a position where we watch and are able to positively influence and help to birth that transformation.

BIBLIOGRAPHY

Rich, Adrienne. "Claiming an Education." In *Open Questions*, edited by Chris Anderson and Lex Runciman. New York: Bedford/St. Martin's, 2005. 608-611.

Shrewsbury, Carolyn M. "What Is Feminist Pedagogy?" *Women's Studies Quarterly* 21, no. 3/4 (1993): 8–16.

Part I

Emotional Work and Ethics of Care

Behavioral Expectations for the Mommy Librarian: The Successful Reference Transaction as Emotional Labor

Celia Emmelhainz, Erin Pappas, and Maura Seale

> "Now girls, I want you to go out there and really *smile*. Your smile is your biggest *asset*. I want you to go out there and use it. Smile. *Really* smile. Really *lay it on*."[1]

> "While not every query will be of interest to the librarian, the librarian should embrace each patron's informational need and should be committed to providing the most effective assistance. Librarians who demonstrate a high level of interest in the inquiries of patrons will generate a higher level of satisfaction among users."[2]

Every librarian[3] who has worked with the public probably has stories about challenging patrons: the one who critiqued the librarian's typing skills, the one who asked if the librarian was pregnant (she was not), the aggressive patron, the know-it-all patron, the crying patron, the stalker patron. Each time, the librarian is expected to answer the

---

1 Delta Airlines Trainer, quoted in Arlie Russell Hochschild, *The Managed Heart: Commercialization of Human Feeling*. (Berkeley: University of California Press, 1983), 4. Emphasis in original.

2 "Guidelines for Behavioral Performance of Reference and Information Service Providers," Reference & User Services Association, 1996/2013, http://www.ala.org/rusa/resources/guidelines/guidelinesbehavioral.

3 Although everyone who works at a public service point may not technically be an MLIS-holding librarian, we follow the RUSA *Guidelines* and use "librarian" to refer to anyone who provides "reference and informational services directly to library users" (RUSA, *Guidelines*), and similarly note that this discussion is not limited to the reference desk, but applies to "any type of reference interaction" (RUSA, *Guidelines*).

patron's reference question to the best of her ability, and to do so with a smile, or with at least the bare minimum of civility.

In this chapter, we consider how reference librarians are explicitly taught to center their work on the performance of emotional labor through the Reference & User Services Association / RUSA's "Guidelines for Behavioral Performance of Reference and Information Service Providers" (hereafter *Guidelines*). Using a discourse analysis of the *Guidelines*, we uncover the expectation that librarians perform authentic emotional labor in reference interactions and highlight the ways in which such expectations are gendered. We begin with a qualitative content analysis of how often emotional labor is mentioned in the *Guidelines*, then move on to a close reading of these guidelines for librarian interactions with the public. As we show below, the *Guidelines* serve three distinct purposes: first, they act as a professional litmus test through which any employer may assess the outward performance of a reference librarian; second, they provide a set of aspirational standards for the ideal reference encounter; and finally, they set explicit expectations for professional behavioral labor that the librarian should, over time, internalize as her own authentic feelings.[4]

EMOTIONAL LABOR AND THE LIBRARY: LITERATURE REVIEW

The Managed Heart by Arlie Hochschild is the foundational work on emotional labor. In this key text, Hochschild contrasts an extensive qualitative study of (mostly female) flight attendants with a smaller study of bill collectors, framing the discussion around *emotional labor*, as when she argues that the flight attendant:

> [I]s also doing something more, something I define as *emotional labor*. This labor requires one to induce or suppress feeling in order to sustain the outward countenance that produces the proper state of mind in others–in this case, the sense of being cared for in a convivial and safe place. This kind of labor calls for a coordination of mind and

---

4 We use "she" as the pronoun for "librarian" as librarianship is unquestionably dominated by women. When we use "women," we include anyone who presents or identifies as a woman. We follow Judith Butler in understanding gender as fluid, constructed, and performative, rather than as binary and fixed. Judith Butler, *Gender Trouble: Feminism and the Subversion of Identity* (New York: Routledge, 1990).

feeling, and it sometimes draws on a source of self that we honor as deep and integral to our individuality.[5]

As Hochschild notes, the harnessing of emotion to evoke a certain state of feeling in another person may occur in private contexts as well.[6] Yet when compensated labor is involved, the tenor of emotional work changes. We adopt Hochschild's terminology here:

> I use the term *emotional labor* to mean the management of feeling to create a publicly observable facial and bodily display; emotional labor is sold for a wage and therefore has exchange value. I use the synonymous terms *emotion work* or *emotion management* to refer to these same acts done in a private context.[7]

Further research has considered the cognitive, emotional, and psychological effects of emotional labor in the service professions.[8] This literature on emotional labor can easily be applied to the work done by public service librarians.[9] Multiple scholars make the argument that

---

5 Hochschild, *The Managed Heart*, 6-7.

6 Hochschild, *The Managed Heart*. See also: Erving Goffman, *The Presentation of Self in Everyday Life* (New York: Anchor Books, 1959); Nicole Molé, *Labor Disorders in Neoliberal Italy: Mobbing, Well-Being, and the Workplace* (Bloomington: Indiana University Press, 2011); Andrea Muehlebach, "On Affective Labor in Post-Fordist Italy," *Cultural Anthropology* 26 no. 1 (2011): 59-82; Kathleen Stewart, *Ordinary Affects* (Durham, NC: Duke University Press, 2010).

7 Hochschild, *The Managed Heart*, 7. Emphasis in original.

8 Karla A. Erickson, *The Hungry Cowboy: Service and Community in a Neighborhood Restaurant*, (Jackson: University Press of Mississippi, 2009); Alicia Grandey, Su Chuen Foo, Markus Groth and Robyn E. Goodwin, "Free to Be You and Me: A Climate of Authenticity Alleviates Burnout from Emotional Labor," *Journal of Occupational Health Psychology* 17 no. 1 (2012): 1-14; Mary Ellen Guy and Meredith A. Newman, "Women's Jobs, Men's Jobs: Sex Segregation and Emotional Labor," *Public Administration Review* 64 no. 3 (May 2004): 289-298; Ute Hűlsheger and Anna F. Schewe, "On the Costs and Benefits of Emotional Labor: A Meta-Analysis of Three Decades of Research," *Journal of Occupational Health Psychology* 16 no. 3 (2011): 361-389; Sharon O'Dair, "Superservicable Subordinates, Universal Access, and Prestige-Driven Research," in *Over Ten Million Served: Gendered Service in Language and Literature Workplaces*, ed. Michelle A. Massé and Katie J. Hogan (Albany: SUNY Press, 2010); Amy Tyson, *The Wages of History: Emotional Labor on Public History's Front Lines* (Amherst: University of Massachusetts Press, 2013).

9 Celene Seymour, "Ethnographic Study of Information Literacy Librarians' Work Experience: A Report from Two States," in *Transforming Information Literacy Programs: Intersecting Frontiers of Self, Library Culture, and Campus Community*, ed. Carroll W. Wilkinson and Courtney Bruch (Chicago: Association of College and Research Libraries, 2015).

emotional labor is a key aspect of labor within the library,[10] whether this takes place in library instruction, at the circulation desk, or during the reference encounter.[11]

Although librarianship is predominantly female, the scholarly literature has yet to consider the role of gender in our expectations for emotional performance as librarians and in our experiences of emotional labor. Lisa Slonowski critiques immaterial labor, situating it within feminist, Marxist, post-Fordist, and post-Structuralist paradigms; in the context of higher education, the affective work performed by academic librarians easily falls within that sphere.[12] Miriam L. Matteson and Shelly S. Miller similarly recommend research into how gendered emotional labor is performed in librarianship, an especially important topic given that they report women experience more stress in undertaking emotional labor than men do.[13] From a service perspective, Nancy Fried Foster calls attention to the professional model of service that inheres in the *Guidelines,* as well as the internalized norms of full customer service in general.[14] Sherianne Schuler and Nathan Morgan, as well as Matteson

---

10 Kathryn Arbuckle, "Emotion and Knowledge: Partners in Library Service?" *Feliciter* 54, no. 5 (2008): 219-221; Miriam L. Matteson and Shelly S. Miller. "Emotional Labor in Librarianship: A Research Agenda," *Library and Information Science Research* 34 no. 3 (2012): 176-183; Miriam L. Matteson and Shelly S. Miller. "A Study of Emotional Labor in Librarianship," *Library & Information Science Research* 35 no.1 (January 2013): 54–62; Miriam L. Matteson and Shelly S. Miller. "What Library Managers Should Know about Emotional Labor," *Public Library Quarterly* 33 no. 2 (2014): 95-107; Miriam L. Matteson, Sharon Chittock, and David Mease, "In Their Own Words: Stories of Emotional Labor from the Library Workforce," *The Library Quarterly: Information, Community, Policy* 85 no. 1 (2015): 85–105; Yu-Ping Peng, "Buffering the Negative Effects of Surface Acting: The Moderating Role of Supervisor Support in Librarianship," *Journal Of Academic Librarianship* 41 no. 1 (January 2015): 37-46.

11 Heidi Julien and Shelagh K. Genuis, "Emotional Labor in Librarians' Instructional Work," *Journal of Documentation* 65 no. 6 (2009): 926-937; Chen Su-May Sheih, "A Survey of Circulation Librarians' Emotional Labor and Emotional Exhaustion: The Case of Difficult Patron Service in University Libraries," *Journal of Educational Media & Library Sciences* 50 no. 1 (Fall 2012): 5-39; Sherianne Shuler and Nathan Morgan, "Emotional Labor in the Academic Library: When Being Friendly Feels Like Work," *The Reference Librarian* 54 no. 2 (2013): 118-133.

12 Lisa Sloniowski, "Affective Labor, Resistance, and the Academic Librarian," *Library Trends* 64 no. 4 (Spring 2016): 645-666.

13 Matteson and Miller, "Emotional Labor in Librarianship: A Research Agenda."

14 Nancy Fried Foster, "The Mommy Model of Service," in *Studying Students: The Undergraduate Research Project at the University of Rochester,* ed. Nancy Fried Foster and Susan Gibbons (Chicago: Association of College and Research Libraries, 2007).

and Miller, specifically note the *Guidelines* as a place where the often underspecified practices which make up emotional labor are codified —yet do not analyze the gendered ideas embedded in them.[15] And to presage some practical or applied solutions for those who are now thoroughly depressed, Matteson and Miller suggest strategies of deep acting, reframing, and mindfulness to help librarians cope with the ongoing social expectations of emotional labor in our workplaces.[16]

Methods: Content Analysis and Close Reading

In thinking through the expectations of emotional labor in reference work, we became interested in how the *Guidelines* implicitly and explicitly codify emotional labor as a normal part of any reference interaction. Although the *Guidelines* set up a reference encounter as occurring free of context, circumstance, or qualification, these same guidelines locate the success of the interaction in the (female) librarian's successful performance of emotional labor. Our analysis of the *Guidelines* shows that personal and emotional labor is both expected and reproduced in each reference encounter, which is nominally framed as an abstract interaction between the librarian and a person seeking information. After our initial review and discussion of the *Guidelines*, we follow Jeffery L. Loo and Elizabeth A. Dupuis in coding emergent themes with *qualitative content analysis*,[17] using a spreadsheet to open code every guideline against a set of themes which emerged from the text as a whole (See figure 1).

By coding recurring themes in columns, as above, we could estimate the proportion of the *Guidelines* that reinforced expectations of emotional labor, as well as observe particular subsets of embodied or affective labor that are expected of librarians.

However, estimates of theme frequency do not engage deeply with the themes of the text; for this reason, we moved to a *close reading* of the text as a group. Each author drew on her experiences as a feminist,

---

15 Matteson and Miller, "Emotional Labor in Librarianship: A Research Agenda."; Shuler and Morgan, "Emotional Labor in the Academic Library: When Being Friendly Feels Like Work."

16 Matteson and Miller, "What Library Managers Should Know about Emotional Labor."

17 Jeffery L. Loo and Elizabeth A. Dupuis, "Organizational Learning for Library Enhancements: A Collaborative, Research-Driven Analysis of Academic Department Needs," *College & Research Libraries* 76 no. 5: (July 2015).

Number	Text from Guidelines	Approachable / Visible	Affirm, Comfort, Encourage	On their timing	Focus on them	Friendly / Bodily labor	Service Orientation
1.1.1	Is to be found in a **highly visible** physical or virtual location (the library, outreach locations, or the library website). **Proper signage** or notification that indicates the location, hours, and availability of in-person and remote assistance is available.	y		y			
1.1.2	Is poised and ready to engage patrons. The librarian is aware of the need to **stop all other activities** when a patron approaches and **focus attention** on the patron's needs.			y	y		
1.1.3	Acknowledges patrons by using a **friendly greeting** to initiate conversation.		y			y	
1.1.4	Acknowledges others waiting for service.						y
1.1.5	Employs a system of question triage to identify questions and service priorities.			y			y
1.2.1	Establishes an **approachable presence** by being **easily identifiable** in compliance with institutional and professional norms and policies.	y					
1.2.2	Acknowledges patrons by making initial eye contact, employing **open body language**, or using a friendly greeting to initiate conversation.					y	
1.2.3	Remains visible to patrons as much as possible.	y					
1.2.4	Identifies patrons needing or wanting help.				y		
1.2.5	Occasionally roves through the reference or public areas offering assistance. To rove successfully, the librarian:	y					y
1.2.5.1	Uses cues, verbal or nonverbal, to determine which patrons need help, and approaches patrons and offers assistance with lines such as:	y		y			
1.2.5.2	Gets the patron started on the initial steps of his/her search, then moves on to other patrons. Offers to provide more assistance if needed.						
1.2.5.3	Checks back on the patron's progress.		y	y			y

Fig. 1. *Qualitative content analysis of the RUSA Guidelines*

a member of the labor force, and a reference librarian to produce a more nuanced understanding of the social origin and performative impacts of the *Guidelines*. In combining a qualitative content analysis with the practices of close reading employed in the humanities, our methods draw together the literature on emotional labor in academia, the *Guidelines*, and our own embodied experience as humans who engage in reference work within a particular set of sociocultural circumstances.

Qualitative Content Analysis: Stepping into the Guidelines with Common Themes

Before examining each set of specific guidelines, we surveyed the themes most commonly emerging from the text as a whole. The *Guidelines* assign every introductory section and set of specific behavioral guidelines to one of five broad *categories of labor* (**visibility, showing interest, listening and inquiring, demonstrating search techniques,** and **follow-up**) expected of librarians engaging with patrons in person or online. We coded each paragraph separately, resulting in 60 blocks of text which were marked with either the presence or absence of themes of 1) broad-scale emotional labor, 2) meeting patron needs, 3) offering referrals or soliciting follow-up interactions, 4) orienting to service, 5) performing an embodied friendliness, 6) keeping full focus on others, 7) accommodating the patron's timing, 8) comforting and encouraging, and 9) being approachable. The chart below (Figure 2) summarizes how often a guideline met any of the emotional labor themes below, so that e.g. 32% of guidelines encouraged librarians to comfort and encourage patrons:

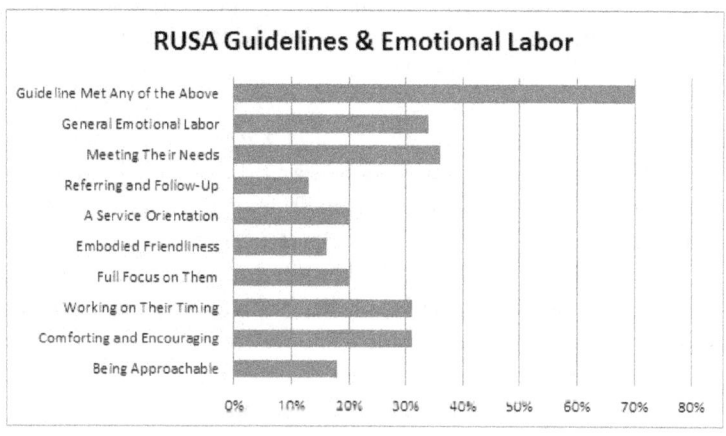

Fig. 2. *RUSA Guidelines and emotional labor*

Each broad theme above was found in at least 20% of the *Guidelines*, and most guidelines were coded with multiple themes resonant of emotional labor. At least 70% of the 60 text blocks demonstrated some expectation of emotional labor, whether the paragraph was ostensibly focused on search behavior, spoken words, or physical interaction. Our qualitative content analysis, then, suggests that the *Guidelines* formalize an expectation that librarians perform emotional services for other people, even as the formal nature of their work is framed as skilled research guidance or professional consultation. In the close reading that follows, we further explore the emotional content and gendered nature of these expectations for reference librarians.

Close Reading: The Nurturing Reference Librarian

It is not surprising that the American Library Association (ALA) and its section on reference work (RUSA) would choose to outline a successful reference interaction, as the reference interview is a repeated responsibility with some elements that can be standardized. What is arresting about the *Guidelines* is that they focus not just on the *procedure* of reference, but on the *behavior* of the librarian. This moves the *Guidelines* beyond documenting tasks ("what to do"), and into the realm of telling professionals "how to be."

The RUSA *Guidelines* were created by an ad hoc committee, revised by the MOUSS Management of Reference Committee in 2004, and again by the RSS Management of Reference Committee in 2011.[18] As these committees suggest, the *Guidelines* are not just guides for individual librarians, but also train *managers* what to look for in employees. Indeed, the goal is framed as "to assist in the training, development, and/or evaluation of librarians and staff who provide information."[19] The *Guidelines*, then, serve to connect the observable behavior of the librarian to whether her interactions are deemed successful or not. In this way, both her behavior and her demeanor become a site of judgment, in which "the positive or negative behavior of the librarian (as observed by the patron) becomes a significant factor in perceived success or failure" of the interaction.[20] This echoes Hochschild's flight attendants, who were taught that "the *emotional style of offering the service is part of the service itself.*"[21]

Within the *Guidelines*, librarian behavior is repeatedly articulated and evaluated in terms of attending to the *emotional* state of the patron. The set of guidelines on **Visibility/Approachability** frame the "first step" of any reference interaction as "to make the patron feel comfortable in a situation that can be perceived as intimidating, confusing, or overwhelming" (1.0). In order to provide comfort, information professionals should use "a friendly greeting" (1.1.3),

---

18 RUSA, *Guidelines*.

19 RUSA, *Guidelines*.

20 RUSA, *Guidelines*.

21 Hochschild, *The Managed Heart*, 5.

"open body language" (1.2.2), and to "acknowledge" (1.1.3, 1.1.4) patrons while maintaining an "approachable presence" (1.2.1) so that people around them feel comfortable.

In the guidelines on **Interest**, emotional service intensifies. The librarian is told to "embrace each patron's informational need" and commit to "providing the most effective assistance. Librarians who demonstrate a high level of interest in the inquiries of patrons will generate a higher level of satisfactions among users" (2.0). Once again, the goal of performing verbal or physical interest is not to form rapport and answer a question effectively, but to make patrons *feel* good and satisfied (presumably in a way that can be quantified in later assessment measures). Rather than show the natural reserve inherent to some personalities or professions, the librarian is encouraged to provide her "complete attention" (2.1.1) and "[signal] an understanding of the patron's needs" (2.2.4) through regular backchannel signaling of "verbal and non-verbal confirmation" (2.2.3) which indicates ongoing interest and attention as the patron talks. In this way, "seeming to 'love the job' becomes part of the job."[22] Here, *interest* is less about conveying a genuine interest in a fascinating question, and more about performing a demonstrative fascination so that a patron can experience "genuine" interest.

In the third section, **Listening/Inquiring**, the librarian is made further responsible for a patron's emotions. She is asked to identify information needs "in a manner that puts the patron at ease" (3.0), and to ensure all her communications remain "receptive, cordial, and supportive" (3.1.1). She is asked to "clarify confusing terminology and [avoid] jargon" (3.1.6), again showing consideration for the patron. Our critiques here are not of any particular recommendation, given that all of these are good professional practice for public services in general. Rather, it is with the implications, specifically regarding the covert consequences, that a prescriptive set of guidelines may have for a feminized profession as a whole.

Finally, the section on **Searching** is similarly framed around responding to and managing a patron's emotional needs. The introduction reminds us of the affective aspect of research, as when a search is not effective, "patrons may become discouraged," but seems to then place the responsibility for the patron's emotional and

---

22 Hochschild, *The Managed Heart*, 6.

technical skills with the librarian: "Many aspects of searching that lead to accurate results are dependent on the behavior of the librarian" (4.0). This section is of particular interest insofar as it collapses the distinction between the technical skills of the librarian and her ability to perform emotional labor. The mechanical act of searching—as well as the intellectual knowledge of resources and methods likely to produce results—becomes conflated with the patron's own capacity to self-regulate and manage their emotions. Throughout the process, the information professional is asked to "encourage" the patron as well as to focus less on whether the patron obtained needed information, and more on whether they are "satisfied with the results of the search" (5.0). One would expect the product of a reference interaction to be positive rapport and a more informed and educated patron; instead, "the product is a state of mind."[23] The end user is taught to value the successful search not as one that produces an accurate result, but as one where all their potentially negative feelings are mitigated.

Throughout each reference transaction, then, the librarian is asked to focus on the *emotions* of the patron while simultaneously suppressing any emotions of her own—a textbook example of emotional labor in the service professions. She is also explicitly reminded that her *behavior* and not her *expertise* is what determines the success of an interaction and her subsequent success in the profession. If her response "sets the tone for the entire communication process" (1.0), then her normal emotional and interpersonal needs must always be subsumed or reframed to meet the needs of another. As she manages many other responsibilities or projects, as well as the normal ups and downs of a personal life, and the complex tenor of interactions between colleagues and supervisors, the librarian is also asked to perform additional labor: to always be approachable, always visible, always "poised and ready to engage patrons" (1.1.2). To be so attuned to others, of course, she is encouraged to tune out from herself, as she is "aware of the need to stop all other activities when a patron approaches and [to] focus attention on the patron's needs" (1.1.2). In this way, the white-collar professional comes to resemble what modern-day North Americans expect of service professionals: a stewardess, a waitress, or even a mother.

---

23 Hochschild, *The Managed Heart*, 6.

This set of *Guidelines* for professionals also, ironically, discourages the librarian from offering interpretations or value judgments of her own. A successful librarian "demonstrates a high degree of objective, nonjudgmental interest" (2.0), "an understanding of the patron's need" (2.3.3), "objectivity" (3.1.9), and avoids "value judgments" (3.1.9). She provides her "complete attention" (2.1.1) and "assurance" (2.3.2) to the user's perspective. Her genuine level of interest and professional assessment are made irrelevant. As a blank slate, she is asked to assume neutrality in order to further support the patron's own development. These expectations to be approachable, receptive, polite, supportive, encouraging, and attuned to patrons as well as social norms all require the librarian to suppress her own emotions, needs, and evaluations of her environment, managing competing priorities with no evident strain or stress. The *Guidelines*, in other words, articulate reference interviews as a human interaction in which one party sets herself aside in order to address other humans' emotional and developmental needs.

And in many libraries, this is all performed in public. The intense *visibility* expected of a librarian further reinforces the gendered labor at the heart of the *Guidelines*. As Iris Marion Young argues:

> [T]he woman lives her body as object as well as subject... An essential part of the situation of being a woman is that of living the ever-present possibility that one will be gazed upon... as the potential object of another subject's intentions and manipulations, rather than as a living manifestation of action and intention.[24]

In a patriarchal culture, women's bodies—and so their approachability and visibility—are seen as belonging to the public or to another person, rather than to the woman as autonomous agent. Even if this understanding of woman as visual object is not intended by the *Guidelines*, they reinforce "a high level of visibility" (1.0) for a woman that is "approachable" (1.0), "poised and ready" (1.1.1), and "easily identifiable" (1.2.1), and who makes "eye contact," focuses "complete attention" (2.1.1) on strangers, and uses "open body language" (1.2.2) —even in potentially threatening public spaces. All of this reinforces the idea that librarians' embodied presence exists in large part to meet the emotional needs of others.

---

24 Iris Marion Young, *On Female Body Experience: "Throwing Like a Girl" and Other Essays* (New York: Oxford University Press, 2005), 44.

In reading these guidelines, the curious librarian may rightly ask: where is the patron's responsibility for behavior, emotional resilience in the face of setbacks, and self-management? Where is their responsibility for containing outbursts or being courteous to service professionals who cannot easily leave a dehumanizing or abusive interaction? Under these guidelines, the *librarian* is the sole key to the success or failure of the interaction, and she must behave and emote in the right ways. A librarian's objectivity and interest is of course a great asset—yet when she erases her own needs, emotions, and opinions, the ideal reference interaction appears to occur in a perfected, Stepfordian void, outside the real messiness of the social world. It is curious that a librarian's performance of *approachability* only counts when judged sufficient by highly variable patrons with highly variable motives. Her *interest* could be borne out of her own internal sense of professional pride, autonomy and integrity[25] — yet is instead judged by the patron. The librarian is to be a "good communicator" (3.0), yet communication is fundamentally interpersonal, dyadic, and interactive. If it happens between two people, then why do both parties not bear responsibility for the successful outcome? In many human interactions, cultural expectations are laid out for all parties. But the result of the *Guidelines* is the impression that a patron's role is to *perceive* and *feel*, while the librarian's is to provide the right *feeling* and *presence*.

The challenge, of course, is that patron behavior and perceptions do not exist in a vacuum devoid of social or cultural contexts. Like all interactions, the librarian-patron interaction is embedded in multiple matrices of context, with no one given outcome or interpretation. As Anne Boring, Kellie Ottoboni, and Philip B. Stark have shown, gender bias figures heavily in student perceptions of professors and other academic authority figures.[26] Jennifer L. Bonnet and Benjamin McAlexander further show that "patrons do consider demographic categories such as gender, age, and race when assessing the

---

25 Barry Schwartz, *Why We Work* (New York: TED Books, 2015).

26 Anne Boring, Kellie Ottoboni, and Philip B. Stark, "Student Evaluations of Teaching (Mostly) Do Not Measure Teaching Effectiveness," *ScienceOpen Research*: 2016, accessed June 20, 2017, doi: 10.14293/S2199-1006.1.SOR-EDU.AETBZC.v1

approachability of reference librarians"[27] Consequently, the librarian's gender plays into patron perceptions of how successful a reference interaction has been. How, then, can a librarian be made responsible for the emotive success of a reference interaction, if evaluations of her professional success are influenced by the gendered social roles expected of her?

In the end, then, even these carefully ordered guidelines cannot avoid the messiness of the social world. On the surface, the *Guidelines* describe a neutral reference interaction in a neutral space — yet their descriptions of the reference ideal are pervaded by gendered language and ideas. We take for granted that people in this female service profession will provide gendered emotional labor — and indeed our analysis found that over 70% of the *Guidelines* explicitly prescribed one of the nine themes indicating emotional labor. What's more, the emotional labor required of the reference librarian in the *Guidelines* is uncanny in its resemblance to the emotional labor required of mothers, girlfriends, wives, hostesses, and servers, and flight attendants. In each of these gendered roles, women are hired "because they are seen as members of the category from which mothers come... are asked to look out for psychological needs more than men are. The world turns to women for mothering, and this fact silently attaches itself to many a job description."[28] In both personal and professional roles, American women are obliged to manage the emotions of others, to satisfy the needs of others, and above all to conform to subtly gendered social norms and cues.[29] It is women—90% of librarians—who are asked to ensure that other human beings feel safe, supported, and nurtured —often by serving as "protomothers."[30] In the *Guidelines*' ideal reference interaction, a librarian has sole responsibility for the patron's happiness and satisfaction. The expectation of fulfillment of neutral information requests by a nurturing reference librarian mirrors the expectations that a wife, mother, or girlfriend must sympathetically

---

27 Jennifer L. Bonnet, and Benjamin McAlexander, "Structural Diversity in Academic Libraries: A Study of Librarian Approachability," *The Journal of Academic Librarianship* 38, no. 5 (2012): 284.

28 Hochschild, *The Managed Heart*, 170.

29 Hochschild, *The Managed Heart*, 20.

30 Hochschild, *The Managed Heart*, 176.

listen to a person's troubles and feelings while meeting their other needs—and all the while affirming their essential validity.

We arrive at a strange tension here, between how the ALA and other advocates assert the librarian's *authority* as a professional librarian, and how the *Guidelines* de-emphasize that same expertise and skill so that a patron may *feel* self-sufficient, comfortable, capable, powerful, and smart. As the *Guidelines* frame it, the ideal interaction is not about challenging patrons to think differently or teaching them the skills to be self-sufficient. Instead, it is about making them think they did the work themselves, and leaving them satisfied with the provision of ongoing service. Here, the *Behavioral Guidelines* evoke our culture's existing behavioral guidelines for dating, for pleasing a husband, for attending to the needs of children, and for attending to the needs of customers, bosses, and colleagues. In trying to ensure that librarians perform (gendered) service adequately, the *Guidelines* arrive at a double bind: they over-articulate what the librarian should do, as though she cannot perform professional labor on her own terms. They imply that how she handles her job should be regularly scrutinized, regulated, and policed. And the *Guidelines* ultimately brush aside the educational and informational goals of a reference transaction, in order to highlight the need for a pleasantly gendered affect, emotional sensitivity to insensitive patrons, and fulfilling the needs of others, as the (female-gendered) librarian performs (gendered) emotional labor in her office or at the reference desk.

Conclusion: Smiling is Success

What is the role of a reference librarian, and what is she specifically responsible for? In the memorable phrasing of Nancy Fried Foster, patrons often approach the reference desk looking for a "Mommy Librarian," someone who can offer emotional support, reassurance, sociality, answers, and interventions at points of pain or need.[31] In this chapter, we have considered how reference librarians are explicitly taught to foreground emotional labor in patron interactions. By focusing on how to manage patrons' emotional (rather than informational) needs, the *Guidelines* reinforce the gendered service role of reference work, and constrain the professional autonomy

---

31 Foster, "The Mommy Model."

of librarians as knowledgeable and understanding facilitators of independent research. "Success" in the reference transaction is then determined by the patron, based on the librarian's ability to manage the patron's reactions to their experiences: not "how well did this answer your question?" but "how good did this make you feel?"

And so we come to a tension: as professionals we are aware of the interplay of education, role, gender, race, class, and past experience in every unique interaction. And yet, we still want to guide patrons well, to listen well, and to make meaningful human connections. In line with our feminist philosophy, we wish to extend an "ethics of care" to patrons and students, while caring for ourselves by calling on patrons to take full responsibility for their own actions and emotion management. An ethics of care focuses on the "relatedness of persons" rather than on people as fundamentally autonomous individuals.[32]

The *Guidelines* place responsibility for the success of a reference interaction solely with the librarian, her self-conduct, and her emotional labor. By contrast, an ethics of care emphasizes that *both* the librarian and patron contribute to the success of the reference interaction, in a process similar to Goffmanian participant interaction.[33] Thus, the participants and their particular circumstances come to bear on each instance of interaction, and are wholly interdependent. In her work on feminist pedagogy, Maria Accardi notes the tension between the goal of educating and challenging students to think differently about how they inhabit the world, in stark contrast to the fact that students are not always receptive to a progressive pedagogy.[34] The tension between patron-centered librarianship and meaningful professional autonomy for the librarian becomes evident: if we erase ourselves, how can we be seen?

How can we advocate for the continued value of investing in libraries and librarians, when the successful interaction as outlined in the *Guidelines* has the patron believing that they've done it all by themselves? And perhaps some of this comes out in the process of training patrons itself. In our ideal reference interaction, patrons are

---

32 Virginia Held, *The Ethics of Care: Personal, Political, and Global* (Oxford: Oxford University Press, 2006), 14.

33 Goffman, *The Presentation of Self in Everyday Life*.

34 Maria T. Accardi, *Feminist Pedagogy for Library Instruction* (Sacramento, CA: Library Juice Press, 2013), 3.

not "passive consumers of knowledge and culture" but rather active and empowered learners.[35] This attitude towards learning, even in a brief encounter at the reference desk, has to be cultivated. We see a way forward in highlighting the affective dimension of *all* learning as it comes to bear on even mundane human interaction.[36] Only through such a process we can attend to the emotional aspect of our human selves, both by empowering the patron to take responsibility for their own emotions while searching for information, and through the self-care, autonomy, subversion, and self-definition that the feminist librarian provides to herself.

---

35 Accardi, *Feminist Pedagogy*, 25.

36 Accardi, *Feminist Pedagogy*, 3.

Bibliography

Accardi, Maria T. *Feminist Pedagogy for Library Instruction.* Sacramento, CA: Library Juice Press, 2013.

Arbuckle, Kathryn. "Emotion and Knowledge: Partners in Library Service?" *Feliciter* 54, no.5 (2008): 219-221.

Bonnet, Jennifer L., and Benjamin McAlexander. "Structural Diversity in Academic Libraries: A Study of Librarian Approachability." *The Journal of Academic Librarianship* 38, no. 5 (2012): 277-286.

Boring, Anne, Kellie Ottoboni, and Philip B. Stark. "Student Evaluations of Teaching (Mostly) Do Not Measure Teaching Effectiveness." *ScienceOpen Research*: 2016. Accessed June 20, 2017. doi: 10.14293/S2199-1006.1.SOR-EDU.AETBZC.v1

Butler, Judith. *Gender Trouble: Feminism and the Subversion of Identity.* New York: Routledge, 1990.

Erickson, Karla A. *The Hungry Cowboy: Service and Community in a Neighborhood Restaurant.* Jackson: University Press of Mississippi, 2009.

Foster, Nancy Fried. "The Mommy Model of Service." In *Studying Students: The Undergraduate Research Project at the University of Rochester,* edited by Nancy Fried Foster and Susan Gibbons, 72-78. Chicago: Association of College and Research Libraries, 2007.

Goffman, Erving. *The Presentation of Self in Everyday Life.* New York: Anchor Books, 1959.

Grandey, Alicia, Su Chuen Foo, Markus Groth and Robyn E. Goodwin. "Free to Be You and Me: A Climate of Authenticity Alleviates Burnout from Emotional Labor." *Journal of Occupational Health Psychology* 17, no. 1 (2012): 1-14.

Guy, Mary Ellen, and Meredith A. Newman. "Women's Jobs, Men's Jobs: Sex Segregation and Emotional Labor." *Public Administration Review* 64, no. 3 (May 2004): 289-298.

Held, Virginia. *The Ethics of Care: Personal, Political, and Global.* Oxford: Oxford University Press, 2006.

Hochschild, Arlie Russell. *The Managed Heart: Commercialization of Human Feeling*. Berkeley: University of California Press, 1983.

Hűlsheger, Ute R. and Anna F. Schewe. "On the Costs and Benefits of Emotional Labor: A Meta-Analysis of Three Decades of Research." *Journal of Occupational Health Psychology* 16, no. 3 (2011): 361-389.

Julien, Heidi, and Shelagh K. Genuis. "Emotional Labour in Librarians' Instructional Work." *Journal of Documentation* 65, no. 6 (2009): 926-937.

Loo, Jeffery L., and Elizabeth A Dupuis. "Organizational Learning for Library Enhancements: A Collaborative, Research-Driven Analysis of Academic Department Needs." *College & Research Libraries* 76 no. 5 (July 2015): 671-689.

Matteson, Miriam L. and Shelly S. Miller. "Emotional Labor in Librarianship: A Research Agenda." *Library and Information Science Research* 34, no. 3 (2012): 176-183.

———. "A Study of Emotional Labor in Librarianship." *Library & Information Science Research* 35, no.1 (January 2013): 54–62.

———. "What Library Managers Should Know about Emotional Labor." *Public Library Quarterly* 33, no. 2 (2014): 95-107.

Matteson, Miriam L., Sharon Chittock, and David Mease. 2015. "In Their Own Words: Stories of Emotional Labor from the Library Workforce". *The Library Quarterly: Information, Community, Policy* 85, no. 1 (2015): 85–105.

Molé, Nicole. *Labor Disorders in Neoliberal Italy: Mobbing, Well-Being, and the Workplace*. Bloomington: Indiana University Press, 2011.

Muehlebach, Andrea. "On Affective Labor in Post-Fordist Italy." *Cultural Anthropology* 26, no. 1 (2011): 59-82.

O'Dair, Sharon. "Superservicable Subordinates, Universal Access, and Prestige-Driven Research." In *Over Ten Million Served: Gendered Service in Language and Literature Workplaces*, edited by Michelle A. Massé and Katie J. Hogan, 35-53. Albany: SUNY Press, 2010.

Peng, Yu-Ping. "Buffering the Negative Effects of Surface Acting: The Moderating Role of Supervisor Support in Librarianship." *Journal of Academic Librarianship* 41, no. 1 (January 2015): 37-46.

Reference and User Services Association [RUSA]. "Guidelines for Behavioral Performance of Reference and Information Service Providers." 1996/2013. http://www.ala.org/rusa/resources/guidelines/guidelinesbehavioral

Seymour, Celene. "Ethnographic Study of Information Literacy Librarians' Work Experience: A Report from Two States." In *Transforming Information Literacy Programs: Intersecting Frontiers of Self, Library Culture, and Campus Community*, edited by Carroll W. Wilkinson and Courtney Bruch, 45-71. Chicago: Association of College and Research Libraries, 2015.

Schwartz, Barry. *Why We Work*. New York: TED Books, 2015.

Sheih, Chen Su-May. "A Survey of Circulation Librarians' Emotional Labor and Emotional Exhaustion: The Case of Difficult Patron Service in University Libraries." *Journal of Educational Media & Library Sciences* 50, no. 1 (Fall 2012): 5-39.

Shuler, Sherianne and Nathan Morgan. "Emotional Labor in the Academic Library: When Being Friendly Feels Like Work." *The Reference Librarian* 54, no. 2 (2013): 118-133.

Sloniowski, Lisa. "Affective Labor, Resistance, and the Academic Librarian." *Library Trends* 64, no. 4 (Spring 2016): 645-666.

Stewart, Kathleen. *Ordinary Affects*. Durham, NC: Duke University Press, 2010.

Tyson, Amy. *The Wages of History: Emotional Labor on Public History's Front Lines*. Amherst: University of Massachusetts Press, 2013.

Young, Iris Marion. *On Female Body Experience "Throwing Like a Girl" and Other Essays*. New York: Oxford University Press, 2005.

"Nothing More than a Gear in your Car:" Neutrality and Feminist Reference in the Academic Library

Nina Clements

It is a truth, universally acknowledged, that a librarian must be a neutral and objective professional.[1] At least, Jane Austen aside, this was the impression I received while in library school. I know I'm not alone in looking back on my MLIS as a challenge to my sanity. I learned from one of my favorite professors, Elizabeth Mahoney, that librarians did not use Wikipedia. I grew to love her anyway, though I disagreed with at least this one seemingly undeniable tenet of the profession. For the most part, my internships and my reference classes affirmed my decision to pursue a career in librarianship, and they motivated me to be my best self, because I had this idea that librarians were the best kind of professional. They were knowledgeable and professional and objective and neutral—all of the things that I was not. I vowed to *transform* myself into a librarian to *do* reference and instruction. I was going to be a person who knew things. I was going to read the newspaper—in print—every day, local and national, and become fluent in current events and politics. I had no idea then how necessary that familiarity (not that I completely achieved it) would be in today's pseudo-information landscape.

---

1 For an interesting discussion of the differences between neutrality and objectivity, see Rory Litwin, "Neutrality, Objectivity and the Political Center," *Progressive Librarian*, no. 21 (December 15, 2002): 72–77.

Yet even at my most idealistic about the profession, the idea of the neutral reference librarian rankled. The idea of neutrality clashed with my version of feminism. Consider feminism as defined by bell hooks: "Feminism is the struggle to end sexist oppression."[2] Maria Accardi, in *Feminist Pedagogy for Library Instruction*, defines it this way: "Feminism is about, among other things, decentering oppressive power relations and transforming them into something egalitarian and democratic."[3] Feminism focuses on sexist oppression but also on the intersection of multiple oppressions. It inherently questions authority, or the dominant hegemonic power. Where does that power sit in the library, I wondered? With the librarian? With the library administration? With the American Library Association (ALA)?

Although not explicitly mentioned in the Reference and User Services (RUSA) *Guidelines for Behavioral Performance of Reference and Information Service Providers*, we spent a great deal of time in my MLIS program discussing the idea of neutrality as it pertained to both services and collections. Neutrality in these areas, however, seemed unattainable. I understood the idea behind it—that our own biases should not cloud or interfere with the quality of help we offer to our reference questioners. But as a feminist, I thought objectivity and neutrality especially were hyper-rational constructs. They were ideas that had no place in the reality of the library.

My career has been entirely in the land of academic librarianship, so my discussion of neutrality will be centered there, though much of the literature discusses neutrality in the realm of the public library. I argue that libraries are "inextricably bound up with the life of a community," regardless of whether the library is public, special, or academic.[4] Furthermore, neutrality is fundamentally incompatible with feminisms. I also argue that neutrality is incompatible with personal authenticity, of which our feminism is an aspect. I will later

---

2 Cathia Jenainati, *Introducing Feminism: A Graphic Guide* (London Icon Books Ltd, 2014), 3.

3 Maria T. Accardi, *Feminist Pedagogy for Library Instruction* (Sacramento: Library Juice Press, 2013), 9.

4 Douglas John Foskett, *The Creed of a Librarian: No Politics, No Religion, No Morals*, 3 (London: Library Association, 1962). Qtd. In Paul T. Jaeger et al., "Democracy, Neutrality, and Value Demonstration in the Age of Austerity," *The Library Quarterly: Information, Community, Policy* 83, no. 4 (2013): 369, doi:10.1086/671910;).

discuss how *The Framework for Information Literacy* might be a way to unpack the library's authority and examine it in context.

Ultimately, neutrality has no place at the feminist reference desk, or any other reference desk for that matter. It is an impossible and potentially damaging concept that does not serve librarians or their patrons. As Desmond Tutu said, "If you are neutral in situations of injustice, you have chosen the side of the oppressor."[5]

In Which the "Antiquated" Notion of Neutrality Is Discussed and Subsequently Dismissed

There is nothing universal about the concept of neutrality. As mentioned above, the word "neutral" does not appear in the RUSA *Guidelines for Behavioral Performance of Reference and Information Service Providers*, though the concept is very much there. Neutrality undergirds what makes us "poised and ready to engage patrons" (RUSA 1.1.2) as we confront an information need. Protocol demands that "the librarian acknowledges patrons by using a friendly greeting to initiate conversation" (1.1.3) but also be "in compliance with institutional and professional norms and policies" (1.2.1).[6] The librarian is present, professional, and in compliance. But what are librarians complying *with* exactly? The dominant ideology of the institution—in my case, the very politicized space of higher education.

But let's back up a moment. What do I mean by the word "neutral"?[7] There are any number of definitions, but let's go to my favorite source, *The Oxford English Dictionary*. The first definition listed for neutrality is "an intermediate state or condition, not clearly one thing or another." This makes neutrality sound like

---

5 Qtd. in Nicole Pagowsky and Niamh Wallace, "Black Lives Matter! Shedding Library Neutrality Rhetoric for Social Justice," *College & Research Libraries News* 76, no. 4 (2015): 196–214.

6 "Guidelines for Behavioral Performance of Reference and Information Service Providers," Text, *Reference & User Services Association (RUSA)*, (September 29, 2008), http://www.ala.org/rusa/resources/guidelines/guidelinesbehavioral.

7 For an excellent discussion of neutrality in the library profession, see Heidi R. Johnson, "Foucault, the 'Facts,' and the Fiction of Neutrality: Neutrality in Librarianship and Peer Review," *Canadian Journal of Academic Librarianship* 1, no. 1 (January 28, 2016), http://www.cjal.ca/index.php/capal/article/download/24304.

a phase or a bad cold. Another definition further down states that neutrality is "abstention from taking any part in a war between other states." Another manifestation of this type of neutrality is a lack of participation in the political sphere—for example, deciding not to vote in the U.S. presidential election. This is, in part, how we elected Donald Trump as our president. Perhaps the definition with which we are most familiar is still further down: "'The state or condition of not being on any side; absence of decided views, feeling, or expression; indifference; impartiality; dispassionateness." [8] This *condition* is not one that we encounter; I maintain that it is a choice, and that choice is antithetical to our authenticity as feminist human beings. As Alison Lewis describes it in her introduction to *Questioning Library Neutrality*, neutrality "too often lapses into what might be better termed 'indifference.'"[9] Jaeger goes further and says that "the very notion of neutrality seems somewhat antiquated."[10] Do we really want to be indoctrinating future librarians in MLIS programs with such antiquated concepts? The idea of neutrality does not fit with the reality of our postmodern world.

But how does this relate to reference services? True impartiality is neither possible nor desirable in the reference interview. This desired neutrality or objectivity prevents us from sharing our experiences and opinions with students and faculty and prevents us from connecting to them on an empathic level. Are we really expected to begin each interaction with a student or professor *tabula rasa*? I don't believe that's precisely the intention of the RUSA guidelines, and yet they don't leave much room for an authentic interaction and experience. Coming to a reference interview with empathy and compassion is one strategy for "decentering oppressive power." If that is the goal of feminism, neutrality is at odds with it. The reference interview needs to be a conversation building toward a shared goal: meeting the questioner's information need. But perhaps we need to go one step

---

8 "Neutrality, n.," *OED Online* (Oxford University Press), accessed December 29, 2016, http://www.oed.com.ccl.idm.oclc.org/view/Entry/126461.

9 Alison M. Lewis, "Questioning Library Neutrality: An Introduction," in *Questioning Library Neutrality: Essays from Progressive Librarian*, 2008, 4, http://eprints.rclis.org/handle/10760/15071.

10 Jaeger et al., "Democracy, Neutrality, and Value Demonstration in the Age of Austerity," 370.

further. We need to inspire students to be aware of the world around them and take part in making it a better place.

The professional literature abundantly discusses the role of neutrality in the profession. According to Sandy Iverson, "librarians tend to see themselves as neutral service providers, rejecting any stated political stance, and certainly their training encourages this position."[11] Iverson goes on to quote Henry Blanke: "Librarianship's reluctance to define its value in political terms and to cultivate a sense of social responsibility may allow it to drift into an uncritical accommodation with society's dominant political and economic powers."[12] Mark Rosenzweig helpfully reminds us that the origins of librarianship had nothing to do with neutrality: "History, however, reminds us, with regards to neutrality, that the very emergence of the library profession was intimately associated with ideologically-informed efforts to place the whole development of education and mass enlightenment under the aegis of elite business interests," and that libraries were agents of "social integration and control."[13]

As Jenson states so succinctly, the idea of a "neutral professional" is "a way to neutralize professionals."[14] Jensen goes on to say that:

> Neutrality is impossible. In any situation, there exists a distribution of power, overtly endorsing or contesting that distribution are, of course, political choices; such positions are not neutral. But to take no explicit position by claiming to be neutral is also a political choice.[15]

Thus, we are aspiring to an ideal that is antiquated and impossible. It seems like a recipe for frustration and failure.

Many librarians, especially progressive librarians, argue against the idea that neutrality is really a tenet of our profession.[16] As Chris

---

11 Sandy Iverson, "Librarianship and Resistance," in *Questioning Library Neutrality*, 2008, 26.

12 Ibid.

13 Mark Rosenzweig, "Politics and Anti-Politics in Librarianship," in *Questioning Library Neutrality*, 2008, 5.

14 Robert Jensen, "The Myth of the Neutral Professional," in *Questioning Library Neutrality*, 2008, 90.

15 Ibid., 91.

16 Julie Biando Edwards, "Neutrality in Context: Principles and Rights," *Information for Social Change,* Summer 2011, no. 31 (2011): 17.

Bourg definitively states, echoing Rosenzweig: "libraries are not now or have they ever been merely neutral repositories of information." Bourg goes on to say that she "think[s] of neutral as really nothing more than a gear in your car."[17] This was a powerful metaphor for me, especially since I drive a car with a manual transmission and conveniently shift into neutral all the time. That is the only kind of neutrality that I welcome in my life. Bourg quotes nina de jesus, who reminds us that "libraries as institutions were created not only for a specific ideological purpose, but for an ideology that is fundamentally oppressive in nature."[18] Neutrality has no place in a profession that should have a mission grounded in social justice:

> The historical debate in LIS suggests that an overarching position of neutrality—if it is interpreted as a middle position, even a weak position, with total freedom from bias—is inconsistent with a social justice orientation, which requires that librarians hold positions on issues that affect access for library users.[19]

Johnson continues to argue that "it is important to have a social justice orientation first and foremost in every context within librarianship," which "aligns with the overarching mission and purpose of libraries to make information freely available to all people, especially those most in need of that information."[20] Litwin says that "the idea of neutrality is a definite evil, because it supports the balance of power, and does it invisibly, in cases where caring individuals, armed with objective information, likely would not."[21] So librarians should be working toward goals of social justice while being authentic, caring individuals. Perhaps Durrani and Smallwood put it best: "There is no way that librarians are or can be neutral in the social struggles of their

---

17 Chris Bourg, "Never Neutral: Libraries, Technology, and Inclusion," *The Feral Librarian*, accessed December 29, 2016, https://chrisbourg.wordpress.com/2015/01/28/never-neutral-libraries-technology-and-inclusion/.

18 Ibid.

19 Johnson, "Foucault, the 'Facts,' and the Fiction of Neutrality," 32.

20 Ibid., 33.

21 Litwin, "Neutrality, Objectivity and the Political Center," 77.

societies" because everything "is a reflection of their class position and their world outlook."[22]

The RUSA guidelines do make explicit use of the word "objectivity," specifying that the librarian "maintains objectivity; does not interject value judgments about the subject matter or the nature of the question into the transaction."[23] Why is the reference interaction considered to be a transaction, which suggests a capitalist exchange of goods or services for money? The reference interview is a *conversation*, a dialectical exchange between two people with an exchange of ideas and information with the goal of meeting the information need. Secondly, this guideline suggests that the librarian has no opinion of her own, that she is not a political actor in the politicized space of the library or in higher education. Engaging in the self-denying myth of neutrality squashes our personal and political selves, which is a disservice to us and those we serve.

But what does this mean, on a practical level? Our insistence as a profession on neutrality plays out in a variety of different ways. During the 2015 student-led protests about the lack of diversity and under-represented groups on campus, my library extended its hours in order to be a safe, supportive space for students. This was a wonderful idea, but we didn't really announce or publicize it. Our Diversity Committee also wanted to issue a statement reiterating our commitment to diversity and our role as a safe space on campus, but they were not permitted to issue such a statement. This would have been an easy way to reaffirm our solidarity with the protesting students while letting everyone know that the library was a safe space, but it was deemed to be too "political." It was more important to remain "neutral."

This kind of fear of stepping away from the neutral ideal ends up serving no one and allows social progress to stagnate. As seen above, the library's role in social justice is a potentially divisive issue within the profession, but we need to do more, especially in light of the violence and prejudice that many of our library patrons face in the real world.

---

22 Shiraz Durrani and Elizabeth Smallwood, "The Professional Is Political: Redefining the Social Role of Public Libraries," in *Questioning Library Neutrality*, 2008, 123.

23 "Guidelines for Behavioral Performance of Reference and Information Service Providers."

In Which We Contemplate the Concept of Authenticity and How It Pertains to Feminism and Reference Services

According to the *Stanford Encyclopedia of Philosophy,* authenticity "describes a person who acts in accordance with desires, motives, ideals or beliefs that are not only hers (as opposed to someone else's) but that also express who she really is."[24] Authenticity is living a certain kind of truth. In my own practice, it means letting my feminist self shine through. Sometimes I don't even know that the light is shining, like when I demonstrate databases during instruction sessions by using feminist or gender-related examples. Or when I talk to students asking to "rent" library materials and I explain the difference between "borrowing" and "renting," trying to get students to see beyond the capitalist transaction and realize that a library can be a space that counters the dominant capitalist economy.

Authenticity and feminism on the job can be a challenge, however. The RUSA guidelines don't necessarily leave much space for authenticity in the reference interview. We are meant to approach the interview with a "friendly greeting," but there is something that strikes me as forced and impersonal about this. Also, why shouldn't we engage in a conversation about our biases with our reference questioners? If a student had approached me during the U.S. presidential campaign seeking information about Donald Trump, I may or may not have brought up my opinion (which I still stand by) that he was not a viable candidate for office. That opinion, stated or not, will likely influence the sources I suggest to the student.

As librarians, we help others find the information they need. The *Framework for Information Literacy* instructs that we teach our students the process of inquiry. Students use the information we help them find and incorporate it into their assignments, their minds, and their lives. How can we help students in this process of becoming information-literate individuals if we are not fully ourselves?

---

24 Somogy Varga and Charles Guignon, "Authenticity," in *The Stanford Encyclopedia of Philosophy*, ed. Edward N. Zalta, Summer 2016 (Metaphysics Research Lab, Stanford University, 2016), https://plato.stanford.edu/archives/sum2016/entries/authenticity/.

As Litwin says, "There is no getting around having opinions if we are authentic beings."[25] Furthermore, "there is no escape from our connection to the rest of society and our ultimate involvement in every issue that affects it."[26] Authenticity leads us to action and political change, as does feminism. According to Bales and Engle, "ours is not a position of neutrality as imagined by the ALA 'Code of Ethics,' but one of social and moral responsibility to challenge the academic library as an ISA [ideological state apparatuses], to contribute to the creation of knowledge and history, not simply the reiteration of canonical indoctrination."[27]

So we've established that being politically neutral is incompatible with at least a few forms of feminisms. And that being a feminist, for many, is an authentic choice. One cannot maintain both feminism and neutrality; one cannot be authentic and neutral at the same time. But one can be "professional" and neutral, at least in theory. And this is what is valued. Professionals who want to be taken seriously "are encouraged to accept and replicate the dominant ideology."[28] But as Jensen states in "The Myth of the Neutral Professional," "the ideology of political neutrality, unfortunately keeps professionals such as journalists, teachers, and librarians—as well as citizens—from understanding the relationship between power and the professions."[29]

In Which We Contemplate the Notion of the Feminist Reference Desk Sans Neutrality

Let us turn our attention to the *Framework for Information Literacy for Higher Education,* specifically the first frame: Authority is constructed and contextual. Perhaps we can use this frame to reimagine reference services. For example, in the reference interview, the librarian's "authority" or position of privilege is constructed and contextual. If the reference librarian's position (and perspective) is constructed and

---

25 Litwin, "Neutrality, Objectivity and the Political Center," 73.

26 Ibid.

27 Stephen E. Bales and Lea Susan Engle, "The Counterhegemonic Academic Librarian: A Call to Action," *Progressive Librarian*, no. 40 (Fall/Winter 2012): 20.

28 Jensen, "The Myth of the Neutral Professional," 92.

29 Ibid., 95.

contextual, how can it also be neutral or objective? If the reference librarian occupies the privileged position of *expert*, how is that a neutral position? As history has shown us, neutrality can be dangerous. In today's political landscape, neutrality can be a tacit acceptance of neoliberalism and oppressive capitalism.

As Donna Haraway describes it, "feminist objectivity means quite simply situated knowledges."[30] This sounds a lot like "authority is constructed and contextual." So is knowledge creation. The issue of neutrality really impacts the services and level of compassion we can offer our students, and isn't compassion something that we, as feminists, offer each other as authentic human beings? Johnson argues that neutrality is opposed to the social justice mission of librarianship, and that mission aligns directly with feminism and its desire to decenter oppressive power.[31]

Neoliberalism is very much alive on campus, and the library is one potential place to combat it, or to reinforce it. Recently, my library underwent a major and costly renovation project. When I showed the mockups of the new space to a business professor, she responded enthusiastically, commenting that the new space, complete with collaborative spaces and SteelCase MediaScapes (places to plug in devices and project onto large screens that a group of students can see), was more "corporate" and would help students to be "job ready." I realize that it is now a luxury to care about knowledge for its own sake, but isn't that the luxury of education? To believe in an intrinsic value in learning? I argue that the space, within which we are encouraged to hold reference interviews, sends a mixed message to students. Its sleekness and impersonality reproduce the corporate world. It is an interesting setting in which to inspire our students toward social change.

What is needed is a comfortable space with adequate technology that facilitates a conversation instead of simulating a board meeting. But what are we to do? How do we eviscerate neutrality from the reference desk? Neutrality is something to deconstruct and discuss while in library school, not something to accept without questioning. We didn't have *The New Librarianship Field Guide* when I enrolled in my MLIS program in 2006. More emphasis in MLIS programs needs to focus on librarians as radical change agents so that we can inspire the same behavior in our

---

30 Qtd. in Iverson, "Librarianship and Resistance," 26.

31 Johnson, "Foucault, the 'Facts,' and the Fiction of Neutrality," 33.

library patrons. As Iverson reiterates, "librarians continue to be educated to progress in their careers with the belief that their role, while critical to a democratic society, is not in the least political."[32] This depoliticization has no place on today's campus or today's world.

By embracing neutrality, we send the silent message to our patrons, especially those from underrepresented groups, that we support the status quo. Neutrality is "the logical conclusion of moral relativism."[33] According to Johnson, "claiming complete neutrality is neither realistic nor ethical. In librarianship, it is more ethical to embrace one's positions and rely on them, which can lead to a stronger value system and more just actions."[34] She concludes, "Neutrality is indeed a myth, and this is something that LIS professionals should acknowledge as well as embrace....it is both appropriate and necessary for LIS professionals to have a political position."[35] Pagowsky and Wallace interrogate neutrality by asserting that:

> the ongoing existence of institutional racism and white privilege substantiates the importance of being aware of how neutrality functions in both higher education and in libraries. If we understand that there is a false construct of neutrality in libraries, and that libraries can even reinforce institutional oppression, we should ask ourselves how our collections, organizational schemes, interfaces, instructional practices, and learning objects impact our communities."[36]

Neutrality is "effectively supporting the existing balance of power."[37] Is that something we have the luxury of doing in today's political landscape, both within higher education and in the country more broadly? Is that something that we, as librarians, want to support? As Joseph Good writes, "If the librarian cannot be motivated to take a stand on pressing social issues out of a sense of moral duty, certainly the

---

32 Iverson, "Librarianship and Resistance," 29.

33 Joseph Good, "The Hottest Place in Hell: The Crisis of Neutrality in Contemporary Librarianship," in *Questioning Library Neutrality: Essays from Progressive Librarian*, 2008, 144.

34 Johnson, "Foucault, the 'Facts,' and the Fiction of Neutrality," 34.

35 Ibid., 40.

36 Pagowsky and Wallace, "Black Lives Matter! Shedding Library Neutrality Rhetoric for Social Justice."

37 Litwin, "Neutrality, Objectivity and the Political Center," 73.

librarian should break his or her neutrality in the name of self-interest."[38] By supporting the status quo—in my case, the neoliberal state of higher education—we are rendering ourselves obsolete. The status quo means budget cuts, means not thinking critically, means we are not necessary. It is in our interest to buck against the commodification of education and fight for the inherent good of helping students to learn.

As Durrani and Smallwood advocate in "The Professional Is Political," libraries should be "people-oriented."[39] They state: "The choice is simple: if the information profession does not acknowledge its social responsibility and act upon it, it will no longer have a social role."[40] While Durrani and Smallwood are specifically discussing the public library, this is true of all libraries. If libraries do not take social responsibility within their communities, how will they advocate for themselves, and who will stand with them?

Librarians need to be "transformative intellectuals" even within our professional lives, which often reflect the dominant ideology. Bales and Engle quote Aranowitz and Giroux, who argue that librarians should "define their political terrain by offering to students forms of alternative discourse and critical social practices whose interests are often at odds with the overall hegemonic role of the school and the society it supports."[41] This is what a feminist reference desk looks like. We are not just purveyors of information in exchange for our salaries, but we work together with reference questioners to create a culture of knowledge and social change.

Ultimately, the question is this: "Are libraries disciplinary agents of the state, or proponents of cultural equality?"[42] Practicing feminisms is one authentic way in which librarians can de-center the status quo and promote equality. There are no universal truths when it comes to libraries and librarians—they are constructed and contextual, and we need to be more intentional about how we construct our roles, services, and spaces.

---

38 Good, "The Hottest Place in Hell," 144.

39 Durrani and Smallwood, "The Professional Is Political," 125.

40 Ibid., 137.

41 Ibid., 23.

42 Jenny Bossaller, Denice Adkins, and Kim M. Thompson, "Critical Theory, Libraries and Culture," *Progressive Librarian*, no. 34/35 (2010): 31.

Bibliography

Accardi, Maria T. *Feminist Pedagogy for Library Instruction*, 2013.

Bales, Stephen E. and Lea SusanEngle. "The Counterhegemonic Academic Librarian: A Call to Action." *Progressive Librarian*, no. 40 (Fall/Winter 2012): 16–40.

Bossaller, Jenny, Denice Adkins, and Kim M. Thompson. "Critical Theory, Libraries and Culture." *Progressive Librarian*, no. 34/35 (2010): 25.

Bourg, Chris. "Never Neutral: Libraries, Technology, and Inclusion." *The Feral Librarian*. Accessed December 29, 2016. https://chrisbourg.wordpress.com/2015/01/28/never-neutral-libraries-technology-and-inclusion/.

Durrani, Shiraz, and Elizabeth Smallwood. "The Professional Is Political: Redefining the Social Role of Public Libraries." In *Questioning Library Neutrality: Essays from Progressive Librarian*, edited by Alison Lewis, 119-140. Duluth: Library Juice Press, 2008.

Edwards, Julie Biando. "Neutrality in Context: Principles and Rights." *Information for Social Change* Summer 2011, no. 31 (2011).

Good, Joseph. "The Hottest Place in Hell: The Crisis of Neutrality in Contemporary Librarianship." In *Questioning Library Neutrality: Essays from Progressive Librarian*, edited by Alison Lewis, 141-146. Duluth: Library Juice Press, 2008.

"Guidelines for Behavioral Performance of Reference and Information Service Providers." Text. *Reference & User Services Association (RUSA)*, September 29, 2008. http://www.ala.org/rusa/resources/guidelines/guidelinesbehavioral.

Iverson, Sandy. "Librarianship and Resistance." In *Questioning Library Neutrality: Essays from Progressive Librarian*, edited by Alison Lewis, 25-32. Duluth: Library Juice Press, 2008.

Jaeger, Paul T., Ursula Gorham, John Carlo Bertot, and Lindsay C. Sarin. "Democracy, Neutrality, and Value Demonstration in the Age of Austerity." *The Library Quarterly: Information, Community, Policy* 83, no. 4 (2013): 368–82. doi:10.1086/671910.

Jenainati, Cathia. *Introducing Feminism: A Graphic Guide.* Icon Books Ltd, 2014.

Jensen, Robert. "The Myth of the Neutral Professional." In *Questioning Library Neutrality: Essays from Progressive Librarian,* edited by Alison Lewis, 89-96. Duluth: Library Juice Press, 2008.

Johnson, Heidi R. "Foucault, the 'Facts,' and the Fiction of Neutrality: Neutrality in Librarianship and Peer Review." *Canadian Journal of Academic Librarianship* 1, no. 1 (January 28, 2016). http://www.cjal.ca/index.php/capal/article/download/24304.

Lewis, Alison M. "Questioning Library Neutrality: An Introduction." In *Questioning Library Neutrality: Essays from Progressive Librarian,* edited by Alison Lewis, 1-4. Duluth: Library Juice Press, 2008.

Litwin, Rory. "Neutrality, Objectivity and the Political Center." *Progressive Librarian,* no. 21 (December 15, 2002): 72–77.

"Neutrality, N." *OED Online.* Oxford University Press. Accessed December 29, 2016. http://www.oed.com.ccl.idm.oclc.org/view/Entry/126461.

Pagowsky, Nicole, and Niamh Wallace. "Black Lives Matter! Shedding Library Neutrality Rhetoric for Social Justice." *College & Research Libraries News* 76, no. 4 (2015): 196–214.

Rosenzweig, Mark. "Politics and Anti-Politics in Librarianship." In *Questioning Library Neutrality: Essays from Progressive Librarian,* edited by Alison Lewis, 5-8. Duluth: Library Juice Press, 2008.

Varga, Somogy, and Charles Guignon. "Authenticity." In *The Stanford Encyclopedia of Philosophy,* edited by Edward N. Zalta, Summer 2016. Metaphysics Research Lab, Stanford University, 2016. https://plato.stanford.edu/archives/sum2016/entries/authenticity/.

Purposeful and Productive Care: The Feminist Ethic of Care and the Reference Desk.

Sara Howard

Background & Narrative

Students approach the reference desk at an academic library for a myriad of reasons, but arguably, at the most basic level they are in search of something. Whether it is the restroom, a book in the stacks, assistance with technology, or research support, the process of getting to the crux of the question and identifying what the student is looking for is commonly referred to as the reference interview. Ross and Dewdeny describe the reference interview as "a conversation between the librarian and the user in which the librarian asks one or more questions (a) in order to get a clearer and more complete picture of what the user wants to know, and (b) link the user to the system."[1] I like this definition two-fold for this project, in that it lays a good foundation on the topic and that the quote from Ross and Dewdeny is from 1989, and it serves as a foundational piece on reference services. There is a proliferation of books and articles on the subject of reference services in the LIS field about styles and methodologies to best accomplish this task. As librarians we are told to practice superb customer service skills and to present ourselves as open and inviting to questions. This requires a dual emphasis on both presentation and process.

---

1 Joan C. Durrance, "Factors that Influence Reference Success: What makes Questioners Willing to Return?" *The Reference Librarian* 23, no. 49-50 (1995): 243.

Much of the literature suggests using neutral or open-ended questions and active listening to take the necessary next steps to get the student closer to the desired information whether that be in the physical form of a book, savvy search skills for a particular database or a referral. For many, these are some of the basic tenets of the reference interview and are important for successful navigation reference services.

Building off the work of Brown,[2] the above methodologies and strategies strike me as, at best, formulaic and not interested in a holistic or transformative outcome in the reference interview. And at worst, as is the case with neutral questions, they are problematic, as noted by Powell & Guadagno.[3] Of course, in the field many of us quickly adapt to the needs of our students and use these methods as more of a template versus strict instructions. In the process of adapting and moving away from these formulaic reference interview methods, newer literature, by Elmborg[4] and Doherty,[5] is looking at the collaborative nature of reference services. What is lacking is an additional focus on a holistic transformation that seemed to be better represented in the literature when looking at one-on-one or in-class instruction, for an example see Franks' 2010 work on "grand narratives."[6]

When examining all of these parts together, I was drawn to working in elements of the feminist ethic of care into reference services, which I argue can have a productive and transformative effect on the reference services. At the start of this project I was a newly minted librarian at an institution where classroom one-shot sessions and one-on-one research sessions with students are all initiated by faculty or student request. I saw my time at the reference desk as the

---

2 Stephanie Willen Brown, "The Reference Interview: Theories and Practice," (2008), *Published Works,* retrieved from *digitalcommon.uconn.edu.*

3 Martine B. Powell, and Belinda Guadagno, "An Examination of the Limitations in Investigative Interviewers' Use of Open-Ended Questions," *Psychiatry, Psychology and Law* 15, no.3 (2008): 382-95.

4 James K. Elmborg, "Teaching at the Desk: Toward a Reference Pedagogy," *Portal: Libraries and the Academy* 2, no. 3 (2002): 455-464.

5 John J. Doherty, "Reference Interview or Reference Dialogue?" *Internet Reference Services Quarterly* 11, no. 3 (2006): 97-109.

6 Sara Franks, "Grand Narratives and the Information Cycle in the Library Instruction Classroom," *Critical Library Instruction: Theories and Methods* (2010): 43-54.

most consistent opportunity for me to reach students and felt I was missing out on enriching the library experience for them.

The Feminist Ethic of Care

Before moving into specifics of practicing reference services via a lens of the feminist ethic of care, I will first share some insights on care ethics and what this transformative effect may look like. In the early 1980s, both Carol Gilligan and Nel Noddings were investigating new ways of exploring their respective disciplines that focused more on communication and care.[7] Throughout the literature, their works are described as care ethics, ethics of care, feminist ethics and care as feminist ethic. Because I will be taking pieces from both theorists and schools of thought[8], I will be using the term the feminist ethic of care or feminist care ethics throughout this chapter. Gilligan's work underscores "the way people talk about their lives is of significance, that the language they use and the connections they make reveal the world that they see and in which they act."[9] Central themes concentrate on communication, collaboration, fluidity and a focus on the person needing care.[10] Other repeated themes include equality and justice, which are important values for many of us involved in library services.[11] These themes easily translated to providing research and reference services.

The notions of equality and justice are also present in other LIS publications that examine transformative experiences.[12] The

---

7 Maureen Sander-Staudt, "Care Ethics." *Internet Encyclopedia of Philosophy: A Peer-Reviewed Academic Resource*, 2016, retrieved from http://www.iep.utm.edu/care-eth/#SH1a

8 Eve Browning Coleand Susan Margaret Coultrap-McQuin, *Explorations in Feminist Ethics: Theory and Practice*., Vol. 697, Indiana University Press, 1992.

9 Carol Gilligan, *In a Different Voice: Psychological Theory and Women's Development*, (Cambridge, Mass: Harvard University Press, 1982).

10 Daryl Koehn, *Rethinking Feminist Ethics: Care, Trust and Empathy*, 1st ed. (New York; London: Routledge, 1998).

11 Grace Clement, *Care, Autonomy, and Justice: Feminism and the Ethic of Care* (Boulder, Colorado: Westview Press,1996).

12 Mandy Lupton, and Christine Bruce, "Windows on Information Literacy Worlds: Generic, Situated and Transformative Perspectives," *Practising Information Literacy: Bringing Theories of Learning, Practice and Information Literacy Together* (2010): 4-27.

concept of the transformative experience has been getting a lot of buzz lately in LIS circles. Besides being the topic of articles and book chapters, the transformative nature of library instruction has also made it into the vocabulary of the ACRL compiled Framework for Information Literacy for Higher Education. Lupton and Bruce view the transformative piece as a "critical focus with more of an emphasis on the emancipatory nature of information literacy for the individual and society."[13] While I love this piece from Lupton and Bruce, I concentrate more on the individual transformative effect that takes place between the librarian/library and student. What I am maintaining, and Hamington makes a similar claim, is that the shared experience in itself is the transformation, "that we experience one another, particularly those who are unfamiliar to us, which in itself is a radical imperative."[14] Hamington further notes that "Caring habits, knowledge, and imagination are such basic parts of the human condition that they can help create these fruitful linkages."[15] It is my hope practicing the feminist ethic of care at the reference desk helps students to see linkages between themselves and the library, in terms of the library as both physical space and a space where knowledge is created, questioned, and critiqued.

I will now propose some strategies for incorporating the feminist ethic of care into day-to-day reference services interactions. I will use personal experiences with students at the reference desk and incorporate statistics from my former academic institution as examples of the most common reference desk scenarios that our specific reference team encountered.

THE FEMINIST ETHIC OF CARE IN PRACTICE
Why it was needed/Why I needed it

When I began this project I was working at a private liberal arts university. Below is a quick synopsis of the way the reference desk operated and a common reference desk encounter.

---

13 Ibid. 5.

14 Maurice Hamington, *Embodied Care: Jane Addams, Maurice Merleau-Ponty, and Feminist Ethics* (Urbana: University of Illinois Press, 2004).

15 Ibid., 32.

One's time on the reference desk was referred to as shifts, you took over from someone else, coupled with the stats one was to record when at the desk, especially the length of your interactions with patrons, what quickly occurred to me was my time on the reference desk was transactional versus collaborative. I felt the need for a more collaborative method of providing reference services and certainly a new terminology to describe our work on the desk, but I felt vulnerable in my temporary position and certainly did not want to make waves.

Using 2015 statistics from libstats, an open source tool used to record reference encounters (https://code.google.com/archive/p/libstats/), the most common reference interaction at my former academic library was students needing help finding a book in the stacks. This takes on several incarnations. Sometimes students need help navigating the library catalog to find a book before heading to the stacks or other times they have searched in the stacks and come up empty. Depending on the specifics of the situation, some described above, this interaction time was recorded under one of these set time metrics from libstats; *under one minute, 1-5 minutes. 5-10 minutes* or *10+ minutes*. The interaction can be categorized as *directional, referral, skill based* or *strategy based*. Overwhelmingly, most of the instances of students looking for a book in the stacks, often described as "looking for a book" or "finding a book" in the notes section was recorded as taking *under one minute* or *1-5 minutes* and *directional*. As a new librarian I used these metrics and notes as a road map for providing reference services at the desk. What I took away as the norm was speed of service and minimal assistance.

After being in my position for a year and gaining both more confidence in my appointment and reference desk savvy, I set out to put into practice pieces of the feminist ethic of care into reference services.

Time is on our side

Both the concept and "reality" of time were barriers in providing reference services with a focus on feminist care ethics. Issues of time seem to be omnipresent in librarianship, from critics discussing the lack of time to provide critical pedagogies in library one-shot sessions to the larger cut-backs regarding time references services are even offered at many colleges and universities. With regards to reference services, time is like a hurdle we are constantly jumping, bypassing or

65

knocking down. On macro-level, there is the time the reference desk/offices are open and staffed, then, at least at my former institution time is used as a main metric when recording reference statistics. Time of day and length of the interaction both at the desk and in one-on-one environments is recorded. The recording of time statistics made me very aware of "time" in my reference interactions. I also became aware that I felt time very differently when providing assistance at the desk versus a research collaboration in my office. From a feminist ethic of care perspective this makes sense due to the important role of dual interaction, arguably stronger in person and in a less-public environment.[16]

I will now provide some examples to take the reference exchange to reference encounter focusing on collaboration and creating a shared experience.

Using the feminist ethic of care perspective when looking at time, I shifted my investigative lens from my own feelings to those of the students. Students, and other patrons, are coming to the reference desk at a point of need. Within the feminist ethic of care, the time students are coming to us, is their "care" moment. Beck and Turner, in examining teaching from the reference desk note, "Studies indicate that students are most receptive to learning at the point of need, which most often occurs at the reference desk." [17] Because students are in this receptive space, perhaps we can work to create more time at the desk. When first practicing this, I felt a great deal of discomfort; this was a space for quick answers versus lengthy transactions. As I continued to breakdown this discomfort I realized that the attention I was paying to time was feeding into feelings of imposter syndrome.

The discomfort piece was coming out of imposter syndrome because it was going against what I observed as the status quo of the quick answers expected to be delivered at the reference desk. As I continued to sit in this discomfort, in this extra time zone, I realized it was not really taking all that much more time, and that the discomfort is arbitrarily created and giving into that was more detrimental to the student than to me. I started to employ some strategies such as having some extra chairs around for students to either come around the desk

---

16 Koehn., *Rethinking Feminist Ethics*.

17 Susan E. Beck, and Nancy B. Turner, "On the Fly BI: Reaching and Teaching from the Reference Desk," *The Reference Librarian* 34, no. 72 (2001): 83-96.

or offering them up as places to put down backpacks or coats. As a faster talker myself, I would try to be aware of my own cadence and not add any sense of urgency to the situation. As students were taking out laptops or notebooks with questions or as I was bringing up a particular database or website, I would attempt to start casual conversations unrelated to classes or assignments. Once this stage is set, as free of distractions as one can make it, I then let the student drive, jotting down a note or two if need be but not stopping to clarify until the student has introduced the situation fully and in their own language. Here, I was not focusing using open-ended questions but focusing on the student being heard.

In some of the scenarios above, I discuss some of the discomfort I first experienced when employing a feminist care ethics at the reference desk, getting out of the mindset of librarian as expert, or perhaps better said, appearing as a non-expert[18], and the way I felt and perceived time in these reference encounters. Processing this initial discomfort allowed me to realize that it was largely internal. However, there is a larger student focused concern that must be taken into consideration when practicing feminist care ethics at the reference desk. What happens when we provide care that was not asked for? What about the negative repercussions that can be an aftermath of that? Some issues include adding to stress or alienating a student from the library and librarians. I think with all care work we have to open for times we do not succeed and take these opportunities to think about ways to avoid these missteps in the future. I think we also have to be open to calling out these moments with our students. It is my hope in the shared experience model, along with focus on listening and allowing space for student contributions all aspects of practicing feminist care ethics, will help to prevent these moments.

Elmborg, when examining a reference [desk] pedagogy, underscores the fact "the librarian needs to make some very sophisticated decisions very quickly."[19] Practicing the feminist ethic of care requires the same skill set. As we practice feminist care ethics more, with its emphasis on listening and shared communication, we will be better able to discern those moments when a student is not

---

18 Mark Stover, "The Reference Librarian as Non-Expert: A Postmodern Approach to Expertise," *The Reference Librarian* 42, no. 87-88 (2004): 273-300.

19 Elmborg. "Teaching at the Desk."

in a space to have this transformative experience and will leave this space open for a student to a return another time when she might be more receptive. I argue that this is also a moment of care, because communication and focus on the student has helped to register where the student is.

Self-Care and Feminist Care Ethics

I could not end this chapter about feminist care ethics without looking at preventing against burnout while performing care work. As Fox & Olson note[20], care work takes work. As budgets, staff, and reference hours are cut, are we giving ourselves more to do? In all honesty, I think we are, but not necessarily in terms of measured time, tasks, or actions. By co-experiencing the reference moment with our students, we are giving that energy into the process each time. This is also noted in the work of Koehn, "Our very selves are at stake when we care because we are working at creating a shared self, invented as we proceed." [21] One way I see us practicing our own self-care is realizing care work cannot be done in a vacuum. Throughout this chapter I have focused on the collaborative nature and shared experience with the student but others can be included in these moments. In practice this could be the simple act of referring the student to a subject specialist or another colleague who might have a more extensive knowledge. By providing space and time for the student to be heard in their initial question at the desk, might we be imparting in the student confidence about the continued assistance they will receive?

The Personal is Political and Extension of Care Ethics

I think we also need to work on a language and methods that remind our supervisors that care work is work that does not often fit into the rubrics of performance reviews. In a recent article posted on the *Chronicle of Higher Education* site, the author suggests that the extra

---

20 Melodie J. Fox and Hope A. Olson, "Essentialism and Care in a Female-intensive Profession," *Gender, Sexuality, Information: A Reader, Los Angeles: Library Juice Press* (2013).

21 Koehn. "Rethinking Feminist Ethics."

mentoring and advising work that female faculty and faculty of color take on (and I believe the same to be true for female and librarians of color, along with LQBTQIA librarians) needs further illumination as "listening, empathizing, problem solving, and resource finding take an enormous amount of time and energy." [22] In this article, the author highlights how this work is done on-top of class time, prep time, publication and service duties, and office hours (which many librarians have on their plates as well). As a librarian, I could use these exact words from the article above, "listening, empathizing, problem solving, and resource finding take an enormous amount of time and energy," to describe reference services collaborations.[23] Arguably, reference interactions are built into our day-to-day structure and overall time when reporting back to supervisors for employment reviews and promotions, but the time and energy components are important to underscore. I understand that many hesitate to ask supervisors to take into account care work because it is difficult to quantify. Might we use reference consultations measurement devices like libstats in our favor in these instances. Discussing with supervisors that instead of a sixty second directional interaction, you took the time to really collaborate with a student, arguably more work? I do not think this will be easy work to do and there are very real concerns for asking for assessment of care work including the fact it could be manipulated by those who negatively work to feminize the field of librarianship. This has very real implications in terms of the role of librarians and pay scales. But perhaps this is a place to start where we are simultaneously working to step out of our comfort zones as librarians for the benefits of our students and asking those in upper management to step out of their comfort or traditional zones and value care work in the academic library environment.

---

22 Green, Myra. "Thanks for Listening." *The Chronicle of Higher Education.* (2015) *Retrieved http://chronicle.com/article/Thanks-for-Listening/233825*

23 Ibid., 1.

Bibliography

Beck, Susan E., and Nancy B. Turner. "On the Fly BI: Reaching and Teaching from the Reference Desk." *The Reference Librarian* 34, no. 72 (2001): 83-96.

Brown, Stephanie Willen. "The Reference Interview: Theories and Practice."*Published Works* (2008). Retrieved from *digitalcommon.uconn.edu*

Clement, Grace. *Care, Autonomy, and Justice: Feminism and the Ethic of Care.* Boulder, Colorado: Westview Press,1996.

Cole, Eve Browning, and Susan Margaret Coultrap-McQuin. *Explorations in Feminist Ethics: Theory and Practice.* Vol. 697. Indiana University Press, 1992.

Doherty, John J. "Reference Interview or Reference Dialogue?" *Internet Reference Services Quarterly* 11, no. 3 (2006): 97-109.

Durrance, Joan C. 1995. "Factors that Influence Reference Success: What Makes Questioners Willing to Return?" *The Reference Librarian* 23, no. 49-50 (1995): 243-265.

Elmborg, James K. 2002. "Teaching at the Desk: Toward a Reference Pedagogy." *Portal: Libraries and the Academy* 2, no. 3 (2002): 455-464.

Fox, Melodie J., and Hope A. Olson. "Essentialism and Care in a Female-intensive Profession." *Gender, Sexuality, Information: A Reader, Los Angeles: Library Juice Press. Refereed* (2013).

Franks, Sara. "Grand Narratives and the Information Cycle in the Library Instruction Classroom." *Critical Library Instruction: Theories and Methods* (2010): 43-54.

Gilligan, Carol. *In a Different Voice: Psychological Theory and Women's Development.* Cambridge, Mass: Harvard University Press, 1982.

Green, Myra. "Thanks for Listening." *The Chronicle of Higher Education.* (2015) *Retrived http://chronicle.com/article/Thanks-for-Listening/233825*

Hamington, Maurice. *Embodied Care: Jane Addams, Maurice Merleau-Ponty, and Feminist Ethics.* Urbana: University of Illinois Press, 2004.

Koehn, Daryl. *Rethinking Feminist Ethics: Care, Trust and Empathy.* 1st ed. New York;London;: Routledge, 1998.

Lupton, Mandy, and Christine Bruce. "Windows on Information Literacy Worlds: Generic, Situated and Transformative Perspectives." *Practising Information Literacy: Bringing Theories of Learning, Practice and Information Literacy Together* (2010): 4-27.

Powell, Martine B., and Belinda Guadagno. "An Examination of the Limitations in Investigative Interviewers' Use of Open-Ended Questions." *Psychiatry, Psychology and Law* 15, no.3 (2008): 382-95.

Sander-Staudt, Maureen. "Care ethics." *Internet Encyclopedia ofPphilosophy: A Peer-Reviewed Academic Resource.* (2016). Retrieved from http://www.iep.utm.edu/care-eth/#SH1a

Stover, Mark. "The Reference Librarian as Non-Expert: A Postmodern Approach to Expertise." *The Reference Librarian* 42, no. 87-88 (2004): 273-300.

FEMINIST REFERENCE SERVICES: TRANSFORMING RELATIONSHIPS THROUGH AN ETHIC OF CARE

Sharon Ladenson

How can feminism revitalize reference services? How can we utilize feminist practices to cultivate a supportive instructional environment in reference which will help empower our students to become critical thinkers? How can we elicit and build on the knowledge and experiences that students bring to the reference process? This chapter explores how using a feminist educational approach, focusing on an ethic of care and active student engagement, can transform the reference process, and provide support for student learning.

ETHIC OF CARE

What comprises an ethic of care? Based originally on analysis of female development and reasoning, care ethics subvert and provide an alternative approach to dominant moral theories focused on rules and rights.[1] Carol Gilligan's groundbreaking and controversial work, *In a Different Voice*, focuses prominently on the concept of care. Investigating human development through interviews, she finds that girls and women often share distinct perspectives, emphasizing relationships and connection. For example, two eleven-year-olds (Amy and Jake) share their thoughts on an ethical dilemma. Part

---

1 Maurice Hamington, "A Performative Approach to Teaching Care Ethics: A Case Study," *Feminist Teacher*, 23no. 1, (2012): 32.

of a series developed by psychologist Lawrence Kohlberg to measure moral development, the ethical problem involves a man (Heinz), and his fatally ill wife. While a new drug may save her, they cannot afford it (despite Heinz's attempts to borrow money and negotiate a lower price). Consequently, Heinz steals the drug. In response to the dilemma, Amy and Jake express contrasting views. While Jake is firmly convinced that Heinz should steal the drug, Amy is concerned that Heinz may have to go to jail, which would ultimately prevent him from taking care of his wife in the future. Amy emphasizes the importance of communication, stressing that Heinz should appeal further to the druggist to understand the significant consequences of not supplying the drug for an affordable price, or seek further help from others if that approach fails. Gilligan notes that Amy views the dilemma as "a narrative of relationships that extends over time," and her "judgments contain insights central to an ethic of care."[2] Gilligan is careful to point out that while her female research subjects share distinct perspectives, she does not seek to make generalizations about either sex.[3] Noddings reinforces and further develops a framework for an ethic of care shaped by perspectives of women, with an emphasis on context and concrete situations. She asserts:

> "It is not the case, certainly, that women cannot arrange principles hierarchically and derive conclusions logically. It is more likely that we see this process as peripheral to, or even alien to, many problems of moral action. Faced with a hypothetical moral dilemma, women often ask for more information. We want to know more, in order to form a picture more nearly resembling moral situations. We need to talk to the participants, to see their eyes and facial expressions, to receive what they are feeling. Moral decisions are, after all, made in real situations; they are qualitatively different from the solution of geometry problems."[4]

When describing features of care, Lindemann also emphasizes the importance of connection, relationships, context, and concrete

---

2 Carol Gilligan, *In a Different Voice: Psychological Theory and Women's Development* (Cambridge: Harvard University Press, 1982): 26-30.

3 Ibid., 2.

4 Nel Noddings, *Caring: A Feminine Approach to Ethics and Moral Education* (Berkeley: University of California Press, 1984): 3.

situations. Caring practice must involve "an expression of a caring relationship... (which) requires an engagement of another's will."[5] Lindemann notes, "if you care about the person... you interact with (her) not simply as an object of your care, but as someone with wants, intentions, and desires of (her) own."[6] Furthermore, being sensitive to context leads effective caregivers to "pay attention to the particulars (of a specific situation) rather than being guided by abstract thinking."[7] Held also explores the concept of caring relations, highlighting the importance of how recipients respond to those who care for them.[8]

Some feminist scholars adopt a broader interpretation of the concept of care, extending the process beyond individual relationships to liberating experiences of healing and transforming the world. According to Fisher and Tronto, "caring can be viewed as a species activity that includes everything we do to maintain, continue, and repair our 'world' so that we can live in it as well as possible."[9] Held notes that "the ethics of care as a feminist ethic offers suggestions for the radical transformation of society. It demands not just equality of women in existing structures . . . but equal consideration for the experience that reveals the values, importance, and moral significance, of caring."[10] Transforming personal relationships *and* working to improve society as a whole are critical to feminist theory and practice. As Held states, "we are trying to construct the kinds of feminist cultural reality which encourage human connection yet discourage domination and that we seek these changes both in the family and friends and gradually in the community, the society, and the world."[11]

---

5 Hilde Lindemann, *An Invitation to Feminist Ethics* (Boston: McGraw-Hill, 2006): 92-93.

6 Ibid., 93.

7 Ibid.

8 Virginia Held, *The Ethics of Care: Personal, Political, and Global* (New York: Oxford University Press, 2006): 36.

9 Berenice Fisher and Joan Tronto, "Toward a Feminist Theory of Caring," in *Circles of Care: Work and Identity in Women's Lives*, ed. Emily K. Abel and Margaret K. Nelson (Albany: State University of New York Press, 1990): 40.

10 Held, *Ethics of Care*, 12.

11 Virginia Held, *Feminist Morality: Transforming Culture, Society, and Politics* (Chicago: University of Chicago Press, 1993): 2.

Ethic of Care and Education

Hence, key tenets of a feminist ethic of care include developing and nurturing caring relations, valuing concrete experiences, and healing and transforming society as well as personal relationships. Feminist educators embrace these principles, cultivating an environment which facilitates making meaningful connections with students, and valuing their experiences as part of the learning process. When describing a feminist ethic of care in the classroom setting, Accardi shares the importance of "taking the time to listen to students, to honor their voices, to rely on them for examples, and to encourage them to listen to each other."[12] Crabtree, Sapp, and Licona describe how feminist instructors demonstrate concern and communicate care "through treating students as individuals, (making) connections between their studies and personal lives, and guiding students through the process of personal growth that accompanies their intellectual development."[13] In order to bring women's distinct voices from the margins to the center, feminist instructors also empower female students to share their ideas and experiences.[14]

Building on the knowledge and experiences of students is critical to feminist education, which also embraces caring. As Accardi notes, feminist instructors who adopt a caring approach view their "students as whole human beings, not vessels to be filled with information and knowledge."[15] Consequently, feminist educators also cultivate an

---

12 Maria T. Accardi, *Feminist Pedagogy for Library Instruction* (Sacramento: Library Juice Press, 2013): 44.

13 Robbin D. Crabtree, David Alan Sapp, and Adela C. Licona, "Introduction: The Passion and Praxis of Feminist Pedagogy," in *Feminist Pedagogy: Looking Back to Move Forward*, ed. Robbin D. Crabtree, David Alan Sapp, and Adela C. Licona (Baltimore: Johns Hopkins University Press, 2009), 4-5.

14 See Crabtree, Sapp, and Licona, "Introduction: The Passion and Praxis of Feminist Pedagogy,"5; Berenice Fisher, *No Angel in the Classroom: Teaching through Feminist Discourse* (Lanham, MD: Rowman & Littlefield, 2001); 44, and bell hooks, *Teaching to Transgress: Education as the Practice of Freedom* (New York: Routledge, 1994), 15.

15 Accardi, *Feminist Pedagogy for Library Instruction*, 44.

environment which facilitates active learning and critical inquiry.[16] Parry underscores this point by describing how a feminist approach "promotes the awareness that knowledge is not a discrete body of 'truths' that the instructor knows and imparts to students."[17] The approach instead suggests "that students themselves are capable of active learning and that this, rather than passive receiving, is what works best."[18] In the context of reference services, stimulating active inquiry is also a key component of a feminist approach. For example, when a student approached the desk to find a specific book about Dr. Martin Luther King, Jr., beyond helping her locate the title, we talked about her questions: What is Dr. Martin Luther King Jr.'s legacy? Was he more radical than conventionally perceived?

Empowering Students as Critical Thinkers

In order to embrace a caring philosophy in reference services, we need to empower students to become substantive critical thinkers. A feminist approach involves working with students to raise thoughtful questions about their topics and to reflect on the social impact of what they choose to investigate. Learning to engage in critically reflective practice is important not only for independent information seeking, but also for broader efforts to produce positive social change. A feminist approach also involves engaging in dialogue with students to solicit and build on their knowledge, experiences, and interests. For example, as gender studies librarian, a student contacted me for guidance on investigating the impact of religion and conservative activism on policies specific to health care and reproductive rights. She was also interested in researching the subsequent impact of such policies on diverse groups of women. During our meeting, we talked about what motivated her to explore the topic. Sharing information about her background, the student explained that she was fascinated

---

16 See Sharon Ladenson, "Paradigm Shift: Utilizing Critical Feminist Pedagogy in Library Instruction" in *Critical Library Instruction: Theories & Methods*, ed. Maria T. Accardi, Emily Drabinski, and Alana Kumbier (Duluth: Library Juice Press, 2010), 105; and Shirley C. Parry, "Feminist Pedagogy and Techniques for the Changing Classroom," *Women's Studies Quarterly* 24, no. 3/4 (1996), 45.

17 Parry, "Feminist Pedagogy and Techniques for the Changing Classroom," 45.

18 Ibid., 45.

by public policy, describing herself as a "policy nerd." Her strong interest and previous study of public policy led her to reflect on and raise questions about the Affordable Care Act, coverage of contraception for women, and how changes in policy could affect the lives of women, particularly those with limited resources.

Using instructional techniques to facilitate active learning is essential for stimulating critical thinking as part of the reference process. Colleagues who promote instructional approaches in reference recognize how the process fundamentally changes the dynamic with students and influences their learning. Beck and Turner assert:

> "Just as college and university faculty are rethinking their roles in the classroom, moving from the traditional teacher-oriented, lecture-driven classroom to the student-centered activity-based session, so should reference librarians reinvent themselves. Academic reference librarians need to take heed of this paradigm shift in higher education by seeing themselves not as mere answer machines but as learning facilitators."[19]

While discussing the importance of instruction at the reference desk, Elmborg also promotes a necessary shift away from simply providing information to helping students develop and answer questions independently. Supplying information without instruction takes "the question away from the student," and fostering such dependence weakens the learning process.[20] Furthermore, Kissane and Mollner argue that when we do the work of selecting sources for students at the desk, we deny those students "full control of their searches and the full measure of insight their questions could give them were they to have gone through that stage themselves or in partnership with the librarian."[21]

When sharing instructional approaches for reference work, colleagues typically describe strategies for demystifying the research process and for teaching students how to locate and access relevant

---

19 Susan E. Beck and Nancy B. Turner, "On the Fly BI," *The Reference Librarian*, 34 no. 72 (2001): 84.

20 James K. Elmborg, "Teaching at the Desk: Toward a Reference Desk Pedagogy," *portal: Libraries and the Academy* 2, no. 3 (2002): 459.

21 Emily C. Kissane and Daniel J. Mollner, "Critical Thinking at the Reference Desk: Teaching Students to Manage Technology," *RQ* 32, no. 4 (1993): 486.

resources.[22] While working with students on such concepts is important, a feminist approach goes a step further by using techniques to elicit critical questions that students have about their topics and sources they find. For example, if a student approached the reference desk to investigate African American identity in contemporary film, we might ask her the following questions: "What movies have you seen with African American characters and/or African American actors?" "What questions do you have about the representation of African Americans in those movies?" Using this technique would also facilitate building on the knowledge and experiences that the student would bring to the reference desk.

In order to embrace a feminist ethic of care and cultivate an empowering and supportive environment for teaching and learning in reference services, we need to focus not only on what information students seek, but also *why* they want to locate it. What generates their interest in the topic? How is the information personally meaningful? While working with a patron at the reference desk who was inquiring about information on the choreographer Alvin Ailey for a class project, I asked what motivated her to seek information about him. This led to conversation about her background and interest in dance. The student's experience as a jazz dancer inspired her to explore the evolution and relationship among various dance styles, including traditional African dance, jazz, and modern ballet. Her passion for dance also motivated her to explore the experiences of other dancers and their sources of inspiration. Learning from the student about how and why the topic was personally meaningful facilitated the process of working with her to start discovering relevant sources. The feminist instructional approach involves not only sharing guidance on how to use library resources, but also encouraging the process of making connections between personal experience and academic inquiry.

Using a feminist ethic of care to facilitate connecting experiential knowledge with discovering outside sources can help with assessing the needs of our patrons more thoroughly. When a patron approached the desk to inquire about finding information about Nigerian history,

---

22 See Beck and Turner, "On the Fly BI," 84-88; Christina M. Desai and Stephanie J. Graves, "Cyberspace or Face-to-Face: The Teachable Moment and Changing Reference Mediums," *Reference & User Services Quarterly* 47, no. 3 (2008): 249; and Edward J. Eckel, "Fostering Self-Regulated Learning at the Reference Desk," *Reference & User Services Quarterly* 47, no. 1 (2007): 17-19.

we started by doing some searches for books. As our conversation evolved, she talked about how interacting and developing friendships with Nigerian refugees in Lansing, Michigan inspired her to learn more about current political and social conflicts in the country (she was curious about what motivated the refugees to leave). Consequently, our dialogue shifted the collaborative process from searching for books about Nigerian history to locating more current sources of general background information and politics of the area. Learning from the patron about her background and personal experiences helped us to locate sources targeted more specifically to her needs and interests.

CARING RELATIONS AND EMPATHY

In order for students to feel comfortable raising critical questions at the reference desk, we need to cultivate caring relations with them. One technique for establishing caring relations is to use self-disclosure in the reference conversation.[23] When students share confusion or anxiety about doing research, we can let them know about challenges we also encounter when trying to locate information. Kern also recommends connecting with patrons by reassuring them (for example, letting students know that the questions they share are good) and by using "inclusive language" to engage students in the search process (inviting them to "see what we can find").[24] Being caring and empathetic also involves exercising patience and helping to meet individual needs. Some students may not be ready to articulate critical questions about their research during the initial reference interview. Working with students to identify and address their specific needs and encouraging them to come back to us for help will promote and facilitate ongoing caring relations.

---

23 See M. Kathleen Kern, "The Reference Interview Revisited," in *Reimagining Reference in the 21st Century*, ed. David A. Tyckoson and John G. Dove, (West Lafayette: Purdue University Press, 2015), 65-66, and Marie L. Radford, "Encountering Virtual Users: A Qualitative Investigation of Interpersonal Communication in Chat Reference," *Journal of the American Society for Information Science and Technology* 57, no. 8 (2006): 1050.

24 Kern, "The Reference Interview Revisited," 66.

CONCLUSION

In order to embrace an ethic of care, we need to reflect and reconsider how to conduct reference interviews with students. This involves building connections by engaging students in conversation not only about what information they seek, but also why information is important to them. Discovering why information is personally meaningful for our students involves building on their knowledge and experiences, which facilitates a personalized, caring approach to the reference process. As we communicate genuine compassion and empathy for students, we model caring behavior that they may seek to emulate in their interactions with others, which also contributes to a collective process of healing and positive transformation beyond the library. Empowering students to become critical thinkers is also a key component of a caring, feminist approach in reference. Encouraging students to raise critical questions about their topics as they search and engage with sources promotes active inquiry in reference, and shifts the role of the librarian from information provider to facilitator of teaching and learning. Rethinking the reference process and adopting a feminist approach not only revitalizes our relationships with students, but also contributes to a positive transformation beyond the library by empowering our patrons to be empathetic, critically-engaged citizens.

BIBLIOGRAPHY

Accardi, Maria T. *Feminist Pedagogy for Library Instruction*. Sacramento: Library Juice Press, 2013.

Beck, Susan E. and Nancy Turner. "On the Fly BI." *The Reference Librarian* 34, no. 72 (2001): 83-96.

Crabtree, Robin D., David Alan Sapp, and Adela C. Licona. "Introduction: The Passion and Praxis of Feminist Pedagogy." In *Feminist Pedagogy: Looking Back to Move Forward*, edited by Robbin D. Crabtree, David Alan Sapp, and Adela C. Licona, 4-5. Baltimore: Johns Hopkins University Press, 2009.

Desai, Christina M. and Stephanie J. Graves. "Cyberspace or Face-to-Face: The Teachable Moment and Changing Reference Mediums." *Reference & User Services Quarterly* 47, no. 3 (2008): 242-255.

Eckel, Edward J. "Fostering Self-Regulated Learning at the Reference Desk." *Reference & User Services Quarterly* 47, no. 1 (2007): 16-20.

Elmborg, James K. "Teaching at the Desk: Toward a Reference Desk Pedagogy," *portal: Libraries and the Academy* 2, no. 3 (2002): 455-464.

Fisher, Berenice. *No Angel in the Classroom: Teaching through Feminist Discourse*. Lanham, MD: Rowman & Littlefield, 2001.

Fisher, Berenice and Joan Tronto, "Toward a Feminist Theory of Caring." In *Circles of Care: Work and Identity in Women's Lives*, edited by Emily K. Abel and Margaret K. Nelson, 35-62. Albany: State University of New York Press, 1990.

Gilligan, Carol. *In a Different Voice: Psychological Theory and Women's Development*. Cambridge: Harvard University Press, 1982.

Hamington, Maurice. "A Performative Approach to Teaching Care Ethics: A Case Study." *Feminist Teacher* 23, no. 1 (2012): 31-49.

Held, Virginia. *The Ethics of Care: Personal, Political, and Global*. New York: Oxford University Press, 2006.

———. *Feminist Morality: Transforming Culture, Society, and Politics*. Chicago: University of Chicago Press, 1993.

hooks, Bell. *Teaching to Transgress: Education as the Practice of Freedom*. New York: Routledge, 1994.

Kern, M. Kathleen. "The Reference Interview Revisited." In *Reimagining Reference in the 21st Century*, edited by David A. Tyckoson and John G. Dove, 61-74. West Lafayette: Purdue University Press, 2015.

Kissane, Emily C. and Daniel J. Mollner. "Critical Thinking at the Reference Desk: Teaching Students to Manage Technology." *RQ* 32, no. 4 (1993): 485-490.

Ladenson, Sharon. "Paradigm Shift: Utilizing Critical Feminist Pedagogy in Library Instruction." In *Critical Library Instruction: Theories & Methods*, edited by Maria T. Accardi, Emily Drabinski, and Alana Kumbier, 105-112. Duluth: Library Juice Press, 2010.

Lindemann, Hilde. *An Invitation to Feminist Ethics*. Boston: McGraw-Hill, 2006.

Noddings, Nel. *Caring: A Feminine Approach to Ethics and Moral Education*. Berkeley: University of California Press, 1984.

Parry, Shirley C. "Feminist Pedagogy and Techniques for the Changing Classroom." *Women's Studies Quarterly* 24, no. 3/4 (1996): 45-54.

Radford, Marie L. "Encountering Virtual Users: A Qualitative Investigation of Interpersonal Communication in Chat Reference." *Journal of the American Society for Information Science and Technology* 57, no. 8 (2006): 1046–1059.

A Woman's Work is Never Done: Reference outside the Library

Kelly McElroy

A man may work from sun to sun, but woman's work is never done.
(Maybe a colonial American saying)

Over a recent weekend, I received two reference requests. One came through my personal email account, from my cat sitter. The last time she had taken care of my cat, she had noticed an intriguing book with a red cover sitting on a table. She thought it looked like a good fit for her lesbian and bisexual women's reading group. Could I remember the title and author? Another request came by text, from a new faculty member I'd met socially. Could I track down the name of a particular Nina Simone song, something about a little girl who isn't allowed to play with another little girl because of her race?

Both of these requests are standard reference questions—reader's advisory and basic trivia—of a kind I almost never encounter during my workday as an academic librarian. Sometimes, as with the cat sitter, I find myself calling on my training for these off-the-desk requests, asking a series of questions to determine the book at hand, and ending my response with a spoonful of read-alikes. ("If you like the book with the red cover, you might like...") For the other question, it took more of a stubborn persistence through tedium: I clicked through two or three pages of Youtube clips of Nina Simone recordings (incidentally, not a bad way to spend a Sunday evening). This type of reference work off the desk—even outside the library's *virtual* spaces—has occupied my thinking lately. I generally love to get questions from my friends, family, and pleasant acquaintances;

even strangers seem to sometimes recognize that I'm a librarian, and ask for directions or recommendations.

And yet, not all off-duty reference requests are welcome. Last fall, I treated myself to a massage. Sitting at a computer all day can lead to neck and shoulder pain for me, so I was very much looking forward to the relief of some serious kneading. I tend to prefer women health providers, but since there was only one appointment available at the last minute, I took it anyway. As we made small talk after I lay down on the table, I mentioned that I was a librarian on campus. The massage therapist, who had done doctoral work in psychology, launched into a series of intricate and clearly preformed questions. He had already asked for help from the campus library, but wanted to confirm—and express his displeasure for—the answers. Even as I agreed that yes, it was problematic that, due to his peculiar staff classification, he could not access electronic resources from his desk, I found myself wishing he would just leave me in peace. I answered his questions—as best as I could while face down on a massage table—but with resentment.

For what had been intended as a relaxing and satisfying hour, I left annoyed and confused. And I found myself wondering, what exactly made me so angry? I like being a librarian. I like how people respond when they hear what I do; I like much of my day-to-day work; I like the ideas and values of our profession. I like answering reference questions, and completing a difficult reference transaction is probably when I feel most like a librarian. Indeed, I often miss reference, as my job duties have shifted to outreach and engagement. I treasure the questions that pop up when I'm tabling at a community event or having coffee with a colleague in student affairs, these traces of traditional library work in a more nebulous new world.

But "librarian" is also a role I play to pay the bills. Being asked to work after hours and without compensation, even within my campus community, can, as it did on the massage table, spur both annoyance and guilt, not to mention lousy service. Richard Bopp and Linda Smith state that, "the central ethical principle guiding reference librarians is 'equality of access.'"[1] And yet, when access occurs outside of the library, it can be difficult to determine how equitable it is. I was struck by a fleeting anecdote in Susan Hildenbrand's review of library women's

---

1 Richard E. Bopp and Linda C. Smith, *Reference and Information Services: An Introduction* (Englewood, Colo.: Libraries Unlimited, 2001), 40.

history. While many library historians have presented (white) women librarians as using their gutsy commitment to overcome low budgets and other adversities, Hildenbrand calls for an intersectional approach: "It might help to explain the experiences of Annie L. McPheeters, who, as a small child, was ejected from a whites-only library by a truculent white woman librarian who was undoubtedly underpaid and overworked and possibly even nurturing and compassionate—to some."[2] When the success of a profession depends on its practitioners' willingness to give, their choices about when and to whom to keep giving may reflect their social prejudices and systematic discrimination. McPheeters herself went on to become a librarian, despite this early negative experience. But I am wary of my own unseen weaknesses, particularly in the work I do beyond my stated job duties.

These overlapping threads—compensation and love, connection and access—inform this conversation. I like my work, but do I really have to do it all the time? I welcome new avenues for authentic connections with my community, but what does it mean if my availability is always assumed? How does gender (alongside race, socio-economic class, and other categories of identity) shape the expectations of when and to whom my labor is available? How can I use reference off the desk to build community, while also maintaining personal boundaries? This chapter will explore off-desk reference work in the context of impoverished feminized professions, unconscious bias and segregation, and the value of taking time for our communities.

Do What You Love, Despite How it Pays

In her examination of the profession and identity development of librarians in turn-of-the-century Utah, Suzanne Stauffer writes that white, middle-class women "were drawn to the profession by this emphasis on the moral and cultural aspects of librarianship, which were in accordance with their socially accepted roles as guardians of morality and disseminators of culture."[3] I circled these words several

---

[2] Suzanne Hildenbrand, "Library Feminism and Library Women's History: Activism and Scholarship, Equity and Culture," *Libraries & Culture* 35, no. 1 (2000), 61.

[3] Suzanne M. Stauffer , "The Intelligent, Thoughtful Personality: Librarianship as a Process of Identity Formation," *Library & Information History* 30, no. 4 (November 2014): 257, doi:10.1179/1758348914Z.00000000067.

times when I first read them. Like many librarians, I love to read and talk about books and other cultural artifacts. To echo Lloyd Dobler from the film *Say Anything*, I also wanted a career where I didn't have to sell, buy, or process anything. Though the specific issues may have changed, the moral and cultural elements of library work remain a strong draw. Even in my first job in a library as a teenager, our training included significant sections about intellectual freedom, equitable access, and privacy, all of which are found in the ALA Code of Ethics and had almost no concrete impact on my work as an on-call shelver.[4]

Librarians often speak of what we do as a vocation, more than simply a wage job. And yet, there can be a tension between a labor of love and the sometimes grim reality of library work. I remember feeling queasy after a screening of the documentary *The Hollywood Librarian* at my graduate school. Scenes of a dire financial crisis in the Salinas Public Library cut to superstar librarian Nancy Pearl espousing her love for her work with no acknowledgement by the filmmakers of the dissonance between these positions.[5] Even when cynicism emerges, it is often resigned: yes, I am struggling to pay off my student loans amid budget cuts and stressful work conditions, but I wouldn't be here if I didn't love it.[6] A quick glance at the angry letters that poured into *American Libraries* after Mark Plaiss' polemical 1990 editorial "Libraryland: Pseudo-intellectuals and semi-dullards" shows that little has changed in this discourse over the past quarter century. Where Plaiss indicated that "deep down, you *know* that any schlemiel can be a librarian,"[7] angry letter writers responded that librarianship is more than just a job. One writer declared, "I am not certain that I'd class librarians with grocery clerks in a blanket sense; I would class,

---

[4] "Code of Ethics of the American Library Association," accessed March 30, 2016, http://www.ala.org/advocacy/proethics/codeofethics/codeethics.

[5] Ann Seidl et al., *The Hollywood Librarian: A Look at Librarians through Film* (Northampton, MA: Media Education Foundation, 2009).

[6] See, for example, Rita Meade, "5 Reasons Being a Librarian Is Stressful," *Screwy Decimal* (blog), January 4, 2013, http://www.screwydecimal.com/2013/01/5-reasons-being-librarian-is-stressful.html.

[7] Mark Plaiss, "On My Mind: Libraryland: Pseudo-Intellectuals and Semi-Dullards," *American Libraries* 21, no. 6 (1990): 588.

well, myself, anyway, with grocery clerks who have a real calling to clerk in a grocery store."[8]

Of course, workers who feel called to clerk in a grocery store aren't required to get a graduate degree to do that work. In 2012, Forbes listed the MLIS as the worst graduate degree to invest in, noting the low mid-career median pay and relatively small projected growth of the field.[9] The reactions against this piece reflect that tension between the powerful story of vocation and the concrete details of frustrating pay. As the frequently divisive Annoyed Librarian put it in their *Library Journal* blog, "We librarians aren't in it for the money. We're in it for the relaxation and the goodwill."[10] I mostly don't disagree with that, for myself. And yet, what does it mean for our professional identity if we're all doing this because we love it, and in spite of the pay? As the job outlook for librarianship stagnates—2% growth expected over the next decade, compared to 7% for all jobs in the United States—and the job market tightens, fewer of us will be able to do what we love for pay.[11]

Feminists have long recognized both that women's work tends to be underpaid, and that women often do additional work on top of whatever they're being paid for. Miya Tokumitsu neatly draws gender into her critique of the exhortation from Steve Jobs and others to Do What You Love and Love What You Do.[12] Some types of labor (janitorial work, fast food preparation) are hard to imagine loving: who would want to scrub toilets when you could be designing iPhones? Although some people in these industries may enjoy their work, they tend to be low paid and have challenging or degrading working

---

8 Ann Welton, "A Vocation, Not a Profession," *American Libraries* 21, no. 8 (1990): 717.

9 "The Best And Worst Master's Degrees For Jobs–Forbes," accessed December 18, 2015, http://www.forbes.com/sites/jacquelynsmith/2012/06/08/the-best-and-worst-masters-degrees-for-jobs-2/2/.

10 The Worst Master's Degree for Jobs," *Annoyed Librarian* (blog), *Library Journal*, June 15, 2012, accessed December 18, 2015, http://lj.libraryjournal.com/blogs/annoyedlibrarian/2012/06/13/the-worst-masters-degree-for-jobs/.

11 Bureau of Labor Statistics, U.S. Department of Labor, "Librarians" in *Occupational Outlook Handbook*, 2016, http://www.bls.gov/ooh/Education-Training-and-Library/Librarians.htm.

12 Miya Tokumitsu, "In the Name of Love," *Jacobin*, 2014, https://www.jacobinmag.com/2014/01/in-the-name-of-love/.

conditions and physical effects.[13] And, these types of service support work are disproportionately done by women, particularly by women of color.[14] The pathways that lead fewer Latinas to management and fewer white men to housecleaning are complex. As one Bureau of Labor Statistics report drily notes, "Labor market differences among the race and ethnicity groups are associated with many factors, not all of which are measurable."[15] In the case of librarianship, the required MLIS degree represents a notable barrier: in 2013, only 3% of Latinos had attained a Master's degree in any subject, compared to 6% for African-Americans, 8% for Whites, and 15% for Asians.[16]

Even for those who can afford it, the notion that one should do what one loves can lead to unpaid internships, precarious adjunct or temporary positions, and other forms of exploitation, all commonly advised to folks considering how to break into librarianship.[17] The recommendation to suck it up and do unpaid work—perhaps on top of other paid, non-professional work—is often lamented, but rarely challenged.[18] The summer before I started graduate school, I subscribed to a number of librarian listservs and set up a series of informational interviews with professionals in my area. The contrast was jarring. The people I met in person emphasized the joy they got from their work and their warm professional community, while online

---

[13] Bureau of Labor Statistics, U.S. Department of Labor, "Janitors and Building Cleaners" in *Occupational Outlook Handbook*, 2016, http://www.bls.gov/ooh/building-and-grounds-cleaning/janitors-and-building-cleaners.htm#tab-3; Bureau of Labor Statistics, US Department of Labor, "Food Preparation Workers" in *Occupational Outlook Handbook*, 2016, http://www.bls.gov/ooh/food-preparation-and-serving/food-preparation-workers.htm#tab-3.

[14] Bureau of Labor Statistics, U.S. Department of Labor, "Labor Force Characteristics by Race and Ethnicity, 2014," *BLS Reports 1057* (November 2015): 4-5.

[15] Ibid., 1.

[16] Deborah A. Santiago, Emily Calderón Galdeano, and Morgan Taylor, *The Condition of Latinos in Education: 2015 Factbook* (Excelencia in Education: 2015), 10.

[17] Tokumitsu, "In the Name of Love."

[18] See, for example, "Work Nights at a Paying Job While You Work a Crappy Unpaid Internship during the Day – and I Know This Sucks, but – Just Do It, If That's Your Only Option.," *Hiring Librarians (blog)*, December 28, 2014, http://hiringlibrarians.com/2014/12/28/work-nights-at-a-paying-job-while-you-work-a-crappy-unpaid-internship-during-the-day-and-i-know-this-sucks-but-just-do-it-if-thats-your-only-option/.

I saw newly minted librarians lamenting their 90-minute commutes to unpaid gigs and declaring they'd decided not to have children because of the working conditions. The sum total of this was still a vision of love, even if a fraught or dysfunctional one. And, I still went to library school in the fall.

Identity and Access

Besides the shared moral and cultural interests that draw us to librarianship, I have some other things in common with the turn-of-the-century librarians that Suzanne Stauffer wrote about. Like them, and like the bulk of librarians today, I am also a white, English-speaking, middle-class woman.[19] Looking at reference outside the library, this longstanding homogeneity of librarianship has an unexpected effect: as our demographics remain glaringly white, most opportunities for reference off the desk likely occur between white librarians and other white people.

Annie L. McPheeters, who had been turned away from the library as a child, went on to become one of the first Black librarians in the Atlanta Public Library.[20] In writing about segregation in Georgia libraries, she points out that laws and regulations providing for libraries rarely included explicit statements on racial exclusion. Instead, the local authorities overseeing library programs simply "for reasons of their own administered service according to their own likes or biases."[21] While there's obviously a huge difference in scale between having any access at all to a public library and access to occasionally ask a question of an off-duty librarian, the fact remains that access can be shared or denied depending on the whims of those with power. Perhaps it seems frivolous (or merely pompous) to suggest that getting extra help from an off-the-clock librarian is any kind of special boost—instead, let's consider it as

---

19 *Diversity Counts* (American Library Association: 2012). ALA does not provide statistics about language of origin or SES of librarians – however, accredited LIS programs in the US and Canada are almost entirely conducted in English, and obtaining a graduate degree is arguably in itself a marker of middle-class status.

20 *New Georgia Encyclopedia*, s.v. "Annie L. McPheeters (1908-1994)," accessed March 30, 2016, http://www.georgiaencyclopedia.org/articles/education/annie-l-mcpheeters-1908-1994.

21 Annie L. McPheeters, *Library Service in Black and White: Some Personal Recollections, 1921-1980* (Scarecrow Press, Inc., 1988), 131.

simply one more element of the invisible constellation that eases things for people with unearned privilege.

Research on implicit associations and bias suggest that people may consciously or unconsciously disguise socially unacceptable beliefs such as feelings of racial superiority.[22] While I might consciously feel annoyed by a man asking me questions while he treats my sore back, I might also make some decisions about who to help based on unconscious bias. We might imagine that the troubling concept of the "problem patron" has a corollary outside the library—someone in your life asking you questions who you wish would just leave you alone.

However, negative bias is far from the only barrier. Like most white Americans, I live a life largely segregated by race and class, among other identity categories. According to the UCLA Civil Rights Project, the typical white public school student today might have about eight classmates out of a class of thirty who are not white.[23] This is actually *more* diverse than my public school classes ever were as a child. I grew up and now live and work in Oregon, a state originally founded with laws to exclude Black people and which remains disproportionately white compared to the rest of the country.[24] The student body at the university where I work is a little more racially and ethnically diverse than the town it is located in, thanks in part to a large international student population.[25] The Public Religion Research Institute found that 75% of white Americans have no people of color among their social network; combined with the overwhelming whiteness of librarianship, this suggests that opportunities for informal reference interactions can differ starkly by race.[26]

---

22 Anthony G. Greenwald and Linda Hamilton Krieger, "Implicit Bias: Scientific Foundations," *California Law Review* 94, no. 4 (2006): 945–67, doi:10.2307/20439056.

23 Gary Orfield et al., Brown at 60: *Great Progress, a Long Retreat and an Uncertain Future* (Civil Rights Project/Proyecto Derechos Civiles, 2014), 12.

24 Walidah Imarisha, "A Hidden History," Oregon Humanities (2013): 13.

25 U. S. Census Bureau, "American FactFinder–Results," accessed March 30, 2016, http://factfinder.census.gov/faces/tableservices/jsf/pages/productview.xhtml?src=CF; Office of Institutional Research, Enrollment Summary (Oregon State University: 2015), 1.

26 Daniel Cox, Juhem Navarro-Rivera, and Robert P. Jones, *Race and Americans' Social Networks* (Public Religion Research Institute: 2016).

And of course, there are many factors that shape this access. When my best friend asked me for help finding information to guide her vote on a recent ballot initiative, she had a lot of other options available. She has Internet access at home, access to some databases through the well-funded public library in her city, and working knowledge of how to navigate those systems. She has a Masters degree in Education, she has asked other librarians for help before, and she has a sense of what is possible to get from a librarian. Given that I can choose who I share my expertise with, I need to think about who has access, and who may not have a librarian around just to help.

Authentic Relationships and Community-building

Beyond questions from my closest friends and family, which I will almost certainly just answer, I get questions from acquaintances somewhat further afield: a new faculty member I met at a party, a fellow member of a community organization, a neighbor. In a college town like the one where I live, no one is very far from the university. If you don't attend classes or work there, you likely know someone who does. In that sense, even strangers may be members of my library community, and this is even truer as I work at a land-grant institution. So the people around me are our users, whether I'm at work or not. I think about this more, as my job duties have evolved away from traditional library work to more ambiguous outreach and engagement. I don't do any reference on the desk anymore, although I do some virtual reference from my own workspace. So, pretty much all the reference I do is off the desk, but not all of it is off-duty. And, considering our community as the state as a whole, nearly all the off-duty reference I do is still in-scope, in the sense of serving "our" users.

As the student outreach and engagement librarian, my job is to better connect the library to students, with a particular focus on those from historically marginalized communities. One assumption behind this work is that students who feel comfortable using the library (including the reference desk), already do. Another assumption is that the library has something to offer all students, particularly marginalized students, to shore up retention and graduation rates. The idea of informal, off-the-desk reference becomes particularly interesting here. Students from marginalized communities—first generation college students, low-income students, students of color at majority white institutions—may be particularly likely to benefit from high-touch personal connections with staff and faculty.[27] In some ways, the characteristics of effective mentorship match the comfortable pace of off-duty reference I do with people I know. My friends and acquaintances feel free to just reach out whenever they need something, without having to schedule an appointment or go through any formal channels. A reference question can simply emerge through casual conversation. In their study of the impact that faculty and staff have on high-risk students, Laurie Schreiner et al. noted that students "seemed to value even small investments of time and energy, particularly when they perceived that the investment was not what other staff or faculty usually did. Taking time for students may be one of the ways that institutional agents can communicate most clearly to students that the institution values them and is committed to their welfare."[28] Again, I'm haunted by the story of little Annie L. McPheeters turned away by a harried white lady librarian. Perhaps it is important that we take time—from other work tasks, or from our personal time—for the most vulnerable members of our community. So it is worthwhile to explore how to create more informal opportunities for off-desk reference even—perhaps especially—while I'm at work.

Some of my most enjoyable reference questions have come at outreach events: for example, when I was tabling at the Study Abroad Fair, I had an extended conversation with a staff member about regional DVDs, and ended up emailing him later with information about our streaming video services to pass along to his wife, a language instructor. At that same event, I connected with a Latina student who wants to become a librarian, but had struggled to find a volunteer position. I was there to promote a library study abroad course, but the richest interactions I had were rooted in reference questions. Even just attending campus events is another way to build these informal connections. A colleague who came

---

27 Laurie A. Schreiner, Patrice Noel, and Linda Cantwell, "The Impact of Faculty and Staff on High-Risk College Student Persistence," *Journal of College Student Development* 52, no. 3 (2011): 322; Samuel D. Museus and Kathleen M. Neville, "Delineating the Ways That Key Institutional Agents Provide Racial Minority Students With Access to Social Capital in College," *Journal of College Student Development* 53, no. 3 (2012): 437, doi:10.1353/csd.2012.0042.

28 Ibid., 333.

to libraries from student affairs often points out that, in that field, jobs explicitly build in this kind of community participation. In her previous job, she was expected to attend one campus event each week, and compensate with flextime. What if all librarians were given this opportunity? Although individual librarians may be able to advocate (or make stealthy decisions) about how to spend their work time, communicating the importance of taking time upwards through administration can lead to more structural changes, such as regular participation in events like student Move-In day, revisions to position descriptions, or inclusion in strategic planning. Given current—admittedly complicated—focus on student retention and success, building new ways to support students on their own terms may even be slipped into existing aims.

We can also create more off-desk environments to connect with our users. At my library, we hold a monthly Crafternoon in the foyer, where we bring a simple craft activity and materials where anyone can drop in and participate. In these sessions, I am often surprised at how many reference and service questions come up. Students tell me what they want to learn; what they're writing papers about; the projects they're excited to work on. I've connected with students about voter registration outreach; students tell me about what stresses them out and what they'd like to see the library do. It is a place where the library can make time for students, whether reference is explicitly part of the mix or not. This is true for all the public events our library participates in. When we bring a bookmobile out to the dorms or table at the Earth Day fair to promote our new composting program, we are also librarians making ourselves available outside the library. The last time I tabled at a public event, reference questions led to conversations about Open Access publishing, genre fiction, Sci-Hub, and the rumor that the ghost of our first university librarian still haunts campus. Reference is a task that people recognize as something librarians do, and it can be an entry point leading to the many other things we do. A purposeful, reflective approach to participating and seeking out community events is one way for libraries to recognize who is not coming in, and to come to them.

A feminist approach to outreach might build on the community-led approach developed in Canadian public libraries. Although public libraries are generally recognized as inclusive, and services quite highly rated, socially excluded people and communities are much less likely to use the library.[29] Rather than develop outreach and marketing *for* socially excluded people, the community-led approach asks library staff to build and maintain relationships *with* them. By listening to the community as the experts in what they need, librarians can collaborate on services to meet those needs, in a loop that incorporates feedback and new ideas from users. For example, a librarian in Halifax found out that certain foods often spoiled at their city food bank, because users did not know how to prepare them. These foods were then labeled with a note that the Halifax Public Library could help you find tasty recipes, if you call the reference desk.[30] In this elegant solution, a persistent type of off-desk question simply got rerouted back to the desk. Recognizing issues out in the community doesn't need to mean developing onerous new activities—in some cases, it can be addressed by a creative application of existing services. However, without the relationship between the librarian and food bank users and staff, the issue would not have been identified, least of all as a reference question. By building relationships with marginalized users, we also have the chance to build awareness of what libraries and librarians can do.

Conclusions

Lately, a quotation attributed to former Simmons LIS professor Allen Smith came across my Tumblr dashboard: "In order to be really good as a librarian, everything counts towards your work, every play you go see, every concert you hear, every trip you take, everything you read, everything you know. I don't know of another occupation like that. The more you know, the better you're going to be." As of the time I'm writing this, the original post had over 800 notes, either reblogs or likes. I feel ambivalent about this sentiment, although it resonates, because I also resent the idea that my personal life serves to enrich my work, as if it is just a value-added aspect of my employment. In some ways, it comes down to the same old bind: Do What You Love, Love What You Do.

---

29 Brian Campbell et al., *Community-Led Libraries Toolkit* (Working Together: 2008): 4.

30 Kenneth Williment, "It Takes a Community to Build a Library," *Public Libraries Online* (blog), April 26, 2013, accessed July 19, 2016.

When I think back to my presumptuous massage therapist, I wish I had simply said no, this isn't the time for this. Setting boundaries on how and when I do work in my personal time is an ongoing and organic process: something that is overwhelming right now might be okay this time next week. Along with this comes reflection: who is asking? Why am I resistant? What are the patterns? Reflection provides a chance to look for my own likes and biases, as well as for potential points of professional service. If I always get asked questions at the grocery store or the bike shop, perhaps there's an opportunity for my work to step in, to bring the reference desk there. My colleagues recently discussed whether we should record off-desk interactions in our reference statistics—if I'm doing work at the bus stop, I should be able to make that labor visible. Recognizing off-desk reference doesn't mean I have to always answer the questions—in some cases, it can be a way to refer people back to my colleagues who are at work, back at the desk.

Bibliography

Bopp, Richard E, and Linda C. Smith. Reference and Information Services : An Introduction. Englewood, Colo.: Libraries Unlimited, 2001.

Bureau of Labor Statistics, U.S. Department of Labor. "Food Preparation Workers." In Occupational Outlook Handbook. Accessed March 24, 2016. http://www.bls.gov/ooh/food-preparation-and-serving/food-preparation-workers.htm#tab-3.

———. "Janitors and Building Cleaners." In Occupational Outlook Handbook Accessed March 24, 2016. http://www.bls.gov/ooh/building-and-grounds-cleaning/janitors-and-building-cleaners.htm#tab-3.

———. "Librarians." In Occupational Outlook Handbook. Accessed March 24, 2016. http://www.bls.gov/ooh/Education-Training-and-Library/Librarians.htm.

———. "Labor Force Characteristics by Race and Ethnicity, 2014." BLS Reports 1057 (November 2015).

Campbell, Brian et al. Community-Led Libraries Toolkit. Working Together: 2008.

"Code of Ethics of the American Library Association." Accessed March 30, 2016. http://www.ala.org/advocacy/proethics/codeofethics/codeethics.

Cox, Daniel, Juhem Navarro-Rivera, and Robert P. Jones. Race and Americans' Social Networks. Public Religion Research Institute, 2016.

Diversity Counts. American Library Association, 2012.

Greenwald, Anthony G., and Linda Hamilton Krieger. "Implicit Bias: Scientific Foundations." California Law Review 94, no. 4 (2006): 945–67. doi:10.2307/20439056.

Hildenbrand, Suzanne. "Library Feminism and Library Women's History: Activism and Scholarship, Equity and Culture." Libraries & Culture 35, no. 1, 2000, 51–65.

Imarisha, Walidah. "A Hidden History." Oregon Humanities (2013), 12–19.

McPheeters, Annie L. Library Service in Black and White: Some Personal Recollections, 1921-1980. Scarecrow Press, Inc., 1988.

Museus, Samuel D., and Kathleen M. Neville. "Delineating the Ways That Key Institutional Agents Provide Racial Minority Students With Access to Social Capital in College." Journal of College Student Development 53, no. 3 (2012): 436–52. doi:10.1353/csd.2012.0042.

Office of Institutional Research. Enrollment Summary. Oregon State University, 2015.

Orfield, Gary,et al. Brown at 60: Great Progress, a Long Retreat and an Uncertain Future. Civil Rights Project/Proyecto Derechos Civiles, 2014.

Plaiss, Mark. "On My Mind: Libraryland: Pseudo-Intellectuals and Semi-Dullards." American Libraries 21, no. 6 (1990): 588–89.

"Population Estimates, July 1, 2015, (V2015)." Accessed March 28, 2016. //www.census.gov/quickfacts/.

Santiago, Deborah A., Emily Calderón Galdeano, and Morgan Taylor, The Condition of Latinos in Education: 2015 Factbook (Excelencia in Education: 2015)

Schreiner, Laurie A., Patrice Noel, and Linda Cantwell. "The Impact of Faculty and Staff on High-Risk College Student Persistence." Journal of College Student Development 52, no. 3 (2011): 321–38.

Seidl, Ann. The Hollywood Librarian: A Look at Librarians through Film. Northampton: MA: Media Education Foundation, 2009.

Stauffer, Suzanne M. "The Intelligent, Thoughtful Personality: Librarianship as a Process of Identity Formation." Library & Information History 30, no. 4 (November 2014): 254–72. doi:10.1179/1758348914Z.00000000067.

"The Best and Worst Master's Degrees For Jobs - Forbes." Accessed December 18, 2015. http://www.forbes.com/sites/jacquelynsmith/2012/06/08/the-best-and-worst-masters-degrees-for-jobs-2/2/.

Tokumitsu, Miya. "In the Name of Love." Jacobin, 2014. https://www.jacobinmag.com/2014/01/in-the-name-of-love/.

U. S. Census Bureau. "American FactFinder - Results." Accessed March 30, 2016. http://factfinder.census.gov/faces/tableservices/jsf/pages/productview.xhtml?src=CF.

Welton, Ann. "A Vocation, Not a Profession." American Libraries 21, no. 8 (1990): 717–717.

Part II

Ways of Doing and Rethinking the Work

Seeing Writing Center Practices through a Feminist Lens & Applying the Lessons Learned to Reference Desk Practice

Dory Cochran

Introduction

With only a week separating my graduation from library school and the beginning of a graduate degree program in English, I felt like I was balancing two identities; one identity being the budding academic librarian, and the second, the determined literature detective. I especially struggled with maintaining this balance after I joined the staff at the university writing center. Perhaps naively I saw this as an opportunity to connect to my library roots and bring tricks of the reference trade to the writing session. I was soon designated as the library liaison and asked to discuss information literacy with my fellow tutors. Given how I was positioned as the "library person," it's no surprise that as a tutor I reflected constantly on how my library experience could inform my tutoring work. Now several years later, I realize that I never thought about how my own experiences as a writing tutor could positively inform and reshape the work I do as a reference librarian.

Driving my reflection on these experiences is my ongoing exploration of what feminist pedagogy means to me and to the library profession. As a young girl, I observed the strong women in my life working to make their communities better, and at the same time, fighting for equality. My grandmother, a single parent, supported my mother in her pursuit to become a musician and tenured professor. My mother then continued the fight, and though taken too early by cancer, battled her way to equal pay and benefits. As an academic, my mother loved teaching and learning. Her struggles taught me of the inequities within higher education, but they also taught me not to give up on academia and that with determination and a passion for learning, positive change can happen. I see my mother's story as a feminist embodiment of the power found in action through reflection. In this way, I wanted to reflect on my own experiences with writing center practice and, through a feminist lens, explore how these ideas can promote action at the reference desk.

There are collaborations happening between writing centers and libraries across the country and the prevalence of these partnerships indicates that pairing the two together is now a best practice. I love that the number of opportunities for librarians and writing tutors to learn about each other's services is growing; however, the reciprocity of these partnerships is not always explored. As librarians, we are excellent at sharing ideas and the willingness to share is crucial to fostering a feminist ethic of care. Just as important, though, is the skill of listening. Ideas are being shared about what librarians can teach writing tutors and, as librarians, we can balance the conversation by listening to ideas emerging from writing centers. In this way, not only can we pedagogically rethink our practice at the reference desk by engaging with new approaches, but we can also bring a feminist ethic of care into our practice through deliberate reflection, sharing, and listening.

In efforts to listen to writing center voices and reflect on implications for our work as librarians, together you and I will explore connections between writing center and reference desk practice by reflecting on four different feminist strategies that can be implemented at the reference desk: active learning, valuing experience, decentering authority, and building community. Taken together, each of these strategies builds interactions that support a feminist ethic of care, or, in other words, a community of librarians who help serve others not only with their minds, but also with their hearts.

As a final welcome, I'd like to share with you words from *The Everyday Writing Center: A Community of Practice*. The authors write, "we hope to put you in dialogue with us. This requires considering your own personal awareness, practice, and inquiry."[1] I echo this call and as I share my own memories and reflections, please join me by working through the reader reflection questions at the end of each section. In sharing our lived experiences together, we both validate multiple voices, while engaging in a feminist act that supports reflection on current practices and how they can change for the better.

Play as Active Learning

A Reference Desk Memory

It was the last shift of the day and I was thinking about dinner. With only ten minutes left on the clock, a student came to the desk and described her troubles finding sources for a paper on American fashion. I walked her through a search in our catalog and while we found a few interesting books I could tell she wasn't inspired. By then my shift was over and I told her to try the search strategies we used on her own and to come back with any other questions the following day.

A Writing Center Memory

I walked into the tutor training session and I saw that there was a small container of Play-Doh on every single chair. I quickly spotted a yellow container and claimed the accompanying seat, happy that I had Play-Doh in my favorite color. Kylie Kinley, a friend and fellow writing tutor, was presenting on creativity in preparation for her presentation later that month at the International Writing Center Association Conference in San Diego.[2] Kylie is a wonderful creative writer and I knew that the day's session would be fun. She first asked us to imagine our favorite animal and then to sculpt that animal with the Play-Doh. What followed was an engaging and thoughtful practice in how creativity can be used to help students write with more description and to help students see writing as an imaginative and fun practice. After that session, I went out and bought some Play-Doh.

---

1 Anne Ellen Geller, Michele Eodice, Frankie Condon, Meg Carroll, and Elizabeth Boquet, *The Everyday Writing Center: A Community of Practice* (Logan: Utah State University Press, 2006), 3.

2 Kylie Kinley, "Drawing Lines in the Sand is Fine, but Building Sandcastles is Better: The Value of Play in the Writing Center" (presentation, International Writing Centers Association, San Diego, CA, October 25-27, 2012).

Taken Together

While these memories come from different settings and interactions, they both revolve around helping a student achieve a goal, whether that be in adding description to a narrative or finding the resources needed for a paper. However, one major difference between the two is that Kylie's session harnessed play as an active learning strategy, while my experience at the reference desk was decidedly without play. In discussing the benefits of integrating play into a writing session, Denise Stephensen argues that play helps students by drawing upon skills, including verbal, visual, spatial, and kinesthetic, that otherwise might not be incorporated into a tutoring session.[3] Essentially, in this approach, toys and play are used as tools to support active learning for students in a tutoring session.

Bringing play to reference work can be risky, but feminist pedagogy pushes us to try new things without a guarantee of success or control. So, how might we use this push to explore connections between active learning in the writing center and feminist implications for reference work? First, let's look at conversations surrounding why play is used in writing centers. Two common themes that emerge are the integration of play to get away from ingrained writing habits and the use of play to imagine something in a different way. Both of these themes draw upon active learning strategies to help students disrupt "the *ready* of a 'ready, set, go'" approach.[4] In connection to feminist pedagogy, this act of disrupting the learning process resembles the use of student-centered teaching as a way to dismantle a "banking" approach to learning. Reference librarians often talk about "teaching moments" at the desk, but in reality, our practice more often resembles a transaction more similar to a bank visit, rather than a classroom.

Transforming our teaching moments at the desk to active learning moments doesn't require radical changes to our practice, but can be started through a slow integration of a few interactive items to the desk. For example, dry erase boards, word magnets, or dice could all be used in creative ways. Perhaps a student might roll a die and

---

3 Denise Stephenson, "Constructive Toys: More than a Good Time," *The Writing Lab Newsletter* 26, no. 2 (2001): 8.

4 Anne Ellen Geller, Michele Eodice, Frankie Condon, Meg Carroll, and Elizabeth Boquet, *The Everyday Writing Center: A Community of Practice* (Logan: Utah State University Press, 2006), 22.

then use that number as a goal for how many keywords to brainstorm before working through a search with the librarian. Or, the letters on wooden blocks could be used to help students brainstorm keywords. Or, if a student is having trouble verbally identifying a research question, using word magnets could be a kinesthetic way to refocus ideas. Though simplified, using these tools to support moments of active learning at the desk can also support a feminist ethic of care by offering service that focuses on interactions with moments for students to reflect, share, and listen. Bringing elements of play to the desk can push us as librarians to make the reference interview more about creative learning and less about simply providing transactional answers.

Reader Reflection

How could I have used an element of play to better help the student who asked for resources on American fashion?

Valuing Experience at the Desk and Thinking About the Questions We Ask

A Reference Desk Memory

A student walked away from the desk and I turned to my co-worker and said, "phew, I need some M&M's after that one." My co-worker laughed with me and asked what happened. I replied by saying, "oh nothing, just one of those times when the student had no clue what they needed. They didn't even know the name of their professor." We shook our heads, laughed, and then went back to work.

A Writing Center Memory

A graduate student in geography was struggling with the clarity and format of her thesis and contacted the director of the writing center to schedule recurring meetings with a tutor. I was selected as that tutor and after being introduced to the student, I met with her about every two weeks for two semesters. She was an international student and we both shared stories about where we grew up and the expectations our families had for our education and careers. Since we were both graduate students, I was hesitant to be overly prescriptive in our conversations. This hesitancy revealed itself in my approach and I used non-directive tutoring strategies, meaning that I almost always asked open questions and shied away from offering decisive opinions. There were several instances where the student replied to a nondirective approach with "What do you mean? Tell me what I should write and where." While the student successfully completed her thesis, our conversations included many moments where something didn't feel quite right in how we were communicating with each other.

Taken Together

As reference librarians, our end goal is to help students, but the way we talk about helping students doesn't always reflect an ethic of care. For example, in her article on the theories and practice of reference work, Stephanie Brown states several times that patrons don't really know what they need and writes that "human memory can be a tricky thing, so it is important to be wary of specific details that the patron provides."[5] As a practice, this is problematic. Not listening to students means that we are forgetting a key element of feminist pedagogy, which is that students are experienced human beings. In fostering an ethic of care, we must check ourselves, and our colleagues, when we start to use language that questions patron knowledge. In this action, we recognize the "we" of learning in feminist pedagogy and value the student as a person with experience.

It's easy to say we will respect student's ideas, but trickier in practice. Integrating flexibility into our work is one way to develop this form of feminist listening. Flexibility can be considered in how we ask questions, or in employing a directive or non-directive tutoring style to better respond to students' preferred way of learning. A writing example in the directive style might be telling a student, "you need to add a transition sentence here." While, a non-directive approach could be, "how could we connect these two paragraphs to make it easier for the reader?" For many years, non-directive tutoring was couched as the better tutoring style and its collaborative focus aligns well with feminist pedagogy. Given students' diversity of learning though, there has been a shift in writing center practice that favors a flexible style that integrates both non-directive and directive approaches as preferred by

---

[5] Stephanie Willen Brown, "The Reference Interview: Theories and Practice," *Library Philosophy and Practice* Paper 164 (2008): 6.

a student.[6] I love thinking about a librarian's role as flexible, because it highlights that questions can be explored in alternative ways, which in turn helps students better communicate their experience.

In practice, though, how are we supposed to know when to be directive or non-directive? One possible writing center strategy (and value of feminist pedagogy) draws upon transparency and calls tutors to acknowledge moments where something doesn't feel quite right when working with a student. In *The Writing Lab Newsletter* Rebecca Babcock talks about this experience as "pragmatic impairment," which refers to the idea that we all respond better to different communication styles. As I was reading Babcock's words, I thought back to memories of working with the geography graduate student. In our sessions together, I insisted on being non-directive, when all she wanted was specific guidance. While taking a directive approach might feel controlling, when balanced with a non-directive approach it can serve as a way to respond to students' needs and encourage a "more open, welcoming, and productive learning environment," or in effect, an environment with a feminist ethic of care.[7]

Now as a reference librarian, I still feel anxious when I take a directive approach, but Babcock offers a useful strategy that also reflects the value of transparency in feminist pedagogy. Specifically, she calls upon tutors—and I would say librarians—to explain why we are offering certain ideas and questions when working with a student.[8] Transparency is overlooked at the reference desk – it's easier to give an answer, rather than an explanation for its accuracy. For example, imagine that a student comes to the reference desk and is trying to research a really broad topic. In order to help a student narrow their topic, I might first ask them about their interests. However, in this process I don't always verbalize to students why I'm asking these types of questions or indicate why it would be helpful to refine their research

---

6 Peter Carino, "Power and Authority in Peer Tutoring, " in *The Center Will Hold: Critical Perspectives on Writing Center Scholarship*, ed. Michael A. Pemberton & Joyce Kinkead (Logan: Utah State University Press, 2003), 110.

7 Kristin Boyd and Ann Haibeck, "We Have a Secret: Balancing Directiveness and Nondirectiveness During Peer Tutoring," *The Writing Lab Newsletter* 35, no. 5-6 (2011): 15.

8 Rebecca Babcock, "When Something Is Not Quite Right: Pragmatic Impairment and Compensation in the College Writing Tutorial," *The Writing Lab Newsletter* 35, no. 5-6 (2011): 9.

question. For some students, this type of non-directive conversation can help them refine their question, but for others they might get frustrated about why I'm questioning their topic instead of helping them find resources. Given this variation in how our students might respond to the questions we ask, embracing flexibility in our questioning and being clear in why we are asking our questions can help us better respect our students' needs. In sum, by asking and responding to questions that value students' experience and engaging in these conversations with flexible and transparent language, we can more explicitly align the reference interview with feminist pedagogical values.

Reader Reflection

Consider the example above where a student is researching a broad topic. What kinds of directive comments might you share to help that student narrow their topic and how would you explain why you are asking those questions?

Rethinking Authority at the Desk by Fostering a Beginner's Mind

A Reference Desk Memory

It was the beginning of the Fall semester and every other question at the desk involved students asking if their textbook was at the library. The first few times I was asked this question I showed students how to search for their book in the library catalog and then if we had the book, I pointed them in the direction of our Course Reserves department. After the fifth or sixth time answering the same question, I just started directing them to Course Reserves.

A Writing Center Memory

It was a Sunday night and I was working at the two library tables my fellow tutors and I had designated as our writing center space for the evening. The first student I worked with was writing a book review, and as an English major myself this session flew by. My second session, however, placed me out of my element. An engineering major was wanting to talk about a lab report. I soon found out that his content and the lab report format were way over my head. After we had been talking for a few minutes I told him that I was unfamiliar with much of the content and format, but that with his guidance we could talk through the areas he wasn't sure made sense. Not only were we able to talk through some of his questions, but I also learned a thing or two about engines.

Taken Together

As ALA president for 2016-2017, Julie Todaro's theme is "Expert in the Library." In a 2015 *Library Journal* interview, Todaro describes the core initiative for her presidency as focusing "on the librarian, the credentials of people working in libraries, the critical skill set that we need, and how we represent not only what the library does but what we do and who we are. You can have the perfect library... but if you don't have a librarian you don't have the expertise to connect the constituents with what they need."[9] While I value Todaro's efforts in explicitly arguing for the value of our profession, the need to reify librarians as experts sends a slight shiver down my spine. What concerns me is the finite nature of this classification and its perspective as one that does not reflect the views of the patron.

Here I'm drawn to rethinking our authority at the desk by considering how the values of creativity and openness within feminist pedagogy foster empathy. In *The Everyday Writing Center*, the authors write that, "if we are to cultivate in ourselves and in our tutors an awareness of teaching as learning, as *becoming* rather than as a display of *being* knowledgeable, we will be well on our way to creating a sustainable learning culture within our writing centers."[10] I love the use of "becoming" in describing librarianship because it paints our practice as an ongoing journey. However, as librarians, sometimes our abilities can make it hard to empathize with student struggles. I struggled with this in my reference desk memory and instead of walking students through a search, I just answered without a conversation. While this could be called efficient, I missed opportunities for interactions with real connection.

---

9 Lisa Peet, "ALA President-Elect Julie Todaro on Transforming Librarians," *Library Journal*, last modified June 18, 2015, http://lj.libraryjournal.com/2015/06/organizations/ala-organization/ala-president-elect-julie-todaro-on-transforming-librarians/#_.

10 Anne Ellen Geller, Michele Eodice, Frankie Condon, Meg Carroll, and Elizabeth Boquet, *The Everyday Writing Center: A Community of Practice* (Logan: Utah State University Press, 2006), 59.

In countering this attitude of static expertise with empathy, how do we develop creativity and an openness to learning anew? Geller et al., ask tutors to foster a "beginner's mind" by engaging in activities where a new skill or idea is taught.[11] In a sense, I experienced this sensation in my writing center memory when I worked with a student in a discipline and format that were new to me. In this scenario, I cultivated a beginner's mindset by working with another person, and one of the best ways to spark this openness and creativity is through collaborating with others. At work, my reference department asked a creative student worker to help lead an activity on openness at the desk using Play-Doh and in the coming months another student will hopefully visit us during a department meeting and teach us how to make origami swans. Engaging in creative and reflective opportunities like these doesn't have to be time consuming and the activities don't necessarily have to connect to library work, but remembering what it feels like to stumble in a task can help us check our over-eager expertise at the library desk. Not only does this approach help us learn from others, but it is also a way to break down barriers of expertise that make it difficult to empathize with our patrons in the library.

Reader Reflection

When was the last time you learned something new? How did that experience make you feel?

Building Community at the Desk Through Reflection

A Reference Desk Memory

The *Summer Citizen* program had begun at my university and most of our questions at the desk were from retired town visitors who were looking for something fun and entertaining to read. An older gentleman approached the desk and asked for a book. We found the title in the library catalog and after a quick scan I said, "Unfortunately, it looks like we don't have it in print. Is there another title you're interested in?" The gentleman replied, "Well, you do have it as an e-book, I see. That's what I want anyway–it looks like I can

---

11 Ibid., 60.

just download it here right onto my smart phone from my Overdrive app." With a grin, he said thank you and went on his way.

A Writing Center Memory

A student was studying for his TOEFL exam and working towards finishing his program and returning to Ecuador to teach. He was a well-known face in the writing center and had a reputation with the tutors for being demanding and drawing sessions over their allotted time. Working with him in a tutoring session was extremely emotionally draining. He constantly vocalized feelings of struggling with his work and he became known as a difficult student to tutor. Unfortunately, because of working with him, many tutors were wary of encountering the same struggles while tutoring other students studying for the TOEFL. I remember feeling this way and going into tutoring sessions with other international students wondering if it would be an easy or hard session. Though unintentional, I let experiences with one student foster an unfair prejudice towards other students.

Taken Together

Considering my memories together, unfair assumptions emerge as a clear theme. In thinking about why these experiences occur, Geller, et al. write that "the racism in our writing centers, like racism across our institutions, communities, and across the social, political and economic landscape of our lives, is not a series of aberrations, but the everyday manifestation of deeply embedded logics and patterns."[12] A feminist pedagogical approach requires that these systemic issues are addressed in our teaching. In order to do this at the reference desk, librarians need to consider how everyday behaviors and interactions might be unknowingly prejudiced and hurtful. Though I didn't intend to enter tutoring sessions with a prejudice or show ageism in a reference interview, these are the types of everyday interactions that call for greater attention and reflection.

In order to empathize and really listen to others we must first know our own thoughts, and practicing deliberate reflection on our own is an important feminist strategy for supporting an ethic of care not only in writing centers, but also in a library. Though not a practice specific to writing center theory, many centers are encouraging tutors

---

12 Ibid., 87.

to individually read marginalized voices and reflect in writing on what that reading means to them.[13] In deliberately engaging with this feminist strategy as a community, several co-workers from my department and I started a reading group, where we read a social justice piece and then talk about our ideas and feelings about the work over treats and coffee. In reading the work before we meet, we all have an opportunity to reflect individually, and then as a group we get to discuss connections not only to our department and library, but also the broader profession. Creating space for this type of reflection fosters a community with heart, where we will hopefully become more aware of daily patterns that lead to prejudice and also more willing to call out unjust interactions when we see them.

Though simplified, living a feminist practice calls upon librarians to *do* something that connects values with actions. Reflection is a key part of this praxis, but we must first reflect on where things stand in our own libraries before we can reflect on what we want to change. The authors of *The Everyday Writing Center* push for this type of reflective action through a discussion of "transformational change" in the workplace and they suggest that strategies for better understanding our environments can be found by drawing upon an assessment model for business managers.[14] In modifying the language and context of this model, they transformed its original corporate agenda to one that focuses on learning spaces. In this way, the tool itself becomes representative of a feminist act in how it was transformed to promote inclusion through reflection. The new model, referred to as a "Writing Center Audit," has two columns, one labeled "pro-learning culture" and the other "anti-learning culture," and includes a list of different attributes to be ranked on a 1-5 scale. Example attributes of the pro-learning culture are "experimentation is encouraged" and "together, directors and tutors explore underlying assumptions about the theoretical underpinnings of their practice." Examples of anti-learning culture are "there is a hierarchy between clerical and tutorial staff" and "annual reports are primarily quantitative in nature and written exclusively for an external audience."[15] These are examples of attributes the authors created for writing centers and I would urge

---

13 Ibid., 97.

14 Ibid., 104.

15 Ibid., 52.

reference librarians to come up with their own attributes, even if only informally. For example, you could start by drawing a line down the middle of a piece of paper. On one side, describe the characteristics of a socially just community where you'd like to work and then vice versa on the other side of the paper. The same process could be done regarding the reference interview or the physical reference space in which we work. The key to this reflection though is to not only reflect individually, but also collaboratively. By working with our co-workers to define what we'd like our work culture to look and feel like, we can begin to take the steps to make sure we're creating an environment that's not only inclusive for librarians, but also for our patrons. In this way, we also take the first step in determining how we will bring our values and actions together and identify with specificity how our work environments will reflect a feminist ethic of care.

Reader Reflection

What would be the top three inclusive attributes or practices of your ideal reference community?

Conclusion

In reflecting on my own experiences in the writing center and at the reference desk, it has been my goal to explore how one practice might inform the other. Together, we reflected on how play can help us bring active learning to the desk and that through flexibility in communication we can value students experience and needs at the desk. And, being attuned to how we communicate can help us remember what it's like to tackle a difficult task with empathy. Combining these strategies, along with practices of critical reflection and discussion, can help build an inclusive community not only in writing centers, but at our reference desks.

Now, I look for others to join me in this conversation. Hopefully, the memories, ideas, and strategies I've shared have sparked a memory or experience of your own that you could use to reshape your own reference practice. If so, write it down, put it into words, and share it with a colleague. By drawing upon and sharing our memories, both good and bad, we can engage in a feminist ethic of care and find ourselves seeking new practices that can help us reshape ourselves and revitalize the work we do as reference librarians.

Bibliography

Babcock, Rebecca. "When Something Is Not Quite Right: Pragmatic Impairment and Compensation in the College Writing Tutorial." *The Writing Lab Newsletter* 35, no. 5-6 (2011): 6-10.

Boyd, K. and Ann Haibeck. "We Have a Secret: Balancing Directiveness and Nondirectiveness During Peer Tutoring." *The Writing Lab Newsletter* 35, no. 5-6 (2011): 14-15.

Carino, Peter. "Power and Authority in Peer Tutoring." In *The Center Will Hold: Critical Perspectives on Writing Center Scholarship*, edited by Michael A. Pemberton & Joyce Kinkead, 96-113. Logan: Utah State University Press, 2003.

Geller, Eodice, Condon, Caroll, and Elizabeth Boquet. *The Everyday Writing Center: A Community of Practice*. Logan: Utah State University Press, 2006.

Kinley, Kylie. "Drawing Lines in the Sand is Fine, but Building Sandcastles is Better: the Value of Play in the Writing Center." Presentation at the International Writing Centers Association, San Diego, CA, October 25-27, 2012.

Peet, Lisa. "ALA President-Elect Julie Todaro on Transforming Librarians," *Library Journal* Last modified June 18, 2015. http://lj.libraryjournal.com/2015/06/organizations/ala-organization/ala-president-elect-julie-todaro-on-transforming-librarians/#_.

Stephenson, Denise. "Constructive Toys: More than a Good Time." *The Writing Lab Newsletter* 26, no. 2 (2001): 6-8.

Willen Brown, Stephanie. "The Reference Interview: Theories and Practice." *Library Philosophy and Practice* Paper 164 (2008): 1-8.

Margaret Fuller's Legacy Interpreted for the Postmodern Library

Mellissa J. Hinton

Nearly two centuries removed from the transcendental legacy left by Ralph Waldo Emerson and Henry David Thoreau, their often overlooked colleague, Margaret Fuller (1810-1850), stands as an icon for paternalistic overtones permeating traditional notions that inform underpinnings of the modern library. As author of the first American feminist tract, *Woman in the Nineteenth Century*, Fuller struggled against the imposed mores of her society and dreamt of a more equitable world. Fuller was an advocate for *all* people. She was a feminist, a radical, a revolutionary, a writer, a teacher, a library user, a social advocate, a mom. She was equally comfortable reading works of the classic writers (the result of the demanding tutelage of her critical father) and the popular culture materials of her contemporary literary moment. Consequently, Fuller might serve as an analogical figure from which to examine feminist themes in user service in the evolving modern academic library.

Although we may think of time as linear, in reality, time has a way of weaving in and out on itself; common themes resonate across the reaches of the ages. Looking backward to our somewhat forgotten feminist forebears provides an opportunity to examine contemporary library service and practice within a feminist pedagogical framework. It also provides an opportunity to participate in the continuing feminist recovery project that was launched in the twentieth century by reintroducing Margaret Fuller to an audience outside of traditional literary or historical scholarship forums. In this essay, I will offer a very brief biographical sketch of Fuller and present her as an early espouser of feminist pedagogy. While placing Fuller within this model may seem somewhat anachronistic, considering her within this realm provides an alternative lens by situating her not as an individual isolated in a moment of time but as part of the continuum of struggle for equality and women's rights, a struggle that continues to the present day. Taking this nontraditional approach is in itself a method consistent with feminist epistemology because it offers a unique lens for interpreting Fuller outside of the mainstream historical context. The concept that alternative ways of seeing and understanding the world have value is foundational within feminist pedagogy. Within this framework, I will also consider Fuller's unique position as a user in the Harvard College Library, assess the objectification within literary and library circles that follows Fuller even now, and suggest that Fuller might be seen as a model for marginalized users in the modern library. In addition to providing a unique perspective on library service, I hope to continue the redemption of Fuller's legacy and the restoration of her place in the pantheon of American feminist thought.

Who was Margaret Fuller?

Sarah Margaret Fuller led a rich but ultimately short and tragic life. She was friendly or personally acquainted with many nineteenth-century luminaries still studied today. She was born in 1810 in Cambridgeport, Massachusetts to a prominent family. Her attorney father, Timothy Fuller, served in the United States Congress from 1817 to 1825. Timothy Fuller recognized that Margaret (the name she preferred) was intellectually gifted and he tutored her in ancient Greek and other subjects taught to white, male children. This demanding education was a blessing and yet a curse, because while Margaret was endowed with superior intellect, as a female, the doors to higher education and professional employment were closed to her. She was provided with a paternalistic education with little opportunity to put it to practical use. Alternatively, she began a writing career (one of the few opportunities open to women), and her essays were published in serial publications such as the *Western Messenger*. When her father died suddenly in 1835, she was forced to forego a long awaited trip to Europe and began teaching to help support her family. Financial limitations would plague Fuller the rest of her life. In the late 1830s, she established a friendship with Ralph Waldo Emerson and other members of the transcendentalist circle and was appointed the first editor of the journal, the *Dial*. Never compensated for her editorial duties, her *Dial* essay, "The Great Lawsuit: Man *versus* Men, Woman *versus* Women," was eventually expanded and published in 1845 as a book, *Woman in the Nineteenth Century*. Although it was shrouded in the language of transcendental thought, Fuller's feminist manifesto called for change in the social order. "Woman" and "man," Fuller wrote in her book, are "two halves of one thought. I lay no especial stress on the welfare of either. I believe that the development of the one cannot be effected without that of the other."[1] As a participant in the transcendental movement and versed in Emerson's theme of the perfection of man, Fuller extended the argument to include women. Fuller's statement is in accordance with many proponents of feminist pedagogy who do not endorse the uplifting of women at the expense of men, but rather encourage the uplifting of all.

At the invitation of Horace Greeley, Fuller moved to New York to work as the art and literary editor for Greeley's *New-York Tribune*, an unprecedented activity for a woman. During her tenure there, she addressed not only subjects of art and literature, but used the forum to expand on social issues by including critiques of prisons and institutions for the poor and mentally ill. In 1846, she traveled to Europe with friends where she continued her relationship with the *Tribune* as its first female foreign correspondent. The 1840s brought famine and political upheaval across Europe and the principalities of a not yet unified Italy were not spared from conflict. Enamored with Rome and sympathetic to the nationalist political position, Fuller remained in Italy while her friends continued their European tour. She sent eyewitness reports about the war in Rome back to the United States for publication in the *Tribune* and eventually participated in the revolutionary cause as a nurse.[2] She fell in love with a Roman nobleman, Giovanni Angelo Ossoli, and gave birth to a son, Nino, in 1848 during the height of the Roman hostilities. Some historians assert that Fuller and Ossoli eventually married but

---

1 *The Essential Margaret Fuller* (New Brunswick, N.J.: Rutgers University Press, 1992), vi.

2 For a brief overview of the 1848-49 Italian revolutionary struggles, see Harry Hearder, and Jonathan Morris. *Italy: A Short History* (Cambridge, U.K.: Cambridge University Press, 2001).

no extant documentation has confirmed this fact. Their baby was left with a nurse when Margaret returned to participation in the partisan activities of the revolution. During the war, she continued to develop a manuscript recounting the history of the Italian uprising. As the revolutionaries continued to lose ground and defeat was inevitable, Margaret and Count Ossoli decided to flee with their son to the United States. Since their funds were limited, in 1850 they boarded a technologically outdated packet boat, the ill-fated *Elizabeth*. The *Elizabeth* ran aground off Fire Island, New York, and Margaret, Ossoli, and their son were among the lost; only their son's body was ever recovered. Ralph Waldo Emerson sent Henry David Thoreau to Fire Island in an effort to salvage Fuller's personal effects but little was recovered and her manuscript on the Italian revolution was forever lost to the forces of time and tides.

Following Fuller's death, Ralph Waldo Emerson, William Henry Channing, and James Freeman Clarke, men who had known Margaret, capitalized on her renown and celebrity, and within two years of her death published *Memoirs of Margaret Fuller Ossoli*. Using excerpts from her letters and writings as well as recollections from friends and associates, their collaboration resulted in a project that portrayed Fuller reductively, diminished her work, and ultimately framed her as a second rate author. In their reflections of Fuller published in the *Memoirs*, contributors prefaced their remembrances by describing her physical attributes, objectifying her from a patriarchal gaze. Emerson recalled that when he first met her he was "repelled" by her "extreme plainness," while another Transcendental colleague, F. H. Hedge commented on the "robustness" of her figure and lack of regard for "hygienic principles."[3]

Given the circumstance that Fuller's child was born before her marriage, perhaps the editors considered their book to be an effort to deflect gossip and preserve Fuller's reputation in a society that would have rejected her for having a child outside of marriage. Undoubtedly the editors' use of her married name, Ossoli, helped in this regard. However, in 1895, Fuller's friend, Caroline (Dall) Healey, wrote that the publication of the *Memoirs* had given rise "to many absurd and

---

3 *Memoirs of Margaret Fuller Ossoli* (1857; Project Gutenberg, 2004), vol. 1, http://www.gutenberg.org/cache/epub/13105/pg13105-images.html.

painful rumors."[4] Thanks to the portrayal created by these men, while Emerson, Thoreau, and Hawthorne are household names even today in the United States, Margaret Fuller has been generally forgotten outside of scholarly circles.[5]

Fuller and Feminist Pedagogy

Fuller's life story contains the stuff of blockbuster movies: war, revolution, romance, betrayal. It is easy to overlook her importance as an early American feminist when captivated by the biographical details. More importantly, what relevance does her life have to a discussion about twenty-first century libraries? I would suggest that we begin by examining Fuller's emphasis on the education of women through the lens of feminist pedagogy.

The search for social justice is a foundational construct that drives the practice of feminist pedagogy; the two cannot be separated. Although feminist pedagogy is a late twentieth-century term, Margaret Fuller represents an early proponent of its precepts. She was a believer in social justice for all people, championed women's rights and the importance of education for all women, and supported significant social movements including prison reform and better treatment of the mentally ill. Her radicalism escalated during her time in Europe. Her participation in the Italian revolution and her supportive recounting of it from the perspective of a war correspondent on the pages of the *New-York Tribune* were political acts. Consequently, Margaret Fuller may be viewed as an early espouser of feminist pedagogy.

In her classic essay, Carolyn M. Shrewsbury outlined the tenets of the feminist pedagogical model:

> Feminist pedagogy is engaged teaching/learning–engaged with self in a continuing reflective process; engaged actively with the material being studied; engaged with others in a struggle to get beyond our sexism and racism and classism and homophobia and other

---

[4] Caroline Healey. *Margaret and Her Friends*. (1895; Hathi Trust, 2014), 14, http://hdl.handle.net/2027/hvd.32044011424330.

[5] Major biographies include a scholarly work by Charles Capper, *Margaret Fuller: An American Romantic Life*, 2 vols. (New York: Oxford University Press, 1997-2002) and a more popular work by Megan Marshall, *Margaret Fuller: A New American Life* (New York: Houghton Mifflin Harcourt, 2013).

destructive hatreds and to work together to enhance our knowledge; engaged with the community, with traditional organizations, and with movements for social change.[6]

The theory of feminist pedagogy, Shrewsbury notes, is distinguished by three elements: community, empowerment, and leadership. Fuller's efforts in teaching, articulating a feminist argument that was grounded in equality, encouraging social reforms through her published writings, and actively participating in the Italian revolutionary struggle are striking examples of Shrewsbury's tenets.

Another leading proponent of feminist pedagogy in the twentieth century, bell hooks, wrote: "A liberatory feminist movement aims to transform society by eradicating patriarchy, by ending sexism and sexist oppression, by challenging the politics of domination on all fronts. Feminist pedagogy can only be liberatory if it is truly revolutionary because the mechanisms of appropriation within white-supremacist, capitalist patriarchy are able to co-opt with tremendous ease that which merely appears radical or subversive."[7] A feminist classroom, hooks argued, must reject traditional teaching methods that "reinforce domination."[8] She also noted that providing an opportunity for all students to have a voice is an essential component of feminist pedagogy.[9]

Fuller was a century and a half ahead of Shrewsbury and hooks as an early proponent of feminist pedagogy, although the term had not yet been invented. As one of the most highly regarded skills of the day, oratory was off limits for women as it was viewed as an unseemly activity for women participants. Neither the pulpit nor the political lectern were considered feminine spaces. In 1839, Fuller, who was considered a superior conversationalist, developed an alternative forum where women could develop their ideas and speak of them openly in a safe space, a semi-public forum without the threat of patriarchal

---

6 Carolyn M. Shrewsbury, "What is Feminist Pedagogy?" *Women's Studies Quarterly* (1997), 166.

7 bell hooks, "Towards a Revolutionary Feminist Pedagogy," in *Falling into Theory: Conflicting Views on Reading Literature,* ed. David H. Richter (Boston: Bedford Books, 1997), 76.

8 Ibid., 77.

9 Ibid., 78.

dominance. This forum came to be known as Fuller's "Conversations" series. From 1839 to 1844, the forum's attendees (white, middle class women, originally, although men participated later) paid admission to meet and discuss issues that were usually considered the exclusive domain of highly educated, white, elite males. Groups of twenty to twenty-five women met at a bookstore owned by Fuller's friend and Nathaniel Hawthorne's sister-in-law, Elizabeth Peabody. Other attendees included such notable women as the abolitionist and writer Lydia Maria Child. Admittedly, Fuller's conversations were fee-based, an effort by Fuller to supplement her meager income while providing a forum for women to express their views. Although this forum was limited by race and to some degree, class, in its reach, Fuller's development of the forum provides a nineteenth-century antecedent for feminist pedagogy. While Fuller initiated the topic for conversation, she encouraged variant points of view on topics that included discussion of mythology and the classics, subjects that were typically the domain of white male scholars.

Nancy Craig Simmons described Fuller's techniques: "Through a pedagogy that encouraged participation, not passivity ... Fuller was engaged in cultivating the intellectual capability in every woman and thus countering the effects of male-dominated culture."[10] Fuller facilitated the discussion; she did not take an authoritarian position as lecturer or teacher, a hallmark of a feminist pedagogical method that is in line with decentering the teacher.

Fuller's efforts to encourage various points of view through her conversations series may be likened to the defined role of libraries as described in the *ALA Library Bill of Rights*: libraries are "forums for information and ideas" and must "provide materials and information presenting all points of view on current and historical issues," while preventing removal of materials that are subject to "partisan or doctrinal disapproval."[11] As unique places that span across curricula, academic libraries by mission are expected to privilege no perspective over another. Within this framework, academic libraries

---

10 Nancy Craig Simmons, "Margaret Fuller's Boston Conversations: The 1839-1840 Series." *Studies in the American Renaissance* (1994): 196, http://www.jstor.org/stable/30227655

11 "Library Bill of Rights," American Library Association, last modified June 30, 2006, http://www.ala.org/advocacy/intfreedom/librarybill/.

serve as ideal places for students to explore alternative points of view within a safe setting. In traditional classroom settings, students might hesitate sharing their views because they feel threatened by potentially punitive grading practices. Students attending lectures and discussions sponsored by the library, however, can learn in a safe environment where potential consequences in terms of fear of poor grades are eliminated. Just as Fuller facilitated an open discussion and provided a forum for those who might have been more reticent in other circumstances, this model should serve as an example for programs and forums sponsored in our libraries. Library-sponsored forums might navigate away from a lecture-based model to one where participants share their views without risk of retribution.

Interestingly, when Fuller expanded the series to admit male participants, the conversations series ended. Whether the end of the series can be attributed to the reinstatement of patriarchal authority in a formerly feminist space is a subject of conjecture but evidence indicates it does. Caroline (Dall) Healey noted that when men joined the series, Margaret "never enjoyed this mixed class, and considered it a failure so far as her own power was concerned."[12] And she noted tensions when "Emerson pursued his own train of thought. He seemed to forget that we had come together to pursue Margaret's."[13] With the attendance of such a well-known and esteemed individual as Emerson, the power dynamic shifted to a traditional patriarchal authoritative structure. How this relates to the importance from a perspective of feminist pedagogy is the recognition that power structure within organizations must be considered in all circumstances and venues, including the academic library. Recognizing the vestiges of power is the first step toward alleviating intimidation.

Power structure in an academic library may not be apparent at first observation, especially since it may be obscured by the familiarity of long accepted practices. For example, selection of resources (physical or digital) is wrought with power in collection building because limited financial resources require that decisions to purchase or not to purchase must be made. Whoever makes the final determination about a purchase request wields a significant amount of power that might be reduced through more collaborative decision making. Physical layout

---

12 Caroline Healey, *Margaret and Her Friends*, 13.

13 Ibid., 46.

of the library also reflects power structure. Consider the layout of the reference desk. The placement of a counter or desk between the reference specialist and the patron creates a barrier that suggests an adversarial relationship. Such simple things as moving the furniture, eliminating the barrier of the reference desk, might be implemented to create a more collaborative space between a reference specialist and patrons. Work station installations where information specialists can facilitate research by users without dictating methods level the field.

Fuller and the Harvard Library

Fuller is remembered for a number of achievements. Among them, she was the first woman permitted to use the Harvard College Library to conduct research for her travel book, *Summer on the Lakes, in 1843*. Looking back to his college days, in his 1884 biography about Fuller, Thomas Wentworth Higginson (1823-1911) recalled seeing her over forty years earlier, "sitting, day after day, under the covert gaze of the undergraduates who had never before looked upon a woman reading within those sacred precincts, where twenty of that sex are now employed as assistants."[14] Higginson, who was an abolitionist, commander of the first Union regiment of former slaves, and editor of the poetry of Emily Dickinson, was himself an advocate for social justice. But his recollection points out the anomaly of her presence as well as the progress made toward women's equality by the end of the nineteenth century. Fuller, a thirty plus-year old woman at the time she was doing the research for *Summer on the Lakes*, was clearly a distraction for the privileged young men at Harvard in the antebellum era. The male students of privilege did not know quite what to make of a mature woman conducting research in an exclusively male domain. Sadly, Fuller's response to her unique position is lost to the historical record. Her extant letters and writings are silent about her feelings so we cannot discern if she reveled in the celebration of her milestone or suffered from feelings of isolation. Perhaps Fuller did not write of her feelings on the subject. But perhaps the editors of her *Memoirs* expunged her thoughts on the matter while expurgating entire sections of her letters, erasing her voice and silencing her for posterity.

---

14 Thomas Wentworth Higginson, *Margaret Fuller Ossoli* (1855; Hathi Trust, 2012), 194, http://hdl.handle.net/2027/uc1.31158000310903.

The silencing of Fuller's voice by patriarchal authorities and her singularity within an exclusively male-dominated sphere may be seen as analogs for individuals who might be marginalized from contemporary library service. Contemporary reference service providers should be cognizant of any penchant for isolating potential users and should strive to eliminate physical or intellectual barriers that might negatively impact users. Extending library services remotely is a step toward eliminating physical barriers and librarian participation in social justice activities that equalize access to technology is in line with the social justice initiatives of feminist pedagogy as well as an extension of Fuller's social justice legacy. All voices matter.

In her essay on Fuller's writing of *Summer on the Lakes*, Nicole Tonkovich reflected on the uniqueness of Fuller's situation in the Harvard Library. Tonkovich argued that "Under the scrutiny of the male gaze, within the walls of America's most elite educational institution, Margaret Fuller attempted to write a book that would be worthy of inclusion in that library. In the process of writing ... [Fuller] both contested and reproduced the power arrangements that the library represented: resisting the hierarchies of written texts enshrined in the library, she nevertheless privileged writing and textual preservation over the oral Indian cultures she wrote about."[15]

Writing from her position as a member of a marginalized population (an intellectual woman in the nineteenth-century United States), Fuller's effort to express concern for a marginalized population was a daring one. Her writing might be seen as an analog for scholarly communication in the present day, where established voices are recorded in mainstream scholarly circles while other voices are silenced. While the establishment of peer review among major publishing venues dominated the scholarly record for the better part of the twentieth century, new forms of publications made available through open access venues provide opportunities for marginalized individuals to be heard. Open access initiatives can be viewed as consistent with feminist pedagogy because they extend educational opportunities to a wider population than is possible with subscription-based publications. Followers of feminist pedagogy should celebrate open access.

---

15 Nicole Tonkovich, "Traveling in the West, Writing in the Library: Margaret Fuller's Summer on the Lakes," *Legacy* 10, no. 2 (January 1, 1993): 79, doi:10.2307/25684472.

Because it was ostensibly a travel book, Fuller's *Summer on the Lakes* was considered an acceptable genre for women's authorship at the time. However, Tonkovich asserts that the resulting work, which included extraneous material such as book reviews and translations of other material typically included in an instructive travel genre, could not strictly be classified within the travel genre because of Fuller's incorporation of ethnographic methods. The result was a work that incorporates feminist pedagogical methods of scholarship, one that offers a different way of looking at the world. As Tonkovich noted, Fuller's "book had to assert its originality, its newness, its right to displace or sit adjacent to other, mostly male-authored books already in place in the Harvard Library."[16]

This astute comment by Tonkovich underscores another shrouded power struggle over space in contemporary academic libraries and its impact upon reference service. As shelf space in academic libraries is reallocated to provide real estate in the library for other purposes, deciding which physical materials will remain and which will be withdrawn is a question of power. Undoubtedly, some individuals will disagree with the decision to withdraw any materials. Practical considerations about space often trump retention decisions. When weeding collections, perhaps physical collections can be shaped to accommodate other voices because so many works by patriarchal authors are available digitally. Maybe weeding is an opportunity.

Since Fuller's day, library staffing has been altered significantly. Higginson could scarcely have imagined that nearly two centuries after Fuller's research experience, the Harvard Library would not only employ female assistants, but would also employ female librarians, department heads, full time staff members with established careers that would transform the profession. Fuller might have laughed at his astonishment. In what is perhaps her most famous quote, Fuller wrote in *Woman in the Nineteenth Century*, "But if you ask me what offices they may fill, I reply—any. I do not care what case you put; let them be sea-captains, if you will. I do not doubt there are women well fitted for such an office."[17] Today, nuclear submarine captain or fighter pilot might be corollaries for sea-captain. Clearly, Fuller would have found no limitations in having women working in the libraries and would

---

16 Ibid., 81.

17 *The Essential Margaret Fuller*, 345.

have celebrated the achievements of twentieth-century women such as Constance Winchell and Isadore Mudge who were instrumental in shaping modern library service.

But Higginson's portrayal of Fuller as an outsider, a subject of voyeuristic examination by young men who found her presence distracting, provides another opportunity to consider our library users. We must identify the "outsiders" who might need assistance in our libraries. Perhaps these outsiders are students new to the academy, navigating the intricacies of the seemingly cryptic coding on the spines of the books or struggling to articulate their questions into research-based projects. Perhaps they are first generation college students who might feel intimidated by the grandiose setting of the academic library. Perhaps the outsiders under the gaze of today's students are international students with different styles of dress or culturally driven customs. Perhaps they are students who are differently abled, or gender nonconforming, who encounter barriers to access. In our libraries, we who ascribe to concepts of feminist pedagogy must reinforce for our students, by modeling or more formal methods, through interactions at the reference desk, that all people have a place in our academic institutions. We must acknowledge our own tendencies toward bias and be ever vigilant about reining it in. We must recognize the power structure that exists within the instructor/student relationship and seek to minimize it. At the reference desk, that would include promoting collaborative research assistance while abandoning the insistence that the reference associate is the expert.

Fuller and Appropriation

Finally, we might consider how Margaret Fuller has been appropriated within the patriarchal power system of library organization and consider whether corollaries exist today that might continue such a trend. When they objectified Fuller in the publishing of her *Memoirs*, Emerson and his cohorts appropriated Fuller's agency by using her married last name in the title of their book, even though she was well known to the public by her given name. In their defense, Fuller did refer to herself in at least one letter as the Countess Ossoli, a title she may have adopted out of her own need for self-legitimization, but she was far better known as Margaret Fuller. Since the question about the timing of the birth of Fuller's son was suspect (If a marriage ever took place, it occurred after his birth.), Emerson and the others attempted to deflect potential scandal by focusing on her marriage and motherhood—the expected mores of a respectable white woman in the mid-nineteenth century.

This appropriation by a patriarchal authority continued within the library setting. In classifying Fuller's works, the Library of Congress assigned her a literary number within the letter "O" range rather than the "F" range: PS2500-2508 transcribed as "Ossoli, Sarah Margaret (Fuller)" although she never published any works under that name.[18] Deliberately assigning a classification number to Fuller that privileges her married name may be seen as a political act based on assumptions of patriarchal authority and power.

In 1915, the Library of Congress published its classification schedule in literature, aiming to print its scheme for "administrative purposes and for the convenience of libraries using the Library of Congress classification," setting the stage for other libraries to adopt Ossoli over Fuller.[19] Consequently, assignment of Fuller to this range in the alphabet is fixed, perhaps irrevocably. To this very day, users browsing on the shelves for books within LC classification must navigate to the Cutter numbers in PS for authors' names that begin with "O" in order to locate Margaret Fuller's collected works. The very same classification systems we refer to every day in our professional lives are rife with layers of patriarchal authority. Recognizing those layers is one small step toward rejecting the reinforcement of patriarchal domination for which bell hooks advocated. The next step is sharing the recognition with students that classification systems and associated subject terms are inscribed with sexism, bias, and racism. This activity that may be accomplished during a reference transaction is an activity of feminist consciousness-raising.

The fact that that Fuller/Ossoli's works are shelved in such a deliberate arrangement may not matter for discovery and information retrieval in an age of keyword searching, automatic cross referencing, and electronic retrieval of information. Perhaps this issue is more a matter of classification and cataloging rather than reference. However, in the realm of patriarchal authority understanding of the

---

18 Library of Congress, *Classification. Literature, Subclasses PN, PR, PS, P* (1915; Hathi Trust, 2013),197, http://hdl.handle.net/2027/nyp.33433012274944.

19 Ibid., 3.

political implications matters a great deal. Patriarchal inscriptions assigned within controlled vocabularies are limiting, damaging, and potentially hurtful. Unfortunately, the use of them is not confined to the historical record. The 2016 controversy over Congressional legislation that prohibited the Library of Congress from removing "illegal aliens" from its list of subject headings underscores the political implications of language and power in the library setting and the ongoing need to be vigilant and active.

As librarians we look for ways to categorize, organize, synthesize. But methods that work well in organizing information do not necessarily transfer to people. In the library, whether at the live reference desk or in the online environment, we must be vigilant to avoid categorizing our users, placing them in hypothetical boxes and making assumptions about them. We must strive to treat each as an individual. And while we undertake efforts to get to know about our users in the entirety so we can meet their general needs, we must always remember that they are individuals—each with personal agency. The challenge of striking a balance between providing services and resources for a general population of library users while meeting the needs of the individual is ongoing.

In this essay, I have tried to reacquaint readers with Margaret Fuller in a venue beyond literary and historical studies. By reframing Fuller within the contemporary setting and considering her legacy through a feminist pedagogical lens, I have offered a unique perspective on one of our feminist forebears. In the library world, we have many other models of feminist leaders: Margaret Hutchins (1884-1961), who developed the model for the reference interview and in feminist pedagogical terms, encouraged librarians to serve their patrons with respect; Isadore Mudge (1875-1957), who originated the venerable *Guide to Reference Books*; and Constance Winchell (1896-1983), Mudge's successor.[20] Future research projects could consider these and other eminent librarians within a similar feminist framework to rethink and reappropriate the inherited legacy of the modern library. Looking to the past and rediscovering our feminist forebears can provide a roadmap from the past and help point the way to the future.

---

20 *Dictionary of American Library Biography* (1978), s.v. "Hutchins, Margaret," "Mudge, Isadore Gilbert," "Winchell, Constance Mabel" (supp. 1990).

While the work is far from finished, contemporary American society has made strides in initiatives supported in feminist circles since the days of Margaret Fuller's struggle and her call for equality in *Woman in the Nineteenth Century*. But in many parts of our global community, young women are executed for seeking an education. Libraries are destroyed and collections are abolished because they include materials outside of a prescribed notion of correctness or political agenda. So it matters a great deal that our reference services in the contemporary day skip notions of classification, sorting, placing in boxes. If we heed Margaret Fuller's call for social justice and her interest in the world at large, we can focus better on our users and perhaps take one incremental step toward improving the world at large. And if we adopt the notion of a successor to Fuller, bell hooks, that feminist pedagogy must reduce dominance in the classroom, by correlation, a feminist reference desk must seek to endorse methods that promote equality and reduce uneven structures of power.

I wish to thank my LIU colleague, Bill Roberson, who read an early iteration of this essay and provided very welcome feedback.

Bibliography

American Library Association. "Library Bill of Rights." Last modified June 30, 2006. http://www.ala.org/advocacy/intfreedom/librarybill/.

Capper, Charles. *Margaret Fuller: An American Romantic Life*. 2 vols. New York: Oxford University Press, 1992-2007.

Fuller, Margaret. *Memoirs of Margaret Fuller Ossoli*. 2 vols. Reprint of the 1857 Boston edition, Project Gutenberg, 2004. Vol. 1: http://www.gutenberg.org/cache/epub/13105/pg13105-images.html. Vol. 2: http://www.gutenberg.org/cache/epub/13106/pg13106-images.html.

———. *Woman in the Nineteenth Century*. In *The Essential Margaret Fuller*. Edited by Jeffrey Steele, 243-378. New Brunswick, N.J.: Rutgers University Press, 1992.

Healey, Caroline. *Margaret and Her Friends: Or, Ten Conversations with Margaret Fuller upon the Mythology of the Greeks and Its Expression in Art, Held at the House of the Rev. George Ripley … Boston, Beginning March 1, 1841*. Reprint of the 1895 Boston edition, Hathi Trust, 2014. http://hdl.handle.net/2027/hvd.32044011424330.

Hearder, Harry, and Jonathan Morris. *Italy: A Short History*. Cambridge, U.K.: Cambridge University Press, 2001.

Higginson, Thomas Wentworth. *Margaret Fuller Ossoli*. Reprint of the 1885 Boston edition, Hathi Trust, 2012. http://hdl.handle.net/2027/ucl.31158000310903.

hooks, bell. "Towards a Revolutionary Feminist Pedagogy." In *Falling into Theory: Conflicting Views on Reading Literature*, edited by David H. Richter, 74–79. Boston: Bedford Books, 1997.

Library of Congress. *Classification. Literature, Subclasses PN, PR, PS, PZ. : PN: General Literary History and Collections. PR: English Literature. PS: American Literature. PZ: Fiction and Juvenile Literature*. Reprint of the 1915 Washington edition, Hathi Trust, 2013. http://hdl.handle.net/2027/nyp.33433012274944.

Marshall, Megan. *Margaret Fuller: A New American Life*. Boston: Houghton Mifflin Harcourt, 2013.

Shrewsbury, Carolyn M. "What Is Feminist Pedagogy?" *Women's Studies Quarterly* 15, no. 3/4 (1987): 6-14. http://0-www.jstor.org.liucat.lib.liu.edu/stable/40003432.

Simmons, Nancy Craig. "Margaret Fuller's Boston Conversations: The 1839-1840 Series." *Studies in the American Renaissance* (1994): 195–226. http://www.jstor.org/stable/30227655.

Tonkovich, Nicole. "Traveling in the West, Writing in the Library: Margaret Fuller's *Summer on the Lakes*." *Legacy* 10, no. 2 (1993): 79–102. doi:10.2307/25684472.

Proceed with Care: Reviewing Reference Services Through the Feminist Lens

Elizabeth Hoppe and Karen Jung

Reference services are evolving. As we make changes our best hope is that they are made with intention. While some of the factors that will necessarily affect the future of reference are beyond the control of the librarians who generally provide the services, we do retain the ability to make some choices about our priorities. While each library has different stakeholders and pressures that must dictate some of these choices, the core concepts of feminist theory can offer a lens through which we can make intentional choices about where to focus our energy and attention.

Bowdoin College is a small liberal arts college on the coast of Maine. Our student body is 1805 with a 9:1 student to faculty ratio. We offer over 40 academic disciplines and programs. Bowdoin is an elite institution that prides itself on need-blind admission and financial aid that uses grants instead of loans to ensure that all students who are accepted are able to attend. The low student to faculty ratio is one demonstration for the highly personal nature of a Bowdoin education, which focuses on the individual experience, high levels of contact with faculty, and a commitment to all areas of student support, including our four libraries on campus. Our research and instruction department aligns with these goals by acting as liaisons to academic departments. There are eight liaisons that provide research and instruction support for our scholars–faculty, staff, students, and members of our extended community. Each liaison is also responsible for collection development in their subject areas and coverage of the reference desk in addition to their other duties.

This chapter, using the example of the process undertaken at Bowdoin, will elucidate how a library can engage with various reference models, perform qualitative and quantitative assessment, and balance function and sustainability with feminist-based guiding goals. We will also reflect on the inherent challenges posed by staffing and training needs, space, and budget.

Theory

Within the frame of feminist theory there are many ways of looking at an issue. When reviewing reference services it is important to narrow the focus to those aspects that are most important for your institution and its stakeholders. Based on the priorities identified by the Bowdoin Library, we will focus on the ethic of care, empowerment, anti-hierarchical collaborative interactions, and valuing the experiential knowledge of all members of our academic community.

Ethic of Care

One of the most significant aspects of feminist pedagogy from the perspective of the reference desk is the ethic of care. Consider reference services, as described by James Wyer in 1929 as a "sympathetic and informed personal aid in interpreting library collections for study and research."[1] Margaret Hutchins expanded this definition in 1944 to go beyond traditional library collections and look at other services, including contextualizing the material in a way that can actually be useful for our guests.[2] While many of the modes of providing reference assistance have changed, and indeed the approaches have evolved, the idea of sympathetic and informed service remains. Scholars that have made the decision to come to a reference desk may have traveled different paths, but for most it is not a natural act. To ask for help is to be vulnerable. This is particularly true for students who may belong to marginalized populations. Guardedness often translates as silence or disengagement. It is important to remember that this silence is as

---

1 J. I. Wyer, *Reference Work: A Textbook for Students of Library Work and Librarians*, Library Curriculum Studies (Chicago: American Library Association, 1930), 4.

2 Margaret Hutchins, *Introduction to Reference Work* (Chicago: American Library Association, 1944), 10.

important as the words we hear from others. As Carolyn Panofsky and Lesley Bogard point out, "Silence, then, is not a form of resistance but rather a clue into an identity of marginalization."[3] We must then endeavor to re-center the marginalized, to encourage interaction that does not ascribe to the dominant power structure.

Trust is not a natural state and if the expectations have not been built through years that teachers and librarians and other authority figures are kind, supportive, and willing to help, there will be an additional barrier for these students to seek out help. This kind of trust does not exist without engaged parties with time and resources to devote to student support. Therefore, this tends to be an additional way that marginalized students who may not have had many positive interactions with authority are put at a disadvantage. Even the most prepared students, to say nothing of faculty, don't universally understand the function of a reference desk, or when reference services may be of help, so the value of seeking out services does not outweigh the wariness students might feel towards authority figures, and this wariness might be intense for students who are most in need of support.

Scholars have different preferences in terms of how they want to interact with the library. Recognizing this fact and promoting a variety of mechanisms for interaction is another way to show care for our scholars. While for some the traditional model, a librarian staffing a reference desk, is just fine, for others it can seem very daunting and unwelcoming. Some scholars prefer to contact someone by email or text when they need help, others would rather drop in to an office. Still others opt for working with their peers to solve their problems. Recognizing and respecting this variety of preferences is an important way that reference services can try to promote an ethic of care.

Challenging Authority

The image of a humorless librarian sitting behind a desk shushing patrons, enforcing rules, and providing answers is one that is cemented in the mythos of the library. The librarian is situated as an authority. This hierarchy is an aspect of patriarchal models of engagement in

---

3 Carolyn P. Panofsky and Lesley Bogad, "Hearing Students' Silence: Issues of Identity, Performance, and Recognition in College Classrooms," in *Transforming Classroom Culture: Inclusive Pedagogical Practices*, ed. Arlene Dallalfar, Esther Kingston-Mann, and R. Timothy Sieber (New York: Palgrave Macmillan, 2011), 183.

the academy, and is in itself anti-feminist as it encourages models of behavior and interaction that devalue the experience and authority that members of our community already possess. This authority plays out in two important ways: as a function of our role as librarians and the space we occupy, which we will discuss in another section; and as the nature of the research paradigm.

The traditional model of academic research reifies privilege, and the dominant narrative and power structures. We must push back against the hierarchy of research authority, seeking out voices not represented by the dominant narrative. In her chapter on feminist research, Patricia Ann Lather states, "The overt ideological goal of feminist research in the human sciences is to correct both the *invisibility* and *distortion* of female experience in ways relevant to ending women's unequal social position."[4] In addition to looking at the female experience, it is also important to keep in mind the intersectional aspects of identity and therefore also recognize other voices that are silenced. Academic discourse privileges certain voices. Peer review and scholarly status and other forms of official academic legitimacy are steeped in traditional values that tend to be lacking voices of otherness. Acknowledging this fact requires an openness to research that may not fit that typical model of academia in order to begin to hear otherwise silenced voices.

There are multiple ways that other voices can be included in the library, such as the materials we acquire, the art we display, the signs we post, and the staff we hire. Each of these areas can be an attempt to welcome in those who might otherwise be less inclined to use our services. Attempting to create "… a framework that overrides these forms of disengagement—a cross-disciplinary framework that accommodates multiple identities and oppressions and that suggests connections between academic inquiry and social action" should be encouraged not only to our scholars, but also internally as our library makes choices about space, staffing, collections, and services.[5] This intersectional approach values all voices and encourages engagement with all perspectives, widening the sphere of academic discourse. In

---

[4] Patricia Ann Lather, *Getting Smart: Feminist Research and Pedagogy With/in the Postmodern, Critical Social Thought* (New York: Routledge, 1991), 71.

[5] Joan Hartman and Ellen Messer-Davidow, eds., *(En)gendering Knowledge: Feminists in Academe* (Knoxville: University of Tennessee Press, 1991), 290.

addition, it shows our efforts to support all of our scholars and their multiple identities. While many of the students and faculty that make use of the library in general, and reference services in particular, have never had any formal training in library organization and information systems, each scholar comes with a set of experience and perspectives that should not be discounted. People make decisions about information on a daily basis, and these instincts can be translated into the research process if given the opportunity. The standard reference interview attempts to capitalize on this fact by asking about the previous research attempts of the individual, but falls short by not acknowledging that an understanding of information may come from informal inquiry in addition to research activities. bell hooks's claims that the "assumption that we all bring to the classroom experiential knowledge, that this knowledge can indeed enhance our learning experience"[6] recognizes the value of alternate forms of information sources and evaluation, and encourages us to leverage the value of non-academic experience.

Empowerment

In the ever-popular maxim, if you give people a fish you feed them for a day, but if you teach people to fish you feed them for a lifetime. So too is the search for information. When a reference desk serves to answer questions, we merely hand out fish. This ensures a steady flow of traffic from students and faculty who are never encouraged to explore the reasoning behind the search and therefore become increasingly dependent on the "magic" performed by the librarian, but it does very little to increase the overall agency of the community. While librarians will always be important for guidance, interpretation, and increasingly complicated fishing methods, this empowerment is ultimately to everyone's benefit as the discourse moves beyond introductory and formulaic toward a deeper conversation. In libraries, how we choose to engage with scholars matters; it shows what we believe to be their inherent skill as well as what we think is the most important mode of interaction with information. In this vein, when we focus on tools instead of questions and habits of mind "…students learn only how

---

[6] bell hooks, *Teaching to Transgress: Education as the Practice of Freedom* (New York: Routledge, 1994), 84.

to find information for a specific need rather than how to think about information."[7] This does a disservice not only to our scholars who can benefit from transferable skills, but to ourselves as librarians, as it ignores the important contributions to ways of knowing that we can make in favor of being a point-and-click demonstrator.

Critical pedagogy attempts to address some of these challenges and shifts focus from trying to explain and cover material toward helping people uncover ideas and ways of knowing that become shaped by their exploration and critique. As hooks discusses in *Teaching to Transgress*, "If we really want to create a cultural climate where biases can be challenged and changed, all border crossings must be seen as valid and legitimate."[8] The idea of what is legitimate is steeped in the patriarchy and dominant power structures. To include the ways of valuing certain spheres of discourse and the way that we present materials to scholars is to begin to challenge the idea of academic "legitimacy", and therefore re-draw the borders surrounding academic discourse. In addition, recognizing the academic privilege of "scholarly" work in the academy, but also understanding the value of experience, particularly in traditionally marginalized populations, is vitally important to challenging these structures. According to hooks, "We must return ourselves to a state of embodiment in order to deconstruct the way power has been traditionally orchestrated in the classroom, denying subjectivity to some groups and according it to others."[9] The library is not exempt from this task, in all of the ways that we engage with information creation, organization, dissemination, and evaluation.

Assessment

In the process of becoming a more feminist space, we must attempt to weave together feminist theory and information about our local context. The copious amounts of information that libraries collect about the who, what, when, and where of reference desk transactions

---

7 Barbara A. Quarton, "Teaching in the Margins," in *Informed Agitation: Library and Information Skills in Social Justice Movements and Beyond*, ed. Melissa Morrone (Sacramento, CA: Library Juice Press, 2014), 59.

8 hooks, *Teaching to Transgress*, 131.

9 Ibid., 139.

tell us very little about why and how we should be providing current and future reference services. In addition to looking at the external statistics and factors that have governed our decisions in the past, we need to look from the inside. In her overview of feminist assessment, Joan Polinar Shapiro states, "Rather than an abstraction floating without any ties to the concrete, feminist assessment is action-oriented and encourages social change to be achieved as an outcome of the process."[10] In order to develop an assessment process, we must first figure out what we need to know to make our decisions and, as a result, what actions we might want to take to collect the information.

Gathering and reporting numbers to a variety of institutions and organizations is an annual ritual; the typical annual statistics include the number of transactions at the reference desk within a user demographic and/or within a transaction level, i.e., directional, or reference question. The quantitative data collected and associated analyses provides us with assessment information that serves to compare institutions, to show longitudinal trends in desk usage, and, sometimes, to provide accountability and justification for services. As we approached the assessment process at Bowdoin, we began questioning if we were really collecting the information we needed to make decisions about the future of our reference desk and services and about the transformation that would be necessary to implement our services. Do our reference statistics show the value of our services to our scholars and our institution? What do we really know about those who used reference services and the unheard voices of our non-users? And, do the numbers reflect the needs and voices of the unheard, or only the privileged people who speak or use our services? Most importantly, would we be using the assessment information we had gathered to make our reference services decisions only empower those who already use our services?

Quantitative Assessment

Assessment of reference services is a widely published topic in the library academic literature, and library conferences are devoted to assessment,

---

10 Joan Polinar Shapiro, "What Is Feminist Assessment?," in *Students at the Center: Feminist Assessment*, ed. Caryn McTighe Musil, Association of American Colleges, and National Women's Studies Association (Washington, D.C.: Association of American Colleges/National Women's Studies Association, 1992), 34.

for example, *Biannual Library Assessment Conference* hosted by the Association of Research Libraries.[11] Websites, for example, *Measuring and Assessing Reference Services and Resources: A Guide*,[12] have been created to inform libraries about assessing library and reference transactions. Despite the commonly understood importance of assessment, most efforts to collect information have been focused on statistics.

One of the shortcomings of quantitative data is that the number of "transactions" reflects little about the complexity of the interaction and, most importantly, little about value of the learning experience to the scholar. In an attempt to address the need for more than just "ticks on a sheet," the READ scale (Reference Effort Assessment Data) was developed by Bella Karr Gerlich and G. Lynn Berard in 2003 to record "effort, skills, knowledge, teaching moment, techniques and tools utilized by the librarian during a reference transaction."[13] At Bowdoin we created and implemented an "effort" scale that was modeled after the READ scale. In addition to providing information about levels of support, rating transactions with the scale has given us one way to reflect on the potential value of our services.

Qualitative and Instruction-based Assessment

Assessment of reference services must also acknowledge the place of critical engagement both within academia and in our scholars' lives. Akyea and Sandoval explain that, "Feminist assessment needs to be illuminating and transforming so as to provide knowledge and skills students need to make informed choices in their lives."[14] We must ensure that our assessment processes remain formative and informative instead of perfunctory. Assessment information collected

---

11 "Library Assessment Conference: Building Effective, Sustainable, Practical Assessment," accessed March 30, 2016, http://libraryassessment.org/.

12 "Measuring and Assessing Reference Services and Resources: A Guide," *ALA Connect*, accessed February 23, 2016, http://connect.ala.org/node/97245.

13 Bela Karr Kerlich, "READ Scale (Reference Effort Assessment Data)," accessed March 30, 2016, http://readscale.org/.

14 Stacy Gray Akyea and Pamela Sandoval, "A Feminist Perspective on Student Assessment: An Epistemology of Caring and Concern," *Radical Pedagogy* 6, no. 2 (2005), http://www.radicalpedagogy.org/radicalpedagogy/A_Feminist_Perspective_on_Student_Assessment__An_Epistemology_of_Caring_and_Concern.html.

and the resulting decisions are paramount to not only the scholars' immediate needs, but also future needs and successes.

Feminist instruction assessment practices provide formative processes for assessing references. The practices combined with self-reflection offer essential information about how our scholars perceived the interactions, how we are perceived by the students, the success or outcome of the interaction, and encourage us to assess whether we are empowering students. Radcliff, et al. and Accardi have contributed much to the discussions of assessment in feminist library instruction and information literacy. Although some instruction assessments may not be possible during the short encounters at the desk or in our offices, Radcliff et al., and Accardi describe short methods—interviewing, informal questions, focus groups, and various classroom assessment techniques (CAT), that may be easily incorporated into one-time and continuous assessment of the reference services.[15]

Informal interviewing or asking questions may be implemented at the end of the encounter, for example: "Why did you come to the reference desk today"; "If the reference desk was not open, how would have pursued the information you need"; or "What is one thing you will do differently based on what we talked about today?"

In contrast to interviewing and informal questions, a focus group "takes advantage of people's natural tendency to discuss things" and through discussions can lead to multiple perspectives, viewpoints, and voices, and provides feedback and comments on scholar and programmatic needs.[16] It is important the focus group members be carefully selected from across the academic community, either recruited or self-nominated, so that the information collected from them will leverage and illuminate the value of as many experiences, knowledge, and personal perceptions of our scholars as possible. This egalitarian method of gathering information also has the potential for empowering our scholars.

---

15 Carolyn J. Radcliff, ed., *A Practical Guide to Information Literacy Assessment for Academic Librarians* (Westport, Conn: Libraries Unlimited, 2007); Maria T. Accardi, *Feminist Pedagogy for Library Instruction*, Gender and Sexuality in Information Studies 3 (Sacramento, CA: Library Juice Press, 2013).

16 Radcliff, *A Practical Guide*, 73.

Modified versions of CAT described by Accardi,[17] such as directed paraphrasing, minute (or perhaps 30 sec.) or "muddiest point" paper, could be conducted at the end of even short encounters with a scholar. These reflective assessments would provide opportunities for the scholar to assess her understanding and knowledge and for the reference staff to assess whether the instruction has enabled and empowered the scholar.

REFLECTIVE ASSESSMENT

hooks states that teachers "..... must be actively committed to a process of self-actualization that promotes their own well-being if they are to teach in a manner that empowers students."[18] In our roles as librarians and teachers, self-reflection or self-assessment allows us to look at our own perceptions, feelings, and relationship to surroundings and scholars. Formal surveys and informal interviews, at the reference desk, in the classroom, during reference interactions, or distributed for anonymous input, can encourage narrative comments from the voices of library users and non-users about experiences with reference services, about why various reference desk services were used and not used, and about where research help was obtained if not through the services we offered and responses to these surveys allow us to reflect the services we offer.

At Bowdoin, we have used a variety of survey techniques to collect assessment information. Information from proprietary surveys, such as LibQual+ and MISO (Measuring Information Services Outcomes), provided us with information about scholars' needs and perceptions about our services. Pursuing questions not addressed in other assessments, our carefully constructed local surveys provided information about scholars' needs, expectations, satisfaction, and the perceived importance of the reference services to the research process. These surveys that were distributed to the academic community were purposely developed to encourage candid commentaries of reference services and the perspectives of the unheard voices of our non-users. Responses and results of the surveys help us reflect on more deeply on services for all members of our community.

---

17 Accardi, *Feminist Pedagogy for Library Instruction*, 83–86.

18 hooks, *Teaching to Transgress*, 15.

Examples of other reflective assessment techniques can be found in an inherently patriarchal environment: the corporate world. The goals of assessment in business organizations, i.e. marketing goods and services, are in opposition to the feminist assessment goals that center on ethics of care and the individual user needs. However, the planning practices and process of engaging in techniques such as SWOT analysis can be adopted to provide the opportunity to create a feminist planning and learning environment where librarians may self-reflect and define shared purposes, values, and goals.

The SWOT analysis, initially developed as a planning method for businesses, can be used to organize information from assessment activities in order to broadly examine reference services. The process provides a method for identifying and examining internal and external strengths, weaknesses, opportunities, and threats. For future planning, weaknesses or threats may be leveraged with identified strengths and opportunities.[19] In her chapter on strategic planning, Madden outlines a framework for engaging in feminist strategic planning. She states that "collaboration must be a fundamental component of strategic planning based feminist principles, along with … context, power, agency, and multiple perspectives."[20] As we engaged in the SWOT analysis, this non-hierarchical process provided the opportunity for Bowdoin liaisons to participate in collaborative planning that empowered participants to present a variety of perspectives, relate personal and scholar experiences, self-reflect, and look beyond individual interests and beliefs, as individuals and as a group. This collaborative, consensus-building, and participatory environment is not only important for the planning process, but also essential for the implementation of our transformed services.

Assessing how reference services are being used theoretically and how the services are located and utilized physically, is important to the success and effectiveness of existing and new services and spaces. Elliott Felix, in a presentation given at the ARL Library Assessment Conference, offered guidance for library service design from a

---

19 David H. Jonassen, "Designing for Decision Making," *Educational Technology Research and Development* 60, no. 2 (2012): 350.

20 Margaret E. Madden, "Strategic Planning: Gender, Collaborative Leadership and Organizational Change," in *Women and Leadership: Transforming Visions and Diverse Voices*, ed. Jean Lau Chin (Malden, MA: Blackwell Pub, 2007), 204.

users' perspective. The techniques described by Felix, in particular, visioning, shadowing, journey mapping, and prototyping of spaces, may provide a new perspective for identifying barriers to reference services.[21] Scholars have different ways of using and traversing library spaces. Unobtrusively observing or following our scholars as they research and find information can provide information about the varied preferences for research spaces and inquiry. Removing any unintentional barriers, physical or hierarchical, is critical to creating an egalitarian, user-empowered, environment.

The assessment methods and data described will provide valuable information to reflect on the services and to inform our decision making. As we reflect on the assessment information we have gathered, make decisions, and implement our transformed services, in order to continue to empower our scholars we must be aware of our own well-being and make decisions that are effective and sustainable. We must also be mindful that much of the information we have gathered has been about, and from, the scholars in our academic community. Focus groups and anonymous surveys may provide us with some information about people that do not use our services. Our biggest challenge with assessment is fostering information from the unheard voices. A great number of scholars with authentic needs for our reference services do not approach us. We need to continue to investigate ways to learn about and understand the unheard of our non-users.

SPACES AND SERVICES

As reference services can be broken down to both the *service* and the *space* it is important to think of both and how they affect one another. After figuring out the current state of references services and our priorities we must consider the space in which these services will be offered and the ways that each option will reflect the feminist principles toward which we are striving. As mentioned previously, space is one way that we can affect the perception of authority within the library, and as we consider our guiding principles of care, empowerment, and

---

21 Elliott Felix, "Designing and Assessing Library Services," in *2012 Proceedings* (Library Assessment Conference Building Effective, Sustainable, Practical Assessment, Charlottesville, VA: Association of Research Libraries, 2012), http://bit.ly / LAC12_services.

collaboration, we can begin to see how each major research space and staffing model affects our attempts.

The traditional reference model consists of a librarian at a desk providing assistance. This model has been the standard for a long time due to its efficacy in providing answers to those in need. It ensures that a highly trained expert is available to perform an in-depth reference interview and provide the best possible service for every query. It does not, however, reflect the changes to the information landscape that have occurred over the last decades. There is less need for a gatekeeper to the library, someone to assist with the card catalog or to guide through a print reference collection. The role of the reference librarian has expanded beyond selection of materials to education in information organization, research question development, pursuing and engaging with lines of inquiry, interpretation of text and data sources, and research ethics. Therefore, changes to the traditional model seem appropriate.

One such change is that many libraries are providing service at reference desks with non-reference staff. Over time the balance between reference librarians and other librarians and staff has shifted, the availability of hours to dedicate to reference duty has necessarily decreased, both for better and worse. While this encourages more one-on-one appointments between librarians and our community members, the just-in-time questions are now either not being answered or are being answered by other members of the library staff who may not have the training needed to determine where a seemingly simple question could become a more in-depth reference interaction.[22] This model, while acknowledging the value of non-librarian staff, does not provide the same level of care for our scholars, placing a barrier to in-depth consultation and making some modes of interaction less accessible, which may disadvantage certain populations from using our services.

The peer reference model that is being explored by many academic libraries attempts to leverage the power of student-to-student interaction. Students may be more likely to go to a peer for help. When student assistants can be trained to provide reference service there is a chance that they will be more effective at reaching their

---

22 Scott Kennedy, "Farewell to the Reference Librarian," *Journal of Library Administration* 51, no. 4 (April 22, 2011): 319–25.

peers who might otherwise be unlikely to ask for help.[23] This depends on the assumption that student assistants can navigate the subtleties of a reference interview and be conscious of when a referral becomes necessary. Training to this degree requires a substantial investment of time and energy and the return may not be of proportionate value.[24] The amount of oversight may become daunting to librarians, and we are worthy of care as well. This model, while encouraging positive peer interaction and the empowerment of student assistants, continues to place a barrier between scholars and specialized service provided by librarians.

The on-call model, where librarians are available in their offices and can be consulted as needed, frees librarians from sitting at a desk while still designating librarians as the appropriate respondent. This model assumes that another service point, usually a circulation desk, is available to field basic direction and technical questions as well as connecting scholars with librarians, which may increase the need for staffing and training at that desk. This model loses the just-in-time quality of a reference desk, as patrons are asked to wait for assistance. It is only marginally more convenient for librarians as there is still a need for time that is scheduled as being available, affecting the other demands on their time. As with other models that do not have a librarian visible and available, you also lose the questions that may arise from proximity, where a student may not feel like it is worth the added effort to go to another desk and have a librarian called on their behalf. It also doesn't leverage the work done by librarians in the classroom to increase trust, recognition, and visibility, which can increase demand for reference assistance.

Making reference services available only by appointment places another barrier between librarians and the immediate needs of our scholars. While this model seemingly benefits from the amount of personal and instructional connections built by librarians, it dismisses

---

23 Brett B. Bodemer, "They CAN and They SHOULD: Undergraduates Providing Peer Reference and Instruction," *College & Research Libraries* 75, no. 2 (March 1, 2014): 162–78.

24 Diane M. Hogan and R. H, "Implications of Vygotsky's Theory for Peer Learning," in *Cognitive Perspectives on Peer Learning*, ed. A. M. O and A. King, The Rutgers Invitational Symposium On Education Series. (Mahwah, NJ, US: Lawrence Erlbaum Associates Publishers, 1999), 49; Keith Topping and Stewart Ehly, *Peer-Assisted Learning* (New York: Routledge, 1998), 12.

the needs of our scholars who may not have had the opportunity to work with a librarian and therefore will be unlikely to make an appointment. Making an appointment depends on the agency of the scholar, which can't always be assumed with those who may not have positive associations with authority. It also has many of the same drawbacks as the on-call model with the only benefit being a less structured schedule for librarian availability.

The lab or learning commons model attempts to create a space that encourages both formal and informal learning interactions. Librarians and our scholars occupy the same space and our scholars can drift from independent work to asking a question with minimal disruption. Other services can also be represented within the space for holistic support of student work. Given the emphasis of collaboration and informal interaction, the lab model depends less heavily on scheduled librarian availability.

This lab model is intriguing from a feminist perspective on many levels. Both our scholars who have had a formal opportunity to work with a librarian as well as those who may not feel comfortable approaching a desk can easily utilize the space as it is open to all. This can serve to level the playing field, encouraging people to interact with librarians who may not have had an opportunity to build a relationship previously. This also breaks down the traditional authority of the reference desk, as it encourages scholars and librarians to share a communal space.

Most discussions and evaluations uncover the idea that our scholars work amongst themselves and ask each other for help on their path to learning.[25] Learning communities that place educators and learners in the same space allow for both this type of peer-to-peer collaboration, as well as modeling research activities and socially supported inquiry, which benefits all members of the community.[26] This model encourages scholars to develop their own ways of knowing, which is in line with our other efforts to challenge the traditional power structure and to empower our scholars. This also leverages the value of both formal and informal interactions. While social interactions may not directly affect the learning outcomes of a student, the ability

---

25 Keith Topping, "Trends in Peer Learning," *Education Psychology* 25, no. 6 (2005): 631–45.

26 Anastasia Tryphon and J. Jacques Vonèche, eds., *Piaget-Vygotsky: The Social Genesis of Thought* (Hove, East Sussex, UK: Psychology Press, 1996).

to interact in an informal way with educators creates a sphere of discourse and trust that then lends itself to collaboration in service of learning and showing care for our scholars. As the relationship grows and our scholars become increasingly aware of and comfortable with the discourse, their ability to act as influencers and educators also increases, widening the network of those able to assist with the act of inquiry.

The learning commons model also recognizes reference services as an arm of our instructional program. Our time in the classroom and our time working one-on-one with students and faculty are inextricably related. It is important to acknowledge this relationship as it provides benefits to both programs. The more classes that librarians work with, the more we foster trust and understanding, which can lead to more reference activity. Conversely, the more work we can do with students in a one-on-one setting, the more time we can spend in classes on questions of deeper engagement and critical inquiry.

Implementation

Creating and sustaining reference services enlightened by feminist theories and based on the ethic of care may require more than designing new learning spaces and points of service. Crucial to the success of integrating feminist principles is the transformation of the culture of individuals, departments, and the library as a whole. Transparent challenges such as budget, space, training, and appropriate staffing often have concrete approaches. Other challenges are more opaque and difficult to define, and may have less tangible solutions. These challenges include melding differing service principles, cultures and philosophies, transforming perceptions of services for scholars and library staff, and empowering them to engage in inquiry.

Traditionally libraries have centered the primary reference service model on a large intimidating reference desk. This desk was THE point of reference service. Planning and creating flexible reference services in many libraries may take years of planning, design, and construction, and will require a significant financial investment. However, it is possible and desirable to begin to cultivate and nurture the internal, and external feminist culture before the work on the physical changes commences. These changes may even be incorporated in environments where physical changes are not planned or plausible.

Several of the reference services models discussed, the reference desk, on-call, and alternate staff models, create an environment that reinforces the traditional power structure between librarian and information seeker, and between the reference librarian and other library staff, in particular the circulation desk staff. Although reference and circulation staff both serve as primary public service points, the services offered by these two groups are siloed. In addition, the primary purposes of services offered at these distinct desks greatly differ. Circulation staff are most often expected to provide quick answers to quick questions with a focus on immediate needs. Staff are often required to multi-task, answering directional questions, checking in and out books and study rooms, answering the phone, etc. Generally, the expectation is that reference transactions involve longer exchanges with the goal of identifying and addressing the specific information needs of the student scholar. Reference staff become engaged in the learning process and develop collaborative relationships with students.[27] In order to develop a collaborative culture between reference and circulation staff, it is necessary to recognize and appreciate the differing service philosophies so that all public service staff are able to identify the best space and culture to meet the academic community information needs.

Elmborg cautions librarians against wielding power by developing special skills and withholding information from users.[28] We also must avoid exercising this power over our colleagues. In order to build the collaborative culture there must be a shift of power agency between librarians, staff, and student staff. Just as the constructivist model of education encourages and empowers students, we must reduce barriers to discussion and empower all staff to interact and become engaged. Instead of creating a hierarchy, we need to build a community of practice as introduced by Wenger and Lave[29] and described by the Wenger-Trayners as "… groups of people who share a concern or a passion for something they do and learn how to do

---

[27] Christopher Magee and Perini, Michael, "The Blended Desk and Its Consequences on Collaboration," *Collaborative Librarianship* 6, no. 3 (2014): 125.

[28] James K. Elmborg, "Teaching at the Desk: Toward a Reference Pedagogy," *Portal: Libraries and the Academy* 2, no. 3 (2002): 463, doi:10.1353/pla.2002.0050.

[29] Jean Lave and Etienne Wenger, *Situated Learning: Legitimate Peripheral Participation*, Learning in Doing (Cambridge [England]: Cambridge University Press, 1991), 98–100.

it better as they interact regularly."[30] Librarians and circulation staff who provide all levels of research services, from finding a book on the shelf to a long discourse on the research process, share enthusiasm and excitement for assisting our scholars. We must be mindful that each person, librarian, staff, and student assistants bring talents and experience that we must respect and honor, and we must nurture each other's unique expertise.

Changing established or perceived organizational library structures can be fraught with obstacles. In an article on changing organizations and establishing "learning organizations," Limwichitr, Borady-Preston, and Ellis discuss the need to modify three layers. They emphasize that the most difficult "layer" to modify is "underlying assumptions."[31] This layer may only be changed by involving employees at all levels. The power relationships between the reference librarian, circulation staff, students, and faculty must be broken down by the willingness to challenge assumptions and to work as a group or organization to develop a common language, to express concerns, and to work together to build consensus on a shared understanding of a common purpose. This building and understanding can begin as we work through assessment processes such as a SWOT analysis or focus groups.

By creating a space and culture that encourage scholars to take charge of their own discovery and to interact with information and librarians on their own terms, we begin to empower them to look beyond answers to more critical engagement. This necessitates a relationship with our community based on trust and a shared understanding of a common purpose and requires attention to changes in population and where (and how) inquiry is taking place. Instead of asking scholars to adjust to arbitrary rules and structural barriers that they do not understand or operate within, we should be continuously looking for ways to complement the ways in which these activities are already taking place and provide ourselves as aides in the process.

---

30 Etienne Wenger-Trayner and Beverly Wenger-Trayner, "Introduction to Communities of Practice," April 15, 2015, http://wenger-trayner.com/introduction-to-communities-of-practice/.

31 Saowapha Limwichitr, Judith Broady-Preston, and David Ellis, "A Discussion of Problems in Implementing Organisational Cultural Change: Developing a Learning Organisation in University Libraries," *Library Review* 64, no. 6/7 (September 7, 2015): 484, doi:10.1108/LR-10-2014-0116.

Perhaps partially due to the traditional library organization structure and its place within the academy, our scholars have perceptions and assumptions about reference services and reference staff. As discussed in earlier sections, scholars are not really sure about what reference staff do. Many scholars, even seasoned faculty, do not recognize the multiple roles we embrace: librarian, teacher, and researcher. Until recently at our library, the title "reference librarian" was emblazoned on signs over the reference desk and near our offices, and on literature about the library. We had inadvertently created a culture that could be perceived as authoritative and that involved one way communication: scholars ask questions, we answer them. In addition, our job titles and job descriptions did not accurately reflect our roles and responsibilities within the library and the college. We have now adopted job titles that include the words research and instruction librarian. These titles more accurately describe how we can assist scholars and reflect the potential for collaborative interactions with the academic community.

The two most important outwardly visible roles that we wish to encourage is that of a collaborator and teacher. Changing scholars' perceptions of the reference librarian sitting behind a desk can start in the classroom where we should promote not the banking model of research services and instruction, but rather a model that supports critical engagement. Students and faculty may be more likely to seek out a familiar librarian that demonstrates an ethic of care. Through critical engagement with the students, faculty can also observe that the student interactions with librarians have the potential for enhancing student and faculty research and the learning experience outside of the classroom.

Changing scholar perceptions of librarians and the culture of research services is not limited directly to a classroom. In our research spaces at Bowdoin, we have begun to make small changes to physical space and to reduce barriers and offer choices for how people seek help. For example, when we started the process of reviewing our reference model, we had a multi-height, large L-shaped reference desk that, in our opinion, was hard to miss. The desk, near the entrance to the library, was designed to provide space for consultation at standing and seated heights for differently-abled scholars. As we reviewed the assessment data, it became clear the large desk was not as obvious as we thought. The desk placement and size created a barrier for our scholars. We were often asked, "Is it OK to come around the desk?"

The liaison offices are located in the back of the library, not in direct view of the reference desk. The remote location had created unintentional barriers to our offices, a safe and private space where we were encouraging scholars to seek assistance outside of the classroom. Re-location of our offices has not yet been possible, but we were able to create a reference space without physical barriers that encouraged scholars to sit down and collaborate with the librarian by simply placing a small round table in a space adjacent to our offices. This has created a collaborative space where we can be seen and has encouraged students and groups to enter the "black hole" of the liaison suite of offices.

Proceeding with Care

Integrating feminist principles into reference services requires a cultural shift that has the potential to reshape the service ethic of the library as a whole. Developing a feminist culture of collaboration and community of practice in the library, and in the academic community, can and should begin even when changes in space are not planned or possible. A critical first-step to moving towards the transformation is looking for ways to reduce both physical and perceived barriers: modify our spaces where possible to encourage open discourse, challenge the hierarchy between reference staff, other library staff, and scholars, nurture relationships across campus, and reflect on our role in the lives of our scholars.

With a clearer vision of the potential for a feminist service model and as we work through the challenges of space, staffing, and budget, we have the opportunity to begin to implement a new service ethic and encourage a culture shift. Using elements of feminist theory along with a careful examination of reference services, it is possible for us to create an egalitarian and empowering environment for all members of the academic community.

BIBLIOGRAPHY

Accardi, Maria T. *Feminist Pedagogy for Library Instruction*. Gender and Sexuality in Information Studies 3. Sacramento, CA: Library Juice Press, 2013.

Akyea, Stacy Gray, and Pamela Sandoval, "A Feminist Perspective on Student Assessment: An Epistemology of Caring and Concern." *Radical Pedagogy* 6, no. 2 (2005). http://www.radicalpedagogy.org/radicalpedagogy/A_Feminist_Perspective_on_Student_Assessment__An_Epistemology_of_Caring_and_Concern.html.

Bodemer, Brett B. "They CAN and They SHOULD: Undergraduates Providing Peer Reference and Instruction." *College & Research Libraries* 75, no. 2 (March 1, 2014): 162–78.

Elmborg, James K. "Teaching at the Desk: Toward a Reference Pedagogy." *Portal: Libraries and the Academy* 2, no. 3 (2002): 455–64. doi:10.1353/pla.2002.0050.

Felix, Elliott. "Designing and Assessing Library Services." In *2012 Proceedings*. Charlottesville, VA: Association of Research Libraries, 2012. http://bit.ly /LAC12_services.

Hartman, Joan, and Ellen Messer-Davidow, eds. *(En)gendering Knowledge: Feminists in Academe*. Knoxville: University of Tennessee Press, 1991.

Hogan, Diane M., and R. H. "Implications of Vygotsky's Theory for Peer Learning." In *Cognitive Perspectives on Peer Learning*, edited by A. M. O and A. King, 39–65. The Rutgers Invitational Symposium On Education Series. Mahwah, NJ, US: Lawrence Erlbaum Associates Publishers, 1999.

hooks, bell. *Teaching to Transgress: Education as the Practice of Freedom*. New York: Routledge, 1994.

Hutchins, Margaret. Introduction to Reference Work. Chicago: American Library Association, 1944.

Jonassen, David H. "Designing for Decision Making." *Educational Technology Research and Development* 60, no. 2 (2012): 341–59.

Kennedy, Scott. "Farewell to the Reference Librarian." *Journal of Library Administration* 51, no. 4 (April 22, 2011): 319–25.

Kerlich, Bela Karr. "READ Scale (Reference Effort Assessment Data)." Accessed March 30, 2016. http://readscale.org/.

Lather, Patricia Ann. *Getting Smart: Feminist Research and Pedagogy With/in the Postmodern*. Critical Social Thought. New York: Routledge, 1991.

Lave, Jean, and Etienne Wenger. *Situated Learning: Legitimate Peripheral Participation*. Learning in Doing. Cambridge [England]: Cambridge University Press, 1991.

"Library Assessment Conference: Building Effective, Sustainable, Practical Assessment." Accessed March 30, 2016. http://libraryassessment.org/.

Limwichitr, Saowapha, Judith Broady-Preston, and David Ellis. "A Discussion of Problems in Implementing Organisational Cultural Change: Developing a Learning Organisation in University Libraries." *Library Review* 64, no. 6/7 (September 7, 2015): 480–88. doi:10.1108/LR-10-2014-0116.

Madden, Margaret E. "Strategic Planning: Gender, Collaborative Leadership and Organizational Change." In *Women and Leadership: Transforming Visions and Diverse Voices*, edited by Jean Lau Chin. Malden, MA: Blackwell Pub, 2007.

Magee, Christopher, and Perini, Michael. "The Blended Desk and Its Consequences on Collaboration." *Collaborative Librarianship* 6, no. 3 (2014): 124–29.

"Measuring and Assessing Reference Services and Resources: A Guide." *ALA Connect*. Accessed February 23, 2016. http://connect.ala.org/node/97245.

Panofsky, Carolyn P., and Lesley Bogad. "Hearing Students' Silence: Issues of Identity, Performance, and Recognition in College Classrooms." In *Transforming Classroom Culture: Inclusive Pedagogical Practices*, edited by Arlene Dallalfar, Esther Kingston-Mann, and R. Timothy Sieber, 181–95. New York: Palgrave Macmillan, 2011.

Quarton, Barbara A. "Teaching in the Margins." In *Informed Agitation: Library and Information Skills in Social Justice Movements and Beyond*, edited by Melissa Morrone, 55–72. Sacramento, CA: Library Juice Press, 2014.

Radcliff, Carolyn J., ed. *A Practical Guide to Information Literacy Assessment for Academic Librarians*. Westport, Conn: Libraries Unlimited, 2007.

Shapiro, Joan Polinar. "What Is Feminist Assessment?" In *Students at the Center: Feminist Assessment*, edited by Caryn McTighe Musil, Association of American Colleges, and National Women's Studies Association, 29–38. Washington, D.C.: Association of American Colleges/National Women's Studies Association, 1992.

Topping, Keith. "Trends in Peer Learning." *Education Psychology* 25, no. 6 (2005): 631–45.

Topping, Keith, and Stewart Ehly. *Peer-Assisted Learning*. New York: Routledge, 1998.

Tryphon, Anastasia, and J. Jacques Vonèche, eds. *Piaget-Vygotsky: The Social Genesis of Thought*. Hove, East Sussex, UK: Psychology Press, 1996.

Wenger-Trayner, Etienne, and Beverly Wenger-Trayner. "Introduction to Communities of Practice," April 15, 2015. http://wenger-trayner.com/introduction-to-communities-of-practice/.

Wyer, J. I. *Reference Work: A Textbook for Students of Library Work and Librarians*. Library Curriculum Studies. Chicago: American Library Association, 1930.

Feminist Pedagogy and Special Collections Reference: Shifting the Balance

Melanie J. Meyers

Special Collections Education Thus Far: We Have Been "Carefully Taught"

Special collections have been, for many years, perceived as the province of the rarefied few, primarily dominated by a white male power structure. Traditionally, the perception of rare book libraries and special collections is that the materials are guarded by gatekeepers who are not terribly interested in outreach or reference, and that, by extension, special collections professionals provide very little in the way of public services. Given that special collections are also frequently housed in spaces that are not integrated fully into the library proper [1], this physical isolation adds to the perception that these collections are separate from other library services, and that the rules of equal access and egalitarian policies do not apply [2].

This aura of exclusivity has been reinforced by the formal education received by special collections librarians; as Michael

---

[1] "ACRL/RBMS Guidelines Regarding Security and Theft in Special Collections", last modified 2008, http://www.ala.org/acrl/standards/security_theft.

[2] This perspective has been changing in recent years, see "ALA-SAA Joint Statement of Access: Guidelines for Access to Original Research Materials", last modified August 2009, http://www2.archivists.org/statements/ala-saa-joint-statement-of-access-guidelines-for-access-to-original-research-materials-au.

Garabedian eloquently describes in his article on library school education for special collections librarians, most MLS programs have not offered much for those who choose to pursue rare books and special collections. Therefore, special collections librarians have not been exposed to the same ideas regarding equality of access, the library "as a democratic space, and librarians as public servants"[3.] Additionally, the emphasis on guardianship, rather than access, indicated that proficiency in the principles of librarianship was considered unimportant; "formal training was hardly necessary for 'gatekeepers' whose main responsibility was to keep a very narrow gate closed to the majority of users most of the time."[4] This is largely in contrast to the principles of free and open access that is the primary focus of the modern library system, and by extension, modern library education.

This lack of formal public services education extends to the archival sector as well; while some archivists acquire their professional training through MLS programs that offer an archives or records management specialization, this is by no means universal. Therefore, archives education also can suffer from the same lack of grounding in democracy of access that Garabedian discusses; as many special collections contain archival or manuscript collections in addition to rare books, this lack of education applies to different specializations within special collections as a whole. This is not a new observation; Susan Malbin discussed this dissonance in her article on reference written in 1997 and reviewed how this is treated in the archival literature. She discussed how archives needed to look at users and rethink how reference interviews were conducted, and she parsed out an excellent summary from an earlier article by Carolyn Heald, which concluded, "Much of the difficulty archivists have in providing reference service stems from lack of training. Unlike librarians, archivists are not formally trained to provide reference service, unless

---

3 Michael Garabedian, "You've Got to be Carefully Taught: American Special Collections Library Education and the Inculcation of Exclusivity", *RBM: A Journal of Rare Books* 7 (2006): 56.

4 Garabedian, 58.

they went to library school".[5] As many special collections librarians also traditionally did not go to library school, both the rare book librarian and the archivist can be deficient in training for reference and public services; given that special collections frequently have both rare books and archival collections, this lack of public service training covers a great deal of special collections staff.

Thankfully, over the years this has gradually changed, as both special collections and archives have embraced a more public-services oriented model. Articles by Stam[6] and Priddle,[7] among others, emphasize the importance of outreach and public services in special collections, and moving away from the model of exclusivity. Additionally, the access policies that required credentialing before entry to special collections ensured an elite, if not elitist, base of readers and staff alike.[8] But these policies appear to be less common,[9] and the institutions that enforce policies of viewing materials "by appointment only" are born less of elitist frameworks and more to address the logistical challenges of retrieving the increasing amount of materials held off-site. Off-site storage frequently means that a certain lead time is required in order to accommodate requests for viewing,

---

5 Susan Malbin, "The Reference Interview in Archival Literature", *College and Research Libraries*, 58 (1997): 69-80. Note: I have included archival literature and education in this piece as special collections frequently have large collections of archival materials in addition to printed books and manuscripts. Additionally, one could make the argument that many archives, with the exception of repositories of vital records, maintained the same policies of restrictive access and exclusivity. This has also been ably discussed in newer articles, see Mattie Taormina and Marilyn Rackley, "Reading Room and Reference (Re)Vision: The Transformation of Reader Services" in *New Directions for Special Collections: An Anthology of Practice*, ed. Lynne M. Thomas and Beth M. Whittaker. (Santa Barbara, CA: ABC-CLIO, 2015), 13-30.

6 Dierdre Stam, "Bridge That Gap! Education and Special Collections", *RBM: A Journal of Rare Books*, 7 (2006):16-30.

7 Charlotte Priddle, "Bridging the Internal Gap: Special Collections and "In-Reach", *RBM: A Journal of Rare Books*, 16 (2015):35-47.

8 "Credentialing" was a common practice in rare book libraries; essentially, one needed to provide a letter (or letters) of recommendation from an accepted source in order to gain access to certain libraries or materials. Some libraries still require this to varying degrees.

9 Most institutions require some form of registration, but these primarily the collection of information for identification and security purposes, rather than a subjective judgement on relative scholarly merit.

so requesting materials and appointments in advance is a necessity in order to ensure availability.

However, with the rising number of classes being offered in MLS programs for special collections librarians, there is now an opening to adjust the formal training we offer to new professionals to include public services and instruction.[10] Coupled with an increasing level of visibility for women in special collections librarianship, an opportunity has arisen to challenge these defaults in regards to access and public services for primary sources.[11] As Taormina and Rackley talk about in their article on the changing nature of reference in special collections, perhaps it is time to "lean in" for reference services, and rethink educational offerings to include special collections reference.[12] And, feminist pedagogy, with its roots firmly planted in collaborative learning and dismantling structures of power, is very well-suited as a vehicle to affect these changes in two ways: first, in how we teach reference and public services; and second, how we design our services and frame our interactions with readers at the special collections reference desk.

"How do I Get YOUR Job?": Special Collections Reference in the Classroom Setting

About three years ago, I was approached to host a group of MLS students from the Palmer School, Long Island University, for a tour and discussion of the collections at my institution (The Center for Jewish History). Happy to accommodate my alma mater and always excited to see some new librarians, we scheduled a visit; but unlike the usual materials based "show and tell" session, what we spent the most time discussing was my role as a reference librarian in special collections. We discussed the increasing emphasis put on both reference and instruction as core competencies of special collections librarianship,

---

10 "Educational Opportunities: A Directory", modified December 2015, http://rbms.info/committees/membership_and_professional/educational_opportunities/. RBMS maintains a directory of programs offering specialized SC classes in curation, history of the book, etc…

11 "RBMS membership survey", modified April 2015, http://rbms.info/files/committees/membership_and_professional/2015_RBMS_Membership_Survey_Questionnaire.pdf.

12 Taormina and Rackley, "Reading Room and Reference (Re)Vision," 21-22.

but how the students felt they received very little formal instruction in either, especially as to how reference and instruction were related to special collections. While all students were required to take the standard reference class as part of the MLS program, the prevailing feeling among the students was that the formal reference class was really geared at doing general reference in a public or academic library; which was/is appropriate, as those are the largest types of libraries and therefore the most common employers of librarians. However, these students clearly needed, and desired, more formal instruction in reference and instruction in order to meet the requirements of the positions they were considering for future employment. What was even more encouraging to me was that many of the group seemed to connect with the job I was doing and professed interest in learning about it in a more formal environment. Hearing that students wanted to forgo jobs as curators or bibliographers for reference and instruction? For me, that signaled a very interesting shift in special collections librarianship. Shortly after that class visit, the director of the Palmer School program on Rare Books and Special Collections, asked me if I would be interested in teaching a class on reference and instruction for the program; this class would not replace the standard introductory class (nor should it, as I believe it is essential), but augment that baseline of general reference and concentrate on the nuances and challenges of providing all aspects of public/reader services for special collections.

However, what I quickly discovered is that no one else was teaching such a class, at least not in 2014. There seemed to be no mentions of any in online course listings and schedules, and no syllabi available online.[13] There were many classes on reference, and many classes on instruction, but no class that combined both AND was specifically tailored for special collections librarianship. This presented more of a challenge, as I had nothing to refer to and no examples to assist me in creating this class. But, it also offered more of an opportunity; I could write the class the way I wanted to teach it, which included teaching the class using a feminist pedagogical framework, but also teaching

---

13 I looked at the RBMS Educational Opportunity Directory, which provides a comprehensive list of the library school programs that offer courses of interest to the broad group interested in rare books/special collections/archives. While some archives programs offered classes on reference and outreach, they were largely offered as "special topics".

the actual concept of feminist pedagogy as a tool for the students to use as instructors themselves. I could teach the concept in the abstract, but also model the framework in a very real sense. Part of the reason why I felt this was important is because of the subject matter: public service and instruction. These are career paths which require interacting with diverse populations, possibly in large numbers, possibly over long periods, ideally in a respectful manner. Reference and public service work, done properly, is a short-term exercise in collaborative problem solving. I felt that the feminist pedagogical framework which prioritizes critical thinking, participatory learning, and most importantly, listening to people, would be a great choice for the subject matter and would allow me to model that kind of respectful behavior and listening skills for the students.

The class was divided equally into two basic larger sections; first was reference, and the second was instruction. Within those two larger concepts, the class was further broken down into smaller modules. While some of the units were fairly straightforward, there was always room to assign readings that emphasize change and collaboration in special collections, particularly when discussing reference and public services; one of the first readings assigned was John Overholt's article, "5 Theses on the Future of Special Collections".[14] While this is not an article that specifically advocates a feminist thesis per se, his five points (openness, distribution, disintermediation, transformation, and advocacy) are all concepts that fit very well and provide ample fodder for discussion within a feminist pedagogical framework, particularly when thinking about critiquing existing power structures within special collections. The unit on archives, manuscripts, and finding aids had readings that discussed issues pertaining to archives, power, and representation;[15] when thinking about how finding aids are written and collections are acquired and arranged, a discussion of power dynamics within archives is particularly relevant. The unit on the reference interview delved into the complexity of the personal consultation and interaction, and how we can present ourselves to

---

[14] John Overholt, "Five Theses on the Future of Special Collections", RBM: *A Journal of Rare Books* 14 (2013): 15-20.

[15] Terry Cook, "What is Past is Prologue: A History of Archival Ideas Since 1898", *Archivaria* 43 (1997): 17-63. Also, Terry Cook and Joan Schwartz, "Archives, Records, and Power: From (Postmodern) Theory to (Archival) Performance", *Archival Science*, 2 (2002): 171-185.

be more open and accessible, and to think about the power in those kinds of transactions. We looked at the professional competencies for reference librarians (from RUSA) and for archivists and special collections librarians (from RBMS and SAA), and discussed how they were different and similar; we also examined the ACRL/SAA statements on access to special collections, and discussed practical application of these standards in a reference setting. A unit on genealogy was very well-received, as I felt this was an important and much-maligned user group that needed an in-depth discussion, and a population that is not traditionally discussed in special collections—although some MLS programs are now offering lectures on family history, usually co-sponsored with a genealogical society or local history organization.[16]

I felt that every unit, even ones that explained potentially dry technical information about special collections, offered an opportunity to frame the discussions of reference and public services in a way that was encouraging of collaborative efforts, and to examine current institutional structures with a more critical eye. I included a unit on UX, which for some students was the first time they had been exposed to the concept, but I felt was necessary. Again, while it is not an overtly feminist process, it opens up conversations about designing with readers in mind (applicable to physical spaces, workflows, digital projects, apps, and websites), which has not been a traditional priority in archives or special collections.[17] Discussion of UX, framed properly, also encourages thinking about collaborating with your readers for the best result, rather than just dictating a process. It brings up issues of perception

---

16 As discussed before, since special collections tends to replicate academic models of power that privilege some users and work over others, genealogists are frequently not given much attention by special collections librarians and archivists. The prevailing attitude is that they are not "real scholars", rather they are hobbyists and therefore not doing real scholarly work. Particularly driven by websites like *Ancestry*, which are easy to use even for those with limited technology skills, the fact is that family history is a fast- growing user group, and one that archivists and special collections professionals need to learn to deal with. The L.I.S program at Long Island University will be offering a course on family history in the fall of 2017, and St. John's University has offered a class in the past, but not frequently.

17 This has been changing in recent years, see: "User Driven", RBMS Conference 2015, https://www.slideshare.net/robinmkatz/meeting-researchers-where-they-are-a-userdriven-manifesto. Also, Malbin's article discusses this as a failing of archives; we should think about user behavior and how we can help, rather than trying to change user behavior to mirror ours for our own convenience.

and usability, as well as accessibility; also, thinking about transparency and a willingness to improve both process and design is sorely needed in special collections and archives, which are environments that can be especially confusing and intimidating to the new user. UX is explicitly collaborative in nature and implementation, as the core focus of UX is trying to solve problems by understanding the nature of the problem. This requires, more than anything else, listening to the voice of the audience, rather than just the echo chamber of the practitioners. Good UX design should be intuitive, consistent, and credible; the only way to achieve these goals is by truly understanding the needs of the user. UX design should also be a transparent and collaborative process; these are two of the best processes in breaking down various hierarchical structures. In addition, as some of the core tenets of feminist pedagogy are challenging assumptions, validating personal experience, and understanding the influence of environment, UX design and theory (perhaps inadvertently) embodies many of the principles of feminist pedagogy, and is essential to running a reference service that values readers and access.[18]

The second half of the class was devoted to instruction, with units on various instructional models and working with a variety of different user groups. The first unit was specifically about pedagogy, and discussion of various pedagogical models for instruction. Active learning, informed learning, peer-led discussions, flipped classroom model, and feminist pedagogy were all discussed in readings and classroom sessions; we also discussed the idea of finding your own teaching voice, deciding what teaching style works best, and that you may have to change your pedagogical style depending on what group you are teaching. We discussed instruction with both graduate and undergraduate students, as those are the groups special collections librarians (particularly in academic institutions) most frequently interact with; we also did a unit called "Out of Our Comfort Zone: Teaching and Instruction to Non-Traditional Special Collections Readers." This unit largely focused on instructional work with K-12 populations, not the usual readers in special collections. However, they are an extremely rewarding population to work with, who had been largely excluded from special collections due to preconceived

---

18 Julie Brown, "Theory or Practice–What Exactly Is Feminist Pedagogy?", *The Journal of General Education* 41 (1992): 51–63.

notions about age and appropriate behavior. Feminist pedagogy in special collections should ideally work to combat elitism in its various forms, and the exclusion of the young is a very persistent bias that has (thankfully) started to wane in recent years.[19] I felt it important to aggressively address the biases against K-12 populations, and also family history, because these prejudices tend to affect the young (K-12), and the older (family historians).

One of the wonderful things about teaching this class was that I also had a great deal of support from my own institution, and was able to give the class at my workplace. This also meant that I was not wedded to the traditional classroom model; we could have classes in the reading room, or the scholar's lounge, or the genealogy institute—the building was ours to roam, which also allowed for discussions on the importance of accessibility and inclusion when thinking about design of public spaces, interfaces, and workflows. Having the class at CJH afforded us another important benefit, which is that I was also able to incorporate collection materials into every session. Having the flexibility of different spaces and the freedom to interface with materials made every session far more participatory, opened up much more discussion, and allowed us to dispense with the lecture type format. The room where we did the more formal instruction (where I needed use of the smart board, or to show slides), was also arranged much more casually than a traditional classroom. There was a large table where everyone could sit and look at each other during discussions, but also has a couch at the back where students could sit as well. I encouraged people to sit wherever they felt comfortable, or to move the chairs around, and while I often stood at the front to use the smart board to show examples, I was never more than three feet from the students; I think this gave a more intimate, familiar feel to the class, and also helped to set a tone that was encouraging of participation. When I had two guest speakers come in to talk about K-12 outreach, the three of us sat on the couch and engaged in a very casual roundtable-style discussion that students could jump into at any time. We took great care to be approachable, and not just "talking heads."

---

19 Many articles on working with K-12 populations have been published in recent years-see: Lori Lynn Dekyspotter and Cherry Dunham Williams, "Alchemy and Innovation: Cultivating an Appreciation for Primary Sources in Younger Students", *RBM: A Journal of Rare Books* 14 (2013): 67-81. Also, see Kate Theimer's book on *Innovative Best Practices in Archives and Special Collections: Instruction* (Lanham, MD: Rowman & Littlefield, 2015), has many valuable case studies on working with K-12 groups.

I also deliberately chose materials that were controversial or difficult to look at; looking at anti-Semitic literature and ephemera, for example, opened up frank conversations about oppression and language- "How does this make you feel to look at this? How would you explain this to a student? How can we unpack this to different groups?" The collections at CJH have an enormous amount of materials related to the Holocaust, which can be very shocking and challenging to look at; for example, showing students our collection of Yizkor books, which are memorial books that commemorate towns and the residents of those towns who perished in the Holocaust. Sometimes looking at these and other materials could be very intense, particularly for students who came from Jewish backgrounds. I was asked repeatedly: How I could look at these things all day? How did I not spend every day in tears? Didn't I get depressed? I was very honest about my emotional response to these materials and how they made me feel, and how this informed my practice. The fact that some of these materials did, and do, deeply affect me is actually a strength to my instructional style. Because I feel sorrow and often anger from seeing these materials, I can articulate to others the importance in a way that resonates with them. I also don't need to be seen as a stoic authority; letting people see my reaction to these materials shows my humanity and connects with theirs, which I believe is akin to the concept of consciousness-raising. We look at these challenging items and discuss them, and connect through our shared sorrow and vulnerability. It's actually one of my favorite parts of my job. And in the end, I think I conveyed to the students that being able to handle these types of materials and discuss their creation, context, collection, and preservation as part of the historical record was a fantastic way to open up discussions about power, and representation, and the complexity of the historical record and the objects that comprise it. And that we don't always have to separate our feelings from the process, they are frequently an illuminating part of the endeavor.

Putting Feminist Pedagogy to Work at the Reference Desk

Creating this class for Palmer also afforded me an opportunity to teach my general outlook on reference in special collections as a whole, which has been greatly influenced by my feminism. In the creation of policies and services for my reference environment, we emphasize equality of readers, scholars, and staff. No one's work gets privileged above others, and the rules apply to everyone equally. I had a reader one day who was an undergraduate and new to the world of special collections, and in our discussion of her work I referred to her as a scholar. She immediately demurred, and said that she was not a scholar. I responded with, "Of course you are. Everyone here is a scholar, and all scholarship has to start somewhere." Many institutions give certain readers (could be faculty, or scholars of some renown) special treatment; I am proud to say that we do not provide such indulgences based on perceived stature. This is partially due to practical rather than ideological concerns; we are an exceptionally busy environment (we can accommodate thirty-two simultaneous readers in special collections), so allowing exceptions to the stated policies is really untenable from a staffing and materials supervision perspective. But it is also because we, as a staff and an institution, consider it elitist and unwelcoming. We do not engage in credentialing, or require readers to present letters of recommendation or other "proof" of their academic worthiness; we are free and open to the public, no appointments necessary. Anyone can be a reader; an individual may walk in, fill out the registration form, and have materials in front of them in approximately twenty minutes. We pride ourselves on our egalitarian policies, and are always looking for ways to improve access and foster a collaborative scholarly environment. We are special collections environment with a public library commitment to access and service.

These principles are also important in terms of creating a welcoming environment for user groups within special collections who are not the typical reader population. Since special collections have traditionally been located in academic institutions, they tend to mirror the same power structures and imbalances found within academia; these structures tend to privilege some over others, based on perceptions of status and worth. And, as most higher prestige positions are occupied by men (white and affluent, primarily), this creates both a gendered and racially based stratification, by default. As CJH is not part of a university structure, we don't have a longstanding and entrenched bureaucratic framework and assumptions to overcome. We can (and are) welcoming to all groups, including both high school and junior high school students, researchers engaged with family history, and the general public. We have a large and rapidly growing genealogy program; family history research is one of our most devoted and expanding user groups. This is a reader group that has not traditionally been welcomed by special collections environments, but we have embraced them; at CJH we have a dedicated Genealogy Institute, and two full-time librarians that specialize in family history.

While it is not my area of supervision or specialization, working with Family History program here was a professional turning point for me in terms of critiquing my own practice. I'll be honest, I started with the same prejudices that I enumerated above, espoused by special collections librarians far and wide. "Genealogists are hobbyists and dilettantes, not scholars. They are doing for themselves, not for the humanities or for scholarship, so it's selfish the way they demand my time; people doing IMPORTANT work need my time. I don't even like my own family—why do you think I want to hear about yours?" I was never overtly rude, or refused to help anyone, but I found them to be a nuisance and internally sighed whenever I had to assist one of them. But as I created this class, I started to examine my own practice with a more critical lens, and came to the horrifying conclusion that I was just as bad as the exclusionary practices I had been railing against. I was practicing the worst form of elitism, I was judging my readers and making unfounded assumptions about the worthiness of their research. While I didn't exclude them outright, I was probably offering them a lesser quality of reference help. This is what special collections did for years, and here I was buying into the same power hierarchy because now I had access to the club.

But, when you get granular about it, family history is in essence the natural progression of social history methodology and research. It's not the story of "great (white) men," it's the story of an everyday person. It's using non-traditional sources to reconstruct the history of a life that may have been exceptional, or may have been ordinary—but either way, or the million other degrees in between, the story still has value. I thought about the some of the first people to write women's history, queer history, histories of people of color—those historians all used non-traditional sources in order to tell the stories of everyday people, excluded from history, because they were not who history was written about (or for). Those scholars didn't use speeches, or books written by "great" people—they looked at cookbooks, scrapbooks, notices in newspapers, and ephemera (to name just a few). Family historians use obituaries, ship manifests, public records, fire insurance maps, city incorporation records—the list goes on. There is very little difference in method- the only real difference is the value judgement that is made on the part of the librarian who thinks the research is not worth their time.... like the librarians and archivists probably treated the early pioneers of social history. I gave a short paper at RBMS Conference in Coral Gables recently, in which I talked about this class, and I specifically talked about my own regrettable bias towards family history readers. I had many people approach me afterwards and say how refreshing it was to see someone critique themselves that way. But to me, that is part of the feminist pedagogical process—you cannot exempt yourself from examination, nor become complacent about your own practice. And the class is a constant work in progress; the latest syllabus will address burnout and self-care (very common in reference librarians), trigger warnings, and the devaluation of emotional labor (particularly instruction) in feminized professions.

The traditional viewpoint of special collections and archives has been that restrictive policies and "gatekeeping" are necessary in order to maintain security of the collections (which tend to have a higher monetary value), and a quiet scholarly environment. In my opinion, these restrictive policies were primarily in play in order to maintain an elite status quo; and to refer to Overholt again, a status quo that tended to conflate stewardship of collections with ownership of materials. As he later states, "They were entrusted to us to preserve them, certainly, but preservation without use is an empty victory. It ought to be our primary purpose at all times to minimize barriers to use, so it is all the more shameful when we interpose such barriers ourselves, not out of concern for the health of the collections, but out of the misguided belief that we are entitled to control, even to monetize, their use."[20] These barriers create hierarchical structures that are invariably biased towards those in power, and against those without. However, these structures are slowly being broken down and eliminated, through the changing makeup of the profession, as well as an emphasis on access and distribution rather than gatekeeping. I also believe, based on my own experiences teaching and running a busy reference service, instruction and reference design that prioritizes collaborative learning and doing, the user experience, and encourages the dismantling of structures that privilege some categories of users/readers over others, feminist pedagogy has the potential to inform a great deal of positive change in the special collections environment.

---

20 Overholt, 3.

Bibliography

Brown, Julie. "Theory or Practice–What Exactly Is Feminist Pedagogy?", *The Journal of General Education* 41 (1992): 51–63.

Cook, Terry. "What is Past is Prologue: A History of Archival Ideas Since 1898". *Archivaria* 43 (1997): 17-63.

Cook , Terry and Joan Schwartz,. "Archives, Records, and Power: From (Postmodern) Theory to (Archival) Performance". *Archival Science* 2 (2002): 171-185.

Dekyspotter, Lori Lynn, and Cherry Dunham Williams. "Alchemy and Innovation: Cultivating an Appreciation for Primary Sources in Younger Students". *RBM: A Journal of Rare Books* 14 (2013): 67-81.

Garabedian, Michael. "You've Got to be Carefully Taught: American Special Collections Library Education and the Inculcation of Exclusivity." *RBM: A Journal of Rare Books*. 7(2006): 55-63.

Malbin, Susan. "The Reference Interview in Archival Literature". *College and Research Libraries* 58 (1997): 69-80.

Overholt, John. "Five Theses on the Future of Special Collections". *RBM: A Journal of Rare Books* 14 (2013): 15-20.

Priddle, Charlotte. "Bridging the Internal Gap: Special Collections and "In-Reach". *RBM: A Journal of Rare Books* 16 (2015):35-47.

Stam, Deirdre. "Bridge That Gap! Education and Special Collections". *RBM: A Journal of Rare Books,* 7 (2006) :16-30.

Taormina, Mattie, and Marilyn Rackley. "Reading Room and Reference (Re)Vision: The Transformation of Reader Services". In *New Directions for Special Collections: An Anthology of Practice*, ed. Lynne M. Thomas and Beth M. Whittaker, 13-30. Santa Barbara, CA: ABC-CLIO, 2015.

Theimer, Kate, ed. *Innovative Best Practices in Archives and Special Collections: Instruction*. Lanham, MD: Rowman & Littlefield, 2015.

Filling in the Gaps: Using Zines to Amplify the Voices of People Who Are Silenced in Academic Research

Dawn Stahura

The Beginning is the End

My time at the reference desk involves engaging with students in research consultations on a myriad of topics. Because I am a feminist, my approach to research and reference questions is filtered through a feminist lens. I define feminist pedagogy at the reference desk as *the flattening of the hierarchical and oppressive power structures by challenging the white cis male-dominant narratives that make up our informational and knowledge systems that inherently silence all other voices and perspectives.* While this might seem like an insurmountable task to accomplish at the reference desk, it can not only be done but also done well. In this chapter, I would like to share with you a few ways in which I teach students to not only critically evaluate the information they find but to actively seek out the missing pieces in order to fill in the gaps of their research. Because zines[1] live by the DIY (do-it-yourself) ethos and attempt to dismantle oppressive forms

---

1 Jenna Freedman, "Pinko Vs Punk: A Generational Comparison of Alternative Press Publications and Zines," in *The Generation X Librarian: Essays on Leadership, Technology, Pop Culture, Social Responsibility and Professional Identity*, ed. Martin K. Wallace, Rebecca Tolley-Stokes, and Erik Sean Estep (Jefferson: McFarland & Company, 2011), 150. Zines are defined as "self-published, small print run, motivated by desire to participate in or contribute to a community rather than for fame or profit, on activist or counter culture topics, and created in the do-it-yourself (DIY) tradition" (Freedman, 150).

of knowledge systems, I implore you to read this chapter in whatever way you feel best suits your needs. The dominant way of reading would be to follow along in chronological order but because zines are not part of the dominant landscape, this way of reading holds no real advantage to your learning process. If you are interested in *validation of personal experiences* start there. If you would rather follow in the traditional method of reading, feel free to do so. If we want our students to critically evaluate the research process and the information they find then we must allow them to decide how and where to begin. Sometimes the ending is the middle and the beginning is the end.

Somewhere in the Middle

Many of us lead instructional sessions that teach our students how to find scholarly content by searching the library catalog and utilizing subscription databases. These skills, along with evaluating sources, are imperative if our students are to become the critical thinkers we want them to be, but the problem is the information our students find oftentimes omits any narrative not deemed "valid" by the white-cis-male-dominated view. In current reference settings, the scholarly articles that we hold so near and dear to the research process silence all but the dominant voices. What is worse is that our students are unaware that so many narratives and perspectives are missing. Sure, they might be frustrated with the lack of relevant results when they do a search, but for the most part no one really questions controlled vocabularies or the statistics found in the methodologies section of scholarly work because no one suggested there were inherent issues residing there. Students are unaware of inherent biases in their search results or filter bubbles that prevent them from seeing the full landscape of resources, which does skew their opinion and perspectives on various topics. Our students cannot include what they do not know is missing, and more often than not, they leave the reference desk with only a partial, distorted view of the way things were or really are.

Voices that Zine

I work closely with several undergraduate and graduate courses in Sociology, Women and Gender Studies and Visual Communications whose teaching faculty find immense value in incorporating zines in their classroom. Not only do I talk about zines, but also, in many cases, the students are assigned to create zines as their final projects. I also teach a graduate level course in Information Sources and Services where I talk at length about the power of zines as primary sources. In both cases I show students the ways in which zines represent the oppressed narratives that dominant informational sources sometimes willfully ignore. From zine subject headings, to keyword searching in our zine spreadsheet, I give students the space and opportunity to question the way information is gathered, organized, and disseminated; an opportunity to question who deems what resources are "valid"; who decides who is an "expert" within the traditional publishing circles.

Zine making and zine reading are inherently feminist acts because they apply three very distinct principles of feminist pedagogy: participatory learning, validation of personal experience, and the development of critical thinking skills.[2] By applying these three principles to the research process, zines become more than just supplemental resources. They become the alternative way of critically evaluating and understanding the systems that disseminate our information. Zines shift the lens from periphery to direct focus.

Principle One: Participatory Learning

The research process starts with the basic search for information. A student approaches the reference desk with a topic in mind and after talking in-depth about the student's pre-search results and what resources are still needed, the conversation turns to generating keywords to help in the search process. As I brainstorm keywords with students I take the time to explain the inner workings of controlled vocabulary and subject headings. While there are certainly benefits to zeroing in on these subject headings for more precise results within the library's resources, the Library of Congress Classification is not all-inclusive. In fact, marginalized groups are still cataloged by outdated vocabulary within our databases and catalogs. These institutionalized oppressions usually go unnoticed in typical library searches unless the student is encouraged to question the legitimacy of the construction of

---

2 Kimberly Creasap, "Zine-Making as Feminist Pedagogy," *Feminist Teacher* 24, no. 3 (2014): 156.

subject headings. This consciousness-raising approach allows students the opportunity to be active participants in their learning by not only becoming aware of silenced voices, but also by questioning the overall production and dissemination of information. Furthering this, I really believe consciousness-raising opportunities allow students to critically evaluate their own voices and what roles they play in the production of knowledge and really zero in on internalized biases.

For example, if a student wanted to find information on African American women and sex, we would need to put *African American women* and *sex* as our search terms. Instead of stopping there, I challenge the student to think about what it means if they just put *Women* in the search box. Who are these women? Who are included? Excluded? Who determines this inclusion? What does it imply if the category of *Women* does not include all women? What about *sex*? What does it mean if the results assume you mean heterosexual sex? Or let's say a student is interested in resources that discuss LGBTQ oppressions (not discrimination) or health issues and sexual politics of the queer community, our library databases and catalogs will not provide the full range of resources that accurately address and describe these topics because LCC does not recognize them as "valid" subject headings. I ask students how it makes them feel if they do not see these identities as "normal" or the "dominant" view within controlled vocabularies.

Once light is shed on these issues, students begin to see the problems with controlled vocabulary and will hopefully dig deeper into the search process. Once they grasp the concept of institutionalized oppression within classification systems, they can understand that the results presented to them are partially inaccurate due to these inherent biases. Several of my students have commented that digging deeper in this way validates their experiences in researching in that it becomes clear that they are not searching incorrectly or using the wrong tools, but that the tools are not representative or inclusive of what their informational needs are. These biases will never give the full narrative and this is where zines supplement the research process. The *To the Front Zine Collection* at Simmons College is cataloged based on the Anchor Archive Zine Library's subject classification[3] and the

---

3 "Zine Subjects | Roberts Street Social Centre," accessed July 5, 2016, http://www.robertsstreet.org/subjects.

Alternative Press Index.[4] I personally read each zine that is cataloged in our collection and take detailed notes of the subjects addressed in each zine. While our zines are catalogued with records that are searchable within our library's catalog, they are classified with the Library of Congress subject headings. This is obviously so students can find zines within their search results and since our zines circulate, this helps with visibility but there are problems with the overall classification scheme. To circumvent this issue, I keep a separate zine catalog in spreadsheet form, which is updated every time a new zine is read and evaluated by me. This alternative catalog is a true reflection of what each zine represents, using vocabulary and subject headings that are not only more inclusive but reflect the true nature and language of the non-dominant narrative. This detailed spreadsheet allows our students to find zines on subjects that are not classified or recognized within the Library of Congress Classification system. Zines can be searched by subject headings or keywords within the spreadsheet by using the standard command + F or CTRL + F.[5] In essence, students are able to search by all the keywords, names, and subject headings that truly describe and reflect their topics.

Students can also physically browse the zine collection, taking certain subject boxes off the shelf to peruse the zines. There is a cheat sheet available that explains what each subject code stands for and lists the topics found under each subject heading. This form of classification is not only more personal but allows for real identification of subjects that reflect the true nature of their existence. Once students are aware that not every voice is heard within the databases they undergo a new search within the zine spreadsheet to begin filling in the holes in their research process.

Principle Two: Development of Critical Thinking Skills

It is a fact that scholarly articles can be daunting for our students because of their confusing jargon, endless pages of references, and

---

4 "Alternative Press Center: The Index," accessed July 5, 2016, http://www.altpress.org/mod/pages/display/8/index.php?menu=pubs.

5 Dawn Stahura, "LibGuides: Zines!: Find Zines," 2016, http://simmons.libguides.com/zincs.

the dreaded methodology section that contains graphs, numbers, and intimidating data. For most students, they would rather skip the methodologies section all together. Who could blame them? In fact, how often do we tell students to just skip the methodology section completely? As librarians, our reasoning (and it is certainly valid) is that unless they are recreating the study or instructed by their professors to read this section, methodologies can be ignored. The focus then shifts to the introduction and the conclusion/discussion as being the "must-reads", the areas that contain the research's truth.

To be honest, I have given this very advice to more than one panicked student who was drowning in the idea of wading through a 30-page research article riddled with words and numbers that did not make sense. In those moments of research crisis, I was mindful of where students were at emotionally and in exercising ethics of care, I choose to have them focus on the "must-reads" which on a basic level satisfied the students' need. I hoped that by focusing on the emotional aspect of research that the students would feel comfortable and safe enough to approach me again should the need arise. In actuality, I do my students a great disservice by ignoring the methodology section entirely because it is here where the truth is revealed as to who is missing in the research. By delving into the methodologies section, I teach my students how the results are always filtered through the researcher's lens.[6] That because we cannot avoid this filter, the results are slanted truth, hinging on the notion that all study participants told the absolute truth. In reality, the very nature of being under a watchful eye skews the results thereby compromising the conclusion to some degree. In simple terms, there is bias present in all forms of research whether it is intentional or not.

Who are these participants? By using the methodologies section, students can dig deeper to find out who was included and who was excluded. This allows them to challenge the legitimacy of the overall results, and once students know who is missing they can begin their search for those oppressed narratives by way of zines. They can decide for themselves in having those oppressed voices present, whether or not it affects their viewpoints on the scholarly research findings and

---

6 K Schilt, "'I'll Resist with Every Inch and Every Breath'–Girls and Zine Making as a Form of Resistance," *YOUTH & SOCIETY* 35, no. 1 (September 2003): 78.

what the implications are. In essence, I ask students if zines affect scholarly results.

A big issue I have with methodology sections and scholarly articles in general is that they are already seen as authoritative. The expertise of the authors have to be proven and vetted before their words ever make the published page. Within academia there is sometimes an intense push to publish, not to share information or to make connections with others but rather to gain tenure. The "publish or perish" landscape of academia can lead to publishing articles that are motivated by financial or reputational gain, not a desire to share information. Scandals arise every year where unethical or even faulty research makes its way into databases and scholarly journals. Many librarians spend a lot of energy diverting students' interest from Wikipedia, but at times, scholarly articles are no better. We just do not say that aloud. We teach students to use Google Scholar over regular Google to help them reach more suitable content but we fail to explain the filter bubble that surrounds everything they ever search using the Internet. We never tell them to question what resources reach them and consider what might be missing altogether.

Zines are different in every conceivable way. For one, zines are not written for a profit or recognition but rather for intimate connection, a way to tell one's truth. Because zines are not filtered through a researcher's gaze, they are inherently honest. There are no gatekeepers to keep a zinester's story hidden, no permission to be granted in order to publish. A zinester writes and publishes a zine by their own rules without interference, which means zines can be as radical as they need to be, sharing stories and ideas that are not popular or even considered. I realize that we do not live in a perfect world and yes, sometimes zines are created with hatred, bigotry, misogyny and racist views. With that said, I believe that zines can and do challenge the status quo. Their very existence is a feminist radical act.

Zines show us that we are more than just statistics,[7] that if certain groups are not included in the research design or the results then the conclusion has no impact on oppressed truths. These scholarly results do not represent the oppressed and never will if they are continuously kept out of dominant narratives. Zines share a different version of the

---

[7] Jennifer Sinor, "Another Form of Crying: Girl Zines as Life Writing," *Prose Studies*, August 4, 2003, 249.

story that does not always match the scholarly researcher's conclusion, and this is imperative if we want our students to see the full landscape of their topics.

Secondly, zines give our students unique opportunities to hear their research. Instead of reading a scholarly article on the impact of an experimental drug to cure AIDS, students can supplement that knowledge with a zine written by someone who is actually taking the drug. This humanizes their research, which I think is something that we, as a culture, fail miserably at. We often forget that the participants in scholarly articles are real people with real emotions and feelings. The humanization of research was revolutionary for one student I met with who said, "research articles do not include how the participants feel, what they struggle with on a daily basis, or how they developed an eating disorder." Zines helped this student hear the point of view of the patients, which led to a greater understanding of eating disorders. When we humanize our research, we care, and it is in this caring that students take risks to break the silence of oppressive systems, to institute change that matters outside the walls of academia. This breaking of the silence took a zine form at Simmons College in the Spring of 2016 when the Students of Color Inclusion Council asked me to lead a zine workshop for them. They wanted to incorporate the *Ten Demands* that were presented to the Simmons President as well as their own biographies, essays, reflections, and art. The end result was *#Simscenes*, a powerful testament to the very real grassroots activism on campus that is seeing real, positive change and by sharing their zines with the community (Simmons and the outside) they are making connections and building relationships on a much deeper level. Deeper level understanding is crucial for any type of social change, big or small.

Lastly, zines allow for the examination of power structures in knowledge production. By reading zines students can examine how knowledge is constructed, and the social positions and intent of those who produce and disseminate information. The very impact of dissemination of information by the dominant groups can be critically evaluated. Once students begin questioning the production of knowledge, they realize that zines allow anyone to be an expert of their own lives, feelings, knowledge, and experiences. This powerful realization extends to our own students as they come to understand that their own voices and knowledge matter, that by including oppressed narratives in their research is a radical act, that by breaking the silence, they are changing the power structure.[8] In my opinion, this should be the true reason we conduct research, to institute real change. Research conducted through the lens of feminist pedagogy recognizes the centrality of the intersections of race, class, and gender, which allows for critical and radical critiques of classic, dominant assumptions.

Principle Three: Validation of Personal Experiences

In helping students find relevant articles for their topics, we often tell them to mine the references of the articles they like to see whom those authors consulted to write their papers. Students are encouraged to use databases such as Web of Knowledge and Scopus to uncover citations of worth. While this is certainly valid advice and I still recommend students do this, it ultimately reinforces the legitimacy of scholarly "experts" as being the only voices of worth. This total reliance on vetted experts omits those not included in the dominant knowledge production. Citation backtracking is a useful skill to have, as long as we are teaching our students that it is not the only way that research can happen.

When students incorporate zines into their research, they begin to see citation management as more organic and personal. This process creates a closeness and connection to the zinester. Zinesters recommend other zines and write about which zines inspired them and encouraged them to come forward with their own stories. By using zines, students create a bibliography that is a mixture of scholarly and organic, an empowered bibliography that includes all voices. Because zines discuss the lives and experiences of the non-dominant worldview, students critically evaluate their own lives and experiences and compare it to the discussions and conclusions they read within the dominant scholarly narratives. This is important if we want our students to not only be critical thinkers but critical producers of knowledge. Zines allow for the active cultural production

---

8 Moshoula Capous Desyllas and Allison Sinclair, "Zine-Making as a Pedagogical Tool for Transformative Learning in Social Work Education," *Social Work Education* 33, no. 3 (April 2014): 314, doi:10.1080/02615479.2013.805194.

of information as opposed to passive cultural consumption of that knowledge. This very concept is one that is gaining importance with its inclusion in the ACRL's new information literacy frameworks.

If we teach our students critical information literacy skills by way of zines, they learn to critically evaluate the establishment itself.[9] Our students can then question the publishing process, the exclusion of 'non-experts', institutionalized oppression, and the way in which some have access to information while others do not. In academia, everyone who lends a hand in the publishing process creates legitimacy of the text, from the writer to the editor to the publisher.[10] Zines do not need legitimacy in order to be authoritative.

Students often take for granted the access they have to scholarly resources but it is worth pointing out that non-academics and non-community members do not have access to the same resources. Academia is a world governed by restricted use clauses, language barriers, and Internet connectivity. Access to scholarly resources requires money and privilege, which is a critical social justice issue. Information and access to it is a basic human right and any time a barrier is placed between knowledge and the people, librarians need to implement the tools to break down those barriers. One easy way to dismantle these barriers is through zines. Zines emphasize the dissemination of knowledge instead of access limitations and paychecks, which is why a lot of zines are traded instead of purchased. The point is not monetary gain as found in some scholarly publishing but rather informational gain. Getting the information out there with the least amount of barriers and obstacles is the true intent of zines. If zines are a radical act simply by way of existence then the reference desk is certainly a radical space that provides the opportunity for our students to engage with resources that are not supported by the white-cis-male-dominated power structure. Zines are therefore the ultimate feminist pedagogical tool as evidenced by student responses to using zines in their research. Students embraced the idea of not

---

9 Gina Schlesselman-Tarango, "Cyborgs in the Academic Library: A Cyberfeminist Approach to Information Literacy Instruction," *Behavioral & Social Sciences Librarian* 33, no. 1 (January 2014): 37, doi:10.1080/01639269.2014.872529.

10 Sandra Jeppeson, "DIY Zines and Direct Action Activism," (Paper Presented at the Meeting of the International Communication Association, Suntec Singapore International Convention & Exhibition Centre) 264–281: 267, accessed July 5, 2016, http://www.academia.edu/12691540/DIY_Zines_and_Direct_Action_Activism.

only hearing their research but also positioning themselves within the narrative. This positioning allows for self-reflection and critique, which oftentimes never makes it into the research process. Zines provide a unique way for my students to evaluate their own feelings and sometimes misconceptions about a particular topic. Minds that are changed for the better allow for a greater opportunity for social justice initiatives to succeed.

The Ending is the Beginning After All

By incorporating zines in the research process, our students achieve a deeper and more thorough understanding of their topics. By using zines our students recognize which points of view are omitted from the scholarly resources found within library databases and catalogs. Through zines, students fill in the gaps of their research with voices that represent the uncensored, subjective, creative, social, and political truths that are written by "non-experts whose only true intent is to shed light on various forms of oppression."[11] By doing so, students flatten the dominant hierarchy of knowledge production and begin to shape a truly inclusive feminist narrative that is desperately lacking in scholarly research and agendas.

Zines are a revolutionary concept that encourages students to speak for themselves as opposed to letting dominant voices speak for them. Students can and should be knowledge and cultural producers overwriting the traditional, white-cis-male-dominated knowledge systems and by doing so they challenge the status quo. This feminist act can lead to institutional change. When our students break the silence with their research, real change happens on a micro-level but just like Scopus or Web of Knowledge, that change creates a web. The further out the web, the more macro the changes become.

This change is not just happening in the student realm. Simmons faculty have changed as well by incorporating zines into their syllabi by way of required readings and the creation of zines for class projects. One of the faculty I work with closely stated that it allowed her students to connect with the course material in a real, authentic way which led to really deep, critical learning. This in-depth analysis ultimately resulted in more meaningful class discussions and more

---

11 Desyllas and Sinclair, "Zine-Making," 299.

thoughtful papers. On a personal level, I have changed too in ways I never imagined. Zines exist in my personal life as I create my own zines and collect them but having the opportunity to work with zines on a daily basis with students is really empowering. I feel closer to my students when we are able to discuss really difficult subjects by way of zines in a safe space. Working closely with zines also allows me to be my empathetic self, to be seen as human. Oftentimes the role of the librarian is painted heavy with stereotypes and I love any chance I can get to strip away that color.

On an institutional level, the Beatley Library is becoming more of a safe space for our students. With the zine collection and makerspace, students know that they can come to the library to not only read zines but also make their own zines. This kind of self-publication is not only radical but also extremely liberating. In this context, I act as mentor, assisting students in layout and publishing. There is nothing more rewarding than seeing a completed zine born out of thoughts once only found in the ether.

There are of course challenges to overcome. Faculty are sometimes resistant to using zines as primary sources, prescribing only the scholarly works found within our databases and academic journals. Overcoming this is not impossible but it does take actively seeking out an adventurous faculty member to take a chance on zines. Once they realize how valuable the payoff is, faculty can be your zine cheerleaders, advocating on your behalf. All it takes is for someone in a position of power to stand with you in solidarity.

With all that I have said here, I am in no way advocating that we throw out scholarly articles and only read zines, nor am I saying that one resource is better or more useful than another. What I am proposing is guiding our students through a richer, more well-rounded research process by incorporating zines. By using both resources our students not only fill in the research gaps, they gain a deeper understanding of not only their topics but also knowledge creation and dissemination. What better place to learn this than at the reference desk. If this is not feminist pedagogy, then I do not know what is.

Bibliography

"Alternative Press Center: The Index." Accessed July 5, 2016. http://www.altpress.org/mod/pages/display/8/index.php?menu=pubs.

Creasap, Kimberly. "Zine-Making as Feminist Pedagogy." *Feminist Teacher* 24, no. 3 (2014): 155–68.

Desyllas, Moshoula Capous, and Allison Sinclair. "Zine-Making as a Pedagogical Tool for Transformative Learning in Social Work Education." *Social Work Education* 33, no. 3 (April 2014): 296–316. doi:10.1080/02615479.2013.805194.

Freedman, Jenna. "Pinko Vs Punk: A Generational Comparison of Alternative Press Publications and Zines." In *The Generation X Librarian: Essays on Leadership, Technology, Pop Culture, Social Responsibility and Professional Identity*, edited by Martin K. Wallace, Rebecca Tolley-Stokes, and Erik Sean Estep, 147-162. Jefferson: McFarland & Company, 2011. 147–62.

Jeppeson, Sandra. "DIY Zines and Direct Action Activism." Paper presented at the Meeting of the International Communication Association, Suntec Singapore International Convention & Exhibition Centre, 264–281. Accessed July 5, 2016. http://www.academia.edu/12691540/DIY_Zines_and_Direct_Action_Activism.

Schilt, K. "'I'll Resist with Every Inch and Every Breath'–Girls and Zine Making as a Form of Resistance." *YOUTH & SOCIETY* 35, no. 1 (September 2003): 71–97.

Schlesselman-Tarango, Gina. "Cyborgs in the Academic Library: A Cyberfeminist Approach to Information Literacy Instruction." *Behavioral & Social Sciences Librarian* 33, no. 1 (January 2014): 29–46 18p. doi:10.1080/01639269.2014.872529.

Sinor, Jennifer. "Another Form of Crying: Girl Zines as Life Writing." *Prose Studies*, August 4, 2003.

Stahura, Dawn. "LibGuides: Zines!: Find Zines," 2016. http://simmons.libguides.com/zines.

"Zine Subjects | Roberts Street Social Centre." Accessed July 5, 2016. http://www.robertsstreet.org/subjects.

Information of My Own: Peer Reference and Feminist Pedagogy

Lauren Wallis

In a reflection piece about her work providing research assistance to her peers, one undergraduate student recalls her own experience trying to ask for directions in a country where she didn't know the language: "I was completely lost, with little to no information of my own…I hardly knew what I needed help with, so I had no idea how to convey that to someone who didn't even speak the same language." The student relates her memory of embarrassment, isolation, and vulnerability to similar feelings she notices in her peers who ask for help with their research: "They are nervous about asking for help because they are often not even sure what they need help with…and, just like I was, they are probably afraid of looking unintelligent, or seeming incompetent." She recognizes that when students reach the point of asking for help with research, they are often feeling alienated and silenced by the work they are trying to do.

At a traditional reference desk, there is little opportunity to render visible the power structures of scholarly knowledge production that can make students feel like they are in unknown territory, trying to ask a question in a language they do not speak. This chapter is based on a peer reference program in which I asked reference student workers to engage in a continual process of identifying and questioning the ways they saw their peers engage with—or resist—doing research. I will discuss the work and written reflections of three undergraduate students I hired, trained, and supported as Peer Research Navigators (PRNs) at Christopher Newport University during Fall 2015.

Throughout the semester I facilitated ongoing training sessions for these students, covering traditional strategies for reference interviewing and using library search tools, but also making room for reflection and discussion about their experience with research on the job and in their own coursework. PRNs worked evening and late night hours, and were stationed at a small desk in a high traffic area of the library away from the reference desk, which was still staffed by librarians.

The program was based on methods from feminist pedagogy and concepts from peer learning, which helped me work alongside PRNs to critique the pieces of the academic power structure that often make students feel disconnected from their research. Peer-assisted learning is a natural fit with feminist pedagogy in many ways: It can destabilize a traditional education hierarchy in which professional teachers are the sole authority, it can show value for the knowledge that peer teachers have, and in some iterations it can encourage students to discuss their personal experiences. But while peer-assisted learning values the unique ways that students can teach other students,[1] it tends to focus on the ways that peers make learning more accessible, without critiquing the power issues that make academic knowledge inaccessible in the first place. In the academic library, power is enacted by the reference desk itself, the library tools that are used to organize and access information, and the very concept of expertise. The work of the PRNs highlighted ways that traditional reference service reinforces academic power, and showed how it can be productive to intentionally undermine academic authority in the library.

Academic Power and the Curse of the Expert-Helper

Since I designed the PRN program as an attempt to resist library systems that uphold academic power structures, it is helpful to first take a closer look at the ways library resources, service models, and staff often reinforce systems that alienate students from research. Scholarly

---

[1] See Matthew Wawrzynski, Carl LoConte, and Emily Straker, "Learning Outcomes for Peer Educators: The National Survey on Peer Education," *New Directions for Student Services*, no. 133 (2011): 17; Keith Topping and Stewart Ehly, *Peer-Assisted Learning* (Erlbaum: Mahwah, NJ, 1998), 2.

knowledge production functions by excluding people—and library search tools are designed to support this exclusivity. Search tools limit access in insidious ways, through controlled vocabulary that dictates how information is organized and described in terms that are often so disparate from the patron's natural language that searching for information seems intentionally complex. Beyond access, search tools are designed to highlight traditional markers of scholarly authority, through icons and filters that are meant to separate peer-reviewed, academic sources from other, non-academic types of sources. The tools themselves point to information created by people the academy has deemed authoritative.

For those who achieve a position of academic authority, there is little choice but to produce work that adheres to traditional academic standards for content and style, is published in paywalled journals, and is accessed through library databases. The academy continually defines and perpetuates itself with this system, while simultaneously depending on the presence of undergraduates for its survival. Undergraduates are cast firmly in the position of non-experts, and they are rarely encouraged to critique the mechanisms that produce and define academic expertise. There are many seemingly small, everyday reminders of their lesser status: lecture-based classes, canonical texts that tend to value the white and the male, and rigid divisions between scholarly and non-scholarly texts, to name a few. Library catalogs and databases also belong in this list, because although they are meant to provide access, they often act as barriers, implicitly communicating to students that they do not have enough authority or power to successfully interact with scholarly information, whether they are trying to find it, read it, or apply it.

When I am helping patrons at the reference desk, I often feel like an extension of library search tools. I might be translating complex tools into accessible terms, but I am still supporting the exclusive nature of scholarly knowledge production. While this position feels confusing, it is written into RUSA performance standards, which define a reference librarian as an expert-helper who is simultaneously an information authority, and an objective, friendly service provider. These guidelines establish that a librarian's first goal in a "reference transaction" should be to "make the patron feel comfortable in a situation that can be perceived as intimidating, confusing, or overwhelming."[2] The reasons for these patron perceptions remain unstated because the librarian's expert-helper role erases the issues of access and authority that I discussed above—the pieces of the structure of scholarly knowledge production that are all at play when a student approaches the reference desk for help with research.

This erasure is possible because the RUSA guidelines call for librarians to be aware of the reasons patrons are struggling with research, but not to discuss those observations with patrons. RUSA recommends librarians demonstrate objective interest and understanding of patron needs through verbal and non-verbal confirmation,[3] but this understanding exceeds simply identifying what information the patron needs. Librarians should deliver "materials that will provide the appropriate level of linguistic and conceptual access" for an individual user,[4] which suggests that we need to make observations about the patron's identity to determine the level of complexity they can handle in a source. So while librarians are asked to be neutral in the ways they communicate with patrons, they are simultaneously asked to make judgments about a patron's level of agency within the system of scholarly knowledge production.

When librarians define ourselves as experts at finding information, we condone a system of information production and organization that is designed to alienate students. In fact, this definition of librarian expertise depends on the continued inaccessibility of these systems and the information they contain—information that is certainly not the students' own. In developing the PRN program, I worked with students to destabilize the ways that reference is built on the passivity of librarians and the marginalization of students within the system of scholarly knowledge production.

As I developed the PRN program, incorporating feminist pedagogy and peer learning helped me work against traditional conceptions of student reference, which are often designed to reinforce

---

2 RSS Management of Reference Committee, "Guidelines for Behavioral Performance of Reference Service Providers," *Reference and User Services Association*, May 28, 2013, http://www.ala.org/rusa/resources/guidelines/guidelinesbehavioral.

3 Ibid.

4 RUSA Task Force on Professional Competencies, "Professional Competencies for Reference and User Services Librarians," *Reference and User Services Association*, January 26, 2003, http://www.ala.org/rusa/resources/guidelines/professional.

librarian authority as information experts. For example, Neuhaus discusses a training program at the University of Northern Iowa that teaches students reference interview strategies, but emphasizes that they should see themselves as "traffic control" to route most reference questions to librarians.[5] Stanfield and Palmer reach a similar conclusion in a study of librarians who train reference student assistants, finding that a dual staffing model "provides an opportunity for librarians to use peer learning to further solidify the information literacy skills of all students."[6] The librarians writing both of these articles are willing to admit that student patrons might find student reference providers more welcoming, but argue that librarians are still integral to reference because of their information expertise. These approaches divide the expert-helper role established in the RUSA documents, assigning what they see as the lesser role of helper to students, and retaining the librarian's role as expert.

When discussing the approachability of student reference providers, the implication is often that their visible markers of identity alone will help make reference assistance more accessible to student patrons. While some articles address student age,[7] others discuss approachability based on race.[8] At California State San Marcos, for example, librarians developed a reference student assistant program focused on hiring students of color, in an attempt to reach the school's diverse population more successfully by "build[ing] bridges between students and library faculty."[9] While it is valuable to disrupt the whiteness that is often present at the reference desk, these articles make an assumption that physical markers of identity in reference

---

5 Chris Neuhaus, "Flexibility and Feedback: A New Approach to Ongoing Training for Reference Student Assistants," *Reference Services Review* 29, no. 1 (2001): 56.

6 Andrea Stanfield and Russell Palmer, "Peer-ing into the Information Commons: Making the Most of Student Assistants in New Library Spaces," *Reference Services Review* 38, no. 4 (2010): 636.

7 Allison Faix et al, "Peer Reference Redefined: New Uses for Undergraduate Students," *Reference Services Review* 38, no. 1 (2010): 95.

8 See Barbara MacAdam and Darlene Nichols, "Peer Information Counseling: An Academic Library Program for Minority Students," *Journal of Academic Librarianship* 15, no. 4 (1989); Jacqueline Borin, "Training, Supervising, and Evaluating Student Information Assistants," *Reference Librarian* 34, no. 72 (2001).

9 Jacqueline Borin, "Training, supervising, and evaluating student information assistants," *Reference Librarian* 34, no. 72 (2001).

student workers will automatically signal approachability and facilitate connections to librarians. These metaphors of transportation represent students' disconnection from their research. When librarians ask reference student assistants to function as bridges or perform the "traffic control" suggested by Neuhaus, we are only reinforcing librarian expertise, and reemphasizing that all students—whether patrons or library student workers—do not have a place in the system of scholarly knowledge production.

Some of my initial inspiration for the PRN program came from Bodemer's discussion of the LibRAT program, which was designed to move beyond assumptions about physical markers of identity, focusing instead on the unique ways that students can teach other students. Drawing from research on peer learning, he argues that peer reference providers can "create contiguity between student life as lived and library resources and services and can leverage cognitive and affective learning benefits by virtue of being peers."[10] In the rest of this chapter, I will extend these observations about the educational power of peer learning, applying feminist pedagogy methods and engaging with the reflections of the PRNs to suggest ways to make information power structures visible and open to critique for student patrons, peer reference providers, and librarians.

PRN Experiences with Peer Reference

In the reflections PRNs wrote about their work, two major themes emerged that show how peer reference can intervene in educational and informational power systems. They discussed the ways they empathized with peers who were struggling with feelings of disconnection from academic research, and they described tensions between service and teaching that they felt in their reference work. These themes align with feminist pedagogy, and while I did not expect the PRNs to label their work as feminist, I do think that my training methods influenced their ability to recognize when students lacked agency in relation to academic research, as well as their desire to engage in collaborative teaching and learning rather than a service role.

---

10 Brett Bodemer, "They CAN and they SHOULD: Undergraduates Providing Peer Reference and Instruction," *College & Research Libraries* 75, no. 2 (2014): 176.

My approach to training centered around informal narratives the PRNs and I wrote and discussed throughout the semester. While I still needed to give them traditional training on research tools and reference interviewing, I found that the narratives and discussion helped contextualize this skills-based training. At the beginning of the semester, I asked the PRNs to think about a time when they needed help, inside or outside of school, and consider what it felt like to have to ask. Toward the middle of the semester, I asked them to write about a time when they experienced a "Eureka Moment," in which they had struggled with a difficult concept for a long time and finally figured it out. In conjunction with a training session on the ACRL Framework for Information Literacy, these narratives prompted students to reflect on how frustrating learning can be, and encouraged them to recognize the ways they were seeing peers grapple with threshold concepts as they did research. At the end of the semester, PRNs responded to a series of prompts that asked them to reflect on the effects of peer learning, both for students and for themselves. In this section, I bring in the voices of the PRNs to discuss their experience providing research help to their peers. While I want to privilege the narratives of the PRNs, I will also point to ways that their work pushed against traditional reference service and moved toward feminist practices such as engaging in collaborating learning and critiquing a lack of student agency in relation to research projects.

As they worked to negotiate a role as peer teachers, rather than expert helpers, PRNs showed how they empathized with their peers' feelings toward research, and were sometimes able to use this affective connection to make their work with students more successful. Since research on peer-assisted learning suggests that students have a unique ability to help other students learn, we cannot ignore that this ability is a product of peer educators' own experiences of anxiety and alienation in an academic context. In a reflection on working with a student who "wasn't very confident in her database skills," Haley describes an interaction in which she and the patron are simultaneously using databases and discussing the anxiety these search tools cause: "She sat down next to me and I showed her some of the different subject specific databases, and some of the techniques for narrowing down her search." As Haley is teaching skills for using library search tools, the patron tells her about her lack of comfort with research: "She jotted down some notes and said that sometimes she feels really lost doing research and doesn't always feel comfortable asking the librarians." Haley's description shows that this patron had negative feelings about research stemming from a lack of agency and authority within the system of scholarly knowledge production, represented here through library databases and the reference desk. It is significant that Haley and the patron were able to discuss this lack of agency in a peer reference setting, separated from the academic authority enforced by the traditional reference desk.

Several of Jordan's reflections have a similar focus on lack of student agency, as she discusses the tension between student voice and professor authority and acknowledges the difficulty peers experience expressing themselves in an academic context. In one reflection, she describes working with a student who does not understand her professor's request to explain why a particular scholarly article is valid. Jordan responds by "explain[ing] two ways I would interpret what their professor was asking," offering jargon-free definitions of academic validity. While Jordan recognizes "I was able to calm her" through this act of translation, the patron originally struggled to conceptualize what validity meant as a measure of scholarly authority. Jordan extends this theme of student voice in later reflections, recognizing that when developing research topics to fit a professor's assignment prompt, a major challenge for students is "understanding what they themselves are trying to say." Noting that students are often flustered when she asks them open-ended reference interview questions to get more information about their topics, she explains, "while [students] are trying to figure out what their professor wants and what direction they want to go in and how to reconcile those two issues, they hit a roadblock when it comes to getting started." Jordan describes the student point of view in a situation where professors have the authority to define what counts as legitimate scholarly inquiry, authority, and knowledge. Throughout her reflections, she discusses strategies she has developed to help students take ownership of the ways professors ask them to engage with scholarly information.

Often, students like the two patrons Haley and Jordan describe above are only trying to navigate research tools and decode their professors' directions successfully enough to complete an assignment. Breaking into the cycle of scholarly knowledge production by using databases and referencing correct sources as defined by the professor is hard enough, so it is no wonder that students often cannot conceptualize themselves as legitimate creators of academic knowledge. Carter addresses this issue as he describes working with a patron who needs to find scholarly sources for a paper, but just wants to cite them, rather than engaging with them to build an original argument. Reflecting on this student's resistance to engaging with scholarly discourse, Carter explains, "students sometimes hurt themselves by discrediting the fact that they themselves can have original substantial thought which can be turned into information for others." He even takes on the voice of his peers, showing how "they rationalize this by thinking, 'Oh, I'm just an undergraduate and I don't have nearly the experience or title to come close to producing something original and thought provoking.'" Here, lack of "experience" and "title" directly inhibit the authority to create new knowledge. Carter is close enough to this experience to identify how his peers often lack the confidence and the means to see their assignments as an opportunity to create new information.

As these narratives show, each of the PRNs empathized with the lack of agency their peers felt in relation to academic discourse. Although they were able to identify issues of student agency, the perpetuation of a service desk model made it difficult for them to engage in extended interactions with patrons that would have allowed them to discuss students' experiences in more depth. Their reflections show how acting as peer teachers prompted them to push against the traditional reference service model. For example, Haley describes working with a patron who asks for books on leadership, but then resists responding to Haley's reference interview questions aimed at identifying a narrower focus. Haley recalls explaining that "in order to find the best sources maybe we could come up with the specific question he wanted to answer." Ultimately, she laments that "I gave him the best help I felt like I could, but when he left I just wished that we could have had better communication or understanding." She sees providing service, or "the best help," as far less effective than "communication or understanding."

Carter and Jordan express similar frustrations to the ones Haley describes, but also include stories about times they felt they were successful at pushing beyond a service role in order to teach their peers. Carter recalls working with a patron who needed a book the library did not own, but did not have time to wait for Interlibrary Loan. He shows her ways to see if she can access it at nearby schools or on Google Books, and when those approaches are unsuccessful he shows her how to use library search tools to find other sources on her topic. Carter recalls that the patron told him "she had learned a lot about the research tools we have and how to successfully navigate them," and recognizes, "I think what made this successful was the one on one time we had working together to solve her problem," identifying their collaborative work as a reason this potentially frustrating access issue turned into a teaching opportunity.

Jordan's discussion of the effectiveness of a teaching role over a service role illustrates the concept of peer modeling, as she describes her own process of recognizing the complex, creative thinking required for advanced research and shows how she models her thought process when she helps her peers. In her Eureka Moment reflection she describes an experience taking a calculus test, realizing she does not have the formula she needs to answer a problem, and applying several formulas she already knows in order to come up with the one she needs. She relates this experience of suddenly realizing that she can deduce mathematical concepts on her own, without "formulas for the really hard stuff," to the way that she and her peers struggle with research as a rote series of tasks: "As students, we have been taught for so many years 'how to do research,' and yet so many of us still struggle with it." Her own approach to research draws on what she has been taught about specific research tasks and steps, but she recognizes the need to move beyond a formulaic approach in a way that is similar to her calculus test experience: "I will think of everything I have been taught about finding research, I will think about everything I know about the subject or topic I am looking for, and I will play with my knowledge to find what works." She goes on to make a direct connection to the ways she uses her work as a PRN to teach her peers to move past a reliance on a formulaic approach to research. She describes this as "help[ing] others figure out the puzzle," noting, "When I help them with a question, I make sure to teach them how I did it. I will tell them and show them what I am trying and why, in hopes that they will be able to do this themselves one day." Jordan recognizes that she can teach by modeling her own complex process of inquiry.

The reflections the PRNs made about their work are similar to the critiques that critical reference librarians make toward a traditional service desk model. Jordan's approach to her own research as "play[ing] with my knowledge" and her attempt to model this process to peers are directly related to Elmborg's call for librarians to treat reference interviewing as a "flexible, open-ended educational conference in which language and identity are encouraged and constructive play with ideas is the goal"[11] Elsewhere, Elmborg draws on the social constructivist pedagogy of composition studies, which emphasizes the social nature of knowledge formation, to argue that librarians and writing teachers can act as guides to help students enter the academic discourse community by engaging them in "meaningful talk about their research."[12] This move to encourage inquiry is evident in Carter's description of the student who wants sources to plug into his paper, as well as Haley's experience with the student studying leadership theory. In both cases, the PRNs pushed the patrons to engage in meaningful talk about research, but found that the service desk model made this difficult.

While the literature on reference student assistants places so much emphasis on training, triage, and the ultimate authority of librarians, it is clear that the PRN's non-expert status can be an impetus for collaborative, patron-centered exploration that represents a feminist approach to reference. PRNs were highly motivated to engage their peers in conversations about research skills and strategies, as we saw in Carter's story about guiding a patron through library and online search tools to find access to a book, or in Jordan's discussion of the ways she tries to model her thinking about research for peers. In the critlib Twitter conversation about critical reference, several librarians questioned the identity of librarians as experts, and Halpern tweeted that "a critical reference librarian can say 'I don't know, let's find out together,'"[13] PRNs were often in the position to do just that. Informed by peer learning and supported by feminist pedagogy, the PRN desk was a programmatic way to resist a neutral, service-based model of reference.

---

11 James Elmborg, "Libraries in the Contact Zone: On the Creation of Educational Space," *Reference & User Services Quarterly* 46, no 1 (2006): 62.

12 James Elmborg, "Teaching at the Desk: Toward a Reference Pedagogy," *Portal: Libraries and the Academy* 2, no. 3 (2002): 461.

13 Rebecca Halpern, "A2: a critical reference librarian can say 'I don't know, let's find out Together' #critlib," January 13, 2015, https://twitter.com/beccakatharine/status/555188693414465537

My Experience Designing the PRN Program

As I designed the PRN program and reflected on it in the writing of this piece, I questioned my use of subversive methods, which often felt necessary because of the institutional context of my position as a librarian. Gore's critique of the idea of empowerment in feminist pedagogy speaks to the difficulty I encountered trying to push beyond a traditional reference model while working within the context of institutional and professional expectations. Gore finds it troubling that power is often portrayed as something that a feminist teacher has and can give to students, and argues that the teacher's position within the context of a patriarchal educational system can limit her ability to empower students.[14] Instead, she says that feminist teachers can think about empowerment as a way of exercising what power we do have in an attempt to help students exercise power.[15] Since I had the freedom to design the PRN program and decide what form training would take, my use of written reflections and group discussions was an attempt to exercise my power in a way that would help the PRNs take ownership of their work and see themselves as more than service providers. I could subvert the traditional model to a certain extent through my training approach, but ultimately I was unable to provide the PRNs with a work space that looked much different than a traditional service desk model. In reflections and discussions, they often expressed frustration with the limitations of a service role. These frustrations suggest that a peer reference program like this one could be improved with a different physical setup, perhaps through collaboration with a campus tutoring or writing center.

Even though I was challenged by the work of subverting the traditional expert-helper role of librarians, I was also concerned about undermining my librarian colleagues. I take issue with the ways a traditional reference model can function to reinforce the scholarly status quo, but I do realize that claiming expertise is important for librarianship as a feminized, undervalued profession. In attempting to empower PRNs and student patrons, I often wondered if I was

---

14 Jennifer Gore, "What We can do for You! What Can "We" do for "You"?" In *Feminisms and Critical Pedagogy*, eds. Carmen Luke and Jennifer Gore (New York: Routledge, 1992): 57-58.

15 Ibid., 62.

devaluing the hard-won status of librarians as information experts. Ultimately, I think that a peer reference model like this one suggests an alternative way to value reference work that goes beyond a focus on delivering streamlined, seamless answers. When students are feeling alienated by scholarly information it can be productive to work with a peer who has a similar marginalized status, but has also spent time reflecting on this position and learning about tools and strategies for doing research. Informed by feminist pedagogy, a peer reference model like the PRN program can create a space for reference where it is possible to critique the power structures inherent in library search tools, scholarly sources, and the reference desk itself.

Bibliography

Bodemer, Brett. "They CAN and they SHOULD: Undergraduates Providing Peer Reference and Instruction." *College & Research Libraries* 75, no. 2 (2014): 162-178.

Borin, Jacqueline. "Training, Supervising, and Evaluating Student Information Assistants." *Reference Librarian* 34, no. 72 (2001).

Elmborg, James. "Libraries in the Contact Zone: On the Creation of Educational Space." *Reference & User Services Quarterly* 46, no 1 (2006): 56-64.

"Teaching at the Desk: Toward a Reference Pedagogy." *Portal: Libraries and the Academy* 2, no. 3 (2002): 455-464.

Faix, Allison, Margaret Bates, Lisa Hartman, Jennifer Hughes, Casey Schacher, Brooke Elliot, and Alexander Woods. "Peer Reference Redefined: New Uses for Undergraduate Students." *Reference Services Review* 38, no. 1 (2010): 90-107.

Gore, Jennifer. "What We can do for You! What Can "We" do for "You"?" In *Feminisms and Critical Pedagogy*, edited by Carmen Luke and Jennifer Gore, 54-73. New York: Routledge, 1992.

Halpern, Rebecca. "A2: a critical reference librarian can say 'I don't know, let's find out Together' #critlib." January 13, 2015. https://twitter.com/beccakatharine/status/555188693414465537.

MacAdam, Barbara, and Darlene Nichols. "Peer Information Counseling: An Academic Library Program for Minority Students." *Journal of Academic Librarianship* 15, no. 4 (1989): 204-209.

Neuhaus, Chris. "Flexibility and Feedback: A New Approach to Ongoing Training for Reference Student Assistants." *Reference Services Review* 29, no. 1 (2001): 53-64.

RSS Management of Reference Committee. "Guidelines for Behavioral Performance of Reference Service Providers." *Reference and User Services Association.* May 28, 2013. http://www.ala.org/rusa/resources/guidelines/guidelinesbehavioral.

RUSA Task Force on Professional Competencies. "Professional Competencies for Reference and User Services Librarians." *Reference and User Services Association*. January 26, 2003. http://www.ala.org/rusa/resources/guidelines/professional.

Stanfield, Andrea, and Russell Palmer. "Peer-ing into the Information Commons: Making the Most of Student Assistants in New Library Spaces." *Reference Services Review* 38, no. 4 (2010): 634-636.

Topping, Keith, and Stewart Ehly. *Peer-Assisted Learning*. Erlbaum: Mahwah, NJ, 1998.

Wawrzynski, Matthew, Carl LoConte, and Emily Straker. "Learning Outcomes for Peer Educators: The National Survey on Peer Education." *New Directions for Student Services*, no. 133 (2011): 17-27.

Social Justice in the Stacks: Opening the Borders of Feminism in Libraries

Gina Watts

I have a vivid memory of the joy of pushing open a library's doors for the first time in my life. I was young. The cool air pushing its way out, the tall lines of unexplored shelves, the personality of the place—it was clean and open and modern, with small pockets of pleasantly cluttered tables. And past all the physical properties, there was the underlying feeling of being welcome.[1] For others, it may not have been a library; perhaps it was a community center or a nearby bookshop. Regardless of the exact setting, though, I think many others will relate to the inherent magic in entering a space of learning and welcoming for the very first time. In my case, I never left.

The real backbone of any library is, of course, librarians. The building cannot go about enacting the values of the freedom to learn and unconditional acceptance on its own. It's no use romanticizing library aesthetics unless one is cognizant of the long hours of work and training that go into making the space what it can be for so many people: a place of equitable learning. The Pew Research Center released a study in September 2015, showing that 65 percent of Americans over age 16 think closing their library would have a major impact on their community, and this number goes up when low-income, Hispanic,

---

1 To be clear: this has not always been the case for all people. *Not Free, Not for All: Public Libraries in the Age of Segregation* by Cheryl Knott (University of Massachusetts Press, 2015) is one place to learn more about this. Here, I speak of libraries in this way to promote the spaces that I think they should aspire to be and what they were in my privileged experience.

or African-American families are asked the same question.[2] Based on Pew's other findings, this recognition of a library's importance is based on many things besides being able to check out books: access to internet and technology, free education and workforce training, or even simply providing a safe space to spend time. The reasons are as varied as the people, ranging from seeking out information on their health to attending programming for veterans, but they all revolve around a theme: unconditional and nonjudgmental access to information and freedom to make decisions about one's own learning. Librarians who strive to provide these opportunities are essentially using their position as a way to promote equity and social justice in their communities, and it is my belief that there are few so perfectly poised to do this as librarians.

The American Library Association lists several core values that support this position, with things like Democracy, Intellectual Freedom, Access, Diversity, Lifelong Learning, and Social Responsibility taking up the bulk of the list.[3] Taking this a step further, I posit that following these tenets gives libraries the power to be one of the most powerfully feminist spaces in American communities. Many definitions of feminism abound, including many that limit the movement to supporting equality between men and women, but I have always preferred a broader interpretation that allows more space for intersectionality and diversity. In this paper, I will define feminism based on bell hooks' definition offered in *Feminism is for Everybody: Passionate Politics*: "A genuine feminist politics always brings us from bondage to freedom."[4] Focusing this lens on gender is important because it recognizes patriarchal oppression as a cause of strife, but the conversation can move from gender to, for example, gender and race, or gender and disability, or gender and sexuality. To this list, I want to add gender and information equity. Information accessibility is one of the most powerful vehicles for people to be able to make conscious movement in the directions they want in life. People

---

[2] John B. Horrigan, "Libraries at the Crossroads, " *Pew Research*, last modified September 15, 2015, http://www.pewinternet.org/2015/09/15/libraries-at-the-crossroads/

[3] "Core Values of Librarianship," *American Library Association*, last modified June 29, 2004, http://www.ala.org/advocacy/intfreedom/statementspols/corevalues

[4] bell hooks, *Feminism is for Everybody: Passionate Politics* (Cambridge, MA: South End Press, 2000), 104.

must overcome countless barriers every day: too little or too much information, censorship, or simply difficulty finding what they need. When these barriers persist, people are prevented from accessing the lives they want.

Fortunately, these problems have solutions within the library system. It takes refuting the old tradition of library neutrality in some cases, but as decades of scholarship can point to, many librarians are enthusiastically doing so.[5] With intentional decision-making on an institutional level about how to best serve patrons, libraries can guide people to what they are searching for and become memory keepers for the types of oppression the world would rather forget. Ideally, this allows the library to grow into places free from those oppressions. This environment can only come from librarians committed to open information access and diversity of ideas.

The first part of the formula for equitable learning is that the information must be available. Through a library administration's choices in acquisition, they have the power to cultivate an information environment that is inclusive of all viewpoints, particularly when it comes to painful histories not always taught in schools. If a library opens up a student's eyes to new knowledge with regard to the treatment of the suffragettes prior to getting the vote, for example, that student may be more likely to approach patriarchal or white-washed histories with skepticism. On top of that, it might allow that student to see that they are capable of guiding their own learning. It is crucial for students to have these moments of realization in order for them to move forward as a socially conscious adult. When librarians are able to promote this type of learning in their institutions, it starts to look similar to the method of consciousness-raising, which has a history of being used in feminist activism dating back to the 1960s.

I particularly like the updated theory of "coalitional consciousness building" offered by Keating in 2005. While consciousness-raising as it was first introduced had its strengths in starting conversations that needed to be had, it often focused too heavily on commonalities and not enough on very real differences between the lives of white, middle-class feminists and the lives of women of color or women

---

5 A simple search on libraries and neutrality in journal articles at my library yielded 40,000 results dating back to 1960, with a high degree of relevancy in the results I reviewed; people have been talking about this for a long time and at great length.

from lower socioeconomic classes. Without leaving behind the entire premise of consciousness-raising, Keating offers a theory about how to be more inclusive when sharing these experiences, inspired by Mohanty, Lugones, and Reagon, among others. When discussing life experiences, she advocates for adding questions like "What are the multiple relations of power at play in the scenarios?" and "Whose interests are served and whose are not by the ways that you and others are/were racialized/gendered/classed/sexualized in the experience?"[6] Transformed into library-speak, these would be incredible questions for people to consider as they sought information in a library. In an academic information literacy session, there are similar questions I could see a librarian prompting for students who will be researching in a library.

Creating these moments in a library, though, takes deliberate effort on the part of library staff. One way to approach these types of knowledge is through memory studies scholarship. In order to understand how libraries interact with history, they must first be understood as a memory place. Dickinson, Blair, and Ott explore this concept in their book, *Places of Public Memory*. Public memory is defined as (1) activated by concerns of the present, (2) representing a common identity around certain characteristics and welcoming present individuals to share in that identity, and (3) focused on preserving objects or memories that are considered worthy of preservation through emotional attachment.[7] More traditional memory places might come to mind first, such as museums or battlegrounds, but in the sense that a memory place "proposes a specific kind of relationship between past and present that may offer a sense of sustained and sustaining communal identification," libraries can belong the category as well.[8]

Take the earlier example about women's suffrage. Given that the staff has cultivated a diverse collection through their acquisition policy, an open environment where the reference desk is welcoming

---

6 Cricket Keating, "Building Coalitional Consciousness," *NWSA Journal* 17, no. 2 (2005): 95, 97, accessed July 27, 2016, http://www.jstor.org/stable/4317127

7 Carole Blair, Greg Dickinson, and Brian L. Ott, Introduction to *Places of Public Memory: The Rhetoric of Museums and Memorials*, ed. Blair, Dickinson, and Ott (Tuscaloosa, AL: University Alabama Press, 2010), 7.

8 Ibid., 27

towards questions, and has the resources to educate someone on how to find further related learning, a patron seeking that information will leave with new knowledge and a fresh way of thinking about subjects they may not have been an expert in. To me, this environment means the library as an institution is committed to serving students with both trained expert librarians and collection development policies. It means information literacy for both staff and patrons is prioritized. It means the library integrates themselves into the life of the community around them by knowing what their patrons need. With the library as a support system, patrons can connect the past to their own present and have the opportunity to feel like part of history. The beauty is that patrons make their own choices about their learning and librarians must create a space where they can do so uninhibited. Unlike a museum, which typically has a more specific concentration, a library can be a place of as many memories as can fit in a Dewey Decimal classification heading.

Libraries might be especially well-positioned to serve as a repository for knowledge in areas where our nation has arguably made the wrong choice. In his book, *Shadowed Ground: America's Landscapes of Violence and Tragedy*, Kenneth Foote differentiates between the histories that are memorialized by the state and those that are not. Foote notes that sites of racial violence are often not marked, because "these sites are difficult to assimilate with heroic notions of the national past, and the sites themselves demonstrate a sort of collective equivocation over public meaning and social memory."[9] Instead of being recognized by the state, tragedies that expose problematic national actions are often relegated to other forms of memorialization—including books written by those who do not want the event to be forgotten or local community memorials. Libraries have the power to bring those stories to light through their choices in hosting community events, acquiring new materials, and creating exhibits. A personal favorite was the spotlight on Pride month at University of Texas at San Antonio Special Collections, where I worked in the summer of 2016. During the month of June, the collections that feature LGBTQ+ history were showcased in the staff room, in the library exhibit cases, and on the blog. Features included a collection of t-shirts from past Pride

---

9 Kenneth E. Foote, *Shadowed Ground: America's Landscapes of Violence and Tragedy* (Austin: University of Texas Press, 2003), 35.

celebrations in San Antonio, manuscripts from well-known LGBTQ+ activists, and photographs.

Along the lines of revealing hidden moments in history, I had an experience in this vein in a previous job. As an undergraduate, I worked in my university's library in special collections. One of my largest projects was to index our collection of letters that constituents had written to Texas Senator John Tower in the late 1960s and 1970s. In these letters, I found that I had access to stories that I had never been taught in school. The topics varied widely, from the Vietnam War to debates about taxes and salaries to the Civil Rights Movement. These letters were from a period in which Thurgood Marshall became the first African American man to be appointed to the Supreme Court and some of the letters were blisteringly angry about the nomination. I felt distinctly uncomfortable reading these racist rants, as though the words would stay in my brain after I read them. During my time there, our special collections department received a request from a professor in California. She was researching the Marshall appointment and wanted to know about John Tower's stated opinions on the issue at the time. As a student assistant, it fell to me to find the right documents and send the scans to her to aid with her research. I became fascinated with the way Tower's opinion revealed itself through the documents. He received all those racist letters, imploring him not approve the nomination—but he did. There were no responses recorded for offensive letters and the record shows that he voted yes to appoint Marshall. Our collection helped this story reach the light again through a professor's research project.

The emphasis on refusing to forget or gloss over the painful parts of history is a large part of a library's potential to serve as a feminist space. Marianne Hirsch and Valerie Smith make a strong connection between feminism and memory studies in their essay, "Feminism and Cultural Memory: An Introduction," saying, "Both [feminist studies and memory studies] assume that we do not study the past merely for its own sake; rather, we do so to meet the needs of the present. Both fields emphasize the situatedness of the individual in his or her social context and are thus suspicious of universal categories of experience."[10]

---

10 Marianne Hirsch and Valerie Smith, "Feminism and Cultural Memory: An Introduction," in *Theories of Memory: A Reader*, ed. Michael Rossington and Anne Whitehead (Baltimore: Johns Hopkins University Press, 2007), 226.

This way of looking at the past (as "constructed and contested") lends weight to a feminist understanding of memory spaces.[11] The phrasing and idea also dovetails nicely with the Association of College and Research Libraries *Framework for Information Literacy for Higher Education*: "Authority is constructed and contextual."[12] This frame emphasizes the importance of the background of the information creator and the context in which the information is being used, and it is represented in both feminist literature and library professional standards. Librarians who approach information requests and interactions with patrons with this philosophy are already enacting certain parts of feminist thought into their work.

Moving forward with this understanding of libraries as feminist memory spaces, we can think of developing this approach in libraries where it is lacking as a quiet kind of feminist revolution. I find this terminology useful because it emphasizes the opportunity in cases where a library has not yet unleashed its potential to be a feminist space. The word "revolution" in some cases has a connotation of being overblown and overwhelming, but here I'm referring to the ability for small changes over time to add up to a brand new way of thinking. Theorist bell hooks provides a few guidelines in her book, *Feminist Theory: From Margin to Center*. In her vision of a feminist revolution, she says, "we need to have a liberatory ideology that can be shared with everyone. That revolutionary ideology can be created only if the experiences of people on the margin…are understood, addressed, and incorporated."[13] We can see how this influences modern trends in the missions and programming of libraries. In their mission statements, libraries focus on the need to "provide easy access to information for all ages, through engaging programs and state-of-the-art technology"[14] in order to be "the center of learning for a diverse and inclusive

---

11 Ibid.

12 "Framework for Information Literacy for Higher Education," *Association of College and Research Libraries*, accessed July 27, 2016, http://www.ala.org/acrl/standards/ilframework#authority

13 bell hooks, *Feminist Theory: From Margin to Center* (Cambridge, MA: South End Press, 2000), 163.

14 "About the Library," *Austin Public Library*, accessed March 19, 2016, http://library.austintexas.gov/about-library/vision.

community."¹⁵ This commitment to innovation, diversity of ideas, and open accessibility gets right at the heart of this analysis, and it doesn't stop at mission statements. Libraries are practicing what they preach across the country.

One of the most incredible examples of recent years is the Ferguson Public Library during the protests and racial tension in that area in August of 2014. It started simply: while local schools and businesses were forced to close, the library stayed open. They welcomed everyone from the community searching for a refuge, from students waiting for the schools to open again to community leaders who needed meeting space to discuss solutions for the people of Ferguson. Teachers came to the library to hold impromptu classes during the closures, and the library used generous donations from across the country to put together 'healing kits' for kids to check out, complete with a stuffed animal for them to keep. Scott Bonner, the library's director and only full-time staff at the time, said of the perhaps nontraditional roles the library was playing, "When there's a need, we try to find a way to meet it. I have a very broad definition of librarianship."¹⁶ This openness to community need reaches far beyond the stereotype of a traditional librarian. Librarians can provide community support in any and every way if the resources are available to them, and can serve as a space to share experiences, stories, and ideas when a community has been shaken.

This type of support happens in so many cases it is impossible to catalog them all—but I will give a few examples. In July of 2015, library commissioners stood up for the LGBTQ+ community in Hood County, Texas, by keeping two children's books that educate on LGBTQ+ families and gender nonconformity on the shelves, *This Day in June* and *My Princess Boy*. Despite protests from some community members, the library commissioners decided that the LGBTQ+

---

15 "2012 Report to the Community," *Cleveland Public Library*, accessed March 19, 2016, http://cpl.org/2012annual/our-mission/.

16 Ferguson Library information drawn from 2 articles: (1) Elise Hu, "A Nationwide Outpouring of Support for Tiny Ferguson Library," *NPR*, last modified November 29, 2014, http://www.npr.org/sections/thetwo-way/2014/11/27/366811650/a-nationwide-outpouring-of-support-for-tiny-ferguson-library; (2) Colin Dwyer, "Book News: Despite the Tumult, Ferguson Library Keeps Its Doors Open," *NPR*, last modified June 19, 2015, http://www.npr.org/sections/thetwo-way/2014/11/26/366767946/book-news-despite-the-tumult-ferguson-library-keeps-its-doors-open

community in Hood County needed to be able to find books that educate on those issues in the library.[17] (This is especially important considering 2015 data from the American Library Association indicates that 8 of the 10 most challenged books from 2014 include diversity in their characters.[18] Although there admittedly have been some questions about the methods behind the collection of this data, these challenges are a trend worth paying attention to.) In another show of libraries' strengths, Richard Gunderman and David C. Stevens in August of 2015 shined a light on library's efforts to assist populations who are homeless and mentally ill, learning that many city libraries are hiring specialists who can assist with mental health disorders and giving workshops at homeless shelters to let them know where they can go during the day.[19]

To better provide education in their community, Hartford Public Library became accredited to offer high school diplomas and provides each student with an academic coach who can assist with planning their futures, whether that be advancement in the workforce or continued education.[20] Through their research into inclusion regarding the American Disability Act (ADA), Paul T. Jaeger and John Carlo Bertot found that "the highest average levels of accessibility of websites was found in libraries" and that libraries have been accommodating those with disabilities in their communities for over a century, when other national institutions may not have such a sterling history.[21]

---

17 Stella M. Chavez, "LGBT Books for Kids Will Stay On Hood County Library Shelves, Commissioners Say," *KERA News*, last modified July 14, 2015, http://keranews.org/post/lgbt-books-kids-will-stay-hood-county-library-shelves-commissioners-say.

18 "2014 Books Challenges Infographic," *American Library Association*, last modified 2014, http://www.ala.org/bbooks/frequentlychallengedbooks/statistics/2014-books-challenges-infographic.

19 Richard Gunderman and David C. Stevens, "Libraries on the frontlines of the homelessness crisis in the United States," *The Conversation*, last modified August 18, 2015, http://theconversation.com/libraries-on-the-front-lines-of-the-homelessness-crisis-in-the-united-states-44453.

20 "Career Online High School (COHS)," *Hartford Public Library*, accessed March 19, 2016, http://www.hplct.org/library-services/adults/COHS.

21 John Carlo Bertot and Paul T. Jaeger, "The ADA and Inclusion in Libraries," *American Libraries Magazine*, last modified October 5, 2015, http://www.hplct.org/library-services/adults/COHS.

Each of these interactions, small or large, is a political statement. Carol Hanisch penned the now-famous phrase, "The personal is political," in 1969 and it remains a classic feminist phrase today. In its original context, this phrase was meant to convey that political issues bleed into personal choices, and vice versa, meaning that personal choices have political ramifications.[22] These ramifications are both intentional and unintentional, because when I talk about any political issue, I am coming at it from the perspective of a white, upper-middle-class woman. My opinions and actions are impacted by this just as much as the things that have happened to me in my life. Education and broader perspectives are a way to augment my understanding, but this background will always exist for me. What I choose to do, then, with regard to people around me who come from different backgrounds, makes a political statement. In the context of libraries, we can interpret the phrase through the lens of personal interactions at a library reference desk. When a patron with a disability or a mental illness, or a patron without a place to sleep that night, or a patron who may live on the margin in terms of race, class, or sexual orientation—when these patrons are supported by their librarian, that librarian is standing up for their humanity and their right to learn. It goes back to bell hooks' feminist revolution: by definition, it must represent those on the margin or it is no kind of revolution at all.

With this background in mind, what can individual librarians do to advance equity and inclusivity in their institutions? For decades, librarians have been writing and theorizing about their role in empowering their communities, but as the world continues to change we have the opportunity to update these older ideas. In 1984, Searing wrote: "By training students in the mysteries of information seeking, by putting the tools of discovery in their hands, librarians and faculty can cooperate to prepare them for full and equal participation in the society of the future."[23] But of course, while Searing's ideas about educating students and patrons are still applicable (with some

---

22 Carol Hanisch, "The Personal is Political," CarolHanisch.org, last modified January 2006, http://www.carolhanisch.org/CHwritings/PIP.html.

23 Susan Searing, "Empowerment and Library Instruction," *Feminist Teacher* 1, no. 1 (1984): 9, accessed March 19, 2016, http://www.jstor.org.ezproxy.lib.utexas.edu/stable/25684347.

translation—trade cassette tapes for tablets), her article does not address the strength shown in the litany of library news just cited. What makes libraries really shine is their power to meet patrons where they are and demonstrate care not just by having accessible technology but speaking out on issues that affect their community. External actions (i.e. activism and advocacy) matter just as much as steps taken inside the library (i.e. having accessible computers and resume workshops).

Librarians committed to feminist principles can find opportunities to turn everyday experiences into teaching moments. As a student, I loved seeing what the library staff came up with for events about Martin Luther King Day, programs to encourage good mental health practices, and a visit from author Dave Eggers where he spoke to us about his literacy nonprofit and the impact it has nationwide. From each of these, I came away invigorated and with a renewed love of learning. Every library interaction has the potential for the same result, even on a small scale.

The first time I had the opportunity to create one of those moments myself was after I had left the university library and had started working for a nonprofit, Skillpoint Alliance. The mission of Skillpoint Alliance is to promote industry-led STEM training at all levels, from robotics clubs for kids to rapid workforce training for adults. I was in the robotics department and my days were spent recruiting robotics teams to apply for our available grants. I became as much of a librarian as I could be without being part of a library, running our communications, outreach, and internal organization management. All this gave me access to countless stories from our applicants that gave me a great deal of insight into the importance of information equity. My challenge was to reach the students who are just starting out. I was constantly aware of the high stakes involved. If those students, perhaps young girls or students from low-income families, did not get the opportunity to start STEM early, it was possible they may believe someone who tells them later that engineering is not for them. The National Alliance for Partnerships in Equity (NAPE) offer a training on diversity and micro-messages that I had the opportunity to take while I was at Skillpoint. Their emphasis on unconscious bias, the power of stereotypes, and self-efficacy were huge in making me think about how best to recruit underrepresented populations of students to STEM—and struck me as a great example of feminist pedagogy.[24] Simple strategies like identifying stereotypes that might be affecting patrons can change institutional communication and instruction policies in important ways. A similar training for educators, librarians, and library users could be extremely valuable in places where it is not already present.

Of course, in such a huge program, we could never reach everyone. One of the most infuriating interactions was with a young girl I met at a robotics tournament in March of 2015. I was meeting with team members when I came across one booth that was empty, save for an 8th grade girl. When I asked where the rest of her team was, she said they were fixing the robot and that she wasn't allowed to help. She was clearly upset and sensed the unfairness, but didn't seem to know what to do. I did my best to speak up, telling her that she should talk to her coach about this problem and find a way in wherever she could. Those boys were not to tell her what she could and could not learn. But I wonder how many other girls I didn't meet have this same story. It shouldn't be the case that each girl has to advocate for herself at age 13 in order to learn what she wants to learn, but here we are.

In that situation, though, I feel like librarians can be exceptionally well trained to respond in a helpful and encouraging way. Imagine this girl being told about the history of Ada Lovelace, Caroline Herschel, or Grace Hopper. Imagine the boys in this scenario, having their worldview shaken up. And perhaps the coach as well! These are the situations librarians have the power to create at the reference desk, at a children's event, or while leading a new patron to a book. As public education resources, librarians' mastery of information and research can lead to new discoveries for just about anyone.

There is a lot of talk about the future of libraries, but it is my belief that this conversation bypasses that fact that what libraries do so well already will always be valuable. These reference desk interactions, where patrons walk away feeling validated and empowered, are the future, because they are what has made libraries strong throughout library history. It becomes truer every day that materials are available online, but librarians know that "online" does not by any means equal "accessible to everyone." Librarians' commitment to multiple ways of relaying information when some might be content to just send a link is

---

24 Meagan Pollock (PhD) and Elizabeth Biddle, "Micromessaging to Reach and Teach Every Student," *National Alliance for Partnerships in Equity*, Webinar, June 11, 2015.

a good example of why librarians are so well placed to act as stewards of social justice. Still, when libraries have to defend themselves against budget cuts, it's important to have as many tools as possible. We certainly can't bring about social justice in our communities and support the unsupported without funds to acquire new and exciting materials, buy up-to-date technology for public use, and pay good staff to take care of the community. Focusing on the parts of a library that cannot be delivered online or bought on Amazon is a good place to start.

One solution from within the library world is the Expect More movement and the concept of "new librarianship," which I was introduced to through a presentation from its creator, Dave Lankes. This idea emphasizes a rising need for a community- and conversation-based philosophy over a materials-based one when talking about the value of libraries.[25] In this universe, the value of the library is centered in the librarians who work there instead of solely the physical materials it holds. Librarians become facilitators of the types of conversations that can bring about new knowledge. Those who wonder about a library's future in a world where information is available online might need to be shown the ways in which libraries still make a difference. (This is especially important given that some of those people are legislators and budget writers.) The guidance and support provided in person by a librarian is one of the best examples.

Another suggestion from Lankes is that the relationship between libraries and its patrons goes both ways. Not only do libraries enrich the lives of their communities, communities enrich their libraries. Though I have been using them here, current common terms like patrons or users are strange in that they have negative connotations in other contexts—no one wants to be patronized or used. Thinking about this from a perspective of feminist pedagogy, the labels applied to a person can have a great deal of power over how they feel they can interact with an institution. Expect More advocates for a change in vocabulary to members, allies, or neighbors. Members have a stake in their library and they are a part of it in a way that a user may not be. Considering a change in terms could potentially move the profession closer toward a philosophy of mutual success simply by forcing us

---

25 Dave Lankes, "Expect More: What's In It for the Information Professional?" Webinar, 1 hour, November 4, 2015.

to consider that relationship, where librarians and library members alike will learn, grow, and share things with each other. Incidentally, this is also a great way to facilitate learning and allow all voices to be heard. The expertise of librarians lies in finding information, not knowing everything already. Therefore, it makes sense that a library should be a place where people can seek out information together, even if one of those people is a librarian and one is a visitor. This is exactly the environment that encourages the concept of information literacy. Librarians are united by a love of learning and this often means listening more than talking.

In my opinion, the importance of one-on-one support at the reference desk cannot be overstated, especially for those who might feel less welcome in other places in society. Empowering communities to talk about social justice issues with sensitivity and strength is one of many ways a reference librarian can make their mark on the world. We need to invite communities to take part in that same magical feeling I got from my community library as a child, because a partnership between communities and their libraries makes the hard work of changing the world a little easier.

Bibliography

"2012 Report to the Community." *Cleveland Public Library.* Accessed March 19, 2016. http://cpl.org/2012annual/our-mission/.

"2014 Books Challenges Infographic." *American Library Association.* Last modified 2014. http://www.ala.org/bbooks/frequentlychallengedbooks/statistics/2014-books-challenges-infographic.

"About the Library." *Austin Public Library.* Accessed March 19, 2016. http://library.austintexas.gov/about-library/vision.

Bertot, John Carlo and Paul T. Jaeger. "The ADA and Inclusion in Libraries." *American Libraries Magazine.* Last modified October 5, 2015. http://www.hplct.org/library-services/adults/COHS

Blair, Carole, Greg Dickinson, and Brian L. Ott. Introduction to *Places of Public Memory: The Rhetoric of Museums and Memorials*, edited by Carole Blair, Greg Dickinson, and Brian L. Ott. Tuscaloosa, AL: University Alabama Press, 2010.

"Career Online High School (COHS)." *Hartford Public Library.* Accessed March 19, 2016. http://www.hplct.org/library-services/adults/COHS.

Chavez, Stella M. "LGBT Books for Kids Will Stay On Hood County Library Shelves, Commissioners Say." *KERA News.* Last modified July 14, 2015. http://keranews.org/post/lgbt-books-kids-will-stay-hood-county-library-shelves-commissioners-say.

"Core Values of Librarianship." *American Library Association.* Last modified June 29, 2004. http://www.ala.org/advocacy/intfreedom/statementspols/corevalues

Dwyer, Colin. "Book News: Despite the Tumult, Ferguson Library Keeps Its Doors Open." *NPR.* Last modified June 19, 2015. http://www.npr.org/sections/thetwo-way/2014/11/26/366767946/book-news-despite-the-tumult-ferguson-library-keeps-its-doors-open.

Foote, Kenneth E. *Shadowed Ground: America's Landscapes of Violence and Tragedy.* Austin: University of Texas Press, 2003.

"Framework for Information Literacy for Higher Education." *Association of College and Research Libraries.* Accessed July 27, 2016. http://www.ala.org/acrl/standards/ilframework#authority

Hanisch, Carol. "The Personal is Political." *CarolHanisch.org*. Last modified January 2006. http://www.carolhanisch.org/CHwritings/PIP.html.

Hirsch, Marianne and Valerie Smith. "Feminism and Cultural Memory: An Introduction." In *Theories of Memory: A Reader*, edited by Michael Rossington and Anne Whitehead, PAGES. Baltimore: Johns Hopkins University Press, 2007.

hooks, bell. *Feminism is for Everybody: Passionate Politics*. Cambridge, MA: South End Press, 2000.

hooks, bell. *Feminist Theory: From Margin to Center* (2nd ed.). Cambridge: South End Press, 2000.

Horrigan, John B. "Libraries at the Crossroads." *Pew Research*. Last modified September 15, 2015. http://www.pewinternet.org/2015/09/15/libraries-at-the-crossroads/

Hu, Elise. "A Nationwide Outpouring of Support for Tiny Ferguson Library." *NPR*. Last modified November 29, 2014. http://www.npr.org/sections/thetwo-way/2014/11/27/366811650/a-nationwide-outpouring-of-support-for-tiny-ferguson-library.

Gunderman, Richard and David C. Stevens. "Libraries on the frontlines of the homelessness crisis in the United States." *The Conversation*. Last modified August 18, 2015. http://theconversation.com/libraries-on-the-front-lines-of-the-homelessness-crisis-in-the-united-states-44453.

Keating, Cricket. "Building Coalitional Consciousness." *NWSA Journal* 17, no. 2 (2005): 86-103. Accessed July 27, 2016. http://www.jstor.org/stable/4317127

Lankes, Dave. "Expect More: What's In It for the Information Professional?" Webinar, 1 hour. November 4, 2015.

Pollock, Meagan and Elizabeth Biddle. "Micromessaging to Reach and Teach Every Student." *National Alliance for Partnerships in Equity*. Webinar. June 11, 2015.

Searing, Susan. "Empowerment and Library Instruction." *Feminist Teacher* 1, no. 1 (1984): 8-9. Accessed March 19, 2016. http://www.jstor.org.ezproxy.lib.utexas.edu/stable/25684347.

Part III

Intersectional and Collaborative Work

Intersectionality at the Reference Desk: Lived Experiences of Women of Color Librarians

Rose L. Chou and Annie Pho[*]

Introduction

When it comes to personal identity, social categories, and being a librarian, there are many nuanced aspects of how one operates in libraries. Within the field of librarianship, there has not been a lot of research conducted to understand the connections between how an individual is treated in the workplace based on their perceived gender, race and ethnicity, sexual orientation, and other identities. We sought to answer the questions: How do women of color librarians experience patron interactions, and how do their intersecting identities shape the way they approach public service? Through interviews with women of color librarians working in academic, public, and school libraries, we learned about the lived experiences of women of color librarians who interact with the public in the workplace. The major themes we will explore in this chapter are labor, perceptions of competency and authority, questioning personal identity and sexual harassment, and self-care.

While our questions focused on interactions at the reference desk, we acknowledge that reference interactions happen at other access points and spaces, such as circulation and information desks or online. We chose to focus on one-on-one in person interactions instead of larger interactions, such as instructional classes, because of the intimacy

---

[*] Both authors contributed equally to the research project and chapter. The order of authors is alphabetical.

of those smaller interactions. The reference desk is an established point of connection where patrons and librarians interact and exchange information. There are certain service expectations that come with this space; a librarian should be friendly and approachable and help patrons to the best of their ability. But there are particular power dynamics also at play in this exchange which gives the added potential for oppressive—sometimes racist, sexist, homophobic, or xenophobic—behavior to exhibit itself, putting the librarian in direct line to receive these comments. Sometimes these acts of oppression are subtle, and are expressed through more nuanced ways as we begin to explore in this research project. Honma writes, "All too often the library is viewed as an egalitarian institution providing universal access to information for the general public. However, such idealized visions of a mythic benevolence tend to conveniently gloss over the library's susceptibility in reproducing and perpetuating racist social structures found throughout the rest of society."[1] The reference desk is no exception to this.

Library literature on feminism and gender often excludes the perspectives of women of color;[2] and existing literature on librarians of color mainly focuses on recruitment and diversifying the profession.[3] Recently there has been some research conducted about racism and microaggressions[4]

---

1 Todd Honma, "Trippin' Over the Color Line: The Invisibility of Race in Library and Information Studies," *Interactions: UCLA Journal of Education and Information Studies*, 1, no. 2 (2005): 1-26.

2 Suzanne Hildenbrand, "Library Feminism and Library Women's History: Activism and Scholarship, Equity and Culture," *Libraries & Culture* 35, no. 1 (2000): 51-65; Marie L. Radford and Gary P. Radford, "Power, Knowledge and Fear: Feminism, Foucault, and the Stereotype of the Female Librarian," *The Library Quarterly* 67, no. 3 (1997): 250-266.

3 Kyung-Sun Kim and Sei-Ching Joanna Sin, "Increasing Ethnic Diversity in LIS: Strategies Suggested by Librarians of Color," *The Library Quarterly* 78, no. 2, (2008): 153-177; Barbara Dewey and Jillian Keally, "Recruiting for Diversity: Strategies for Twenty-first Century Research Librarianship," *Library Hi Tech* 26, no. 4 (2008): 622-629; Emily Love, "Generation Next: Recruiting Minority Students to Librarianship," *Reference Services Review* 38, no. 3 (2010): 482-492; and Anjali Gulati, "Diversity in Librarianship: The United States Perspective," *International Federation of Library Associations and Institutions* 36, no. 4 (2010): 288-293.

4 Microaggressions are defined as "the everyday verbal, nonverbal, and environmental slights, snubs, or insults, whether intentional or unintentional, which communicate hostile, derogatory, or negative messages to target persons based solely upon their marginalized group membership." Derald Wing Sue, "Microaggressions: More than Just Race," *Microaggressions in Everyday Life*, November 17, 2010, https://www.psychologytoday.com/blog/microaggressions-in-everyday-life/201011/microaggressions-more-just-race.

in academic libraries[5] and a book published on the experiences of academic librarians of color[6], yet we have been unable to find more in-depth research that focuses on the work experiences of women of color librarians in all types of libraries. There are several ways an individual can experience discrimination and discomfort in how others treat them. A study on librarian approachability in an academic library found that "societal structure influences how patrons perceive librarian approachability,"[7] showing that one's perceived social categories can impact how the public perceives and treats an individual working in public services. Our research builds on current discussions around diversity, microaggressions, and intersectionality in libraries, which range from conference presentations[8], articles,[9] and other

---

5 Jaena Alabi, "Racial Microaggressions in Academic Libraries: Results of a Survey of Minority and Non-minority Librarians," *The Journal of Academic Librarianship* 41, no. 1 (2015): 47-53; Jaena Alabi, "'This Actually Happened': An Analysis of Librarians' Responses to a Survey about Racial Microaggressions," *Journal of Library Administration* 55, no. 3 (2015): 179-191.

6 Rebecca Hankins and Miguel Juarez, eds, *Where Are All the Librarians of Color?: The Experiences of People of Color in Academia* (Sacramento, CA: Library Juice Press, 2015).

7 Jennifer L. Bonnet and Benjamin McAlexander, "Structural Diversity in Academic Libraries: A Study of Librarian Approachability," *Journal of Academic Librarianship* 38, no. 5 (2012): 277-286.

8 Eboni M. Henry et al, "Librarians of Color: The Challenges of "Movin' On Up" (Part II)," Panel presentation at the American Library Association Annual Conference, San Francisco, CA, June 27, 2015, http://alaac15.ala.org/node/28885; Juleah Swanson et al, "From the Individual to the Institution: Exploring the Experiences of Academic Librarians of Color," Panel presentation at the Association of College and Research Libraries Conference, Portland, OR, March 26, 2015, http://acrl.learningtimesevents.org/from-the-individual-to-the-institution-exploring-the-experiences-of-academic-librarians-of-color-2.

9 Juleah Swanson et al, "Why Diversity Matters: A Roundtable Discussion on Racial and Ethnic Diversity in Librarianship," *In the Library with the Lead Pipe*, July 29, 2015, http://www.inthelibrarywiththeleadpipe.org/2015/why-diversity-matters-a-roundtable-discussion-on-racial-and-ethnic-diversity-in-librarianship; Fobazi Ettarh, "Making a New Table: Intersectional Librarianship," *In the Library with the Lead Pipe*, July 2, 2014, http://www.inthelibrarywiththeleadpipe.org/2014/making-a-new-table-intersectional-librarianship-3; Angela Galvan, "Soliciting Performance, Hiding Bias: Whiteness and Librarianship," *In the Library with the Lead Pipe*, June 3, 2015, http://www.inthelibrarywiththeleadpipe.org/2015/soliciting-performance-hiding-bias-whiteness-and-librarianship.

library community projects.[10] As issues of race and gender become more widely acknowledged in the consciousness of librarians, we hope that this research will be beneficial to the field of librarianship, as the profession strives for inclusivity, diversity, and social responsibility in the workplace.[11]

Our interest in this research project stems from our involvement in other projects within the profession of library and information science (LIS). We are both on the LIS Microaggressions team, where we help distribute and promote the project, and the zine associated with it. The purpose of the LIS Microaggressions project is to provide a space which "aims to identify, acknowledge, and overcome the microaggressions that continue to exist in our profession and that are the real, lived, experiences of LIS professionals from marginalized communities today."[12] We are both alumni of the Minnesota Institute for Early Career Librarians from Underrepresented Groups, where intimate conversations between other librarians of color illustrated that many of us have dealt with prejudice and microaggressions in the workplace. These conversations are often held among peers who may have similar experiences, but they're not often communicated to the profession at large. Upon reflection of what feminism and the reference desk would be to us, it became clear that intersectionality would be a key factor in understanding the experiences that other women of color might face in the workplace, and particularly how they interface with the public and their coworkers.

Intersectionality is a term coined by Kimberlé Crenshaw, and she states that the "experiences Black women face are not subsumed within the traditional boundaries of race or gender discrimination as these boundaries are currently understood, and that the intersection of racism and sexism factors into Black women's lives in ways that cannot be captured wholly by looking at the race or gender dimensions of those experiences separately."[13] Intersectionality studies the ways

---

10 *Microaggressions in Librarianship*, accessed August 4, 2015, http://www.lismicroaggressions.com; *#critlib*, accessed August 4, 2015, http://critlib.tumblr.com.

11 "Core Values of Librarianship," *American Library Association*, June 29, 2004, http://www.ala.org/advocacy/intfreedom/statementspols/corevalues.

12 "About," *LIS Microaggressions*, accessed February 10, 2016, http://lismicroaggressions.tumblr.com/about.

13 Kimberlé Crenshaw, "Mapping the Margins: Intersectionality, Identity Politics, and Violence Against Women of Color," *Stanford Law Review* 43, no.6 (1991): 1244.

in which multiple social and cultural identities impact individual experience, allowing for a more holistic view of our lives. Looking at race and gender isolated from each other fails to see the many dimensions in which they intersect and overlap, creating a complicated lived experience that cannot be captured by studying one identity.[14] We felt that it was important to examine and explore the experiences of women of color librarians using intersectionality as our framework for understanding. As we discovered in our interviews, many of the women we talked to were treated differently on the basis of social categories such as their race, gender, and sexual orientation.

Research Methodology

Since this project places a high value on personal experiences, we chose a feminist interviewing methodology where we conducted interviews to hear in-depth accounts from women of color librarians. The qualitative method of interviewing allowed us to gain more insight and nuance into the complexities of race and gender than other commonly used quantitative methods such as surveys. It was very important for us to make the participants feel that they were the experts, not us—we were not there to doubt or question their experiences but to learn about them. Traditionally, studies using interviews often create an unequal power dynamic, where the interviewer is the expert and participants are simply objects in the study. We wanted to ensure that wasn't the case in our interviews, especially since the experiences of people of color and women have historically been doubted and deemed invalid by mainstream society. Furthermore, we believe that building a power dynamic between interviewer and interviewee obstructs learning by creating barriers. Sharlene Nagy Hesse-Biber's work was especially helpful to us as we designed our research study.[15]

Self-reflection was another important aspect of feminist methodology we prioritized. We actively took time to self-reflect throughout the entire research process, from creating our recruitment

---

14 Stephanie Guittar and Nicholas Guittar, "Intersectionality," in *International Encyclopedia of the Social & Behavioral Sciences,* ed. James D. Wright (Amsterdam: Elsevier, 2015), 657-662.

15 Sharlene Nagy Hesse-Biber, "The Practice of Feminist In-Depth Interviewing," in *Feminist Research Practice,* eds. Sharlene Nagy Hesse-Biber and Patricia Lina Leavy (Thousand Oaks, CA: SAGE Publications Inc., 2007), 111.

questionnaire and interview questions to reflecting before and after our interviews. We acknowledged our own identities as "insiders" and "outsiders"—we are insiders in that we are both women of color and librarians, yet we are outsiders in that we are the researchers and may not racially identify with most of our participants. We discussed the balancing act of being completely open to whatever our participants said while also not having a specific agenda to confirm our own assumptions or guesses.

We recruited participants by creating a call for volunteers including an online questionnaire that was sent out to various library listservs and publicized on social media. Using the method of purposive sampling, we selected our fourteen participants based on their recruitment questionnaire responses, specifically their answers to two free response questions.[16] We wanted to interview people who had experiences they were very open to sharing and intersectional themes they wanted to discuss with us. The demographics of our participants were broad, coming from all regions of the United States and identifying as multiracial, African American, Black, Latina, Asian, and Native American. Their years of experience working in libraries range from under one year to over fifteen years. Four of our interviews were conducted in person, and the remaining ten were conducted either by phone or through a video conference call.

We do not believe that objectivity is possible in conducting research or in the practice of being librarians. Everyone comes into their work with their own experiences and biases, and we acknowledge that this research study reflects our own interests. If we were not interested in these themes, we would not have conducted this study. We are two Asian-American women who are early-career librarians and have both worked in public services. Our perspectives going into the research project, conducting interviews, and analyzing data are affected by our backgrounds and experiences. We asked questions and selected participants based on themes we wanted to hear about, but we were also completely open to anything our participants shared with us. While we expected to hear some of the findings discussed

---

16 The two free response questions were: How does your personal identity affect how you approach working at the reference desk?; The purpose of this study is to explore the experiences of women of color librarians who interact with the public, and to understand how their personal identities shape how they approach their work. What themes or topics would you be interested in talking about if selected for an interview?

later in this chapter, our findings are largely things we did not expect or think about when starting this research project.

When we discuss our initial findings in this chapter, we rely heavily on direct quotes from our participants. We believe that the voices of our participants speak for themselves, and it is not always necessary to add our own words, or reference the works of others, to provide further understanding. It is integral to our feminist methodology that we do not have to follow the same traditional scholarly publishing rules that have been so ingrained in our education. We struggled with balancing long-held scholarly impulses with the aspiration to find another way to best share our research.

Findings

A. Labor

Throughout our interviews, we noticed a thread of comments related to the labor involved in being a woman of color librarian. Over half of our participants are either the only librarian of color or one of few librarians of color at their past and current institutions. This lack of a diverse workforce creates a work environment that can feel isolating and discouraging.

What often results from being the only librarian of color is that they are the only person doing "diversity work" or the only person being asked to. Examples of diversity work include conducting outreach to diverse communities, attending workshops related to diversity, serving on diversity committees, creating LibGuides for ethnic studies areas, and forwarding job announcements to ALA ethnic caucus listservs. Our participants do this type of work because it's important to them personally and they care deeply about these issues. One participant explained that while she is known as "the diversity person," she doesn't really mind being asked first to do these types of projects:

> It's a mix of being known as a person that will always take diversity projects, but also that I like diversity projects. For example with the Muslim Student Association, I want to make sure that they feel welcome in their library because sometimes the campus can be you know, not welcoming. So if I can show them that they have an ally in the library or at least with me as a librarian, then I want to do that. I

want to see students succeed to stay and finish their programs, to end their programs, that motivates me in the projects I choose.

More than one participant has stated that it would be great if more white colleagues volunteered to do diversity work. One participant said, "We have a lot of diversity programming but it's always the same people. You're preaching to the choir and so I'm not sure how effective we're going to be able to be if we're on the road to address some of those structural issues, it's really, really challenging." She went on further, "I feel like it has to be everybody's responsibility, and if this is something that we say is important to the library and the university, to me there should be some consequences if you don't participate." Another problem is that even when white colleagues do volunteer to work on diversity initiatives, librarians of color then have the burden of explaining basic concepts, and it becomes more work to collaborate with someone who lacks knowledge of diversity issues. As one participant described:

> Sometimes it can feel like I'm sort of a poster child for all things black…I do feel kind of like when people have questions, or when people need to kind of talk about something uncomfortable, or put someone in the department on the race issue, it's me. And that's fine cause that's what I want, but still it does feel a little like tokenism, it kind of feels like I don't want to necessarily be doing this by myself and when I do want to collaborate, it's with a white colleague who doesn't know as much, and that's not a jab against them, they want to know more, they want to learn, but I'm working with someone who is not quite as knowledgeable on these issues and who doesn't quite even have the rhetoric to approach it from a certain angle. I feel like I'm explaining and trying to validate my experiences to them, then we can move toward this conference proposal, or toward this whatever it is that we're doing. So yeah, it's been a struggle.

Another participant described her work environment when it comes to diversity projects: "I think there is more of a collaborative effort on projects, so it's nice to see that it's not just the same person over and over again. They don't ask me first, for every diverse project that they could ask. They ask certain ones to work on the Black Lives Matter displays, and that's good I don't have to be the person every time and I feel that it's more encouraging to see that every day and everyone is involved actively."

An organization's overall lack of awareness or practice of diversity initiatives can send the message that diversity work is not valued as highly as other library work. Anantachai, Booker, Lazzaro, and Parker observe, "diversity research can often be viewed as 'unofficial work' that is not recognized as fitting into a traditional scholarly paradigm."[17] One participant said:

> I call it the black tax, like it's the extra work that you have to do that is largely unrewarded and uncompensated. It's like, I don't mind the diversity leadership team and serving as a mentor, but I also want to have time to do other things as well and maybe if other people in the library would step up and do some of these things then you wouldn't always be looking to me, so those are the kinds of structural types of things that I think we could do much better jobs to address.

Another dimension of this issue of diversity work being valued less is the perceived lack of competency that many women of color librarians face, which will be discussed in more detail later in this chapter. Furthermore, a recent study on business executives and diversity-valuing behaviors may add some additional troubling context. Diversity-valuing behaviors in this study are defined as behavior that promotes demographic balance within organizations, such as respecting cultural and gender differences and valuing working with a diverse group of people. The study found that "women and nonwhite executives who were reported as frequently engaging in these behaviors were rated much worse by their bosses, in terms of competence and performance ratings, than their female and nonwhite counterparts who did not actively promote balance…We found clear and consistent evidence that women and ethnic minorities who promote diversity are penalized in terms of how others perceive their competence and effectiveness."[18]

---

17 Tarida Anantachai, Latrice Booker, Althea Lazzaro, and Martha Parker, "Establishing a Communal Network for Professional Advancement Among Librarians of Color," in *Where Are All the Librarians of Color? The Experiences of People of Color in Academia*, eds. Rebecca Hankins and Miguel Juarez (Sacramento, CA: Library Juice Press, 2015): 39.

18 Stefanie K. Johnson and David R. Hekman, "Women and Minorities Are Penalized for Promoting Diversity," *Harvard Business Review*, March 23, 2016, https://hbr.org/2016/03/women-and-minorities-are-penalized-for-promoting-diversity.

Other issues with being one of the very few librarians of color include the themes below.

Isolation and Exclusion

> I am the only, as far as I know, queer librarian at my institution that I've met. I'm sure there are some others, but I don't know who they are. I'm definitely the only black queer person. I think I am legitimately the only black person in the library system.

> They were asking me, "what other black librarians work where you do?" I was like "Oh I guess it's just me." It was the first time I really laid out that number. And there might be one other person, but I haven't personally met her. But really it's the fact that I can count on one hand the number of people not only who are black and queer, but who are just black at my library. It's a little disconcerting at the moment.

> I tended to be kind of ostracized by some of my other colleagues. They tended to—they wanted to work together and they didn't really want me to be involved. And so that on top of the fact that I was the only black woman, the black librarian, really the only librarian of color period. It was—it could be very isolating.

Being Judged

One of our participants who identifies as Latina and works with a lot of Latina students in an academic library says that her colleagues constantly criticize, both directly and indirectly, that she has long research appointments with students. She said:

> I feel like Mexican-American women talk about certain things, like you have to chat before you get to the bulk of the question. I've had co-workers say, "well you take so long with them." That's uncomfortable for me, to feel like I'm helping someone but I'm constantly being judged. I've been working in this for about 15 years so I shouldn't have to prove what I'm doing to you.

Structural Racism

> One of the things that I've always been really big on is a job description that is reflective, not of a particular experience but of the work that you need that person to do. So being really realistic about what it takes to do the job I think that's a real struggle. I think people aren't aware of that. You know we complain about not having a diverse library staff,

and we say well we always recruit the same kind of people and to me what that says is that we're reproducing ourselves. We are looking for people like ourselves and what we're looking for isn't really required to do the job, for example, sometimes for our introduction we ask for two years of library experience, and so rather to me two years of post MLS experience for entry level job is a lot. So you gotta really think about what kind of experience someone is going to have, or what, who would have had an opportunity to get that experience.

I remember interviewing a woman…They asked me to serve on the interview panel for the vacancy I had left. She applied for the position, she's Latina, and the question came up, "Where do you see yourself in 5 years?" And she said, "I see myself as a branch manager." And these women that I had worked with for years and years and years, they were just taken aback by the fact that she would be so ambitious as to want to be a branch manager. And I was sitting there like, really? Are you kidding me? And so they did not hire her…I thought to myself now if a white male had come in and sat in the same chair and said he wanted to be the branch manager in 5 years, would they have batted an eye? And it was kind of like oh I guess she was too spicy, I mean that was kind of how they had her sort of framed as being really aggressive, and she wasn't aggressive. But yeah, she was ambitious, and why is that a problem?

I've worked in places where people said "oh it really would be nice if we could find a children's librarian of color. And if only I could find one." To which my response is where are you looking? That idea that we're committed to in theory diversity, but in practice means that one, it's a stated goal somewhere, whether it's in a strategic plan, whether it's in a human resources policy statement. It's a stated goal, but also you build the infrastructure to recruit, but you build the infrastructure to retain and to advance. So you don't have the situation where you have all these people who identify ethnically and culturally as something else, as non-white, but that they all are shelvers or library assistants and then maybe you have one or two or three librarians [of color] in this organization that has 300 people. But that there is a real practice of identifying and retaining and advancing people of color. And that people put their time, energy, and dollars behind it.

Being the only librarian of color, or one of a few, can be a very isolating experience for a variety of reasons. Alabi's survey of academic librarians on racial microaggressions reinforces these comments on exclusion and isolation of librarians of color.[19] However, diversifying

---

19 Alabi, "'This Actually Happened,' 186-187.

the workforce in terms of numbers alone is not the only solution to this problem. Other work has to happen as well, namely, more white librarians need to step up to the plate and do diversity work. If they are intimidated or feel it's not their place, then they should learn to be an ally without placing the burden on people of color to teach them. The profession needs to think beyond recruiting more people of color to become librarians, and as the last quote mentioned, libraries must build infrastructure to better recruit, retain, and advance people of color within their organizations. What we really need to explore is how to create a more inclusive organizational culture. Furthermore, diversity work should be seen as equal to other professional work—or even more so. The following sections discuss additional issues that women of color librarians face that create uncomfortable, and sometimes hostile, work environments.

B. Perceptions of Competency and Authority

In the workplace, many people of color experience having issues with coworkers or patrons questioning their competence and authority. Research that examines racial microaggressions in academic librarianship reveals that many academic librarians of color are more likely to face microaggressions in the workplace and are treated differently than their white coworkers.[20] Faculty of color are also more likely to have their intelligence, qualifications, and authority questioned which can have negative effects over time on one's confidence and mental health.[21] Not surprisingly, these experiences came up frequently during our interviews with women of color librarians. One participant said, "As an early-career librarian and someone who is seen as lesser, I feel like I have to work harder to be like 'I'm a professional'...as the saying goes 'you work twice as hard to get half as far.' Like I have to work so much harder just to stand on the same playing field as other people." For some librarians who were early career, they attributed the perceived incompetency due to looking young, being a person of color, or a being a woman. The insidious nature of condescension that these women faced is sometimes not

---

20 Alabi, "Racial Microaggressions in Academic Libraries,"52.

21 Alabi, "'This Actually Happened,' 181; Derald Wing Sue et al, "Racial Dialogues: Challenges Faculty of Color Face in the Classroom," *Cultural Diversity and Ethnic Minority Psychology* 17, no. 3 (2011): 331-40.

overtly offensive, which makes it hard to pinpoint what exactly made those interactions uncomfortable.

Many librarians mentioned that some patrons were not always confident in the answers that were given to them, making the librarian feel as though they were not being perceived as a trained professional. As a result of this perception that patrons may not be satisfied with the answers given by the librarians, some felt like they needed to be extremely thorough in helping their patrons.

Sustaining a level of high performance for long periods of time can be difficult, especially if one observes that other coworkers are not expected to perform at the same level of rigor and professionalism. Several of the women we spoke to acknowledged that they had to hold themselves to a higher standard because they knew they would be more susceptible to being perceived as less competent than their counterparts.

These feelings of not being treated as someone with the training and authority to be a librarian were not limited to just public service interactions in a space like the reference desk. For some, this extended into the classroom. A number of our interviewees who also teach in their libraries remarked that there are some similarities between providing research assistance one-on-one, and teaching to a larger group, but the dynamic of working with a group does change things, including more interaction with faculty members or other instructors. As one librarian remarked that "it felt a lot more stressful than a reference interaction, which was more one-on-one, and instead in an instructional session where I felt like really it is all eyes on you and you're not just teaching to just one person, you are teaching to an entire room of students."

The quotes below illustrate the experiences of how these women of color librarians' ability and competence have been perceived in the workplace.

Teaching

> I've had times when I'm setting up and prepping, and people sort of look at me like who is this and then they see me with all the documents and things so once they realize I'm the librarian, then some of them still like look at me funny. I don't know, I think it depends on how that session goes to whether or not they trust me. It's like I have to earn it by the end, or if they still aren't convinced at the end, in the workshops I have an hour or so to teach and to I guess

win students over and show them that I'm competent and teach them something new.

Even when I walk into the room to deliver an instruction session, some people have mistaken me for a student aide. It's like no, no, I'm your instructor for the day—I'm your librarian. Sometimes that can be a challenge to navigate, because not only am I navigating blackness and perceived stereotypes and expectations that you have of black folks in general, or preconceived notions you might have, but I'm also navigating the idea that I'm a young black woman in this profession. And you read me as a student and they already assume certain levels of intelligence based on race and identity but add age to that and it feels like another mark against me in some folks' view.

Providing Reference Services

I am on the younger side of the demographic...when an older patron is asking me a question, I can feel that they don't necessarily trust my answer or they're skeptical of how I'm going to go about getting the answer.

I feel like not across the board, but sometimes you can just kinda tell the person that you are helping doesn't have a lot of confidence in what you're offering. And so I feel the need to be really, really thorough with my patrons, and to make sure that I follow up, depending on what your question is.

I chalked up some of the responses of people towards me then to me being young, or me being just out of library school, but I think I have a lot of responses now where I realized it might be some kinds of unconscious things coming in—like, my boss there, reference traffic was really low. It was as if she didn't have confidence with my ability to answer reference questions, so if she was nearby she would make a beeline to the desk. It was as if she wanted to make sure or reassure herself of what I was going to say.

Authority and Management

We spoke to several librarians who were in management positions or positions of authority in their workplace. In our conversations, many recounted times when patrons did not believe that they were the person in charge, sometimes asking to see another manager or being disrespectful. For many of the women, this gave them feelings of discomfort, anger, and invalidation. The quotes below illustrate a couple of librarians' experience, but this sentiment was echoed in several of our interviews.

> I've had plenty of patrons who ask the manager to meet, and when I tell them that is me, they are very dissatisfied and say well I need to speak with the man in charge. So I will hear things like that and it's sometimes a double whammy...from some patrons, it's simply youth more than gender, from a couple patrons, it's been some racial issues in a way that I'm not thrilled with.

> Also, when people come to the reference desk and they ask for the person in charge, and I say "okay well I'm the librarian here today, I'm the person in charge" and they're like "no, no, no" they think it's another woman who's Caucasian who has the same exact position as me, but in my view, well maybe they think she's in charge because she's white and older, but we have the same position.

Because these interactions are not always explicitly discriminatory, it's hard to pinpoint exactly why someone is not willing to believe that librarian's position of authority, which in turn makes it harder to address. One librarian mentioned that the reference desk was located outside of her boss's office and patrons would often mistake her for a receptionist instead of a professional librarian who was trained to provide research help. When we asked how this made her feel, she replied "I was also very angry because I knew that the only reason that they refused to interact with me or refused to believe that I had qualifications to help them was just based on what they saw before them." Patrons asking to speak to a "real librarian" suggests several things to the person who is working at the desk. It suggests that they are not competent or unable to help that patron, even when they are fully capable of doing so. Within the taxonomy of microaggressions developed by Sue, these kinds of comments are seen as microinsults which "represent subtle snubs, frequently outside the conscious awareness of the perpetrator, but they convey an oftentimes hidden insulting message to the recipient."[22] For those on the receiving end of these comments, feelings of frustration, disrespect, and even stress can lead to negative consequences on one's psyche over a prolonged period of time. One has to discern when something is worth speaking

---

22 Derald Wing Sue, *Microaggressions in Everyday Life: Race, Gender, and Sexual Orientation* (Hoboken, NJ: Wiley, 2010): 31.

out against, but many times people end up internalizing these feelings or feel like they must overcompensate for other's misconceptions of their ability to perform well in their jobs.

C. Questions of Personal Identity and Sexual Harassment

As we conducted our interviews, it became more apparent that sexual harassment in the workplace has become normalized and that the woman's body and appearance are up for comment or violation. In several interviews, many women made reference to patron interactions that made them feel uncomfortable. In some instances, this was because they had male patrons who would cross the line and interrogate the librarian's sexuality, gender, and race. This is not particular to women who work in a library, it is a reflection of a larger societal issue; yet the nature of providing public services in a library setting means that one has to have a friendly and approachable demeanor which is either imposed upon the employee through customer service standards in the workplace, or guided by a personal philosophy to perhaps ease any library anxiety. Unfortunately, for many women, this level of friendliness or niceness is misconstrued by patrons as an invitation to comment on the librarian's appearance, to ask personal probing questions that went beyond a reference question, or to ask about the librarian's racial or ethnic background.

In several of the interviews where women mentioned feeling uncomfortable because of sexual harassment, they did not always report the incidents to Human Resources or their supervisors. Unwanted advances towards women in the workplace has become so normalized that it's seen as an inconvenience or frustration but not something that is always taken seriously by those in authoritative positions. As a coping mechanism, some women began to change how they presented themselves at work. One interviewee mentioned that she began to change how she dressed at work so that she would stop receiving comments about her body while at work: "I wear a lot of long cardigans to hide my shape or have my butt covered because I don't want the looks, I don't want the comments on my hips." It is a significant realization that women must pay close attention to how they present themselves in the workplace in order to feel safe, secure, and also respected. The quotes below highlight some of our participants experiences in terms of uncomfortable patron interactions and how they present themselves at work.

Sexual Harassment

Men will presume familiarity and disrespectfulness, commenting on my appearance and sexual overtures.

I feel like guys will ask me for inappropriate things for my reactions so I always usually don't give them a reaction. So for example a guy came up to me and he was like "Hey I want a book on kama sutra," and I was like okay sure, gave him a call number and told him where to find it. And then he was like, "Oh this doesn't freak you out?" And I was like nope. So he goes "Are you into like sexual experimentation?" And I was like, uh nope, not at all.

So there's times when you have to—I have to go to the shelf to show the person where the book is or try to teach them instruction on how to use the library. And they'll just definitely be uncomfortably close and touch me sometimes like on the shoulder and stuff. So for those I end the interaction pretty quickly, like "okay, well there's your book and I'll see you next time." It's never been anything like too—it's things I can handle. I can handle like a pat on the shoulder and stuff like that. But I'm also wondering—I'm like, I don't think you would be doing that for like a male librarian so it can get uncomfortable.

Appearing More Professional

I constantly get asked, "oh do you go to school here, or what are you studying here, or oh can I talk to a librarian" because I think they think I'm a student worker. That's another thing. I don't feel like I'm validated or being taken seriously. So in order to look older I sometimes put more effort into my hair, like when I'm throwing it into a bun, which is what I usually do. I started doing the makeup last year, it's completely new to me and I'm still trying to figure that out. I don't know that it makes a difference, but internally I think that it makes a difference and makes me more confident so I think that might help if I have more confidence in my appearance in looking older. Even wearing my glasses I feel like makes a difference.

I started doing this thing where I wear my hair out as my sort of calling card, but I noticed when I'm trying to do a little bit more professional look, I'll wear my hair back... but I tend to have a little bit more of a professional put-together look where I might wear a little mascara or something like that, but I'm not really, I don't wear a lot of makeup as it is. But I might kind of put it up a notch if I have a big meeting.

Women may feel pressure to present as more feminine or more professional in order to be more accepted by their peers and patrons, and yet also it opens them up to comments about their appearance. As Minh-Ha T. Pham states "Fashion, like so many other things associated primarily with women, may be dismissed as trivial, but it shapes how we're read by others, especially on the levels of gender, class and race. In turn, how we're read determines how we are treated, especially in the workforce—whether we are hired, promoted and respected, and how well we are paid."[23] Even what we as a profession consider as professional does not always account for one's racial and ethnic background, and in turn centers whiteness and heteronormative values. Galvan writes:

> Unpack for a moment what the notion of being 'put together' professionally involves: hairstyles, makeup, becoming comfortable in costuming which may or may not be designed for our bodies, voice coaching to eliminate accents and modify tone, time for exercise to appear 'healthy', orthopedics to address poor posture, orthodontics and teeth whitening, eye contacts if our lenses distort our appearance, concealing body modifications, and the countless ways marginalized librarians modify gesture, develop behavioral scripts, and otherwise conceal their authentic selves in the interest of survival."[24]

As we learned in our interviews, many women of color felt pressure to present themselves in ways that conform to white, heteronormative norms, which sometimes felt at odds with their authentic selves in order to appear authoritative, competent, and professional.

In terms of appearance, our interviews emphasized that certain aspects of a woman's appearance were more questioned than others. Several black women that we spoke to mentioned that the way they wore their hair was often a topic of antagonism. One mentioned a patron who reached over the counter to touch her hair, while complimenting her and asking her about her hair, but never asking for her permission to touch her body. She described it as a dehumanizing

---

23 Minh-Ha T. Pham, "If the Clothes Fit: A Feminist Takes on Fashion," *Ms. Magazine*, Fall 2011, http://www.msmagazine.com/Fall2011/iftheclothesfit.asp.

24 Angela Galvan, "Soliciting Performance, Hiding Bias: Whiteness and Librarianship," *In the Library with the Lead Pipe*, June 3, 2015, http://www.inthelibrarywiththeleadpipe.org/2015/soliciting-performance-hiding-bias-whiteness-and-librarianship.

experience, since she was made to feel like a "circus animal." In a different situation, the same librarian was pulled into an office to talk to a supervisor who complained about another employee's hair, which gave the implicit message to the librarian that she needed to be more aware of how she wore her own hair, in the event that her coworker might talk about it behind her back.

Sharing Personal Identity

The concept of appearing professional at work is not limited to only how one dresses or presents, it can also be related to how much personal information a librarian might share with their colleague or with a patron. A couple of the librarians we interviewed mentioned that they were not out about their sexuality at work. One librarian mentioned she must wear many masks at work, and while her coworkers may not have issue with her being queer, she wondered "can I safely perform my queerness here in a way that won't have people look at me strangely? Can I safely approach these topics?" These issues of perception truly go beyond appearance, and can be tied to issues of personal safety and harassment. Another librarian stated, "I have to sort of play a role that people are comfortable with, which is not really my true personality. So that's the first thing. But I do think I also just generally have to hide my being queer from customers and from staff, or risk harassment basically. And in fact in the times that people have found out that I am queer, it has led to negative consequences."

Race/Ethnicity and Appearance

> Sometimes I feel like when a reference interview starts to go into more personal stuff, like if I've helped the patron and then usually it's a man, wants to ask me more personal questions. Like it starts to really make me feel uncomfortable. And usually they're questions about my hair or my ethnic background. I don't want to, I mean it's obvious, I look different…

Appearance goes beyond how one dresses at work, and extends to assumptions that people make when looking at someone. Many of our participants dealt with comments about their racial and ethnic identity, which made many of the women feel uncomfortable. A couple of participants mentioned that they sometimes pass for white, and while working at the reference desk, they had to listen to patrons say racist comments. Again, for these librarians, they were put into an uncomfortable situation where they were forced to decide whether they should say something and get into a conflict, or let it slide. However, by not saying anything, some women felt like they were being complicit in allowing those comments to go unchallenged, which creates internal tension with their self-identity and outward presentation.

Going beyond physical appearance, one librarian mentioned that because of her last name, she has been automatically interviewed for bilingual job positions even though she did not state on her application that she was bilingual nor did she even apply for those positions. There are many assumptions that can be made about one's racial and ethnic identity through not just appearance, but even one's name. The questioning of someone's race or ethnicity Others that individual and relays the implicit message that they do not belong there; and might even suggest that they do not match what the idea of a professional librarian should look like in that patron's mind.

D. Self-care

We did not initially create questions about self-care in our interview guide, but the topic frequently came up organically in our interviews. Promotion and discussion of the subject of self-care in online media has become more prominent in recent years, but it is more than just a trend or buzzword. Self-care can have different meanings and interpretations, so what we mean by self-care is generally "any intentional actions you take to care for your physical, mental and emotional health."[25] We asked every participant if they had ever experienced a patron interaction that made them feel uncomfortable, and all fourteen women had. After hearing those experiences, we often, though not always, followed up and asked how they felt during the interaction and what actions they took to take care of their mental and emotional health. We sometimes asked if their coworkers or institution provided any emotional support because an unsupportive environment also contributes to our participants needing to practice self-care. Self-care is important because repeated incidents of racism,

---

25 "So What Is 'Self-Care'?," *University of Kentucky Student Affairs*, accessed March 21, 2016, http://www.uky.edu/StudentAffairs/VIPCenter/downloads/self%20care%20defined.pdf.

racial prejudice, and microaggressions have very real effects on mental and physical health.

People who experience racism, microaggressions, and other racial stressors may be at increased risk of mental and physical health effects such as high blood pressure, anxiety, depression, and decreased immune system efficiency.[26] To be clear, we are not diagnosing any of our participants with these or claim to have any sort of expertise in psychology or medicine, but we want to emphasize why it is so important to talk about these issues: racism has a very real effect on the lives of those who experience it. It is not just "in your head," but it affects your everyday life. Psychologist Robert T. Carter has found that "Racism can and does create damage to one's psyche and personality in the same way that being subjected to community violence, being held captive, or being psychologically tortured can create emotional damage."[27] Practicing self-care means that you have to prioritize yourself, and that may seem as if it is selfish or self-indulgent behavior. Women of color particularly are likely to put themselves last: "When we're expected to take care of others emotionally and physically, taking time, energy, and resources for ourselves can feel shameful."[28]

Here are some responses to our questions about self-care.

Burnout

> I find I can burn out a little bit if I don't get a few breaks here and there, it's a frontline customer service kind of thing. I'm on the reference desk about 33 of my 38 hours at work every week and we're very short staffed…I'd say I have less time than others since I have to do some administrative things so it can get very taxing…sometimes I feel that it's hard for me to mask that I'm very stressed with the amount of work that I have to do, so sometimes I dread people coming to ask a question at the reference desk because it interrupts work that I'm doing, which is very unfortunate because that is definitely not how it should be.

---

26 Sue, *Microaggressions in Everyday Life*, 97-100.

27 Robert T. Carter, "Racism and Psychological and Emotional Injury: Recognizing and Assessing Race-Based Traumatic Stress," *The Counseling Psychologist* 35, no. 1 (2007): 83.

28 Sarah Mirk, "Audre Lorde Thought of Self-Care as an 'Act of Political Warfare'," *Bitch Media*, February 18, 2016, https://bitchmedia.org/article/audre-lorde-thought-self-care-act-political-warfare.

Right now I'm at the point where I'm kind of getting burnt out by working with the public, but I don't know if that's because the majority of my hours are at the reference desk, where if I had a full-time job where I maybe had more off desk hours and could recharge and go back to the desk and people, I could handle more situations.

General Self-care Strategies

I try to lay out a really positive self-health plan for myself, which means I should be able to take a day if I need to. I should be able to take a day whether I have a cold or if I wake up and it just doesn't feel like today is the day. That doesn't mean I abuse my days, or take more than I need to, it just means that I'm trying to constantly check in with myself and think about health as more than what we traditionally think about it as.

I think I go home and laugh about it and vent. I just—what I guess is, I feel like growing up, my parents always prepared us that this is the world you're gonna live in…a predominantly white world, so you're gonna have to learn how to adjust and get along with peers and these are your coworkers.

Support Systems

I did have a couple of friends at work who also sort of—they had sort of different experiences, but they understood the difficulties that I was going through with some of my colleagues. I would get together with them for dinner or drinks or we would try to have lunch together most days and just sort of sit and vent and kind of decompress together.

If I can, I try to take a break or rope in a co-worker who may be able to support me and help in that situation so maybe take over the reference desk for a little bit.

I have really good staff, where they'll intervene. We have policies where you can't sexually harass people (one of our patron policies). And I have plenty of other library patrons who would just be like, "You know, that's inappropriate or you need to leave"—and I have really good support it's just I guess I just get upset that because I provide customer service or I'm nice, or in the words of an older gentleman "I'm charming," that people feel the need to cross a line.

Many librarians turn to external library networks outside of their institutions for support within the profession. Anantachai, Booker,

Lazzaro, and Parker suggest conferences and professional organization committees as places to find support, "Finding a community of like-minded colleagues validates an individual's experience, and can help to encourage that individual to move from being a listener to an active contributor to the profession."[29] We have found this beneficial in our own lives but also recognize the privilege in being able to attend library conferences. Many librarians do not receive financial support from their institutions to attend conferences and would have to pay out of pocket in order to have those opportunities. One easy action that institutions can do is to provide more financial support for librarians of color to attend conferences and other professional development opportunities, such as leadership institutes.

While everyone will have different methods and strategies for practicing self-care, a common one is having a strong support network of people who you can vent to, whether these are colleagues, friends, family, or significant others. Even reading through this chapter of other women's voices may be a form of self-care, validating the knowledge and experiences women of color librarians face on a daily basis. It is important to hear others acknowledge and affirm similar experiences you've had, especially when mainstream society wants to deny you that. For us, this project reiterated and reprioritized how truly necessary it is to take time for yourself and to take care of yourself.

Conclusion

Despite the challenges and hardships that women of color librarians face in the workplace, a large majority of our interviewees replied that they genuinely love working with the public and working in the profession. All of our participants find it rewarding to help others find information and answers to questions they are seeking; this is why they became librarians in the first place.

The findings from our research project demonstrate that systems of oppression—namely racism, sexism, and heterosexism—are deeply entrenched in our society. While wildly blatant forms of racism occur less frequently today than in the past, the pervasiveness of microaggressions in the daily lives of women of color show that oppression looks different

---

29 Anantachai et al., "Establishing a Communal Network," 42.

in this modern context. How prejudice expresses itself and is received is dependent on the individual and environment in which they exist. It's not always going to look like an overt display of discrimination, but can be much more subtle and harder to address. When women of color are then placed in the position of serving the public, a unique situation is created where the librarian must balance the value of providing good customer service with the demeaning feelings of receiving racist, sexist, and heterosexist comments on a frequent basis. Does being a good librarian have to be at the expense of oneself?

Going into this project, we had some assumptions about the types of microaggressions that librarians of color face at the reference desk. However, we did not expect the volume and intensity of these microaggressions and the frequency of sexual harassment that women of color librarians experience. During our interviews, there were several times where we felt empathetic to the experiences of the women we spoke to, where it felt like there were no words to really express our empathy. Our profession espouses diversity and inclusion as core values, and yet we need to ask: are libraries even safe spaces for their employees? Libraries as institutions are often complicit in sustaining societal racism, patriarchy, and heteronormativity; and in our interviews we learned about the impact that has on women of color who need to work within this realm. While there might not be much that libraries can do about patrons' actions, libraries can certainly decide what patron behavior is appropriate and allowed by implementing institutional guidelines for intervening in inappropriate situations. Reflecting upon our research findings, we realize there is so much more to be done in this area.

The complexities of these issues does not allow for the simple binary of a problem and a solution. What is important is to start talking about the things women of color librarians face—and to a broader audience than just those of us who identify as that. We are left with many questions to continue exploring as we unpack what we've learned in our conversations with these women of color. Join us in taking on these questions. How does structural oppression reproduce itself in spaces that are touted to be egalitarian and democratic? How does one maintain respect in the library when confronted with oppressive treatment or being stereotyped based on one's race, gender, or other social categories? How can library organizations create better work cultures and environments for staff and patrons to exist as their true selves? What would a feminist reference desk look like?

Bibliography

"About." *LIS Microaggressions.* Accessed February 10, 2016. http://lismicroaggressions.tumblr.com/about.

Alabi, Jaena. "Racial Microaggressions in Academic Libraries: Results of a Survey of Minority and Non-minority Librarians." *The Journal of Academic Librarianship* 41, no. 1 (2015): 47-53.

———. "'This Actually Happened': An Analysis of Librarians' Responses to a Survey about Racial Microaggressions." *Journal of Library Administration* 55, no. 3 (2015): 179-191.

Anantachai, Tarida, Latrice Booker, Althea Lazzaro, and Martha Parker. "Establishing a Communal Network for Professional Advancement Among Librarians of Color." In *Where Are All the Librarians of Color?: The Experiences of People of Color in Academia*, edited by Rebecca Hankins and Miguel Juarez: 31-53. Sacramento, CA: Library Juice Press, 2015.

Bonnet, Jennifer L., and Benjamin McAlexander. "Structural Diversity in Academic Libraries: A Study of Librarian Approachability." *Journal of Academic Librarianship* 38, no. 5 (2012): 277-286.

Carter, Robert T. "Racism and Psychological and Emotional Injury: Recognizing and Assessing Race-Based Traumatic Stress." *The Counseling Psychologist* 35, no. 1 (2007): 13-105.

"Core Values of Librarianship." *American Library Association.* June 29, 2004. http://www.ala.org/advocacy/intfreedom/statementspols/corevalues.

Crenshaw, Kimberlé. "Mapping the Margins: Intersectionality, Identity Politics, and Violence Against Women of Color." *Stanford Law Review* 43, no.6 (1991): 1241-4299.

#critlib. Accessed August 4, 2015. http://critlib.tumblr.com.

Dewey, Barbara, and Jillian Keally. "Recruiting for Diversity: Strategies for Twenty-first Century Research Librarianship," *Library Hi Tech* 26, no. 4 (2008): 622-629.

Ettarh, Fobazi. "Making a New Table: Intersectional Librarianship." *In the Library with the Lead Pipe.* July 2, 2014. http://www.inthelibrarywiththeleadpipe.org/2014/making-a-new-table-intersectional-librarianship-3.

Galvan, Angela. "Soliciting Performance, Hiding Bias: Whiteness and Librarianship." *In the Library with the Lead Pipe.* June 3, 2015. http://www.inthelibrarywiththeleadpipe.org/2015/soliciting-performance-hiding-bias-whiteness-and-librarianship.

Guittar, Stephanie, and Nicholas Guittar. "Intersectionality." In *International Encyclopedia of the Social & Behavioral Sciences,* edited by James D. Wright, 657-662. Amsterdam: Elsevier, 2015.

Gulati, Anjali. "Diversity in Librarianship: The United States Perspective." *International Federation of Library Associations and Institutions* 36, no. 4 (2010): 288-293.

Hankins, Rebecca, and Miguel Juarez, eds. *Where Are All the Librarians of Color? The Experiences of People of Color in Academia.* Sacramento, CA: Library Juice Press, 2015.

Henry, Eboni M., Eileen K. Bosch, Karen Quash, Leslie K. Griffin, Mario Ascencio, Monica Lopez, and Ray Pun. "Librarians of Color: The Challenges of "Movin' On Up" (Part II)." Panel presentation at the American Library Association Annual Conference, San Francisco, CA, June 27, 2015. http://alaac15.ala.org/node/28885.

Hesse-Biber, Sharlene Nagy. "The Practice of Feminist In-Depth Interviewing." In *Feminist Research Practice,* edited by Sharlene Nagy Hesse-Biber and Patricia Lina Leavy, 111-148. Thousand Oaks, CA: SAGE Publications Inc., 2007.

Hildenbrand, Suzanne. "Library feminism and library women's history: Activism and scholarship, equity and culture." *Libraries & Culture* 35, no. 1 (2000): 51-65.

Honma, Todd. "Trippin' Over the Color Line: The Invisibility of Race in Library and Information Studies." *Interactions: UCLA Journal of Education and Information Studies* 1, no. 2 (2005): 1-26.

Johnson, Stefanie K., and David R. Hekma. "Women and Minorities Are Penalized for Promoting Diversity." *Harvard Business Review.*

March 23, 2016. https://hbr.org/2016/03/women-and-minorities-are-penalized-for-promoting-diversity.

Kim, Kyung-Sun, and Sei-Ching Joanna Sin. "Increasing Ethnic Diversity in LIS: Strategies Suggested by Librarians of Color." *The Library Quarterly* 78, no. 2, (2008): 153-177.

Love, Emily. "Generation Next: Recruiting Minority Students to Librarianship." *Reference Services Review* 38, no. 3 (2010): 482-492.

Microaggressions in Librarianship. Accessed August 4, 2015. http://www.lismicroaggressions.com.

Mirk, Sarah. "Audre Lorde Thought of Self-Care as an 'Act of Political Warfare'." *Bitch Media.* February 18, 2016. https://bitchmedia.org/article/audre-lorde-thought-self-care-act-political-warfare.

Pham, Minh-Ha T. "If the Clothes Fit: A Feminist Takes on Fashion." *Ms. Magazine.* Fall 2011. http://www.msmagazine.com/Fall2011/iftheclothesfit.asp.

Radford, Marie L., and Gary P. Radford. "Power, Knowledge and Fear: Feminism, Foucault, and the Stereotype of the Female Librarian." *The Library Quarterly* 67, no. 3 (1997): 250-266.

"So What Is 'Self-Care'?" *University of Kentucky Student Affairs.* Accessed March 21, 2016. http://www.uky.edu/StudentAffairs/VIPCenter/downloads/self%20care%20defined.pdf.

Sue, Derald Wing. "Microaggressions: More than Just Race." *Microaggressions in Everyday Life.* November 17, 2010. https://www.psychologytoday.com/blog/microaggressions-in-everyday-life/201011/microaggressions-more-just-race.

———. *Microaggressions in Everyday Life: Race, Gender, and Sexual Orientation.* Hoboken, NJ: Wiley, 2010.

Sue, Derald Wing, David P. Rivera, Nicole L. Watkins, Rachel H. Kim, Suah Kim, and Chantea D. Williams. "Racial Dialogues: Challenges Faculty of Color Face in the Classroom." *Cultural Diversity and Ethnic Minority Psychology* 17, no. 3 (2011): 331-40.

Swanson, Juleah, Azusa Tanaka, Isabel Gonzalez-Smith, Isabel Espinal, Todd Honma, Ione Damasco, and Dracine Hodges.

"From the Individual to the Institution: Exploring the Experiences of Academic Librarians of Color." Panel presentation at the Association of College and Research Libraries Conference, Portland, OR, March 26, 2015. http://acrl.learningtimesevents.org/from-the-individual-to-the-institution-exploring-the-experiences-of-academic-librarians-of-color-2.

———. "Why Diversity Matters: A Roundtable Discussion on Racial and Ethnic Diversity in Librarianship." *In the Library with the Lead Pipe.* July 29, 2015. http://www.inthelibrarywiththeleadpipe.org/2015/why-diversity-matters-a-roundtable-discussion-on-racial-and-ethnic-diversity-in-librarianship.

Reference and Beyond: Aspiring Librarians and Intersectional Feminist Strategies

Nicole A. Cooke, Jennifer Margolis Jacobs, Katrina Spencer, Chloe Collins, and Rebekah Loyd

Introduction

> Feminist education—the feminist classroom—is and should be a place where there is a sense of struggle, where there is visible acknowledgment of the union of theory and practice, where we work together as teachers and students to overcome the estrangement and alienation that have become so much the norm in the contemporary university.[1]

I have the luxury and privilege to teach a suite of courses related to diversity and social justice, one of which is entitled *Race, Gender, and Sexuality in the Information Professions* (RGS), at the School of Information Sciences (iSchool), at the University of Illinois. In the latest iteration of the class, I had a small, but mighty, group of students, all of whom are aspiring librarians but come from different backgrounds and have differing thoughts about the impact they would like to make on the profession. They may not all end up working at a traditional reference desk, but they are all committed to working with and teaching their patrons through a feminist pedagogy lens.

---

1 hooks, bell. *Talking Back: Thinking Feminist, Thinking Black* (South End Press, 1989), 50.

As a former instruction librarian and trainer, with a subject expertise in adult education and andragogy,[2] my classes are designed to encourage critical discussion and examination of challenging topics, and they require students to participate in hands-on learning whenever possible. While I don't explicitly label my classes as being designed around feminist pedagogy, they are taught and managed from this perspective. In the RGS course the students were explicitly introduced to feminist pedagogy through readings and a guest speaker, and at the conclusion of the session, one of the students exclaimed:

> Oh my god, I just realized that this class is *modeling* feminist pedagogy! On the first day of class I couldn't figure out why we were reading the things we were and why we had to do these assignments. I get it now. You're brilliant!

Maybe not brilliant, but staunchly committed to educating library and information science (LIS) students in a new way – my teaching approach focuses on the development of empathy and cultural competence in students. As I have stated elsewhere, "In this way, I feel I can prepare LIS students of *all* races and creeds to be more effective, understanding and enthusiastic in their service of diverse populations."[3]

During the two-week intensive summer course students completed two oral assignments, engaged in structured critical reflections, and read and watched an interdisciplinary, and perhaps eclectic, collection of articles, chapters and videos, designed to allow them to draw connections between librarianship, race, gender, and sexuality. The main assignment was to reflect on the course content, especially the concept of feminist pedagogy, think about the ways in which they would parlay this new knowledge into a critical professional practice, and then interview one another about the entire experience.[4]

---

[2] Cooke, Nicole A. " Becoming an Andragogical Librarian: Using Library Instruction as a Tool to Combat Library Anxiety and Empower Adult Learners." *New Review of Academic Librarianship* 16, no. 2 (2010): 208-227.

[3] Cooke, Nicole A. "Creating Opportunities for Empathy and Cultural Competence in the LIS Curriculum." *SRRT Newsletter,* 187 (2014): http://libr.org/srrt/news/srrt187.php#9.

[4] Cooke, Nicole A. "Documenting Your Critical Journey". In *Critical Library Pedagogy Handbooks, Vol. 1 & 2,* edited by Nicole Pagowsky, and Kelly McElroy. Chicago: ACRL Press, in press.

In this reflective chapter, the RGS students and I will offer our reflections on this learning experience and discuss the ways in which this formal introduction to intersectional feminist strategies will enable them to incorporate anti-racist and queer approaches into their critical practices as information professionals who will serve and teach diverse populations (through their work in reference and instructional capacities). This joint reflection is an extension of our in-class learning; in true feminist pedagogical fashion, it is hoped that the students with whom I created a learning environment and experience learned as much from me as I did from them. This class is an example of how LIS programs can consider and incorporate feminist pedagogy into the graduate classroom. Leading by example can have a profound and lasting impact on how aspiring librarians learn new content and learn how to teach and interact with others.

The Feminist LIS Classroom

A classroom (whether face-to-face or online) that is steeped in feminist pedagogy will be as unique and dynamic as the people comprising the class; in that way, it is perhaps not possible to have a standard feminist classroom. However, the literature does suggest that there are some fundamental components of such a classroom, the most important of which is that feminist pedagogy offers a particularly relevant space for women and minorities[5] and encourages the creation of new knowledge through a process of engaging with inclusive readings and materials. Webb, Allen, and Walker[6] propose the basic principles of feminist pedagogy as: the reformation of the relationship between professor and student; empowerment; building community; privileging the individual voice as a way of knowing; respect for diversity of personal experience; and challenging traditional views.

When considering the *reformation of the relationship between professor and student,* one must think about the power differential that exists in classroom settings and how that power can be disrupted.

---

5 Shackelford, Jean. "Feminist Pedagogy: A Means for Bringing Critical Thinking and Creativity to the Economics Classroom." *The American Economic Review* 82, no. 2 (1992): 571-572.

6 Webb, Lynne M., Myria W. Allen, and Kandi L. Walker. "Feminist Pedagogy: Identifying Basic Principles." *Academic Exchange Quarterly* 6, no. 1 (2002): 67-72.

Traditional classrooms feature the instructor as the sole expert, who imparts knowledge and wisdom to the learners. This model rests on the expectations of "patriarchal education"[7] and assumes that students are "passive, malleable, modest, inactive, and deferring".[8] This model is long entrenched and to run a classroom that is contrary can be difficult for the instructor and the students. Feminist pedagogy encourages the teacher to become a leader and facilitator, and challenges them and their students to think aloud about questions that would normally be asked intrapersonally and increase "interactions through dialogue,"[9] which in turn accelerates an atmosphere of curiosity and inquiry. To this end Alice Atkinson Christie states:

> A classroom based on feminist pedagogy is a community of learners where power is shared and where participatory democratic processes help learners develop independence. It is an active, collaborative classroom where risk-taking is encouraged; where intellectual excitement abounds; and where power is viewed as energy, capacity, and potential, rather than domination.[10]

Related to this is the next expectation of feminist pedagogy, *empowerment*. Democracy and shared power are difficult things to embrace; however, it should not be perceived that instructors relinquish all of their power (because they are ultimately still evaluating and grading students), but they do minimize their power by recognizing that education is not a "neutral cognitive process,"[11] but is actually a process that benefits from the feelings, experiences, mental schemas, and information needs of students. Jean Shackelford[12] refers to this as "democracy rather than dominance." Restructuring the classroom

---

7 Ibid., 68.

8 Bright, Clare. "Teaching Feminist Pedagogy: An Undergraduate Course." *Women's Studies Quarterly* 21, no. 3/4 (1993): 131.

9 Webb, "Feminist Pedagogy: Identifying Basic Principles," 68.

10 Christie, Alice Atkinson. "Using E-Mail Within a Classroom Based on Feminist Pedagogy." *Journal of Research on Computing in Education* 30, no. 2 (1997): 148.

11 Webb, "Feminist Pedagogy: Identifying Basic Principles," 68.

12 Shackelford, Jean. "Feminist Pedagogy: A Means for Bringing Critical Thinking and Creativity to the Economics Classroom." *The American Economic Review* 82, no. 2 (1992): 573.

in this way can be a painful, emotional, and iterative process that requires ground rules, patience, and a variety of implicit, explicit, literal, and physical steps.[13]

Feminist pedagogy leads to *community building* as it enables learning to occur as a result of relationship building, giving learners an opportunity to be active in their own meaning-making and giving them confidence in their own knowing.[14] This gives students a voice and a stake in the learning process. *Privileging the individual voices as a way of knowing* gives students "a collaborative floor" on which they are afforded "some power over the meaning of words, not usually available to those in a hierarchy who are least powerful and typically muted."[15] Showcasing student voices and experiences is vitally important and is a "critical way of knowing" and learning.[16] Sharon Ladenson[17] continues this notion by suggesting that instructors "seek to actively engage students in learning, and consequently," because in doing so "they value and encourage sharing diverse personal experiences as part of the educational process." The key here is to celebrate, and critically examine, differences, and use those open discussions to spur collaborative learning and growth. This *respect for diversity of personal experience* represents a "multiplicity of truths"[18] that supports the development of empathy and understanding those from diverse backgrounds and experiences (e.g., different social classes, race and ethnicity, gender identification, religions, sexual orientation, etc,).

---

13 Spencer, Leland G. "Engaging Undergraduates in Feminist Classrooms: An Exploration of Professors' Practices." *Equity & Excellence in Education* 48, no. 2 (2015): 198-200.

14 Gawelek, Mary Ann, Maggie Mulqueen, and Jill Mattuck Tarule. "Woman to Women: Understanding the Needs of our Female Students." *Gender and Academe: Feminist Pedagogy and Politics* (1994): 182.

15 Treichler, Paula A., and Cheris Kramarae. "Women's Talk in the Ivory Tower." *Communication Quarterly* 31, no. 2 (1983): 126.

16 Gawelek, Mulqueen, Mattuck Tarule. "Woman to Women: Understanding the Needs of our Female Students," 181.

17 Ladenson, Sharon. "Paradigm Shift: Utilizing Critical Feminist Pedagogy in Library Instruction. In *Critical Library Instruction: Theories and Methods*, edited by Maria T. Accardi, Emily Drabinski, and Alana Kumbier. (Duluth, MN: Library Juice Press, 2010), 106.

18 Foss, Karen A., and Sonja K. Foss. "Personal Experience as Evidence in Feminist Scholarship." *Western Journal of Communication (includes Communication Reports)* 58, no. 1 (1994): 40.

Ultimately, all of these expectations of feminist pedagogy *challenge traditional views* and remind us that teaching and learning are not value-free, nor are they stagnant, monolithic processes.

Michele Paludi[19] extends the aforementioned components of feminist pedagogy by detailing several specific techniques that can be employed in the classroom. They include having students conduct research on a topic of their own choosing; using experiential exercises that draw upon students' personal experiences; arranging classroom furniture into a circular, nonhierarchical seating arrangement; using assorted media to help students make connections between course content and the outside world; and, having students interview a feminist scholar and/or activist. This final suggestion speaks directly to the assignment the RGS students completed, but instead of interviewing already established feminist scholars, they interviewed one another, future feminist scholars and practitioners.

Student Reflections

RGS students were asked to ponder the following prompt: *Reflect on your experience in your class with Dr. Cooke and discuss the ways in which you feel the intersectional feminist strategies (feminist pedagogy) will enable you to incorporate anti-racist and queer approaches into your critical practice as an information professional who will serve and teach diverse populations (via formal or informal work in reference and instructional capacities).* The following are their thoughts on how feminist pedagogy will impact their professional information practices.

Jennifer

School library media specialists are in a prime position to advocate for and include all students. School librarians collaborate with teachers, model information literacy strategies, plan programs, protect privacy, provide access to information, and purchase materials. With these responsibilities come privilege and power, which need to be used wisely. Recognizing this power, I enrolled in three social justice and diversity courses—*Social Justice in the Information Professions,*

---

19 Paludi, Michele A. "Feminist Pedagogy." In *Encyclopedia of Critical Psychology* (New York: Springer, 2014).

Information Services to Diverse Users, and *Race, Gender, and Sexuality in the Information Professions*—at the School of Information Sciences at the University of Illinois at Urbana-Champaign (iSchool). Cooke's modeling of feminist instruction and assessment has inspired me to develop cultural competence and empathy for students in underrepresented groups.[20] Children and adolescents are often exposed to bias and prejudice. School librarians must incorporate anti-racist and inclusive approaches in order to welcome all learners in a safe space.

How can teacher librarians incorporate feminist pedagogy in their services? In the summer of 2015, I took Dr. Cooke's course, *Race, Gender, and Sexuality in the Information Professions.* She has fully embraced feminist pedagogy, which greatly enhances her iSchool instruction. We engaged in tough discussions, presented on diversity-related topics, and read[21] and conducted our own oral histories via the StoryCorps app.[22] Guest speakers helped us to understand the power we hold as librarians and how to include anti-racist and inclusive approaches in our instruction and practice. Additionally, we evaluated how the news media and social media portray minority groups. These experiences have positively impacted my teaching. Since then, I make sure to use resources that can be modified by language and reading level, and I incorporate more group activities.

Prior to taking Dr. Cooke's courses, I often wondered how I could best advocate for and include all students in a school library setting. Guest speakers in her classes provided outreach ideas that helped me to further develop my vision. One speaker described her urban fiction book club, which included discussions in person, via social media, and through journaling. Another guest explained the value in creating transactional relationships, wherein both teacher and student profit from the collaboration. Their ideas are relevant and applicable to school libraries as well.

---

20 Nicole A. Cooke, "Creating Opportunities for Empathy and Cultural Competence in the LIS Curriculum," *SRRT Newsletter Social Responsibilities Round Table, 187,* (2014): 1.

21 Kathleen de la Pena McCook, *Women of Color in Librarianship: An Oral History.* (Chicago: American Library Association, 1998).

22 Robert Schroeder, *Critical Journeys: How 14 Librarians Came to Embrace Critical Practice.* (Sacramento, CA: Library Juice Press, 2014).

As a school librarian I strive to reach all of my students by utilizing inclusive and anti-racist approaches instructionally.[23] My instruction includes hands-on activities, open group discussions, and a variety of presentation format choices. When I purchase materials they will reflect the cultures of my students, and I demonstrate and utilize databases that include a variety of accommodations (e.g., audio, dictionaries, reading levels, and translation). Collaboration is paramount as I learn from my students and their teachers. Like my mentors, I want to provide programming and outreach services with a strong focus on diversity and social justice. Teacher librarians need to welcome all students in a setting that reflects their diverse backgrounds and individual learning needs. I want my students to feel safe, included, and welcomed.

Library and information science programs need to make their students feel safe, included, and welcomed as well. They need to recruit students of color, and support the students throughout their time in the program, and afterward when they enter the workforce. Library science students must learn how to accommodate all users. Diversity courses should be required by all American Library Association accredited programs. Additionally, accredited universities need to show their commitment to inclusion by having specializations in diversity and social justice. My graduate program did not have this specialization, so I tracked myself. All students should have access to diversity tracks and instructors, such as Dr. Cooke, who consistently demonstrates feminist pedagogy.

Katrina

One of the most surprising revelations for me in *Race, Gender, and Sexuality in the Information Professions* course was realizing the extent to which I had already been exposed to feminist pedagogy and the extent to which I had already incorporated its philosophies into my teaching. What was new for me was having the vocabulary—an actual term—that efficiently described the approach used in many seminar-structured courses and my day-to-day interactions at work. We students learned that, from a theoretical perspective, feminist pedagogy resisted hierarchy, acknowledged learners as leaders, and

---

23 Maria T. Accardi, *Feminist Pedagogy for Library Instruction* (Sacramento, CA: LibraryJuice Press, 2013).

promoted a democratic environment. While these tenets are wholly acceptable, there is at least one underlying value I would like to make more explicit: feminist pedagogy also recognizes the validity of multiple truths. How can it not? One of feminism's inherent and fundamental implications is that there are *at least* two gendered means of experiencing reality. A subject looking at the world through a masculine lens and a subject looking at the world through a feminine lens will inevitably encounter different truths. Feminist pedagogy, then, in classrooms and in the library and information science field, actively anticipates a variety of vantage points in the perception of challenges, problem solving, and learning objectives, too. The acceptance of this multiplicity is where this ideology appeals to my ideals of critical practice most. However, theory and practice are at times at odds with each other and one must consider what paradigms of support are necessary to support this set of values that did not predominate in the 20th century, but is being more broadly visited in the 21st.

Employing feminist pedagogy implies allowing time to engage various voices, deeply examining conflicting opinions, and allowing student-initiated detours from the lesson plan as a reflection of proactive learning. Moreover, many practitioners of feminist pedagogy also support the asynchronous extension of the classroom and its discussions beyond the physical walls of a traditional space by creating online discussion forums (Blackboard, Moodle, and other learning management systems), social media groups (Facebook), and digital threads (Twitter). For all of these reasons, embracing this methodology may prove more challenging than a traditional method as feminist pedagogy seeks diversity and ways to support its expression. While a traditional method frequently has a set agenda, one authoritative voice that imparts knowledge, and a set timeframe for completing planned tasks, the classroom following a feminist pedagogy model is flexible, responsive, and sensitive to students' priorities. Instructors who lead this type of learning must take on the additional burden of explicitly and perhaps repeatedly informing students of their expectations and frameworks before and during the course. They must create syllabi that are proto-contracts outlining how learners will interact with one another and the criterion upon which they will be evaluated lest students arrive with a separate agenda and encounter challenges en route to success. Moreover, an instructor supporting this model necessarily requires the support of his or her superiors. As his or her methodologies may be novel, s/he will absolutely need backing from his/her administration. All of these considerations require that students' expectations be changed, learning outcomes be broadly defined, and the learning trajectory reflect frequently individualized and heterogeneous goals as opposed to set, identical outcomes of success. Feminist pedagogy has a promising future as it allows for the success of the many types of students we encounter in our increasingly diverse society. Yet, making this avenue to learning regular and widespread will take time and indeed the energy of many committed practitioners.

Chloe

I was initially drawn to *Race, Gender, and Sexuality in the Information Professions* because of my background in gender studies and the fact that these topics seemed largely lacking in many of my other library and information science classes. While I did broach topics that interested me such as: how libraries can better serve patrons experiencing homelessness and patrons managing mental health issues; issues of appropriation and ownership in museum contexts; Freud's philosophy on discipline, punishment, and spectacle and how his ideas transfer to librarian/patron dynamics and the organization of libraries; and, how groups and individuals construct identities using dress and adornment through the creation of an exhibition proposal, I had not yet encountered a class explicitly taught using feminist strategies and critical practice as a frame of reference.

Watching Chimamanda Ngozi Adichie's TEDTalk "Danger of a Single Story"[24] on the first day of class took me back to the first day of my first women's studies class as an undergraduate and I was excited to have found a space where I could engage in intentional dialogues about intersectionality, privilege, and marginalization within the GSLIS program. Race, gender, and sexuality in the information professions are huge topics to cover in an intensive summer course. However, Dr. Cooke utilized traditionally non-academic platforms such as social media sites, brought in guest speakers, incorporated open discussion, integrated queer and anti-racist materials, and assigned an oral history project during our

---

24 Adichie, Chimamanda Ngozi. "The Danger of a Single Story." TED (video blog), July 2009. Accessed July 1, 2016. https://www.ted.com/talks/chimamanda_adichie_the_danger_of_a_single_story?language=en.

class's short time together, so that we were not just talking about feminist pedagogy, but actively engaging with and practicing it.

Feminist pedagogy is something that can be incorporated into any discipline. It is about recognizing people as individuals with lived experiences operating in larger systems and participating in a maze of cultural constructs. It is a method of teaching that takes both a micro and macro view of the world we live in and the people we interact with. It asks questions. It acknowledges that there are no simple answers. In my career as a librarian, I will implement feminist pedagogy by seeing and listening to my patrons, understanding their needs, creating safer more inclusive spaces, making an effort to bring marginalized topics, experiences, and materials to light, and making every effort to continue learning and expanding my own cultural competence.

Fostering an understanding of feminist pedagogy and how to put it into praxis is something library and information schools can and should be doing. We should be questioning the organizational systems and practices put in place. We should be examining current polices and how they affect our patrons. I do not believe in the idea that librarians are gatekeepers, but we do have a responsibility that should not be taken lightly. We make decisions about what is kept in our cultural memory, who and what are represented, and where and how it is kept. While it is possible for individual instructors to incorporate feminist practices in their classrooms, if LIS programs want to truly prepare students for careers in library science, they will recognize that inserting feminist pedagogy into the curriculum should not be the work of individual instructors, but something that is integrated into the culture and curriculum of LIS programs. Doing otherwise is a disservice to our institutions, our patrons, and ourselves.

Rebekah

At the heart of feminist pedagogy is the acknowledgement that people's experiences are valuable and valid, and this is central to Dr. Cooke's *Race, Gender, and Sexuality in the Information Professions* course. The students in the course mutually respected each other's contributions and learned collaboratively as Dr. Cooke modeled feminist pedagogy in her curriculum and leadership. Feminist pedagogy erases authority and privilege to allow learning to occur more freely between people. All voices had a place at our table, and we learned to understand cultural competence from a feminist pedagogical approach.

As information professionals, librarians encounter and serve an infinitely diverse array of patrons. Moreover, as the caretakers of the community's information, we have a responsibility to relay that information to our patrons. We must be able to take their perspectives and needs into account when building collections, providing reference services, publicizing our holdings, and providing access. This requires cultural competence about our communities and individual patrons. Fortunately, feminist pedagogy gives us a set of principles and practices we can use to pursue cultural competence.

First, we must learn to ignore traditional roles of privilege and authority in order to better view everyone as equals. We therefore must not imagine ourselves in positions of authority as librarians; we are learning as much from the patron as she is learning from us. By approaching a patron as a fellow learner, I can discover as much from a patron's stories about his research as he can discover from the archive.

Second, we must ask patrons what they need and actively listen to their responses. We must find out where our patrons are so we can meet them there. Every patron encounter is a librarian's chance to learn about a need in the community and an individual's experiences. Furthermore, though some voices may seem loud and authoritative when amplified by privilege or numbers, feminist pedagogy reminds us that every voice is equally important and valid.

As we begin to form a broad understanding of the community and its needs, we find ourselves on the path to cultural competence. However, cultural competence has no final answers and requires constant development. There are always new voices joining the community, and we must actively seek them out. Tools like usage statistics give us a blueprint for planning broad outreach to our patrons, but open conversation is our best tool for learning deeper cultural competence. We have to understand our fluctuating community and the groups and individuals that make it up so we can meet patrons where they are, informed by their own desires and ideas about the world through a feminist pedagogical approach.

Concluding Thoughts from a Feminist Pedagogue

Creating a classroom that both espouses and actually incorporates feminist pedagogy requires consistent dedication and hard work. And it requires time, an enormous amount of time to establish and maintain this special brand of classroom environment. However, it is perhaps among the most rewarding experiences I've had as an instructor. Because of my subject expertise in adult education and andragogy, I was previously familiar with the tenets and techniques put forth by Webb, Allen, and Walker and Paludi[25] and incorporated them into my teaching, but not until my self-study of feminist pedagogy and critical pedagogy did I realize the name and full extent of this pedagogical approach. As bell hooks has described in her writing and interviews about her experiences as an educator, implementing a course framed with feminist pedagogy can actually be a painful experience, because of the extra work involved, and because of the entrenched notions of teaching and learning that are held by both instructors and learners. Michelle Bauer summarizes hooks' experiences in the following description:

> She informs her students at the beginning of each semester that they are required to participate in class discussion. Even though students may not have something very important to contribute on a given day, the attempt to ensure that every student's voice is heard, acknowledged, and affirmed is absolutely essential to the inclusive classroom dynamic that hooks is working to achieve. The insistence that students become active and responsible learners has resulted in many complaints from hooks' students. Some of her students have resented the mandatory participation and others have expressed their discomfort with the way she scrutinizes their opinions and challenges them to question their assumptions. This insistence upon questioning one's own beliefs has been stressful not only for her students but for hooks as well. Her attempts to engage students fully have been a difficult and arduous task.[26]

This description is wholly accurate. Such classes can be wonderfully engaging, interesting, and enlightening, but they can also be intense and painful because there are dual streams of new learning occurring – the learning of actual course content and learning how to learn in a new way. What I have found in my teaching is that additional time

---

25 Webb, Allen, and Walker, "Feminist Pedagogy: Identifying Basic Principles," 2002. Paludi, "Feminist Pedagogy," 2014.

26 Bauer, Michelle. "An Essay Review: Implementing a Liberatory Feminist Pedagogy: bell hooks' Strategies for Transforming the Classroom." *Melus* 25, no. 3/4 (2000): 271.

and reflection are essential in order for students *and* instructors to be able to fully ascertain the value and power of a feminist classroom. Post-course reflection is necessary and allows for a fuller realization of the intellectual and personal growth that occurs. So while the title of this volume is the *Feminist Reference Desk*, I am suggesting that the process of being a feminist librarian with a critical practice can and should begin in our graduate LIS classrooms, if not before. In this way aspiring librarians enter the field with important sensibilities and understanding that will enable them to conquer the reference desk and any of the other important roles in the library. Ultimately, my goal is to be one of the "new storytellers" in LIS education:

New Storytellers work diligently to incorporate new stories into the classroom by creating learning environments that accommodate and encourage discussions of race, privilege, social justice, and other necessary and difficult issues. Such environments can be achieved in part by allowing students to contribute their own expertise and experiences to the discussions, and allowing students to be co-creators of the course content.[27]

New storytellers are, in part, those who model feminist pedagogy in their classrooms. We need new storytellers in the classroom in order to produce and inspire "new librarians" who will carry these ideals into the field and reimagine the services they deliver to their communities.

---

27 Cooke, Nicole A. "Counter-Storytelling in the LIS Curriculum." In *Perspectives on Libraries as Institutions of Human Rights and Social Justice* (Emerald Group Publishing Limited, 2016), 340.

Bibliography

Accardi, Maria T. *Feminist Pedagogy for Library Instruction.* Sacramento, CA: Library Juice Press, 2013.

Adichie, Chimamanda Ngozi. "The Danger of a Single Story." TED (video blog), July 2009. Accessed July 1, 2016. https://www.ted.com/talks/chimamanda_adichie_the_danger_of_a_single_story?language=en.

Bauer, Michelle. "An Essay Review: Implementing a Liberatory Feminist Pedagogy: bell hooks' Strategies for Transforming the Classroom." *Melus* 25, no. 3/4 (2000): 265-274.

Bright, Clare. "Teaching Feminist Pedagogy: An Undergraduate Course." *Women's Studies Quarterly* 21, no. 3/4 (1993): 128-132.

Christie, Alice Atkinson. "Using E-Mail Within a Classroom Based on Feminist Pedagogy." *Journal of Research on Computing in Education* 30, no. 2 (1997): 146-176.

Cooke, Nicole A. "Documenting Your Critical Journey". In *Critical Library Pedagogy Handbooks, Vol. 1 & 2,* edited by Nicole Pagowsky, and Kelly McElroy. Chicago: ACRL Press, in press.

Cooke, Nicole A. "Counter-Storytelling in the LIS Curriculum." In *Perspectives on Libraries as Institutions of Human Rights and Social Justice,* pp. 331-348. Emerald Group Publishing Limited, 2016.

Cooke, Nicole A. "Creating Opportunities for Empathy and Cultural Competence in the LIS Curriculum." *SRRT Newsletter,* 187 (2014): http://libr.org/srrt/news/srrt187.php#9.

Cooke, Nicole A. "Becoming an Andragogical Librarian: Using Library Instruction as a Tool to Combat Library Anxiety and Empower Adult Learners." *New Review of Academic Librarianship* 16, no. 2 (2010): 208-227.

Foss, Karen A., and Sonja K. Foss. "Personal Experience as Evidence in Feminist Scholarship." *Western Journal of Communication (includes Communication Reports)* 58, no. 1 (1994): 39-43.

Gawelek, Mary Ann, Maggie Mulqueen, and Jill Mattuck Tarule. "Woman to Women: Understanding the Needs of our Female Students." *Gender and Academe: Feminist Pedagogy and Politics* (1994): 179-198.

hooks, bell. *Teaching to Transgress: Education as the Practice of Freedom.* New York, NY: Routledge, 1994.

hooks, bell. *Talking Back: Thinking Feminist, Thinking Black.* South End Press, 1989.

Ladenson, Sharon. "Paradigm Shift: Utilizing Critical Feminist Pedagogy in Library Instruction. In *Critical Library Instruction: Theories and Methods,* edited by Maria T. Accardi, Emily Drabinski, and Alana Kumbier, 105-112. Duluth, MN: Library Juice Press, 2010.

McCook, Kathleen de la Pena, *Women of Color in Librarianship: An Oral History.* Chicago: American Library Association, 1998.

Paludi, Michele A. "Feminist Pedagogy." In *Encyclopedia of Critical Psychology,* 707-710. New York: Springer, 2014.

Shackelford, Jean. "Feminist Pedagogy: A Means for Bringing Critical Thinking and Creativity to the Economics Classroom." *The American Economic Review* 82, no. 2 (1992): 570-576.

Schroeder, Robert (Ed). *Critical Journeys: How 14 Librarians Came to Embrace Critical Practice.* Sacramento, CA: Library Juice Press, 2014.

Spencer, Leland G. "Engaging Undergraduates in Feminist Classrooms: An Exploration of Professors' Practices." *Equity & Excellence in Education* 48, no. 2 (2015): 195-211.

"StoryCorps." *StoryCorps, Inc.* 2016. https://storycorps.org/

Treichler, Paula A., and Cheris Kramarae. "Women's Talk in the Ivory Tower." *Communication Quarterly* 31, no. 2 (1983): 118-132.

Webb, Lynne M., Myria W. Allen, and Kandi L. Walker. "Feminist Pedagogy: Identifying Basic Principles." *Academic Exchange Quarterly* 6, no. 1 (2002): 67-72.

Feminist Pedagogy and the Critical Catalog

Katherine Crowe and Erin Elzi

Introduction

The problematic nature of the linguistic choices, structure, and the application of the Library of Congress Subject Headings and Library of Congress Classification in regard to race, class, gender, disability, and other categories of identity, is a well-covered issue in the academic literature on cataloging and classification. Despite a relative wealth of coverage in the cataloging literature, reference and instruction librarians and archivists, with the notable exception of Emily Drabinski and her chapter "Teaching the Radical Catalog," in the volume *Radical Cataloging*, have rarely weighed in to address the pedagogical and reference implications of this issue.[1] Reference and instruction librarians and archivists have, however, begun to address how to incorporate critical theory and pedagogy into their instructional design and approach. This chapter draws from literature on critical theory, radical cataloging, and how the authors have integrated these ideas into reference and instruction, which both see as necessarily in partnership with cataloging and technical services work.

The authors' approach is informed by each having worked in the other's field. Prior to working as a reference archivist, Crowe

---

1 Emily Drabinski,"Teaching the Radical Catalog," nn *Radical Cataloging: Essays at the Front*, ed. K.R. Roberto (Jefferson, NC: McFarland, 2008), 198-205.

cataloged and created metadata for archival collections and digitized archival items at the University of Denver (DU), under the umbrella of the Technical Services department. Elzi came to the University of Denver from a small design-history focused school (Bard Graduate Center), where she primarily worked in technical services and also provided reference support. Crowe's work creating metadata for non-bibliographic materials continues to inform her instructional work in the archives, much of which requires students to directly interrogate primary sources—preferably those that center the experiences of people with one or more marginalized identities and directly relate in some way to the student experience—while working together in small groups.

Crowe's approach to instruction, which positions the students as interlocutors and interpreters, requires students to do much of the same kind of interpretive "heavy lifting" that Crowe did (and Elzi continues to do) as a cataloger, asking many of the same questions that catalogers of original material ask themselves during the cataloging process: what is the "aboutness" of this thing? How can it be used to answer a question? What kinds of questions does it elicit? What kinds of questions could it answer? What are its uses? What are its limits? This instructional framework, informed by both authors' experiences in technical services, as well as critical pedagogy theorists like bell hooks, Henry Giroux, and Paulo Freire, requires students to contextualize the item or items themselves during the instruction session, and then —dependent on how the class is structured, re-contextualize the item or items as their research progresses. When possible, these in-class instructional sessions also require the students to bring these same skills to bear as they begin to search for secondary bibliographic and other non-archival sources. During this process, students begin to realize that the metadata applied to secondary sources may not always match up with language present in primary sources, and in many cases, is logically inconsistent even with similar topics represented in secondary sources. For example, when students look for secondary sources on Japanese internment during World War II, the phrase "enemy alien" is not present in the bibliographic metadata for books on the subject, despite being present in many of the primary sources they view in the archives, as it is not an authorized LCSH subject heading. However, if the research topic or question evolved to include questions about undocumented individuals residing in a country where they are not citizens, the instructional experience could easily introduce a conversation about the fact that the term "illegal aliens" is still an authorized LCSH subject heading and why that is.

In this way, the authors draw out and require students to use concepts inherent to poststructuralism and feminist theory—in particular, the de-centering and deconstruction of dominant narratives, the discursive and socially constructed nature of knowledge creation and organization, consideration of race, gender, and other categories of identity that intersect with one another, and the promotion of active learning and dialogue as fundamental components in pedagogy, cataloging, and classification. The authors also pull from concepts covered by legal scholar Kimberlé Crenshaw's "intersectionality theory," which in turn draws from critical race theory, and posits that race, gender, and other categories of identity cannot be considered separately from one another. These theories and our experiences inform the authors' practitioner-focused, pragmatic approach to designing feminist reference and instructional approaches to the construction, deconstruction, and teaching of the library catalog as it is now, with an emphasis on the American academy, academic libraries, and archives. We envision a kind of "meeting in the middle" for catalogers, reference archivists, and instruction librarians—an acknowledgement that the catalog is inherently problematic and may never be truly "radical," but that its problematic nature is precisely what makes it such a valuable tool for teaching about the historically contingent nature of language and knowledge. We also believe that the inherently problematic nature of the catalog should not deter technical services and public services professionals in academic libraries from working to address overt injustice in cataloging practice. A "radical catalog" may never be possible, but we shouldn't shy away from this work.

FEMINISM AND CRITICAL PEDAGOGY IN ACADEMIC LIBRARIES AND ARCHIVES: FOUNDATIONS FOR THE AUTHORS' PRAXES

Crowe and Elzi share a philosophical approach with a small but vocal group of academic catalogers, reference and instruction librarians, and archivists who draw from intersectionality, critical pedagogy, and feminist theory in their work. Intersectionality, which draws from critical race theory and feminist theory most directly but also relates to disability studies and queer theory,[2] has as its focus a desire to deconstruct and question the social constructs of race, gender, sexual orientation, disability, and other identities. These theories can help the instruction librarian, cataloger, or archivist shed light on how power and privilege impact individuals and groups with one or more of these marginalized identities. Feminist theory-based instruction with primary sources can help students connect to research on a personal level, generate empathy for historical actors, and learn to contextualize both primary sources and metadata about both primary and secondary sources as a part of the research process.

Crowe's approach to teaching with primary sources in an academic archives is informed by foundational critical pedagogy theorists Paulo Freire (*Pedagogy of the Oppressed*), bell hooks (*Teaching to Transgress*), and Henry Giroux. Her teaching has also been heavily informed by Maria T. Accardi's application of these and other theorists' work to her feminist pedagogy and instruction in academic libraries.[3] Like Accardi's, Crowe's instructional approach is concerned with the "socially constructed nature of knowledge," and uses analysis of archival primary documents, often in the context of specific course goals and outcomes, to draw this out in classroom discussion.[4] Like Accardi, her process draws on feminist theory, connecting it to critical pedagogy (pedagogy informed by critical theory) in her work as a reference archivist.[5] Crowe's praxis is also informed by a shift, beginning in the

---

2 Richard Delgado and Jean Stefancic, "Critical Race Theory: An Annotated Bibliography," *Virginia Law Review* (1993): 461 ; Arlene Stein and Ken Plummer, "I Can't Even think Straight" "Queer" Theory and the Missing Sexual Revolution in Sociology," *Sociological Theory* 12, no. 2 (July 1994): 178. doi:10.2307/201863; Kimberle Crenshaw, "Demarginzalizing the Intersection of Race and Sex: A Black Feminist Critique of Antidiscrimination Doctrine, Feminist Theory and Antiracist Politics," *University of Chicago Legal Forum*, no. 1 (1989): 141, http://chicagounbound. uchicago.edu/uclf/vol1989/iss1/8.

3 Paulo Freire, *Pedagogy of the Oppressed* (New York: Continuum, 1970); bell hooks, *Teaching to Transgress* (New York: Routledge, 1994); Henry Giroux. *Teachers as Intellectuals: Towards a Critical Pedagogy of Learning* (Granby: Bergin & Garvey, 1988); Maria T. Accardi, *Feminist Pedagogy for Library Instruction* (Sacramento: Library Juice Press, 2013).

4 Eamon Tewell, "A Decade of Critical Information Literacy: A Review of the Literature," *Communications in Information Literacy* 9, no. 1 (2015): 29.

5 Maria T. Accardi, *Feminist Pedagogy for Library Instruction*. (Sacramento: Library Juice Press, 2013), 29.

1970s and 80s, in archivists' approach to their collecting and descriptive practices. During this time, scholars working and teaching in new disciplines like ethnic studies and women's studies (later women's and gender studies) began to request access to primary source materials that documented individuals and organizations which many special collections and archives at institutions of higher education had never considered collecting in any focused, purposeful way: papers of people of color, women, people with disabilities, and other marginalized groups.[6] Dale Mayer, an archivist grappling with how best to collect for 'the new social history' and work with this new breed of historian, dubbed their perspective "history from the bottom up,"[7] a phrase echoed in a 2008 article on the same topic.[8] Related, Crowe has drawn from other archivists' and educators' work—in particular the Brooklyn Historical Society's TeachArchives.org project – to create instructional experiences with archival materials that go beyond "show and tell" to help students generate a deeper intellectual and personal engagement with research.[9] Deborah Mutnick, an English faculty member at LIU Brooklyn who worked with the Brooklyn Historical Society, speaks to many of the goals of the archives instructional experience that Crowe seeks to create: connecting to research on a local and personal level, generating empathy for historical actors through this connection, and creating an "exciting point of entry to the research process."[10] Though Mutnick does not explicitly speak to a grounding in feminist pedagogy, the language Mutnick uses to describe her goals aligns well with this approach to instruction, and has been a source of inspiration for Crowe as she has constructed her own approach to teaching with primary sources. Crowe's approach to reference and instruction is also informed by her prior work as a cataloger of both archival collections and items—

---

6 Dale Mayer, "The New Social History: Implications for Archivists," *The American Archivist* 48, no. 4 (Fall 1985): 390, http://www.jstor.org/stable/40292942.

7 Ibid., 391.

8 Elke Greifender, Melinda Van Wingen, and Abigail Bass, "Reappraising Archival Practice in Light of the New Social History," *Library Hi Tech* 26, no. 4 (2008): 577, http://dx.doi.org/10.1108/07378830810920905.

9 Deborah Mutnick, "The Appeal of the Archives: Engaging Students in More Meaningful Research," *TeachArchives.org*, accessed February 1, 2017, http://wwww.teacharchives.org/articles/more-meaningful-research/.

10 Ibid.

many of her decisions in how to apply cataloging best practices to the primarily visual collections she cataloged were based on a desire to create a user friendly experience which also mitigated some of the "othering" tendencies of LCSH. For example, when cataloging images of University of Denver athletic teams, rather than apply the authorized terms "Basketball" and "Basketball for women," she chose to apply the terms "Men's basketball" and "Women's basketball"—deciding to go against LCSH both in order to create a user experience more aligned with common descriptions for both sports, as well as to blunt the impact of the inherently "othering" LCSH terms.

Like Crowe, Elzi's approach is informed by debate and changing best practices among catalogers in the 1970s and 80s – most notably, Sanford "Sandy" Berman.[11] Rather than focusing on systemic injustice in the structure of LCSH, or a discursive approach to knowledge creation and deconstruction, Berman focused instead on the removal and "improvement" of racist, sexist, or otherwise pejorative terms for groups of people found in LC subject classification.[12] Elzi also draws upon the philosophy behind Drabinski, K.R. Roberto and Amber Billey's advocacy to change the requirement for Library of Congress instructions for Name Authority Cooperative Program (NACO) catalogers to limit themselves to a gender binary when establishing authority records,[13] as well as Billey's critiques of continued LCC issues with racist Cuttering practice. Elzi and Crowe's praxes both draw upon Drabinski's queer theory-inflected critique of LCSH and LCC, in particular Drabinski's discussion of foundational queer theorist Michel Foucault's emphasis on language's "historically contingent" and "discursively produced nature."[14] Elzi's background in small art libraries, where she spent time working in both technical services and reference, has also informed her thinking.

---

11 Sanford Berman, *Prejudices and Antipathies: A Tract on the LC Subject Heads Concerning People* (Jefferson: McFarland, 1993).

12 Steven A. Knowlton, "Three Decades Since Prejudices and Antipathies: A Study of Changes in the Library of Congress Subject Headings," *Cataloging & Classification Quarterly* 40, no. 2 (2005): 125, doi:10.1300/J104v40n02_08.

13 Amber Billey, Emily Drabinski and K.R.Roberto, "What's Gender Got to Do With It? A Critique of RDA Rule 9.7," *University Libraries Faculty and Staff Publications*, paper 19 (2014).

14 Emily Drabinski, "Queering the Catalog," *The Library Quarterly* 83, no. 2 (April 2013): 101, doi:10.1086/669547.

Within the context of feminist and critical theory and with an eye to an intersectional and inclusive approach to both pedagogy and cataloging, the authors present some barriers and suggested approaches to mitigate the continuing marginalization of already-marginalized identities within the catalog, as well as promote a critical understanding and reading of the catalog within reference and instructional spaces.

Barriers to Creating a Genuinely Radical Catalog

What do we mean by the "radical catalog"? It may be easier to define the traditional "non-radical catalog": limited, antiquated, lacking expansiveness – in many ways, it does not "see" or allow for intersectionality. The WorldCat record for the book *Conversations with Audre Lorde*, a collection of previously published interviews with Lorde, provides a helpful example. In one of the interviews, Lorde describes herself as "Black, Lesbian, Feminist, warrior, poet, mother doing my work. I underline these things, but they are just some of the ingredients of who I am."[15] The catalog record found in OCLC lists the following subject headings: Lorde, Audre—Interviews; Poets, American—20th Century—Interviews; Feminists—United States—Interviews; Lesbians—United States—Interviews; African American lesbians—Interviews; African American poets—Interviews; African American women—Interviews. While some of Lorde's self-defined modes of her intersecting identities are represented, others are missing. Some do not exist in LCSH. Others do, which calls into question another issue—that of the efforts of so-called objective catalogers, who may or may not be cataloging with the goal of representing intersecting aspects of a particular work. Of the first category, nowhere is there mention of Lesbian Poets. In fact, the only option for drawing the relationship between lesbians and poetry is the heading "Lesbian erotic poetry". What is one to do with Lesbian poetry on other topics? There is also nothing in LCSH for poets or feminists who are mothers. As for the second category of missing subjects, "African

---

15 Charles H. Rowell, "Above the Wind: An Interview with Audre Lorde," in *Conversations with Audre Lorde*, ed. Joan Wylie Hall (Jackson: University Press of Mississippi, 2004), 195.

275

American feminists" does in fact exist as an LCSH, as does "Lesbian mothers", "African American mothers", "Women poets, American" but are not included here, despite all four being a major topic of the intersectionality discussed Lorde's description of herself in the book.[16] Not only does this show how the subjective interpretation of how to apply LCSH rules might fail to surface relevant subject headings, but it's a blatant example of how the lack of expansiveness prevents the traditional library catalog from addressing issues of intersectionality. Calls for changes to LCSH and LCC as they currently exist, short of complete re-imaginings of their vision of knowledge organization, are unlikely to result in an intersectional or radical catalog, but it is possible to imagine the Library of Congress re-envisioning the groups who comment on standards to be more inclusive–or, as Cherry and Mukunda put it in their discussion of indigenous classification, creating "epistemic partners."[17] While intersectional terms do acknowledge the ways in which certain marginalized identities are interconnected and result in distinct experiences, the mere existence of the terms further emphasizes the "othering" already inherent in LCSH and LCC.

Despite some advances of the representation of marginalized groups in LCSH, the underlying structure of many terms still demonstrate the cis-hetero-white-Christian-patriarchal lens through which the Library of Congress operates when establishing subject headings. Though "Women as…" to "Women…" and the elimination of the relation between Lesbianism and Sexual Perversion are welcome changes,[18] the current set of headings still distinguishes between men and women by, in the vast majority of cases, using a female qualifier (i.e. "Women poets") to distinguish poets who identify as female from "Poets," despite the fact that "Male poets" do not receive their own subject heading and are assumed to fall within the overarching "Poets". The same subjective other-ization of LCSH appears, in reverse, with "Male Primary School Teachers" as distinct from "Primary School

---

16 Library of Congress Authorities, accessed February 14, 2016, http://authorities.loc.gov.

17 Alissa Cherry and Keshav Mukunda, "A Case Study in Indigenous Classification: Revisiting and Reviving the Brian Deer Scheme," *Cataloging & Classification Quarterly* 53, no. 5-6 (2015): 695, doi:10.1080/01639374.2015.1008717.

18 Sanford Berman, *Prejudices and Antipathies: A Tract on the LC Subject Heads Concerning People* (Jefferson: McFarland & Company, 1993), 5.

Teachers." As in the prior example, there are no existing qualified versions of this heading that apply to women—demonstrating the authoritative stance LC takes in stating that if someone is a Primary School Teacher, we are to assume they are not male.[19] The problematic nature of these examples call into question the basic underlying structure of classification and subject application, which underpin the catalog and related systems that libraries use for reference and access. The exclusionary structure and necessarily subjective application of LCSH restricts reference and technical services librarians in one of their primary goals: access for all.[20]

Despite the above issues with the traditional library catalog, the authors question whether it is possible or even desirable to create a "radical catalog," where problematic subject access applications have been "fixed" and intersectionality has been made visible and usable. Crowe and Elzi would argue that both the problems and inconsistency of LCSH, and the problematic language within the text of primary and secondary sources, increasingly visible in the catalog through full text indexing, can provide rich teaching opportunities to "queer the catalog," encouraging students to think critically about their information environment. The authors both struggle with when and how to intervene for this very reason; if knowledge is "discursively produced" and "historically contingent," what would a radical catalog even look like? Both Crowe and Elzi acknowledge that any one "correct" language system or "way of knowing"–what Maria T. Accardi has called "epistemological privilege"[21] is not possible, as it inevitably erases the intersectionality of human experience and identity. Over time and conversation, the authors hit on a middle ground, informed by historical practice and contemporary debate. Like Sandy Berman and the first generation of catalogers who spoke out against the catalog, they favor the replacement of authorized terms when found overtly racist, sexist, or otherwise obviously pejorative. Where this is not possible or advisable, they propose the use of instruction and

---

19 Library of Congress Authorities, accessed February 19, 2016, http://authorities.loc.gov.

20 Helen Murphy and Pauline Rafferty, «Is There Nothing Outside the Tags? Towards a Poststructuralist Analysis of Social Tagging," *Journal of Documentation* 71, no. 3 (2015): 482, doi:10.1108/JD-02-2013-0026.

21 Maria T. Accardi, *Feminist Pedagogy for Library Instruction,* (Sacramento: Library Juice Press, 2013), 18.

reference to highlight and deconstruct the overt "othering" that is intrinsically a part of LCSH and LCC in their current forms, as well as similarly problematic practices in classification and Cuttering.

The authors also acknowledge that a radical catalog would require some mechanism for a continuous deconstruction (or, from a public services perspective, a continual examination and "troubling" of the knowledge structures that make up the catalog), rather than proffering alternative or "improved" solutions in the form of "better" vocabulary or "less offensive" decisions in classification. Drabinski offers a view on this from a queer theory perspective, which challenges the idea that a "correct" vocabulary or knowledge organization is either possible or desirable.[22] The application of queer theory to the catalog challenges the entire structure of knowledge organization—a structure upon which classification and cataloging rests not just comfortably, but relies upon for support. From a queer theory perspective, neither 'correct' terminology nor knowledge organization will ever exist due to language's historically contingent and socially constructed nature.[23] Instead, from a poststructuralist/queer perspective, the "radical" catalog will never exist. Therefore, the public services librarian/archivist, cataloger/metadata librarian, and catalog users should approach the catalog with an eye toward a continual questioning and de-centering/troubling of its inherent authority.[24] Still, the group that lags behind in the application of critical analysis of subject headings and classification in practical application—with notable exception for librarians whose collections are focused around a particular axis of identity or "way of knowing" (re: indigenous knowledge/ontologies) [25]—tends to be the very people doing much of the heavy lifting of the "care and feeding of metadata."[26]

Elzi and Crowe suggest that more cross-training of public services and technical services library staff would begin to, at minimum, create more of an understanding of the underlying structure of the catalog

---

22 Drabinski, "Queering," 96.

23 Ibid., 102.

24 Ibid., 106.

25 Cherry and Mukunda, "A Case Study," 549; Marisa Elena Duarte and Miranda Belarde-Lewis, "Imagining: Creating Spaces for Indigenous Ontologies," *Cataloging and Classification Quarterly* 53, no. 5-6 (2015): 678, doi:10.1080/01639374.2015.1018396.

26 Diane Hillmann, "Metadata Quality: From Evaluation to Augmentation," *Cataloging and Classification Quarterly* 46, no. 1 (2008): 66, doi:10.1080/01639370802183008.

and how public services librarians might play more of a role in this "care and feeding." Elzi's previous roles in art libraries, which tend to be small and rely on all employees to do a bit of everything, have shown her that this kind of cross-training can pay real dividends for researchers. After several reference interactions, she began to realize that researchers' initial search terms did not match those of what she had assigned to works in the collection. Because she had the power to make changes in the metadata that would be beneficial to her research audience, she was empowered to enact change in ways that might not be immediately apparent to a reference and instruction librarian. She could also bring her knowledge of the underlying structure of existing metadata and controlled vocabularies to bear in ways that could benefit patrons in their search strategies. Elzi recognizes that some strategies that she found to be successful in a small, subject-specific collection like an art library—where a critical analysis and subject application more pertinent to the "aboutness" of the work in the context of the collection is more easily achieved—might be harder to scale in a large academic library, where even specialists are often required to be generalists in reference or cataloging to some degree. Still, finding ways for the catalogers to directly learn from researchers how they use the catalog, and ways for public service librarians can be well-adept in, and critical of, the terms and structure of controlled vocabularies would lead to the ideal situation —one in which critical cataloging and robust searches combine to give researchers to the tools they need to navigate the catalog. In addition, it ensures that the staff on both sides of the catalog are working in tandem to ensure that the catalog is constructed in a way that most closely fits the needs of the researchers and supports critical inquiry—even if the catalog itself may never be truly "radical."

Meeting up with Public Services/Pedagogy and the Radical Catalog

Much as the work of making a truly "radical" catalog, when viewed through a poststructuralist lens, will not ever be complete, we also need to view critical library and archives pedagogy as practiced in reference and instruction as discursive and never "finished." In this same sense, teaching the catalog in radical ways so that all patrons have the tools to deconstruct and decolonize libraries' knowledge organization—as Emily Drabinski has put it, "queering the catalog," is work that will also never be "done." Jonathan Cope has noted that librarians with reference, instruction, and information literacy responsibilities can be frustrated with the discursive nature of a poststructuralist approach to instructional librarianship—in other words, that "Foucaultian analysis only leads to more analysis".[27] Despite the difficulty of a practitioner-based approach toward critical library/archives cataloging and pedagogy, we believe that a discursive, de-centering, reflective approach to teaching is possible. In addition, working directly with physical archival sources with language contemporary to the period requires students to engage directly with the historically constructed nature of language. These "keywords" can then be brought to an instruction sessions with a subject librarian as an additional method for both seeking out relevant material and questioning the metadata and classification of the books, newspapers, and journals where the language appears.

This approach to teaching also creates some logistical concerns —namely: "How can I both cover relevant material and engage in activities that encourage students to question the underlying political hegemony of the classroom/library/university/society—in 50 minutes?"[28] Despite the limitations of "one-shot" teaching, which "almost sabotage feminist efforts from the start,"[29] Maria T. Accardi argues that it is "in a sense...better to be on the margins than to be recognized as full citizens of the college or university culture because... within the margins we ironically have more freedom."[30] We've found several approaches that utilize the limited amount of time we have (in our case, typically one 2-hour class period with 50-60 minutes for the librarian and 50-60 for the archivist) to create a critical pedagogical experience for students and faculty in both the archives and the more typical "instruction session" working with the instruction librarian using the library catalog and databases.

In Crowe's instruction at the University of Denver, there have been several approaches that address these concerns. If the class only has time for one in-library session, which is typically the case as the University of Denver is on a 10-week quarter system, having the

---

27 Maria T. Accardi, Emily Drabinski, and Alana Kumbier, eds. *Critical Library Instruction: Theories and Methods*. (Sacramento: Library Juice Press, 2010), 20.

28 Ibid.,71.

29 Accardi, *Feminist Pedagogy,* 69.

30 Ibid.

curator/archivist pair with a subject librarian for a combination of an in-class archives session and an in-class instruction session in a lab working with the resources in the catalog can be very effective. This dual session can meet the goals the teaching faculty has set out for the course, as well as incorporating active learning, de-centering the authority figures in the room (teaching faculty and librarians), introducing destabilizing questions and concepts, and picking up on contemporary-to-the-question "keywords" in the archival sources that can be used throughout the whole of the research process. The instruction librarians and archivists start out with brief introductions of themselves and some contextual information about the items they'll be working with, and then launch right into a brief (20-25 minute) in-class exercise where small groups of students[31] analyze select items from archival collections and answer questions that ask them to consider bias, the socially constructed and historically contingent nature of the items, the uses and limitations of these kinds of sources as evidence, how scholars might use items like these in their own research, and other questions tied to course outcomes that begin the process of critical document analysis. At the conclusion of the exercise in the archives, the subject librarian works with the group of students in a computer lab (another 40-45 minutes) to find related primary sources and secondary sources in the catalog with which to contextualize and, during the time remaining in the class, put in conversation the primary source items that they worked with in the archives.

Many of the classes that we work with are from the Writing Program, which requires students to understand writing and rhetoric from the perspective of many different academic traditions—a focus that lends itself well to this feminist approach to instruction in the archives. After several years of trial and error, we've begun to theme these in-class archives sessions around primary source materials that center the student experience,[32] typically student newspapers, and ideally, center the experience of students in one or more marginalized identity categories. For example, in one of the rhetoric and composition classes, we had groups work with student newspaper articles that incorporated the experience of Japanese and

---

31 Ibid., 35.

32 Ibid., 72.

Japanese-American students who had been relocated to Colorado due to Executive Order 9066, the presidential order that made Japanese internment possible during World War II. Students considered the historical context, the rhetorical situation of the article (which featured a newly arrived Japanese-American student relocated from Stanford being interviewed and declaring his patriotism, love of America, and jazz), and responded with the kinds of research questions that this kind of source could generate, as well as the uses and limitations of this kind of source as evidence for research. Another focused on the school's first national champion in any sport (her championship was in skiing) in 1945, who happened to be a woman, and student newspaper articles which, relative to articles about male athletes at the same time period, focused heavily on personal appearance, plans to marry, and her "favorite outfits" for competition.

Another group of classes that can lend themselves well to working with archival material are the "FSEMs" (Freshman Seminars), which pair students and a faculty member "teaching their passion." One of these classes, which focused on the literature of the Jazz Age, involved students working with a selection of student-related materials in the archives from this period of time (dresses, photographs, letters, etc.), from which they were to generate a creative response—a poem, a play, music, etc. During this particular class, Crowe noticed that one of the students seemed not to be particularly engaged with any of the sources she'd pulled out. When asked more about his background and interests, she learned that he was a veteran, and pulled out a ledger that documented student veterans who had served during World War I—and it was like a light switch had flipped on—he was instantly interested and engaged in the exercise. Even in this short amount of time, because the assignment required only one relevant source, she was able to respond to his needs and tailor his learning experience accordingly. His creative response, which selected three brothers who had served on different fronts, ended up being a fictional epistolary-style novella, featuring fictionalized versions of three actual brothers from the ledger, writing about their experiences to one another during World War I.

Depending on the disciplinary application—for example, if the students are working with newspapers in the archives-based exercise and online in licensed databases—they are exposed to language contemporary to the period of time which they are learning about.

They are also required, as part of the exercise, to consider the context within which the document was created, and in addition, learn phrases which can enable them to locate similar materials in online catalog searches where full text indexing of historical newspaper databases is present. These exercises require the students to engage deeply with the source itself, and the questions are transferrable to their work with online sources and future in-class work as well. While not overtly engaging with feminist or critical theory as a part of the exercise, we have encountered some (not much) student resistance—with some students commenting that they preferred the work with the subject librarian to the in-class exercise because the "secondary sources were so much easier"—but overall, response in our brief assessments has been positive.[33]

Some of these courses have led to interesting conversations about subject heading applications—for example, a Spanish language course focused on the history of New Spain that visited the archives to view some maps also covered the topic of crypto-Jews (Jews who live outwardly as Christians but continue to surreptitiously incorporate elements of the Jewish faith and culture into their lives), many of which have the term "Marranos" associated with them.[34] The students who decided to select this as a topic ended up having a conversation with me, the subject librarian, and the faculty member teaching the course, about how "marrano" is a pejorative Spanish term denoting "pig," (a reference to the Jewish practice of keeping kosher and avoiding pork)—and while the students were able to use this term to collocate many relevant items using this term, they also learned about the history and context of the term as applied within LCSH and historically—evidence that Drabinski's call for "queering the catalog" resulted in a radical teaching application that might not have occurred, had a more contemporary and culturally appropriate term such as "crypto-Jews" (the term more in favor with scholars of this cultural group) been used.

A similar conversation arose from a class on contemporary Native American experience from an in-archives exercise using photogravures from Edward S. Curtis' "The North American Indian."

---

33 Ibid.,28.

34 Library of Congress Linked Data Service, "Marranos," accessed March 20, 2016, http://id.loc.gov/authorities/subjects/sh85081413.html.

The students reviewed the photogravures side by side with Native American mapmaker Aaron Carapella's maps of the indigenous people of North America, as Carapella had used several of Curtis' images on the map to represent different tribal groups.[35] In addition to the conversation about 21st century discourse from the Native American community about this work, we also discussed and viewed specific examples of American Indian languages as represented in subject access in comparison to Carapella's maps, which include the names of the languages as represented by the tribal groups that he interviewed, using their terminology. Though we did not discuss it in that class, it could also have proven to be a fruitful opportunity for discussing the problematic nature of Library of Congress subject access and classification for materials on contemporary American Indians and how the catalog does not incorporate indigenous knowledge/ways of knowing. For example, Debbie Reese, a librarian who is tribally enrolled at Nambe Owingeh, has written a series of blog posts on her site, "American Indians in Children's Literature" critiquing Carapella's maps. Her critique, which uses her nation as an example, illustrates the problematic nature of Carapella's stated goal: to illustrate all pre- and at-contact nations. As she notes, there are currently (as of August 15, 2016) "over 200 federally recognized nations in the US (not counting Alaska). There were a lot more, pre-contact. How, I wondered, was Carapella going to show the locations of those 200+ federally recognized nations in the hundreds and thousands of years prior to contact, or 'at contact'? We didn't all come into contact with Europeans at the same time."[36] Using Reese's critique as an example with a student would have illustrated issues in cataloging the complexity of indigenous ways of knowing, as well as complicating the notion that there is such a thing as a monolithic Native American experience, all while centering the voice and critique of a Native American woman librarian.

---

35 Aaron Carapella, *Tribal Nations Maps*, accessed March 20, 2016, http://www.tribalnationsmaps.com.

36 Debbie Reese "A Second Look at Carapella's Tribal Nations Maps," accessed February 1, 2017. https://americanindiansinchildrensliterature.blogspot.com/2016/08/a-second-look-at-carapellas-tribal.html

Feminist Assessment

The problematic nature of early 20th century outcomes-based assessment has been addressed by a number of scholar-practitioners in the reference and instruction library community.[37] As Accardi put it in *Feminist Pedagogy for Library Instruction*, "the potential exists for learning outcomes and instructional design to be feminist, how these things are deployed determines how nurturing and learner-centered they really are"[38] because, without reflection, they can become "banking method" tools, as well as frame information literacy as a "neutral, apolitical concept."[39] The ACRL Information Literacy Framework is a promising addition to the academic librarian and archivist's toolkits for thinking critically about assessment, as it frames the issue around "threshold concepts" rather than outcomes-based learning, which is perilously close to Freire's "banking model." As Accardi puts it, "a feminist assessment is possible...guided by the principles of feminist pedagogy. It is learner-centered and diverse and validates differing perspectives and voices. It challenges the power relations that govern traditional assessment methods. It seeks to bring about social change and feminist activism. Feminist assessment is inherently reflective, and reflection itself is a feminist act."[40]

The special collections and archives assessment forms we used for the academic year 2015-2016 are brief—three questions total—they ask one yes/no question (have you ever been to a special collections/archives), and two reflective questions (what would you tell someone who had never been to an archives that you think they should know before going? What do you think could have been improved, if anything, about your experience?). Our goal with the second question is to put the students in a mental position of authority—rather than having them assess their own experience, they are in the rhetorical position of giving guidance to another student who might be apprehensive. Our hope in positioning the question in this way, was that students would be more confident and expansive in their responses and give us some insight into what they

---

37 Accardi, *Feminist Pedagogy*, 72; Tewell, "Decade of Critical Information Literacy," 29.

38 Accardi, *Feminist Pedagogy* 72.

39 Ibid., 76.

40 Ibid.

took away from the experience. In general, this was the case – and though we didn't ask for it, many of the students spoke positively of their affective or emotional response to archival sessions, describing them as "magical" or "illuminating." This hasn't substantively changed the way the sessions are taught, as we had an anecdotal sense that the physical and aesthetic experience of working directly with archival materials was an important aspect of the learning experience, particularly in creating the "exciting point of entry" that Mutnick spoke of. It has, however, informed our reconstruction of the assessment form to more explicitly get at the affective component of the instructional experience to see if we can perhaps hone in on this and get a deeper sense of what emotions are being elicited so as to better understand how (or if) they impact engagement and learning, possibly in a future qualitative study.

We've recently created a new set of questions for general assessment aimed at the ACRL Framework, focusing in particular on the frames "authority is constructed and contextual" and "scholarship as a conversation," as these two frames touch on many of our goals in the classroom, and align well with the goals of the writing and rhetoric classes, as well as many of the discipline-specific instruction sessions (history, sociology, languages and literatures, etc.) that utilize archival material. In addition, we plan to work with select faculty across the disciplines to see if we can pull together focus groups of students to have more in-depth information about students' experiences with the material and how it connected not only to the course outcomes, but to their understanding of research and inquiry. In addition, we have added a third question that asks for three adjectives to describe their experience, in hopes that this will more explicitly draw out the affective component of the sessions, which kept bubbling up, despite us never having directly asked for it. Early responses have been enlightening—students in a class on feminism who worked with 1970s era student newspapers used adjectives that suggested discomfort, as many of the articles—on topics like discrimination, campus sexual assault, and student protest—were sometimes upsetting to read. Students in a creative writing class on "the pastoral" who worked with sculptural, natural materials-based artists' books used language also suggesting deep engagement, but instead used more positive adjectives to describe their experiences.

In both cases, the students in these classes appeared to be deeply engaged in the instructional exercises, but the adjectives about the affective responses—especially in the class on feminism—are an important reminder that discomfort with language may sometimes be central to the research process.

Never Neutral, Never "Solved," Always in Process

When viewed through the lens of feminist, queer, critical race theory, and other discursive, de-centering theoretical frameworks, the problematic nature of language and subject headings will never and can never truly be resolved, as language's historically contingent and socially constructed nature is inevitable. This would seem to indicate that a truly radical catalog will never exist and, in a purely post-structuralist sense, it will not because it cannot. Instead, we propose a systematic approach that expands the discursive possibilities of current bibliographic systems, allowing for expansion and change, both ideological and tangible. Simultaneously, we advocate for a continued "queering" of the catalog within the context of library instruction, as called for by Drabinski, so that the never-truly-radical catalog can spark dialogue about structural inequity and power inherent in library knowledge systems. In short, we propose a "critical catalog," constantly in a state of being engaged by librarians and researchers, who do what they can to advocate for solutions that err on the side of social justice, combined with a relationship between technical services and public services that gives both sides a better understanding of how tools are used and how they work, and with library instruction at all levels that stresses the importance of examining the catalog with a critical eye. In this solution, the term "system" is not limited to the catalog, but instead refers to the entire network of information managed and presented by library professionals: cataloging, public services, Library of Congress, software developers, library users, and beyond. Change does not have to start in cataloging—indeed, in order for the catalog to work towards radicalism (something we should work towards, even if it is unachievable), a dialogic approach to knowledge change, creation, and engagement between public and technical services librarians, archivists, and users is necessary. A critical catalog would allow for intervention at any point in the cataloging or research process that the catalog is found to obstruct the teaching or research process. In addition, the individuals doing the majority of this work (and their supervisors, and the library administrators) need to see this critical and discursive approach to the work as non-negotiable—a job requirement, not a luxury. In order for this work to be successful, all of the people who work on all of the moving parts need to be aware, engaged, and fairly incentivized to do this work: developers who build the software that allows for alternative and expanded vocabularies to be applied, catalogers and the users who expand and interrogate terminology, the public services librarians who teach the catalog critically—a continuous circle of change, improvement and expansion. The result: perhaps not a radical catalog, but a radical library.

Bibliography

Accardi, Maria T. *Feminist Pedagogy for Library Instruction.* Sacramento: Library Juice Press, 2013.

Accardi, Maria T., Emily Drabinski, and Alana Kumbier, eds. *Critical Library Instruction: Theories and methods.* Sacramento: Library Juice Press, 2010.

Alemu, Getaneh, Brett Stevens, Penny Ross and Jane Chandler. "Linked Data for Libraries: Benefits of a Conceptual Shift from Library-Specific Record Structures to RDF-based Data Models." *New Library World* 113, no. 11/12 (2012): 549-570, doi:10.1108/03074801211282920.

"Audre Lorde." *Wikipedia.* Last modified August 1, 2016. https://en.wikipedia.org/wiki/Audre_Lorde.

Bates, Marcia J. "Learning About the Information Seeking of Interdisciplinary Scholars and Students." *Library Trends* 45, no. 2 (Fall 1996): 155-164.

bell hooks. *Teaching to Transgress: Education as the Practice of Freedom.* New York: Routledge, 1994.

Berman, Sanford. *Prejudices and Antipathies: A Tract on the LC Subject Heads Concerning People.* Jefferson: McFarland & Company, 1993.

Billey, Amber, Emily Drabinski and K.R.Roberto. "What's Gender Got to Do With It? A Critique of RDA Rule 9.7." *University Libraries Faculty and Staff Publications*, paper 19 (2014).

Carapella, Aaron. *Tribal Nations Maps.* http://www.tribalnationsmaps.com.

Cherry, Alissa, and Keshav Mukunda. "A Case Study in Indigenous Classification: Revisiting and Reviving the Brain Deer Scheme." *Cataloging & Classification Quarterly* 53, no. 5-6 (2015): 548-567. doi:10.1080/01639374.2015.1008717.

Crenshaw, Kimberlé. "Demarginzalizing the Intersection of Race and Sex: A Black Feminist Critique of Antidiscrimination Doctrine, Feminist Theory and Antiracist Politics." *University of Chicago*

Legal Forum, no. 1 (1989): 139-167. http://chicagounbound. uchicago.edu/uclf/vol1989/iss1/8.

Delgado, Richard, and Jean Stefancic. "Critical Race Theory: An Annotated Bibliography." *Virginia Law Review* (1993).

Drabinski, Emily. "Teaching the Radical Catalog." In *Radical Cataloging: Essays at the Front*, edited by K.R. Roberto, 198-205. Jefferson, NC: McFarland, 2008.

Drabinski, Emily. "Queering the Catalog." *The Library Quarterly* 83, no. 2 (April 2013): 94-111. doi: 10.1086/669547.

Duarte, Marisa Elena, and Miranda Belarde-Lewis. «Imagining: Creating Spaces for Indigenous Ontologies." *Cataloging and Classification Quarterly* 53, no. 5-6 (2015): 667-702. doi:10.1080/01639374.2015.1018396.

Evans, Siân, Jacqueline Mabey, and Michael Mandiberg. "Editing for Equality: The Outcomes of the Art+Feminism Wikipedia Edit-a-thons." *Art Documentation: Journal of the Art Libraries Society of North America* 34, no. 2 (Fall 2015). doi: 10.1086/683380.

Freire, Paulo. *Pedagogy of the Oppressed, 30th Anniversary Edition*. New York: Bloomsbury, 2014.

Giroux, Henry. *Teachers as Intellectuals: Towards a Critical Pedagogy of Learning*. Granby: Bergin & Garvey, 1988.

Goggin, Maureen Daly. "Composing a Discipline: The Role of Scholarly Journals in the Disciplinary Emergence of Rhetoric and Composition since 1950." *Rhetoric Review* 15, no.2 (Spring 1997): 322-348. http://www.jstor.org/stable/465647.

Greifender, Elke, Melinda Van Wingen, and Abigail Bass. "Reappraising archival practice in light of the new social history." *Library Hi Tech* 26, no. 4 (2008): 575-585. http://dx.doi.org/10.1108/07378830810920905.

Held, David. *Introduction to Critical Theory*. Berkeley: University of California Press, 1980.

Hillmann, Diane. "Metadata Quality: From Evaluation to Augmentation." *Cataloging & Classification Quarterly* 46, no. 1 (2008): 65-80. doi:10.1080/01639370802183008.

hooks, bell. *Teaching to Transgress.* New York: Routledge, 1994.

Hu-DeHart, Evelyn. "The History, Development, and Future of Ethnic Studies." *The Phi Delta Kappan* 75, no. 1 (1993): 50-54. http://www.jstor.org/stable/20405023.

Jin, Qiang. "Is FAST the Right Direction for a New System of Subject Cataloging and Metadata?" *Cataloging & Classification Quarterly* 45, no.3 (2008): 91-110.

Kenney, Barbara. "Revitalizing the One-Shot Instructions Session Using Problem-Based Learning." *Librarian Publications*, paper 13 (2008).

Knowlton, Steven A. "Three Decades Since Prejudices and Antipathies: A Study of Changes in the Library of Congress Subject Headings." *Cataloging & Classification Quarterly* 40, no. 2 (2005): 123-145. doi:10.1300/J104v40n02_08.

Koford, Amelia. "How Disability Studies Scholars Interact with Subject Headings." *Cataloging & Classification Quarterly* 52, no. 4 (2014): 388-411. doi:10.1080/01639374.2014.891288.

Library of Congress. *Library of Congress Authorities.* http://authorities.loc.gov.

Library of Congress. "Marranos." Library of Congress Linked Data Service. http://id.loc.gov/authorities/subjects/sh85081413.html.

Mayer, Dale . "The New Social History: Implications for Archivists." *The American Archivist* 48, no. 4 (Fall 1985): 388-399. http://www.jstor.org/stable/40292942.

McMillan Cottom, Tressie. *tressiemc.* http://tressiemc.com.

Murphy, Helen, and Pauline Rafferty. «Is There Nothing Outside the Tags? Towards a Poststructuralist Analysis of Social Tagging." *Journal of Documentation* 71, no. 3 (2015): 477-502. doi:10.1108/JD-02-2013-0026.

Mutnick, Deborah. "The Appeal of the Archives: Engaging Students in More Meaningful Research," *TeachArchives.org*, accessed February 1, 2017, http://wwww.teacharchives.org/articles/more-meaningful-research/.

OCLC Research. *searchFAST.* http://fast.oclc.org/searchfast.

Olson, Hope A. «How We Construct Subjects: A Feminist Analysis." *Library Trends* 56, no. 2 (Fall 2007): 509-541.

Reese, Debbie "A Second Look at Carapella's Tribal Nations Maps," accessed February 1, 2017. https://americanindiansinchildrensliterature.blogspot.com/2016/08/a-second-look-at-carapellas-tribal.html.

Rowell, Charles H. "Above the Wind: An Interview with Audre Lorde." In *Conversations with Audre Lorde*, edited by Joan Wylie Hall, 184-199. Jackson: University Press of Mississippi, 2004.

Stein, Arlene, and Ken Plummer, ""I Can't Even think Straight" "Queer" Theory and the Missing Sexual Revolution in Sociology." *Sociological Theory* 12, no. 2 (July 1994): 178-187. doi:10.2307/201863.

Svenonius, Elaine. "Access to Nonbook Materials: The Limits of Subject Indexing for Visual and Aural Languages." *Journal of the American Society for Information* Science 45, no. 8 (September 1994): 600-606.

Tewell, Eamon. "A Decade of Critical Information Literacy: A Review of the Literature." *Communications in Information Literacy* 9, no. 1 (2015): 24-43.

Westbrook, Lynn. "Information Needs and Experiences of Scholars in Women's Studies: Problems and Solutions." *College and Research Libraries* 64, no. 3 (May 2003): 192-209. doi:10.5860/crl.64.3.192.

Zaveri, Paul, and Mukta Atkekar. "Collaborative Tagging in Digital Libraries." *International Journal of Information Dissemination and Technology* 4, no. 2 (April-June 2014): 148-154.

Feminist LibGuides: Towards Inclusive Practices in Guide Creation, Use, and Reference Interactions

Amanda Meeks

Introduction

> "Feminism is about, among other things, decentering oppressive power relations and transforming them into something egalitarian and democratic."[1]

Recently, there has been a great deal of focus on where feminism and librarianship intersect, especially pertaining to pedagogical practices in library instruction. Feminist pedagogy brings to light an emphasis on the empowerment, community building, and respect for diversity of experience in the library classroom. Many feminist teaching librarians, myself included, have found ways to incorporate feminist principles into library instruction. However, recent conversations have revealed that a teaching tool many librarians rely on may not be in line with feminist teaching methods. LibGuides are often utilized as an instructional tool in academic information literacy sessions, but are commonly a go-to reference tool outside of the classroom as well. The LibGuide platform makes it easy for librarians who design them to rely on the banking model of education, which Paulo Freire describes

---

[1] Maria T. Accardi, *Feminist Pedagogy for Library Instruction*, Series on Gender and Sexuality in Information Studies, Number 3 (Sacramento, California: Library Juice Press, 2013), 9.

as "filling" learners with information as if they are depositories and the teacher is the depositor.[2] As Alison Hicks points out in her article "LibGuides: Pedagogy to Oppress?" many LibGuides exemplify the banking model of education because they "move the focus of inquiry from creation to listening, and from problem posing to consumption."[3] LibGuides, as a tool, are inherently designed in a way that limits student engagement and encourages passive learning behaviors. Within the reference context, banking-model LibGuides can present a host of problems for both educators and learners.

Library guides, and pathfinding tools more generally, are designed to help researchers quickly find the "best sources" for their subject of study. Hicks points out that "LibGuides that are structured by librarian-defined understandings of the 'best sources' move the focus of research away from the rhetorical evaluation of evidence."[4] This issue means that the tool does not lend itself to the conversation around feminist and critical pedagogy in the library classroom or at the reference desk so neatly. It may be linked to flaws in the design of LibGuides as a platform, as well as how individual librarians who create the guides are using the tool. An explicit critique of both the platform and one's own or one's library's best practices is necessary to build guides that align with feminist pedagogy.

Many librarians have started to raise critical questions about the oppressive nature of LibGuides. Giullian and Zitser ask whether "LibGuides improve learning or reinforce information inequality in higher education"[5] in their article "Beyond LibGuides: The Past, Present, and Future of Online Research Guides." The authors build a strong argument that the tool does, in fact, reinforce social inequality because LibGuides are discoverable through simple Internet searching, which implies that all have equal access to a nicely packaged reference tool. Oftentimes, librarian-created LibGuides primarily include lists

---

2 Paulo Freire and Myra Bergman Ramos, *Pedagogy of the Oppressed* (New York: Continuum, 1970).

3 Alison Hicks, "LibGuides: Pedagogy to Oppress?" *Hybrid Pedagogy*, April 16, 2015, http://www.hybridpedagogy.com/journal/libguides-pedagogy-to-oppress/.

4 Ibid.

5 Jon C. Giullian and Ernest A. Zitser, "Beyond LibGuides: The Past, Present, and Future of Online Research Guides," *Slavic & East European Information Resources* 16, no. 4 (October 2015): 170–80, doi:10.1080/15228886.2015.1094718, 171.

of resources that are behind a pay wall, making them inaccessible to anyone outside of the academic institution that hosts the guide. Users who find a LibGuide through an Internet search may not be able to access many of the resources they find listed. Furthermore, the authors call attention to the way that librarians who build guides are "treated by the educational institutions that employ them, relegating them to the ranks of service (rather than teaching) staff and mandating the use of Springshare's platform as a way of interacting with the university's 'customers'."[6] This trickles down through the library hierarchy when paraprofessional desk staff and student employees are asked to refer to LibGuides when helping learners at the reference desk.

These conversations encouraged me to look closely at my own LibGuides to identify strategies to transform them into egalitarian and democratic tools that reinforce my ideals as a feminist educator. As bell hooks writes in *Teaching to Transgress*, to share blueprints, as opposed to strategies, "would undermine the insistence that engaged pedagogy recognizes each classroom as different, that strategies must constantly be changed, invented, reconceptualized to address each new teaching experience."[7] In this chapter I will share some approaches that I took to address each unique instance in which I applied feminist pedagogy to LibGuides as a reference tool and highlight a few examples of others' guides that reinforce feminist pedagogy and inclusivity.

My Context

At the time of writing this chapter, I was employed at a branch library of a larger academic art and design institution that shares LibGuides across five international locations (including e-Learning). The combined libraries hosted 234 total LibGuides, including course, subject, topic, and internal guides. The vast majority of our guides are created by the research and instruction team or head librarians across all locations and are based on the subjects taught at the institution. Course guides are primarily used during one-shot information literacy instruction sessions but live online as a reference resource beyond the session.

---

6 Ibid, 175.

7 bell hooks, *Teaching to Transgress: Education as the Practice of Freedom* (New York: Routledge, 1994), 10.

The branch location I worked at has a combination reference and circulation desk model and MLS-holding librarians, circulation assistants, and student library assistants all staff the desk. While a librarian or circulation assistant is always available as "backup," student library assistants are empowered to help other learners who come to the desk with research questions. However, most of our library assistants, and even some of our professional staff, are not always comfortable answering in-depth research questions. This often results in referring those in need of help to the research librarian for a consultation.

The university has an extremely diverse student population, with 49 states and over 100 countries represented; the international student population at the branch campus is 25 percent. Several individuals come from cities and countries where libraries still rely on card catalogs or only print materials. Librarians are often not seen as educators and research experts, but mere attendants, and scholarship may be viewed differently altogether. Our domestic students are also racially diverse and demographically reflect the city in which this branch resides, Atlanta, Georgia.

Despite this high level of diversity, I observed little critical dialogue around race, sex, or class issues at our campus. This might be due to the fact that the institution is an industry-focused art and design school, but I would argue that critical information, visual, and digital literacy are key components of a well-rounded art and design education. Critical dialogue can support all learners as whole individuals in any discipline. Additionally, as artists and designers, just as with any information and content creators, these students hold a significant responsibility to understand how their work will contribute to the status quo or effect positive social change in the world for themselves and their communities. As educators, we must make room for this level of consciousness and push against the institutionalized art practice that has grown with the rise of the corporate university model.[8]

---

[8] Cathy Eisenhower and Dolsy Smith, "The Library as 'Stuck Place': Critical Pedagogy in the Corporate University," in *Critical Library Instruction: Theories and Methods*, ed. Maria T. Accardi, Emily Drabinski, and Alana Kumbier (Duluth, MN: Library Juice Press, 2009), 305–18.

Application of the Principles of Feminist Pedagogy to LibGuides

Webb and Allen's article "Feminist Pedagogy: Identifying Basic Principles" provides six key principles of feminist pedagogy: reformation of the relationship between professor and student, empowerment, building community, privileging voice, respecting diversity of personal experience, and challenging traditional pedagogical notions. I used these principles to help frame my self-evaluation and attempts at applying feminist pedagogy to LibGuide creation, use, and reference interactions.

The reformation of the relationship between professor and student. I aimed to build LibGuides that reflect our undergraduates' research process through fostering a democratic and collaborative relationship with the undergraduate, required courses, ENG123 (composition) and COMM105 (speech). I focused on these two courses because information literacy is built into the course objectives and outcomes. Students in these courses are expected to produce research papers and presentations on topics that interest them in order to explore creative and academic disciplines. Librarians typically provide a one-shot instruction session for these courses, as requested by faculty.

To share the power of teaching, I included some class-generated resources and content on the LibGuides. I used polleverywhere.com, a simple online polling tool that allows anyone to submit answers via their cell phones, to collect everyone's research topics (figure 1). In a separate poll we modeled keyword brainstorming (on one of the students' topics from the first poll) to show how content can be co-constructed in the classroom collaboratively, allowing students some ownership over the guide (figure 2). The classes could see their work and research process reflected in the guides as they used them later to complete their assignments independently, after our initial instruction session. Embedding the polls with student-generated content was meant to validate the learners' personal interests and highlight the value of each individual's ideas and thoughts.

For more in-depth instruction, I find Amanda Scull's work inspiring. She worked with an international education course to develop guides based on a literature review assignment and research. Students were asked to create a LibGuide in teams and each group was asked to evaluate the resources used in their literature review

The Feminist Reference Desk

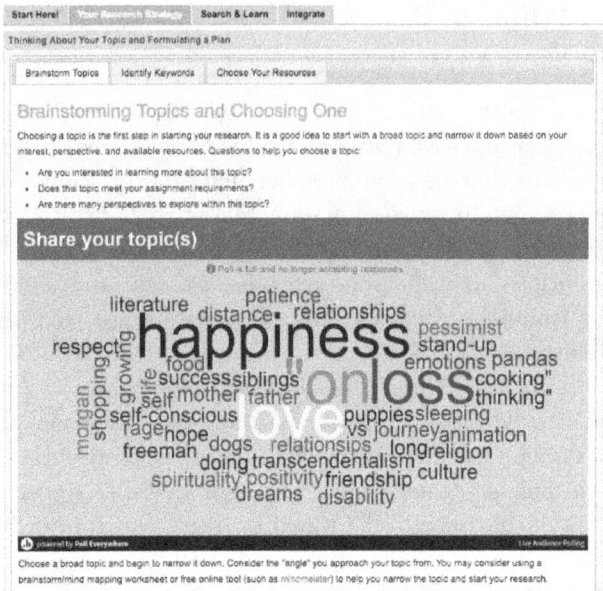

Fig. 1. *Screenshot from ENG123 LibGuide, illustrating class participation and topic brainstorming.*

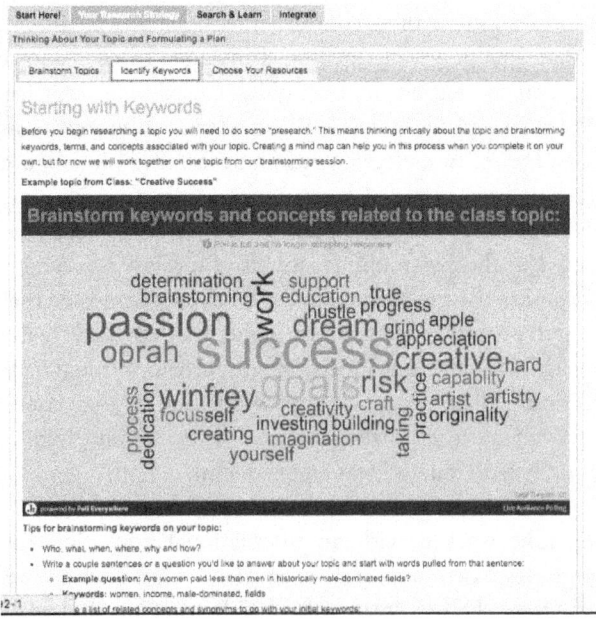

Fig. 2. *Screenshot from ENG123 LibGuide, illustrating class participation and keyword brainstorming for the topic "Creative Success."*

"for the most relevant and reliable sources—the sources that they would recommend to others conducting research on the same topic."[9] The groups were also asked to find nontraditional material for their LibGuide, such as images, videos, audio, and blogs and put care into the design of the pages.

Through collaboratively creating guides and problem posing or critiquing the content, guides become more relevant to learners. Librarians can avoid cognitive dissonance, or the inconsistency or disagreement among ideas (of what is of value to learners) by including students. The instructor may take on the role of guiding learners to discover and explore topics as their research process unfolds collectively. The practice of sharing the research process as a class can "help students learn to raise questions to gain further understanding of each others' perspectives and they can then ask students to marshal evidence to support their ideas. This helps students exercise critical inquiry and hone self-reflective skills."[10] During the courses I noted that many of the topics learners shared were related to affect, popular culture, and creativity and were less academic in nature. Given the range of topics put forth and through more in-depth group-created guides, learners could have the opportunity to consider the resource choices provided as they relate to the topic(s) at hand. Exploring the resources available and responding to the classroom discussion allows learners and instructors to negotiate what would be helpful in the guide and what does not foster learning and exploration. This process helped me be more mindful of who my community of learners are and how they like to learn, which Ruth Baker notes is important for LibGuide designers.[11]

However, there is no guarantee that individual learners using the guide on their own possess the intrinsic motivation (desire for mastery and meaning) one would need to engage with the research process in

---

9 Amanda Scull, "Fostering Student Engagement and Collaboration with the Library: Student Creation of LibGuides as a Research Assignment," *Reference Librarian* 55, no. 4 (October 2014), 321.

10 Alice Lai and Lilly Lu, "Integrating Feminist Pedagogy with Online Teaching: Facilitating Critiques of Patriarchal Visual Culture," *Visual Culture & Gender* 4 (January 2009), 61.

11 Ruth L. Baker, "Designing LibGuides as Instructional Tools for Critical Thinking and Effective Online Learning," *Journal of Library & Information Services in Distance Learning* 8, no. 3/4 (July 2014), 111.

a self-reflective way on their own. Many learners are still driven by the extrinsic motivation of grades and assignment completion because of the corporate and capitalist learning environment of higher education. Even the most feminist of class members have been conditioned to the effects of patriarchal education,[12] which rewards those who follow rubrics and rely on rationalism as opposed to trusting their own way of being, questioning, and learning within any given context.[13]

Empowerment

In my attempt at a more participatory and democratic use of LibGuides with ENG123 and COMM105 students, I made sure that the classes knew that they were contributing to guides that would be used by future sections, giving them the power usually reserved for instructors and librarians. Learners were more engaged throughout class as a result of this shared power. The guides had a significantly higher number of views than previously created course guides, possibly because learners had contributed and understood the guide's value.

In terms of developing the guides further, beyond the course guides mentioned above, I began discussing and reevaluating the LibGuides across our institution. I shared this task with the student library assistants, who typically provide reference help at our combined circulation desk. One question that I have been grappling with is how much should desk staff be expected to rely on guides? How does one empower them to rely on their knowledge of a subject or how to best help learners in need? Authors Webb and Allen provide helpful insight to these questions on education, and in this case training, by stating that, "education either functions as an instrument facilitating students' integration and conformity into the logic of the present system, or it becomes 'the practice of freedom' teaching men and women to deal critically and creatively with reality and to learn to participate in transforming their world."[14] Providing training that is also in line with these principles of feminist education can ensure teaching and learning as opposed to conformity.

---

12 Myria W. Allen Lynne M. Webb, "Feminist Pedagogy: Identifying Basic Principles.," *Academic Exchange Quarterly* 6 (2002): 67–72. 68.

13 Eisenhower and Smith, "The Library as 'Stuck Place'."

14 Lynne M. Webb, "Feminist Pedagogy." 68.

The library assistants, like many, are uniquely situated because they are students themselves and can provide insight into how they learn. They are empowered to answer reference questions and provide research help at the desk, peer to peer. One library assistant pointed out that she builds a rapport with other learners who come in seeking help by letting them know she is also a student and by taking an interest in them and their work. Some learners will accept help from a peer, while others will go straight to a research librarian based on the recommendation of their instructors, but by and large undergraduates at this institution are happy to get help right away, as opposed to wait for a consultation. The library assistants and I discussed the use of the guides and they shared that the desk staff rarely ever used guides in reference interactions. Through our conversations, the student assistants became more interested in how they might be able to use the guides to their benefit. I wanted to approach this conversation carefully and from a position of shared power. My goal was to encourage them to rely on their own intuition and teaching methods on the desk and when helping others, not leave them feeling like they "should" rely on the LibGuides without critical evaluation of the guides as a tool for reference interactions.

After our initial discussion, library assistants were to choose one guide from the many available and critique it by our next meeting. This open-ended assignment allowed each to rely on her unique knowledge of the subject she chose. Their desire to use the guides and to help others gave them motivation to provide high quality contributions to the guides. Each library assistant chose the subject for their respective majors and came back to the group with several ideas for improvements to the LibGuide. Some of the ideas and criticisms they shared overlapped with known issues to the LibGuides, such as there being "too many guides to even know where to start" and wanting "more instructional" content. Other ideas had not been considered by the librarians creating the guides, including providing a thesis tab for all subject guides as opposed to on the guide dedicated to graduate studies. This activity resulted in a lot of positive reinforcement and conversation about the differences between their disciplines and research needs and we agreed that having a student editor for each guide could keep them fresh and relevant. The students found it useful to evaluate the guides and reflect on one of the tools provided to them as learners and employees.

Building Community

One of the tenets of critical and feminist pedagogy is that knowledge is socially constructed and all should have the opportunity and ability to participate. Feminist educators can help make room for marginalized voices within this construction of shared knowledge where it doesn't already exist. Working with library assistants and learners in the classroom has inspired me to continue to move towards building a community around LibGuides creation as opposed to a top-down hierarchy. Ideally, this will foster more collaboration and respect for non-librarian voices within reference and online research help. Incorporating student and classroom-generated content and having student reviewers of guides makes this at least partly achievable. Inviting faculty and all levels of staff in the library to contribute to guides through creation, critique, and group decision-making regarding guide content opens new avenues for collaboration and learning. This level of "collaboration offers intrinsic and compelling rewards including superior work products, sounding boards for ideas, suggestions for improvement, as well as the confirmation and validation of a research community." [15] These initiatives can help create a more open environment with fewer barriers to both teaching and learning within the reference and LibGuide context.

Student and faculty groups on campus that focus on a particular topic could also be involved in guide creation. For example, our Academic Integrity Council of faculty members asked for assistance with compiling resources to help faculty address academic integrity in the classroom. As we discussed a new, more positive approach, we brainstormed activities that could help spark conversations around academic integrity and listed these resources on the internal guide. I initially developed the LibGuide for this group and provided some resources beyond the university's policy and procedures. Ultimately, it seemed appropriate for the group to develop the guide further. After a training session and a discussion among several committee members, I created editor accounts for them and they continued to build the guide on their own. As a community of contributors, with no one

---

[15] Lynne M. Webb, Kandi L. Walker, and Tamara S. Bollis, "Feminist Pedagogy in the Teaching of Research Methods," *International Journal of Social Research Methodology* 7, no. 5 (December 2004), 423, doi:10.1080/1364557032000119599.

person as the gatekeeper, resources are added based conversations and activities meant to empower all learners and educators.

Privileging the individual voice as a way of knowing

The practice of including the student voice could be pushed further by including learners in the process of building guides collaboratively, over time. This builds respect for the personal narrative, intuition, and experiential knowledge.

It seems more natural to privilege individual voices within the classroom, but doing so in a guide is challenging and needs to be explored further. By including collective brainstorming (such as with polleverywhere.com), sharing relevant personal experiences (such as providing a list of FAQs that students ask about the research process and answer for one another), and making decisions by consensus (as to what is included in a guide for specific classes), LibGuides can become more egalitarian and relevant to learning within each unique context.

Springshare recently released blogging and discussion tools with version 2.0. This may provide new opportunities for learners to share resources, openly critique resources on the guide, reflect on their process, and collaboratively come to conclusions on questions posed by others. However, contributors to both the blogging and discussion tools require account creation and email registration, which cannot be accomplished in a one-shot instruction session. There may be other creative uses to explore with these tools as another interactive feature to help privilege the individual voices of learners, but there are definite barriers to doing so in the way Springshare has developed their product.

Respect for diversity and personal experience

In addition to considering how interacting with guides empowers or disempowers reference desk staff, library assistants and librarians alike, conversations around LibGuides have led to the evaluation of the resources we promote as well. LibGuides, and librarians who create them, need to highlight resources that honor diversity of experience and background without falling into tokenism of marginalized groups. "Feminist forms of pedagogy cannot just be feminist in theory; the content of the learning must also be feminist for the pedagogy to have an impact."[16] This means including sources by and about women and historically marginalized populations to help raise consciousness about oppression can increase the impact of feminist perspectives in library instruction and reference. In order to avoid tokenism, it is important to also draw attention to race, sex, and class beyond just simply boasting about inclusion.[17] In order to model feminist perspectives on the guides, I incorporated examples of search queries and topics that would help raise awareness of feminist issues, such as the gender wage gap and LGBTQ issues; these search terms are embedded in the instructional portion of the guides for COMM 105 and ENG 123 for future use. I have also begun thinking of social issues that affect specific majors and industries. For example, lack of diversity in Hollywood and the #oscarssowhite movement could be included on the film and television guides and the ethics behind the fashion industry's working conditions for factory workers could be included on the Fashion guide. Many of these topics, of course, have search terms outside of the controlled vocabulary within library databases and catalogs. In-person reference interactions would be a good time to discuss language and raise awareness of the antiquated and harmful terminology of our systems, but addressing this issue in the LibGuide platform may be more challenging.

In recent years several librarians have raised questions of the neutrality of information, libraries, and education. Accardi states that, "Education is always political; it does not take place in a neutral vacuum."[18] A guide that illustrates the political nature of information and education is Nicole Pagowsky and Niamh Wallace's LibGuide on the events of the shooting of Michael Brown in Ferguson, Missouri. The guide successfully raises awareness of racial injustice and pushes back against the idea of information and library neutrality. On the topic of what was included in the "Black Lives Matter" guide the creators wrote:

> The guide grew organically–as it was shared, we incorporated links as requested, from colleagues in the library, and from faculty and staff on campus. We set out to collect a variety of resources—news, statistics, scholarship, literature, blogs—on not only police violence,

---

16 Accardi, *Feminist Pedagogy for Library Instruction*, 79.

17 hooks, *Teaching to Transgress*, 38.

18 Accardi, *Feminist Pedagogy for Library Instruction*, 68.

but on racial injustice more broadly, from a variety of perspectives, particularly those that are not as frequently heard.[19]

Topical guides, such as this one, can focus on social justice and feminist issues; more librarians are starting to create similar guides on various topics. The LibGuide "Incorporating Indigenous Knowledges Guide," from the Charles Darwin University in Australia, is a topical guide created to help instructors integrate Indigenous teaching and learning methods into their classrooms, which helps Indigenous people maintain their culture and push back against assimilation and colonialism.[20] After Beyoncé released her visual album, "Lemonade," Jenny Ferretti, Maryland Institute College of Art's Digital Initiatives Librarian, created a guide that unpacked the album's influences and references using books, articles, and popular websites.[21] She has also created a guide to "Understanding Civic Unrest in Baltimore 1968-2015," which she also connects and attributes to her interest in critical librarianship, empowerment, and social issues.[22] Bank Street College of Education Librarians provides several great examples of topical guides relevant to teacher education and training including: "Resources for Families of Incarcerated Parents," "Coping with Tragedy," "Feminist Resources for Education," "LGBT Resources," and "Resources for Families of Gender-Variant and Transgender Children." All of these guides highlight issues that are feminist concerns. They provide a starting point for exploration during a reference interaction or self-guided reference while also inviting suggestions and contributions. Each guide also has a particular context to consider—whether that guide is primarily created to support

---

19 Nicole Pagowsky and Niamh Wallace, "Black Lives Matter! Shedding Library Neutrality Rhetoric for Social Justice," *College & Research Libraries News* 76, no. 4 (April 1, 2015): 196–214.

20 Payi Linda Ford et al., "The Incorporating Indigenous Knowledge LibGuide : Charles Darwin University Embedding Australian Aboriginal and Torres Strait Islander Knowledge, Culture and Language," *Australian Academic & Research Libraries* 45, no. 2 (June 2014): 111–20, doi:10.1080/00048623.2014.910859.

21 Jennifer Ferretti, "Art Is Information, Part I: Exploring the Research Methodologies of Artists in Beyoncé's 'Lemonade' #libeyrianship, Other Things That Can Be Gleaned from Formation:," *Medium*, April 29, 2016, https://medium.com/@CityThatReads/art-is-information-part-i-9d0cbc35907c#.8xya3gcbr.

22 Jennifer Ferretti and Sian Evans, "#libeyrianship: Pop Culture and #critlib in Information Literacy Programs," *ACRLog*, May 23, 2016, http://acrlog.org/tag/popular-culture/.

art and design students in understanding how a work of feminist art was created (Ex: the "Lemonade" LibGuide) or whether it is to provide future educators with tools to teach in a way that honors their students' affect and personal experiences (Ex: the Bank Street guides).

As I mentioned in my context description, I worked with a diverse student body. Most of our international population participate in an ESL program throughout their education, but they may still struggle to make sense of how to use the library. The services provided may be new and many have limited or no prior information literacy training. I created a "Guide for International Students" based on the belief that all learners have the right to be provided access to resources and education in their primary language. It broadly covers the topic of understanding the library, includes a glossary of terms, language resources, an overview of library organization, how to start the research process (and get help), academic integrity, and local culture for each campus. Each page of the guide contains a Google Translate widget; this is the only space on the university's site where international students are able to get information in any language other than English. Though there are major issues with the translation tool, many have been thrilled when they first see the guide during orientation or instruction sessions and despite these issues the guide is heavily used.

Challenging traditional views

The selection of LibGuide material and resources is not neutral when done by a single person. That person's experiences and bias will factor in as much as the institution's access to paid databases and resources. LibGuides make information resources seem neutral in the manner they are presented, without transparency about how they were selected, evaluated, and prioritized. Including multiple people in the guide creation can foster more egalitarian LibGuide practices and applications across subject, course, and topic guides. Guide maintenance should be an iterative process with frequent reevaluation so that librarians can ensure that the guides reflect multiple perspectives and ideas as they emerge and evolve. James Elmborg argues that "unfortunately, many librarians today still consider their knowledge the source of their professional power,"[23]

---

23 James K. Elmborg, "Teaching at the Desk: Toward a Reference Pedagogy," *Portal: Libraries and the Academy* 2, no. 3 (2002): 462, doi:10.1353/pla.2002.0050.

but by including our students, staff, and faculty in guide creation, teaching, and learning we can start to chip away at that mentality and challenge traditional power structures in higher education.

Thoughts on LibGuides in Reference Interactions

The number one goal of any reference interaction is to encourage exploration of the topic that the learner is interested in. However, many students expect a simple and straightforward answer because they are used to the banking model of education. In *Feminist Pedagogy for Library Instruction,* Maria Accardi states that "some students at the reference desk would just prefer that I give them the needed call number rather than turning the computer screen to them to demonstrate exactly how I found the call number,"[24] which is a common scenario for desk staff. Kate Adler argues that reference dialogues "cannot be reduced to a mere 'depositing of ideas' but rather it is an act of creation, a generative space that requires and develops critical thinking."[25] James Elmborg also adds, "whenever we answer a student's question without teaching the student how we answered it or why we answered it as we did, we are essentially taking the question away from the student, thereby creating a dependency in that student that undermines rather than strengthens the learning process."[26] It takes time and care to explain a process or encourage critical thinking and exploration. The current rendition of the LibGuide platform makes this student-centered approach to reference interactions and Guide creation a challenge, but it is still achievable.

Overall, the library staff and library assistants I worked with throughout this evaluation understand the idea of guiding others through finding what they need, as opposed to just providing an answer, and the value of proactively asking questions to help draw out pertinent details that help both parties learn. The library assistants noted how the use of subject LibGuides could be a good resource to

---

24 Accardi, *Feminist Pedagogy for Library Instruction,* 48.

25 Kate Adler, "Radical Purpose: The Critical Reference Dialogue at a Progressive Urban College," *Urban Library Journal* 19, no. 1 (December 17, 2013), http://ojs.gc.cuny.edu/index.php/urbanlibrary/article/view/1395.

26 Elmborg, "Teaching at the Desk." 459.

start more general inquiries but the resources may not be relevant for specific questions. One library assistant commented that the guides might hinder reference transactions because "unless I know what's there, I don't know if it will help other students," so it could be a dead end for the conversation.

Several library assistants and staff alike expressed that too much information on the guide becomes overwhelming, even to them, so they felt that the guides would also be overwhelming to the majority of learners. Elmborg writes that "without imparting specialized knowledge to our students we may be overlooked as teachers, and the role of the library is to support the teaching mission of their institution. Reference teaching holds a unique position within the learning environment, in that it allows for library staff to act as 'coaches and collaborators,'" [27] but relying too much on the "kitchen sink" approach of LibGuides made by one librarian may simply perpetuate harmful teaching models, such as banking, during reference and self-guided research. A better approach is to construct meaningful, contextual guides that many have a chance to contribute to over time.

Elmborg also argues that in reference work we need to "understand the ways humans use information, we need to focus on the internal intellectual processes of our patrons rather than on the organizational, conceptual structures of the library."[28] I would make the same case for LibGuides as self-guided learning tools or tools used to aid in reference interactions. The guides that I have developed for COMM105 and ENG123 are both tutorial style guides, with more emphasis on the research process and less on the resources available to learners. Should these be used in reference, both the learner and the desk staff would be guided through the process of finding relevant information without being spoon fed any particular books, articles, or websites. This approach creates an opportunity for more collaborative learning, which, as Lynn Webb writes, assumes that "learning occurs through relationships and dialogue, and collaboratively learning assumes the learner to be active in her or his own meaning-making and to be a knower of her or his own right."[29]

---

27 Elmborg, "Teaching at the Desk," 463.

28 Ibid, 467.

29 Lynne M. Webb, "Feminist Pedagogy," 68.

Final Reflections and More Questions

It is important to remember that Springshare provides a product designed around aggregating a university's "assets" for their "customers," not a tool designed around feminist pedagogy. If librarians want a tool that works with our pedagogical approaches and within our specific contexts then we will need to work with Springshare and push for change in how the platform itself is designed and implemented.

LibGuides are often developed based on a common checklist that focuses on the style, aesthetic, writing, and maintenance of guide links and information. This has resulted in guides that are static and rely primarily on the databases and books found in the library providing the guides. Emphasizing the process of locating, evaluating, and integrating information in an anti-oppressive way is a start to building better guides. From a pedagogical standpoint,[30] particularly a feminist or critical perspective, LibGuides seem to be no more valuable as tools than any other platform available if they are not leveraged in a way that challenges their typical use and exclusive nature. "When we design LibGuides around the key search tools on a topic, we isolate research from the reading and writing processes,"[31] and this reinforces oppressive power structures in higher education.

Several new ideas and questions emerged as I worked to apply feminist principles to LibGuide creation and use: how do we reconcile the assumption that learners "understand how to do research and all librarians simply need to do is to provide access to links to the appropriate resources"[32] with the assumption that they do not have effective and valid ways of researching and learning outside of our ideas of research practices? How do we honor their way of knowing through an overly simplistic tool seemingly designed to rely on the banking model? Research is a messy process; how can guides be developed to reflect that or to help demystify the process? How can LibGuides reinforce reference interactions that are meant to

---

30 Aaron Bowen, "LibGuides and Web-Based Library Guides in Comparison: Is There a Pedagogical Advantage?," *Journal of Web Librarianship* 8, no. 2 (April 2014): 147–71, doi: 10.1080/19322909.2014.903709.

31 Hicks, "LibGuides."

32 Baker, "Designing LibGuides as Instructional Tools for Critical Thinking and Effective Online Learning," 110.

be authentic learning opportunities? These are questions for future exploration as students, staff, faculty, and librarians continue working with the LibGuide platform within our unique contexts. LibGuides are currently part of the "librarians' tool belt" of sorts, and it is up to our profession to lead the efforts to change the way we build guides for and with our communities.

Bibliography

Accardi, Maria T. *Feminist Pedagogy for Library Instruction.* Series on Gender and Sexuality in Information Studies, Number 3. Sacramento, California: Library Juice Press, 2013.

Adler, Kate. "Radical Purpose: The Critical Reference Dialogue at a Progressive Urban College." *Urban Library Journal* 19, no. 1 (December 17, 2013). http://ojs.gc.cuny.edu/index.php/urbanlibrary/article/view/1395.

Baker, Ruth L. "Designing LibGuides as Instructional Tools for Critical Thinking and Effective Online Learning." *Journal of Library & Information Services in Distance Learning* 8, no. 3/4 (July 2014): 107–17. doi:10.1080/1533290X.2014.944423.

Bowen, Aaron. "LibGuides and Web-Based Library Guides in Comparison: Is There a Pedagogical Advantage?" *Journal of Web Librarianship* 8, no. 2 (April 2014): 147–71. doi:10.1080/19322909.2014.903709.

Eisenhower, Cathy, and Dolsy Smith. 2009. "The Library as 'Stuck Place': Critical Pedagogy in the Corporate University." In *Critical Library Instruction: Theories and Methods,* edited by Maria T. Accardi, Emily Drabinski, and Alana Kumbier, 305–18. Duluth, MN: Library Juice Press.

Elmborg, James K. "Teaching at the Desk: Toward a Reference Pedagogy." *Portal: Libraries and the Academy* 2, no. 3 (2002): 455–64. doi:10.1353/pla.2002.0050.

Ferretti, Jennifer, and Sian Evans. 2016. "#libeyrianship: Pop Culture and #critlib in Information Literacy Programs." *ACRLog.* May 23. http://acrlog.org/tag/popular-culture/.

Ferretti, Jennifer. 2016. "Art Is Information, Part I: Exploring the Research Methodologies of Artists in Beyoncé's 'Lemonade' #libeyrianship, Other Things That Can Be Gleaned from Formation:." *Medium.* April 29. https://medium.com/@CityThatReads/art-is-information-part-i-9d0cbc35907c#.8xya3gcbr.

Ford, Payi Linda, John Prior, Barbara Coat, and Lyndall Warton. "The Incorporating Indigenous Knowledge LibGuide : Charles Darwin University Embedding Australian Aboriginal and Torres Strait Islander Knowledge, Culture and Language." *Australian Academic & Research Libraries* 45, no. 2 (June 2014): 111–20. doi:10.1080/00048623.2014.910859.

Freire, Paulo and Myra Bergman Ramos. *Pedagogy of the Oppressed.* New York: Continuum, 1970.

Giullian, Jon C., and Ernest A. Zitser. "Beyond LibGuides: The Past, Present, and Future of Online Research Guides." *Slavic & East European Information Resources* 16, no. 4 (October 2015): 170–80. doi:10.1080/15228886.2015.1094718.

Hicks, Alison. "LibGuides: Pedagogy to Oppress?" *Hybrid Pedagogy*, April 16, 2015. http://www.hybridpedagogy.com/journal/libguides-pedagogy-to-oppress/.

hooks, bell. *Teaching to Transgress: Education as the Practice of Freedom.* New York: Routledge, 1994.

Lai, Alice and Lilly Lu. "Integrating Feminist Pedagogy with Online Teaching: Facilitating Critiques of Patriarchal Visual Culture." *Visual Culture & Gender* 4 (January 2009): 58–68.

Lynne M. Webb, Myria W. Allen. "Feminist Pedagogy: Identifying Basic Principles." *Academic Exchange Quarterly* 6 (2002): 67–72.

Pagowsky, Nicole, and Niamh Wallace. "Black Lives Matter! Shedding Library Neutrality Rhetoric for Social Justice." *College & Research Libraries News* 76, no. 4 (April 1, 2015): 196–214.

Scull, Amanda. "Fostering Student Engagement and Collaboration with the Library: Student Creation of LibGuides as a Research Assignment." *Reference Librarian* 55, no. 4 (October 2014): 318–27. doi:10.1080/02763877.2014.929076.

Webb, Lynne M., Kandi L. Walker, and Tamara S. Bollis. "Feminist Pedagogy in the Teaching of Research Methods." *International Journal of Social Research Methodology* 7, no. 5 (December 2004): 415–28. doi:10.1080/1364557032000119599.

Exploring a Feminist Disability Studies Reference Desk

Brian A. Sullivan and Malia Willey

Theories and practices related to feminism and disability studies can inform and transform the reference desk of the academic library. Feminist disability studies pedagogy enables educators to "explore ways in which society has or has not been constructed physically and socially for particular bodies, minds, and emotions."[1] As a part of our social and educational landscape, reference desks may privilege particular bodies, minds, and emotions. Feminism and disability studies offer a lens for critiquing and changing the physical and social constructions of reference services. Practices related to universal design serve as an important beginning for creating more inclusive environments for all learners. However, accessibility alone is not enough. As critical efforts, feminism and disability studies challenge educators to go beyond universal design to exhibit a transformative pedagogy that expands our students' perception of the world. We explore how feminist disability approaches, such as feminist standpoint theory and disability sitpoint theory, the ethic of caring, and concept of interdependence, empower us to imagine different forms reference services might take.

Access is a prevalent word in the lexicon of libraries, and librarians strive to make their reference desks accessible. Accessibility promotes equality and inclusion, which aligns with the values of

---

1 Kristina R. Knoll, "Feminist Disability Studies Pedagogy," *Feminist Teacher* 19, no. 2 (January 2009): 124.

feminism and disability studies. One method for enabling access is anticipating the diverse needs of library users through universal design. Universal design began as an architectural practice that aims to make spaces as accessible as possible from the start. Diversity in access is anticipated by incorporating accommodating features, such as curb cuts and ramps, into the blueprints. Librarians can use strategies related to universal design to create reference spaces that better accommodate diverse learners and improve accessibility for everyone. Physical and virtual environments should be designed to address the variety of users who seek help at the library. Reference desks should welcome a spectrum of bodies and minds. Flexibility in the structure, configuration, and furniture of the desk lets users easily adapt the surroundings to their needs or preferences. Consultation areas that allow for focused conversations with a librarian can benefit those who excel in less distracting environments.[2] In addition to the physical space, the online presence of the reference desk can be made more accessible through the incorporation of accessibility standards, implementation of sound design, and attention to format.[3]

Pedagogical approaches that use universal design strategies, such as Universal Design for Learning [UDL], go beyond individually meeting "reasonable accommodations" to create more accessible learning experiences for all students. UDL plans for diverse learners by incorporating multiple means of representation, engagement, and action and expression.[4] These three UDL principles respectively represent the what, why, and how of learning.[5] Instructors can use varied materials, instruction approaches, and learning activities to facilitate the different learning needs and preferences of students. Several librarians have detailed their experiences in using pedagogy

---

2 Clark Nall, "Academic Libraries and the Principles of Universal Design for Learning," *College & Research Libraries News* 76, no. 7 (July 2015): 375.

3 Jessamyn West, "Accessibility Is More Than Curb Cuts and ALT Tags," *Computers in Libraries* 36, no. 1 (January 2016): 22.

4 "UDL Guidelines—Version 2.0," *National Center on Universal Design for Learning*, last modified July 7, 2014, http://www.udlcenter.org/aboutudl/udlguidelines.

5 "About Universal Design for Learning," *CAST*, accessed May 6, 2016, http://www.cast.org/our-work/about-udl.html.

informed by universal design in the library classroom.[6] Educators minimize the institutional barriers to student learning through designing accessible learning spaces and curricula as a matter of course.

The three principles of UDL provide further opportunities for everyone to learn at the reference desk. Multiple means of representation of materials in formats and media present more ways to obtain information. Providing handouts, both in print and electronically, anticipates diverse learners. Supplemental audio, visual, and interactive elements in online learning objects can further stimulate learning. Tutorials featuring audio should include subtitles and transcripts. Librarians can promote multiple means of engagement with the reference desk through in-person interactions, text and video chat, phone, and email.[7] Multiple means of action and expression are critical at the reference desk for creating an interactive learning experience. This emphasis on interaction dovetails with the aim of feminist pedagogy to create a collaborative and cooperative classroom.[8] To create such an environment, librarians should guide students through the process of answering their questions through generative conversation, instead of simply handing students the answers. Opportunities for students to express their information needs and participate in their research process should be incorporated throughout a reference interaction. Librarians can encourage students to navigate research tools, brainstorm search terms, or select appropriate subject terms. Universal design advances the reference desk as an accessible and feminist space for shared learning.

While the application of universal design improves accessibility, it is not an end point for altering our notion of the reference desk. The practices of universal design may serve as a starting point for re-conceptualizing

---

6 Ted Chodock and Elizabeth Dolinger, "Applying Universal Design to Information Literacy: Teaching Students Who Learn Differently at Landmark College," *Reference & User Services Quarterly* 49, no. 1 (2009): 24-32; Ying Zhong, "Universal Design for Learning (UDL) in Library Instruction," *College & Undergraduate Libraries* 19, no. 1 (January 2012): 33-45; and Katy Kavanagh Webb and Jeanne Hoover, "Universal Design for Learning (UDL) in the Academic Library," *College & Research Libraries* 76, no. 4 (May 2015): 537-53.

7 Nall, 374-75.

8 Maria T. Accardi, *Feminist Pedagogy for Library Instruction* (Sacramento, CA: Library Juice, 2013), 40-41.

a more inclusive reference desk, but it does not intentionally address the ingrained social and cultural barriers to inclusion. Julia R. Johnson appeals, "It is not enough for educators to create accessible curricula and to create inclusive learning environments. Our curriculum should take us someplace better—someplace more humane and just—someplace in which the material and discursive practices of exclusion are challenged in our efforts to include."[9] Feminist disability studies pedagogy calls for the educator, including the reference librarian, to intentionally foster social and cultural change. Below, we explore how feminist standpoint theory and disability sitpoint theory, the ethic of caring, and the concept of interdependence inspires us to re-envision reference as a transformative endeavor.

Both feminism and disability studies place a value on the importance of different perspectives. Feminist standpoint theory examines insights of persons from subordinate groups.[10] The subsequent conception of disability sitpoint theory considers the knowledge of those whose bodies are perceived as incongruent with their environments.[11] People with disabilities, like other minority groups, can offer alternate viewpoints because of their marginalized position within society. To gain a more varied perspective, individuals with diverse identities and abilities should be consulted as libraries create new spaces and services. As librarians interact with students at the reference desk, it is important not to presume that librarians know what is the best way for each individual student to learn. Instead of relying on official documentation, students with disabilities should be considered the best source on their condition.[12] Paying attention to the affective dimensions of learning creates an environment where students may feel comfortable sharing their learning needs or preferences. Likewise, the feminist ethic of caring encourages librarians to honor the voice of each student through

---

9 Julia Johnson, "Universal Instructional Design and Critical (Communication) Pedagogy: Strategies for Voice, Inclusion, and Social Justice/Change," *Equity and Excellence in Education* 37, no. 2 (June 1, 2004): 146.

10 Anita Silvers, "Feminist Perspectives on Disability," in *The Stanford Encyclopedia of Philosophy*, ed. Edward N. Zalta, sec. 3. Last modified February 17, 2015, http://plato.stanford.edu/archives/spr2015/entries/feminism-disability.

11 Rosemarie Garland-Thomson, "Integrating Disability, Transforming Feminist Theory," *NWSA Journal* 14, no. 3 (Fall 2002): 20-21.

12 Heather Mole, "A US Model for Inclusion of Disabled Students in Higher Education Settings," *Widening Participation & Lifelong Learning* 14, no. 3 (December 2012): 73.

listening.[13] In our experience, something as simple as asking students if they have a preference in the format of materials can result in students sharing their individual learning styles. As the conversation progresses, we find it helpful to ask students if they are comfortable with moving on to the next part of the question or how they are feeling about the research process. These moments create an opportunity for students to articulate their individual thoughts beyond a librarian providing an answer.

Interdependence is a concern of feminism and disability studies. In conversation with Judith Butler, disability activist Sunaura Taylor comments, "Somehow disabled people are perceived as more dependent, when in actuality we are all interdependent, that is, dependent on different structures and on each other."[14] Both feminism and disability studies recognize that individuals rely on the knowledge and care of others. Interdependence thwarts the neoliberal notion that independence, including independent learning, is inherently more valuable to society. Librarians can further demonstrate the ethic of caring and exemplify interdependence during the reference interaction by acknowledging and practicing reciprocity. Students bring their own background knowledge and feelings to the reference desk. When librarians and students mutually engage in a conversation about the research process, the experience and expertise of both the student and the teacher is valued. Enabling students to express how they feel about their progress shows that the librarian cares about the intellectual and emotional growth of the individual student.

Peer tutoring is another opportunity for cultivating and promoting interdependence at the reference desk. Academic libraries have a long history of employing students to provide additional reference assistance, and now libraries have begun to adopt peer tutoring programs for the purpose of collaborative learning.[15] The relative

---

13 Accardi, *Feminist Pedagogy*, 44.

14 Judith Butler and Sunaura Taylor, "Interdependence," in *Examined Life: Excursions with Contemporary Thinkers*, ed. Astra Taylor (New York: New Press, 2009), 187.

15 Brett B. Bodemer, "They CAN and They SHOULD: Undergraduates Providing Peer Reference and Instruction," *College & Research Libraries* 75, no. 2 (March 2014): 162-178; Allison Faix, "Peer Reference Revisited: Evolution of a Peer-reference Model," *Reference Services Review* 42, no. 2 (April 2014): 305-319; and Mary Ann O'Kelly et al., "Building a Peer-Learning Service for Students in an Academic Library," *portal: Libraries & The Academy* 15, no. 1 (January 2015): 163-82.

parity of the students allows them to more easily communicate ideas with one another and come to an understanding together.[16] Students are taught and mentored by librarians to provide research help for their fellow peers. Traits of effective peer tutors include the affective qualities of nurturing, encouraging, and counseling.[17] Librarians who work with a peer consultant program at Grand Valley State University emphasize, "Training is designed to instill confidence in the ability to help, even if specific information literacy skills still need development. Deep engagement with peers is the priority."[18] The emotional and social process of learning is key in peer tutoring. From the perspective of feminism and disability studies, this prioritization of meaningful exchange between students reinforces that learning is interdependent. It is especially promising that the peer tutoring model encourages the ethic of caring between students.

The reference desk is an opportunity for librarians to create a more equal learning space. Maria T. Accardi, the editor of this book, has advocated that the marginal role of the library within the academy actually positions librarians to be critical and creative educators.[19] This is particularly true in the context of disability in light of feminism. Academic libraries must certainly meet the letter of the law in terms of accessibility, but librarians are positioned to go beyond the "reasonable accommodations" of the standard classroom. Libraries can start to realize inclusive and transformative possibilities as librarians begin to explore what forms the reference desk might take when modeled after a feminist disability perspective.

---

16 Bodemer, 163.

17 Bodemer, 164.

18 Mary Ann O'Kelly et al., 168.

19 Maria T. Accardi, "Teaching Against the Grain: Critical Assessment in the Library Classroom," in *Critical Library Instruction: Theories and Methods*, ed. Maria T. Accardi, Emily Drabinski, and Alana Kumbier (Duluth, MN: Library Juice Press, 2010), 252, 262; and Accardi, *Feminist Pedagogy*, 69.

BIBLIOGRAPHY

"About Universal Design for Learning." *CAST.* Accessed May 6, 2016. http://www.cast.org/our-work/about-udl.html.

Accardi, Maria T. *Feminist Pedagogy for Library Instruction.* Sacramento, CA: Library Juice, 2013.

Accardi, Maria T. "Teaching Against the Grain: Critical Assessment in the Library Classroom." In *Critical Library Instruction: Theories and Methods*, edited by Maria T. Accardi, Emily Drabinski, and Alana Kumbier, 251-64. Duluth, MN: Library Juice Press, 2010.

Bodemer, Brett B. "They CAN and They SHOULD: Undergraduates Providing Peer Reference and Instruction." *College & Research Libraries* 75, no. 2 (March 2014): 162-78.

Butler, Judith and Sunaura Taylor. "Interdependence" In *Examined Life: Excursions with Contemporary Thinkers*, edited by Astra Taylor, 185-213. New York: New Press, 2009.

Chodock, Ted, and Elizabeth Dolinger. "Applying Universal Design to Information Literacy: Teaching Students Who Learn Differently at Landmark College." *Reference & User Services Quarterly* 49, no. 1 (2009): 24-32.

Faix, Allison. "Peer Reference Revisited: Evolution of a Peer-reference Model." *Reference Services Review* 42, no. 2 (April 2014): 305-19.

Garland-Thomson, Rosemarie. "Integrating Disability, Transforming Feminist Theory." *NWSA Journal* 14, no. 3 (Fall 2002): 1-32.

Johnson, Julia. "Universal Instructional Design and Critical (Communication) Pedagogy: Strategies for Voice, Inclusion, and Social Justice/Change." *Equity and Excellence in Education* 37, no. 2 (June 1, 2004): 145-53.

Knoll, Kristina R. "Feminist Disability Studies Pedagogy." *Feminist Teacher* 19, no. 2 (January 2009): 122-33.

Mole, Heather. "A US Model for Inclusion of Disabled Students in Higher Education Settings." *Widening Participation & Lifelong Learning* 14, no. 3 (December 2012): 62-86.

Nall, Clark. "Academic Libraries and the Principles of Universal Design for Learning." *College & Research Libraries News* 76, no. 7 (July 2015): 374-75.

O'Kelly, Mary Ann, Julie Garrison, Brian Merry, and Jennifer Torreano. "Building a Peer-Learning Service for Students in an Academic Library." *portal: Libraries & The Academy* 15, no. 1 (January 2015): 163-82.

Schroeder, Robert, and Christopher V. Hollister. "Librarians' Views on Critical Theories and Critical Practices." Behavioral & Social Sciences Librarian 33, no. 2 (April 2014): 91–119.

Silvers, Anita. "Feminist Perspectives on Disability." In *The Stanford Encyclopedia of Philosophy*, edited by Edward N. Zalta. Last modified February 17, 2015, http://plato.stanford.edu/archives/spr2015/entries/feminism-disability.

"UDL Guidelines—Version 2.0." *National Center on Universal Design for Learning*. Last modified July 31, 2014. http://www.udlcenter.org/aboutudl/udlguidelines.

Webb, Katy Kavanagh, and Jeanne Hoover. "Universal Design for Learning (UDL) in the Academic Library: A Methodology for Mapping Multiple Means of Representation in Library Tutorials." *College & Research Libraries* 76, no. 4 (May 2015): 537-53.

West, Jessamyn. "Accessibility Is More Than Curb Cuts and ALT Tags." *Computers in Libraries* 36, no. 1 (January 2016): 22-24.

Zhong, Ying. "Universal Design for Learning (UDL) in Library Instruction." *College & Undergraduate Libraries* 19, no. 1 (January 2012): 33-45.

LIS Graduate Student Workers, Feminist Pedagogy, and the Reference Desk: Praxis and a Narrative

Raina Bloom

Where We Begin

I say the same thing, nearly word for word, every time we interview a prospective graduate student worker. The staff members in the room introduce ourselves, I refer to our library as a "teaching library," and then I say -

> We put the people in the position that you're applying for in an interesting spot. We ask them to embody the teaching mission of the library by working with novice researchers at our information desk. At the same time, we see the position as a constant learning experience and do a lot of teaching, mentoring, and support of the people in it. It's an interesting tension -

I'm usually making a gesture with my hands at this point, suggestive of an object being acted on by two opposing forces, holding it in balance.

> - We want this position to be as much like real professional experience as we can make it. And that includes this interview. We're going to ask you the same kinds of questions that are asked in professional-level academic librarian interviews. We know you haven't started library school yet, but we're interested in your thought process. If you have questions or need clarification, please don't hesitate to ask, okay? Let's start with question one:
>
> Why did you decide to become a librarian?

A Consideration of LIS Literature

In the library literature, it is evident that much thought and planning has gone into the training and role of student workers at academic library reference desks. Writing and research have been done on the design of student work opportunities at the reference or information desk and the design and delivery of such programs.[a] Woodward assessed the performance of students on the reference desk at the University of Illinois in Urbana-Champaign, discovering that, with adequate training and integration into library staff culture, graduate student workers can attain a level of accuracy and reliability on par with a professional reference librarian.[b] Nahl obtained similar results in a pre- and post-test study of fieldwork students, finding that they were able to score 85% on a skills and information test, where their librarian colleagues scored 91%.[c]

The literature also reflects an interest in the perceived quality of graduate student workers' experience in academic libraries and the relevance of said experience to their eventual professional goals. For example, Hoffmann and Berg surveyed a group of Canadian library school students engaging in service learning experiences across a variety of departments and found that four themes emerged in the students' observations—the relationship between theory and practice, the importance of training outside of the LIS classroom, the authenticity of the experience, and the importance of an equal relationship with professional librarians.[d]

If librarians charged with the training of graduate student workers begin with the supposition that we want to develop future colleagues,[1] and not simply train cheap or free labor to fill out a desk schedule, we must ask ourselves what that means. What is a reference librarian? What is her function? Undeniably, as suggested above, one important function is to accurately and reliably respond to patron inquiries, but we want more than that for early-career professionals. We should want to cultivate a reflective way of thinking and being a professional in a library that can guide practice more effectively

---

1 Cheers to that! I want to be seen as a professional-in-training, not just a warm body at the desk. – Angie Schiappacasse

than a mere understanding of policy, procedure, and resources.² A consideration of the provocation of a reflective, engaged mindset is lacking in LIS literature.

Ball connects practicums and service learning experiences in LIS to the broader concepts of experiential and service learning, citing Dewey, Freire, and Donald Schön, among others. Ball writes that "service learning provides a much richer experience than traditional class work because it enables students' self-examination and personal growth through civic engagement."ᵉ If we want to take full advantage of the opportunity that hands-on learning affords library school students, even as we financially compensate them for their time, we require a method, a path that leads us past the strictly pragmatic.

Feminist pedagogies are an appropriate, even ideal, method for encouraging and supporting the self-reflection and self-awareness we hope for in early-career academic librarians. Feminist pedagogies are a method and a worldview with flexible boundaries, but we can locate some common threads. In a literature review on feminist teaching in multiple settings and at multiple grade levels, Webb, Allen, and Walker frame their analysis with Shrewsbury's assertion that feminist pedagogy is "a theory about the teaching/learning process that guides our choice of classroom practices by providing criteria to evaluate specific educational strategies in terms of the desired goals and outcomes."ᶠ While this could be said of most, if not all, pedagogical methods, Webb, Allen, and Walker identify six common themes specific to feminist pedagogy in their literature review: reformation of the relationship between professor and student, empowerment, building community, privileging the individual voice as a way of knowing, respect for diversity of personal experience, and challenging traditional views.ᵍ

For our purposes, and with the support of other thinkers and doers in feminist teaching, we will combine and reduce these themes to three guiding concepts – an interest in and awareness of power/empowerment, the value of lived and past learning experiences, and an awareness of and willingness to interrogate systems of domination and control that affect learning.

---

2 It is pretty great when a supervisor encourages you to remind a patron desperate for a reserve item about the library's handy book scanners rather than the vagaries of IP law.
– Samantha Link

Using the example of the emerging, increasingly conscious feminist teaching method employed by myself and my colleague, Trisha Prosise, at College Library at the University of Wisconsin–Madison, I will provide concrete examples of what feminist pedagogies for graduate student workers look like in action. Graduate student workers from College Library, past and present, will comment upon, support, and complicate these examples in the footnotes. Given their number, their busy lives, and my inability to provide financial compensation for their work here, I put forth footnoting as a method by which they could be heard without having to commit an excess of time that they can neither financially nor logistically afford, and they concurred with the suggestion.

About College Library

College Library is one of approximately forty libraries on the campus of the University of Wisconsin-Madison. It is the undergraduate library for the University of Wisconsin-Madison General Library System and the only twenty-four hour library on campus. It was established as part of the post-World War II undergraduate library movement in the United States and has maintained that focus since it opened in September, 1971. Described in an internal, collaboratively written document, College Library's mission is, in part, facilitating "discovery and learning by creating a welcoming environment for all, especially those new to academic research." The mission concludes, " . . . through a strong sense of community and a deep commitment to undergraduate education, College Library promotes an atmosphere of inclusion and independence that fosters lifelong learning." Though the permanent staff have a variety of worldviews and experiences that have contributed to the creation and execution of this mission, its disinterest in the hierarchies rampant in higher education and its focus on undergraduates, a community whose information needs often get overlooked or dismissed as less urgent or legitimate, is undeniably, if not explicitly, feminist-minded.

A significant part of this commitment to undergraduate education is College's status as a twenty-four hour library. In response to a student governance request, College began operating as a twenty-four/ five library during the fall and spring semesters in 2003. Committed to providing research help in the evening and late evening hours, a program of employing graduate student workers from the School of Library and Information Studies (SLIS) has been in steady development since that time. In the program's current form, a group of five or six graduate student workers are hired, trained, and supervised by two librarians. Known as Reference Student Assistants (RefSA), students are hired and trained before their first semester of library school. The students hold their position during their entire degree program. Together with permanent library staff, the students are responsible for staffing the reference desk Sunday through Thursday from 8 p.m. until midnight, and without permanent staff on Friday and Saturday from 5 p.m. until 11 p.m. During their weekend shifts, the students are the supervisors, responsible for security as well as student circulation and computer lab staff in the building in the evening.

This program is in constant evolution, responding to reference traffic, staffing needs, and the personal visions of the librarian supervisors, who are given freedom to shape the training and mentoring program as they see fit. Given this flux, identifying core principles and areas of focus for RefSA training and mentoring is important. In its current iteration, it has become apparent that a feminist-minded pedagogy is our central operating principle.

As I described in the introduction, we begin with incoming RefSA with the notion that College Library is a teaching library. We understand our reference desk to be a classroom and the persons who staff and visit it to be a community of learners. Our hope is to confront library anxiety and foster self-sufficiency. Given this context, the application of the feminist pedagogical principles we have identified—power/empowerment, lived and past learning experience, and a reflective awareness of systems of domination and control—creates a complex engagement among staff, patrons, and professional practice that enriches, supports, and complicates every interaction.

Power/Empowerment

Shrewsbury suggests that we embrace power in the feminist classroom as a "creative community energy," freeing it from traditional notions of power connected to domination and control.[h] She offers a series of strategies to achieve empowerment of learners, including creating opportunities for students to reflect on learning goals, developing independence (including skills related to the ability to be independent), reinforcing competence, and the importance of the learners' role in the classroom.[i] Brown, without using the word "power," writes of a "transfer of authority," and, like Shrewsbury, lists a series of tactics to bring such a transfer about—group discussion, small group work, collaborative projects, journaling, and peer tutoring.[j]

Traditional, domination-centered concepts of power are at play at a library reference desk. Radford and Radford, relying on Foucault's notions of discursive power and citing a variety of examples from popular culture and literature, write that "the library and librarians are a prevalent metaphor of power and knowledge within popular culture,"[k] while dissecting how gendered stereotypes of librarians themselves are used to defuse our fear and anxiety about knowledge, information, and the power of discourse.[l] The complexity of the power relations at a reference desk is only intensified by the presence of a graduate student worker, whose simultaneous role as a learner and a teacher is apparent to all involved (including the student worker herself).

To dismantle these traditional notions of power, librarians can choose—and, in doing so, teach others to choose—Shrewsbury's understanding of power as a vital, creative force available to us at our reference desks. Visibly tampering with perceived, traditional power dynamics in a reference interaction—namely, the perception of the librarian as the all-knowing oracle of a complex, inscrutable system—can change what patron, student worker, and librarian alike can expect from one another.[3][4] It can also teach graduate student workers to aspire to something different than the received and hostile image of the reference librarian as stuffy, shushing, obsessive gatekeeper, as described by Radford and Radford.

---

3 One of the best things I've learned to express at the reference desk is the answer "I don't know. Let's find out together!" It's honest, it's direct, and it tells the patron in no uncertain terms that my objective is to learn along with them. – Angie Schiappacasse, seconded by Jenny McBurney

4 In my first professional librarian position, I worked mostly with undergraduates who were first-generation college students and often first-generation Americans. Many expressed, in one way or another, feelings of insecurity and deference towards me as an authority figure. Because of my experience at College Library, I have the training to recognize these insecurities and how they negatively impacted my students' ability to succeed in the assignment at hand. I also developed the skills to be able to break down the mystique around searching for resources and finding information. – Lori Steckervetz

Like Shrewsbury and Brown, I will provide some concrete examples of different ways to use and reinterpret power/empowerment at the reference desk, based on our experiences at College Library.

We repeatedly refuse the concept of "correct." As noted above, one of the most damaging assumptions made about librarians is that we are all-knowing and in possession of correct answers to questions.[5] This is both an unreasonable belief and a dangerous one – if this is the standard to which librarians are held, we cannot help but fail. An early career professional who continues to believe that this is true about librarians will struggle to be effective at the reference desk. What librarians truly possess is the ability to locate a possible correct answer and defend the choices we make when arriving at that answer with support from sources and past experience.[6] We teach our graduate student workers and re-teach ourselves this by openly, respectfully, disagreeing with one another;[7] by discussing individual interactions in depth at meetings; and by being open with patrons about the limits of our own knowledge. Saying "I don't know, let's find out together" to a patron in front of a graduate student worker can open the way for profound lessons for all learners involved (patron, graduate student, and librarian).[8]

We make decisions collaboratively and change policy based on graduate student worker expertise and input. Our graduate student workers are responsible for weekend evening supervisory shifts. During the regular semester, these are the only nights on which the library closes, the only nights without permanent security staff on

---

5 I try to apply this to my own pedagogy with students in the classroom or at the reference desk. I demonstrate that searching for resources, and research as a whole, is messy and at times very frustrating. I show my students that the first search, and often the next few searches, will not yield the desired results. I try to make it clear to students this is just as true for librarians as it is for them. My hope is for them to start to understand that research is a process, one that they can engage in without fear of "doing it wrong." – Lori Steckervetz

6 One of the most important skills I gained from College Library is not only the ability to defend my choices, but also the mindset that I had the right to. – Sam Becker

7 This has become one of my favorite parts of this whole mentoring and learning experience. Moving myself from having a fear of disagreeing in front of graduate students to fully embracing and encouraging diverse solutions has been very empowering for me as a mentor. Diverse teams get things done! –Trisha Prosise

8 I swear I hadn't read this far before commenting above. It's like I picked up the lesson or something. – Angie Schiappacasse

hand, and the only nights without permanent reference staff on hand. As such, when we are asked questions about policy or practice on those nights, we often open it for discussion before proposing an answer, reinforcing student worker competence, as Shrewsbury suggests.[9] [10]

Our training and hiring processes invite collaboration that make power a communal, shareable object. When we interview potential student workers, we pose thought-problem questions that require them to think critically, out loud, and on the fly. Once hired, our training experience for our new graduate student workers is only successful with the support of their involvement and contributions. They are taught about campus-specific resources and tools through hands-on experience. They are asked to locate information on various websites and in various databases and to describe the processes by which they arrived at their answers. Returning students are asked to participate in the training as well, taking significant responsibility for training their new colleagues on chat reference, our most heavily-trafficked service point, and security.[11] [12]

---

[9] And it feels good to be heard! – Angie Schiappacasse

[10] This inclusion has turned out to be very empowering for me as a new professional. I have entered a professional position feeling confident that yes, I should speak up, that my opinions and perspectives are of value, and that I am indeed an equal at the table with my colleagues. – Lori Steckervetz

[11] This was beneficial on a number of levels. As a first-year RefSA, I saw the second-years as my role models. They had been just like me a year ago, and now look how awesome they were! Maybe someday I could be awesome too. And later, as a second-year RefSA, I gained experience in mentoring newer colleagues, which served me well when I became a professional librarian and began supervising my own students. This collaborative training also demonstrated to me that we all had something to offer to the group, no matter our level of experience, and we could share and learn from one another without feeling intimidated or incompetent. – Jenny McBurney

[12] Seconded! As one of the new colleagues that Jenny mentored, it was such a useful experience to have second years come in and help with the training. It fostered from the beginning the feeling that I could go to them with questions. It also gave the job a feeling of community and togetherness. You weren't just filling a spot for two years. You helped to train and worked with your colleagues, you were engaged in a community rather than just working a job. – Sam Becker

Respecting Lived Experience

Crabtree, Sapp, and Licona write that feminist pedagogy respects our ability to become knowledgeable or assert authority through personal experience.[m] At our reference desk and in our related work, we should show regard for our own lived experiences and for the lived experiences of our graduate student workers and patrons.

Power/empowerment and lived experience are symbiotic, requiring one another to thrive. As such, the importance of lived experience to the work of graduate student workers at library reference desks has already emerged in the previous section of this chapter. But we can put a finer point on it with additional examples and strategies that make central a conscious regard for personal experience. Crabtree, Sapp, and Licona write that "Feminist teachers demonstrate sincere concern for their students as people and as learners and communicate this care through treating students as individuals, helping students make connections between their studies and their personal lives, and guiding students through the process of personal growth that accompanies their intellectual development."[n] If librarians who are responsible for graduate student workers demonstrate this sincere concern and reinforce the same habit of mind for our student workers when they are learners for whom we are responsible, we can have hope that they will do the same when they are teachers, responsible for our patrons and the patrons they will encounter throughout their careers.[13]

College Library's RefSA training relies heavily on the notion of the reference interview. We teach our new graduate student workers the five step process of

- Greeting and listening completely
- Asking open-ended and clarifying questions
- Paraphrasing often
- Providing an answer
- Establishing a feedback loop/following-up

---

13 I can testify to this! I came to library school through a process of finding my values while exploring the field of organic gardening. I expected I'd be an odd duck when applying to be a RefSA with just one recent work reference: my boss at an urban farm in Cleveland, OH. The connection between that experience and my desire to work in libraries makes total intuitive sense to me, but I imagined I'd have to justify or brush over it in front of "academic" staff. Instead, Trisha and Raina have been interested to hear about my background and help me contextualize my time at College in terms of my goal to be a public librarian, sharing stories with lots of different people. – Samantha Link

and all of the complexities and subtleties that this seemingly straightforward process entails. We urge our new graduate student workers to rely on this format as they learn to negotiate the often awkward and transgressive experience of making an effort to understand completely what another person wants or needs in an educational setting.

This may not seem particularly feminist-minded at first glance, but, when exploring the reference interview, we place emphasis on the repeated use of open-ended and clarifying questions and attentive, total listening.[14] Placing ourselves and our student workers in dialog with our patrons with questions about their experience of research (both cognitive and affective) cannot help but create regard for and awareness of our patrons and ourselves as individuals, with knowledge to bring to bear on information seeking. We encourage our student workers to ask questions about a patron's process, where they have searched so far, what they hope to find, and where they have encountered problems or challenges. We encourage them to affirm and support learning without making choices for a patron. Simultaneously, we encourage our student workers to not immediately steer patrons away from resources that seem less helpful or research topics that are too broad or inappropriately framed. We strive to create a dialog between librarian/student worker and patron, wherein experiences and knowledge can be shared mutually.

After engaging with patrons in this way, we ask our graduate student workers to write about it, at least for their first year of employment. Our approach was inspired, in part, by the Critical Incidents Protocol, a collaborative and reflective activity for education professionals.º Though it is not described as such, the Protocol has a decidedly feminist flair, given its interest in the lived experiences of professionals and the creation of a mutually respectful environment in which to share them. It uses writing exercises and small-group discussion to support teachers as they examine seemingly minor

---

14 College Library, more than any other job I've held, has shaped my professional values and habits. It continues to inform how I think about learning spaces and working with students. Open-ended questions to help students think about their thinking and structure their research is a crucial piece of my teaching as well as my reference desk interactions. Consistent, attentive listening is something I had to work on as a RefSA, but it's a skill I think I'm better at, at least when working with students. Open-ended questions help me to not accidentally lead students or make an interaction about what I know rather than what they know. – Sam Becker

incidents or interactions to understand their own decision-making processes.

Similarly, we ask RefSA to tell us stories, no matter how trivial the circumstance may have seemed at the time, to raise questions about their choices, but not to question them (again, this illustrates the fragile boundary between practices associated with power/empowerment and lived experience). Through this approach, we acknowledge that the skills and understandings of a professional are the sum total of her experiences and her understandings of her experiences. As Schön suggests in *The Reflective Practitioner*, professionals may struggle to come into consciousness of their own processes and awareness – they do not know what they know or how to explain it to others.[15] [p] Using a feminist approach of regard for the lived experience of the learners at the reference desk creates a heightened awareness and begins to address the struggle for professional awareness and respect.

Interrogating Systems of Domination and Control

Student workers who understand the role that power/empowerment plays at a library reference desk and who have learned to rely upon and speak from their lived experiences will inevitably arrive at questioning the power structures that are at play in their work as teachers and learners.[16] Accardi writes that "the cultural apparatuses that serve to oppress women and perpetuate oppression of marginalized peoples do not disappear once a teacher or a student walks into a classroom."[q] At

---

15 Reflection is an important part of understanding your choices and processes. It's also key for intentional, mindful growth to occur. In the first year, reflection was really difficult for me because I was (and sometimes still am) very attached to notions of correctness. It helped me to better understand why I was directing students the way I was and why I was making the decisions I was making. It required me to slow down and think about my shift. It's also an exercise I've asked my own reference student workers to employ at the end of their shifts. Reading their reflective writing has been a learning experience for me as they reflect on their own processes and I learn things from them about the university, engineering research, and student life at my new school. – Sam Becker

16 So much of what I learned in RefSA also gets applied to how I teach in a classroom. Possibly because of the emphasis on College as a teaching library, I've taken the lessons I've learned about the importance of experience and the power structures at play in learning environments and applied it to other spaces outside of the reference desk.
 – Sam Becker

College, we understand that our library, and especially our Reference and Information Desk, is a classroom. We strive to remain mindful of our position as perpetuators of the liberatory and oppressive possibilities of both libraries and higher education.[17][18]

We engage our graduate student workers in discussions about the tension between what our patrons need to know to complete assignments and the flaws in the systems of scholarly communication that we have to teach to help our students. We discuss shortcomings in databases, the true complexity of source evaluation, how to unpack the meaning of citation metrics, and how to understand and internalize these things while still informing and educating patrons in a way that meets their (often introductory) needs.

As noted earlier, College Library is the University of Wisconsin-Madison's undergraduate library. Our mission brings our practices into constant contact with young adults who are encountering new people and ideas daily. We work to make our space more inclusive, while respectfully acknowledging the cognitive stage many of our patrons occupy. RefSA participates in the staging of the Helen C. House Party each fall, an indoor carnival that turns cotton candy, face painting, and carnival games into tools in our effort to confront library anxiety.[19][20] RefSA staff meetings include discussions on microaggressions and appropriate practices for serving patrons whose appearance does not match the information on

---

17 It's true! Mindfulness is a pillar of reference at College Library. One example that we talk about a lot is our shared response to "Where's the bathroom?" We have a women's bathroom in one direction and a men's bathroom in the other, and instead of sizing up a patron and assigning them a gender, we always say something like, "The men's room is that way and the women's room is that way." Who you are is up to you; we're just here to help. – Angie Schiappacasse

18 I second Angie's comment and feel the need to add that various members of College Library staff have been pushing for an All Gender bathroom for years. Given that we are working within an entire library and higher education system of which we do not have full control, we cannot always get what we want. So, we do what we can with what we have now and continue to seek improvements. – Trisha Prosise

19 Yes! Welcoming new undergrads to the library and saying "Psst—the pizza's upstairs," while wearing zebra-striped face paint helps to convey that we are not scary and that they should come back some time. – Angie Schiappacasse

20 And, the Helen C. House Party is unique among library parties in that there is no underlying secret objective where we trick students into learning something "useful." There are no call number scavenger hunts or citation races. The goal is to get students through the library doors in order to have fun, full stop. – Jenny McBurney

their campus identification. On one notable occasion in 2014, College Library was host to the largest on-campus protest since the 1960s anti-war protests that consumed UW's campus. During finals, our busiest time in the semester, students associated with the Black Lives Matter movement held a die-in that covered the library's floors.[r] While RefSA were not working during this protest, we held a discussion about it in our next meeting, reflecting on our director's decision to welcome the protestors; permit them to lie anywhere on the floor, including behind the Reference and Information Desk; and engage individually with students who contacted her to complain.[21] [22]

Most of the students who have been employed through the RefSA program are women, reflecting demographic realities of librarianship. At College Library, they are women sitting in a public space whose job is to be visible and approachable. As people who serve others know, this can lead to negative, sexualized, or otherwise unwanted attention from patrons. We teach our graduate student workers, of any gender, to understand and respect their own limits, to end chat conversations that have taken a turn for the worse, and to sidestep a patron's attempt to be overly familiar and continue the reference interaction. When they have had to enforce their boundaries, we affirm their choice to do so, even when they question or criticize their own decisions.[23]

---

21 Being invited to openly process your work experiences with your supervisors/mentors is something that I never even dreamed I'd get to do. Not only have these conversations shaped my professional development, but they're also practices that I'll take with me wherever I go. – Angie Schiappacasse

22 I second Angie, and it ties into the anecdote here! One of my first shifts as person-in-charge of the library was two evenings before said protest. A campus police officer approached the desk to inform library staff about it (although they already knew, of course...). I hadn't even formally met Carrie Kruse (the director) yet and am not sure I would've known how to handle the information without our internal staff wiki, which being in place let me confidently tell the officer I would pass along the message to those who needed to know. Our discussion in the next meeting made me glad to have followed my gut and not made a huge deal of it. I realized then how much responsibility is given to RefSA to represent the library, just freshly learning the library's policies and procedures as we are! – Samantha Link

23 As a woman and a librarian, I think I am often doubly-subject to this self-criticism. Women are socialized to be "nice," which can sometimes mean allowing unacceptable behavior to continue because we feel we can't/shouldn't make a fuss about it. And librarians are supposed to help without judging, which further enforces the idea that we need to be accommodating. Learning to enforce my own boundaries when necessary and be okay with doing so was, and still can be, hard. Being able to talk through these situations with trusted mentors was essential for me. – Jenny McBurney

The Feminist-Minded Librarian

Training and mentoring new professionals using the feminist pedagogical methods described here will yield a specific type of librarian. Crabtree writes that "feminist teachers also engage actively in the exploration of how *who* we are within these environments necessarily impacts *what* and *how* we teach."⁵ The supervisors of the RefSA program hope that students who complete it will be professionals with a strong understanding of who they are in a professional context and in possession of the ability to think, speak, and act from that understanding, even when knocked sideways by a job search postgraduation or weathering the first year at a new institution whose practices and mission may not match what our students came to expect when working with us.[24] [25]

As of this writing, students who have worked at College Library as RefSA are employed at the University of Wisconsin-Madison, the University of Minnesota-Twin Cities, the University of Minnesota-Duluth, the University of California – Berkeley, Worcester Polytechnic Institute, Drake University, the University of Michigan – Ann Arbor, and Red Lake Nation College, just to name a few.[26] They are metadata analysts, social science liaisons, reference and instruction librarians, and directors. Two have such fondness for and belief in the mission and methods of College Library that they have returned to supervise the RefSA program and are my colleagues, Ian Benton (past supervisor of the program and current coordinator of our Reference/Information

---

24 Librarianship is not my first profession, but it is the first that, in part due to being mentored with feminist pedagogy, I feel that I have a strong sense of who I am within this profession. This has been my most important asset since earning my MLS. I have been able to assert myself where in the past I would have held back. I have felt empowered and have been able to more clearly define my professional philosophies, as a librarian and as a teacher, all of which are heavily informed by a feminist perspective. – Lori Steckervetz

25 Basically, I have always "been a feminist" but it felt like a personal interest. I was mocked for minoring in Women's Studies in college, and I assumed that the real/career world would be equally as uninterested in my personal beliefs. Luckily I was wrong, and I have since discovered like-minded colleagues and friends and learned a ridiculous amount from being a RefSA. I love that my feminism is now intertwined with my opinions and knowledge of librarianship, and I think that I am a better person and a better librarian because of it. –Jenny McBurney

26 Dang, way to go people. You all rock. – Jenny McBurney

and Circulation Desk) and Trisha Prosise (current supervisor). College Library cannot take full credit, but the profession seems to want these enthusiastic, thoughtful, assertive, early-career professionals.

The Feminist-Minded Librarian Starter Kit

As I have mentioned, this program of hiring, training, and mentoring graduate student workers has been in evolution for over a decade at College Library. As we encourage our students to reflect, we, too, reflect on our work with them. Our approach is not one-size-fits-all. It works for us because it is responsive to the library's needs, the graduate students' needs, and our abilities as supervisors and busy professionals.

If you would like to attempt something similar at your library, however, we have some suggestions connected to our three major themes of power/empowerment, respecting lived experience, and interrogating systems of domination and control:

- *Empower your student workers* – Trisha writes, "If I had to suggest one thing, it would be to help graduate student workers feel supported in being reflective about themselves and their own practice, so that they know **why** they are making certain choices and could explain if necessary. I believe this leads to better decisions and speeds professional growth. I suggest continuing to support graduate student workers in their choices even if you would have done it differently. In some circumstances it might still be useful to explain what you would have done and why, but if they are well trained and can be reflective, you can be confident they will have a basis for their choices grounded in who they are and what they know about a given situation."

- *Respect their lived experience* – Encourage graduate student workers to tell stories about their work, whether it be to you, to one another, in writing, or out loud. Ideally, it will be all of the above at one point or another. Figure out how you are best able to hear those stories and how they are best able to share them. Tell them stories about your work. Tell them when you're wrong. Tell them when you don't agree with something with all of the generosity and regard you can muster. Ask their opinion and advice about policy decisions that directly impact their work.[27]

- *Interrogate systems of domination and control that benefit you* – Ask yourself why you're hiring graduate student workers. What are they for? What are *you* for, relative to them? Ask yourself what they're getting from the experience. Ask yourself how they could get more. Teach them how to explain to others what they've gotten from the experience in a way that others will be able to hear. Think long and hard about who you hire and why. Demonstrate your regard for your patrons, especially patrons who belong to marginalized groups. Learn enough that you can explain to your graduate student workers why you need to demonstrate this regard. Explain it to them.

Who We Need to Be Right Now

Working for the University of Wisconsin in the 2010s is an exercise in learning how to defend what you believe about higher education both philosophically and practically. Slashed budgets and pervasive misunderstandings concerning the use and role of publicly-funded higher education have left colleges and departments scrambling to protect and promote what they have. Libraries confront this challenge while also responding to wider cultural and market forces that misunderstand the work that librarians do, drive the cost of materials up, and erode the publicly available scholarly record.

---

[27] So I think my biggest "RefSA implementation" has simply been opening up dialogue and letting students ask questions and work through issues without judgment. In my first job at MERIT (UW-Madison), our group of desk students was bigger than RefSA so we could only occasionally fit group meetings into everyone's schedules. When I was a RefSA, those biweekly group meetings were my safe space to ask questions, share ideas, and learn from everyone else. I wanted my own students to have those same benefits even without the opportunity for regular group meetings, so I cultivated one-on-one interactions instead. I tried to check in with each student at least once a week during their shifts and see how they were doing, what issues had come up, what were they struggling with or wondering about. These conversations could range from the mundane (how do you do a microfiche lending request again?) to the complex (how do you create a social media plan? why? what are the goals/limits?). We need to give students a chance to think about what they're doing and why, and for me that has been asking the questions and then offering a safe space for them to wonder. – Jenny McBurney

So. We have a meeting. We have another. We tell RefSA about the budget and changes to public service policy, about the impacts on their work. We tell them we want to start collaborating with another library to increase the number of people staffing chat and we'd like their help to provide training. We tell them we will soon be answering questions from the university system's two-year campuses in the evenings, to provide support to our colleagues there. We tell them we're too short-staffed to cover the summer reference shifts without them, even though they've never worked summers with us before. A discussion ensues about quality of service, our primary patrons, respecting differing service models among libraries, and the practicalities of creating a new training program, serving patrons who are new to us. They say yes, yes to all of it, that they want to share what we do and how we do it with other students, other libraries.[28] [29] [30] They are exactly who we need right now. They are exactly who we need to be right now.

---

28 This is so true, even/especially after graduating—when I was at MERIT, I wanted to train my info desk students the way Raina and Trisha trained me. Of course, because of our size and unique services at MERIT, our desk model was very different in a lot of ways from College's, but I really appreciated the perspective I had and how I was able to apply my experience to fit a new situation. As I mentioned above, I deliberately worked to create open dialogue between myself and my students so that they would feel the same level of comfort discussing questions and problems with me that I had felt as a student at College Library.

I also loved the opportunity we had last year, to combine some of our reference training with College's RefSA training. Our students benefited greatly from Trisha and Raina's expertise and well-organized training, and they also got to know other campus librarians and libraries outside of MERIT. It was the perfect supplement to and expansion on our internal training. – Jenny McBurney

29 When I arrived at my first job, I was asked to create a peer-to-peer learning model at the desk. The first thing I did was pull from what I knew from RefSA. The libraries are very different so the desk looks very different, but particularly in how I train, schedule, and mentor my undergraduates I'm thinking very intentionally of RefSA. I couldn't agree more with the idea that RefSA want to share what we do and how we do it. – Sam Becker

30 In a past position, I inherited a reorganized department that unified both Circulation (as well as Reserves and ILL) with the Research Help Desk (formally the Reference Desk). Without my training as RefSA at College Library, specifically without THIS type of training, I would have been at a complete loss for what to do. I would have been aware that there were unhealthy power structures left over from the previous admin. While the new administration encouraged change to flatten hierarchies and increase transparency and collaboration, the gap I saw was a lack of empowerment among the staff I am now overseeing and how that trickled down into how student employees were treated, with very simple tasks meant to "keep the kids busy." I credit the training I received at College Library with giving me a way to view the missing pieces and figure out a way to help my staff grow into their new identities of empowerment. – Lori Steckervetz

Acknowledgements

The thoughtful and heartfelt engagement of former RefSA was central to the experience of writing this chapter and the finished product. In so many ways, this work could not exist without them. They are –

- Sam Becker, Campus Engagement Librarian, Drake University
- Samantha Link, Program Services Library Assistant, Columbus Public Library (Columbus, WI) and Education Officer, Madison Community Cooperative
- Jenny McBurney, Research Services Coordinator/Liaison Librarian, Wilson Library, University of Minnesota-Twin Cities
- Trisha Prosise, Public Services & E-Learning Librarian, College Library, University of Wisconsin-Madison
- Angela Schiappacasse; Resident Librarian for Reference, Educational Technology, and Instruction; MERIT Library, University of Wisconsin-Madison
- Lori Steckervetz, Research & Instruction Librarian, Gordon Library, Worcester Polytechnic Institute

I would also like to acknowledge my partner and colleague, Dave Bloom (Science and Engineering Librarian, Wendt Commons Library, University of Wisconsin-Madison), for his keen editing skills and insight, and for continuing to know what I'm talking about.

I have the honor to be your obedient servant. R. Bloom

BIBLIOGRAPHY

Accardi, Maria T. *Feminist Pedagogy for Library Instruction.* Sacramento, CA: Library Juice Press, 2013.

Arriga, Alex. "Hundreds of Students Fill College Library to Protest Racial Injustice 'Die-In' Demonstration." *The Badger Herald,* December 14, 2014. https://badgerherald.com/news/2014/12/14/hundreds-of-students-fill-college-library-to-protest-racial-injustice-in-die-in-demonstration/.

Ball, Mary Alice. "Practicums and Service Learning in LIS Education." *Journal of Education for Library and Information Science* 49, no.1 (2008): 70-82.

Brown, Julie. "Theory or Practice: What Exactly Is Feminist Pedagogy?" *The Journal of General Education* 41 (1992): 51-63.

Crabtree, Robbin D., David Alan Sapp, and Adela C. Licona, eds, *Feminist Pedagogy: Looking Back to Move Forward.* Baltimore: Johns Hopkins University Press, 2009.

Hoffmann, Kristin and Selinda Berg. "'You Can't Learn it in School': Field Experiences and Their Contributions to Educational and Professional Identity." *Canadian Journal of Information and Library Science* 38, no.3 (2014): 220-238.

Hole, Simon and Grace Hall McEntee. "Reflection Is at the Heart of Practice." *Educational Leadership* 56, no.8 (1999): 34-37.

Leonard, Barbara G. and Donna Z. Pontau."Sculpting Future Librarians through Structured Practicums: The Role of Academic Librarians." *The Journal of Academic Librarianship* 17, no.1 (1991): 26-30.

Nahl, Diane, Ann Coder, Janet Black, and Marge Smith. "Effectiveness of Fieldwork at an Information Desk: A Prototype for Academic Library-Library School Collaboration." *The Journal of Academic Librarianship* 20, no.5/6 (1994): 291-294.

Radford, Marie L. and Gary P. Radford. "Power, Knowledge, and Fear: Feminism, Foucault, and the Stereotype of the Female Librarian." *The Library Quarterly* 67, no.3 (1997): 250-266.

Schön, Donald. *The Reflective Practitioner.* New York: Basic Books, 1983.

Shrewsbury, Carolyn M. "What Is Feminist Pedagogy?" *Women's Studies Quarterly* 21, no.3/4 (1993): 8-16.

Webb, Lynne M., Myria W. Allen, and Kandi L. Walker. "Feminist Pedagogy: Identifying Basic Principles." *Academic Exchange Quarterly* 6 (2002): 67-72.

Woodward, Beth S. "The Effectiveness of an Information Desk Staffed by Graduate Students and Nonprofessionals." *College & Research Libraries* 50 (1989): 455-467.

Woodward, Beth S. and Sharon J. Van Der Laan. "Training Preprofessionals for Reference Service." *The Reference Librarian* 16, (1987): 233-254.

Wu, Qi (Kerry). "Win-Win Strategy for the Employment of Reference Graduate Assistants in Academic Libraries." *Reference Services Review* 31, no.2 (2003): 141-153.

Notes

a. Diane Nahl et al., "Effectiveness of Fieldwork at an Information Desk: A Prototype for Academic Library-Library School Collaboration," *The Journal of Academic Librarianship* 20, no.5/6 (1994): 291-294; Beth S. Woodward and Sharon J. Van Der Laan, "Training Preprofessionals for Reference Service," *The Reference Librarian* 16, (1987): 233-254; Kristin Hoffmann and Selinda Berg, "'You Can't Learn it in School': Field Experiences and Their Contributions to Educational and Professional Identity," *Canadian Journal of Information and Library Science* 38, no.3 (2014): 220-238; Beth S. Woodward, "The Effectiveness of an Information Desk Staffed by Graduate Students and Nonprofessionals," *College & Research Libraries* 50 (1989): 455-467; Barbara G. Leonard and Donna Z. Pontau, "Sculpting Future Librarians Through Structured Practicums: The Role of Academic Librarians," *The Journal of Academic Librarianship* 17, no.1 (1991): 26-30; and Qi (Kerry) Wu, "Win-Win Strategy for the Employment of Reference Graduate Assistants in Academic Libraries," *Reference Services Review* 31, no.2 (2003): 141-153.

b. Woodward, "Effectiveness."

c. Nahl, "Effectiveness," 292.

d. Hoffmann, "'You Can't Learn," 227-232.

e. Mary Alice Ball, "Practicums and Service Learning in LIS Education," *Journal of Education for Library and Information Science* 49, no.1 (2008): 72-73.

f. Lynne M. Webb, Myria W. Allen and Kandi L. Walker, "Feminist Pedagogy: Identifying Basic Principles," *Academic Exchange Quarterly* 6 (2002): 67-72; and Carolyn M. Shrewsbury, "What Is Feminist Pedagogy?" *Women's Studies Quarterly* 21, no.3/4 (1993): 8-16.

g. Webb, "Feminist Pedagogy."

h. Shrewsbury, "What Is," 10.

i. Ibid.,10-11.

j. Julie Brown, "Theory or Practice: What Exactly Is Feminist Pedagogy?" *The Journal of General Education* 41, (1992): 54.

k. Marie L. Radford and Gary P. Radford, "Power, Knowledge, and Fear: Feminism, Foucault, and the Stereotype of the Female Librarian," *The Library Quarterly* 67, no.3 (1997): 259.

l. Ibid., 261.

m. Robbin D. Crabtree, David Alan Sapp, and Adela C. Licona, eds, *Feminist Pedagogy: Looking Back to Move Forward* (Baltimore: Johns Hopkins University Press, 2009), 4.

n. Ibid.,4-5.

o. Simon Hole and Grace Hall McEntee, "Reflection Is at the Heart of Practice," *Educational Leadership* 56, no.8 (1999): 34-37.

p. Donald Schön, *The Reflective Practitioner* (New York: Basic Books, 1983).

q. Maria T. Accardi, *Feminist Pedagogy for Library Instruction* (Sacramento, CA: Library Juice Press, 2013), 24-25.

r. Alex Arriga, "Hundreds of Students Fill College Library to Protest Racial Injustice 'Die-In' Demonstration," *The Badger Herald*, December 14, 2014, https://badgerherald.com/news/2014/12/14/hundreds-of-students-fill-college-library-to-protest-racial-injustice-in-die-in-demonstration/.

s. Crabtree, *Feminist Pedagogy*, 5.

Feminist Pedagogy and the Reference Desk: A Conversation

Jeremy McGinniss and Angela Pashia

When co-authoring works, the editing process often includes a final smoothing over to ensure that the entire piece reads as a single, unified voice. While this mode of authorship is valuable for many purposes, converting a polyvocal text to a single voice can erase nuance that may be useful to readers in different contexts. From an intersectional feminist perspective, it's useful to examine the ways different social positions and institutional contexts influence our work at the reference desk.

There are several examples within critical pedagogy which demonstrate the value of writing as a dialogue instead of a monologue. Paulo Freire and Myles Horton came together to "talk a book," *We Make the Road by Walking,* reflecting together that "knowledge grows from and is a reflection of social experience."[1] bell hooks situated her dialogue with Ron Scapp in *Teaching to Transgress*[2] within the context of "border crossing," and the need for conversations between "individuals who actually occupy different locations within structures, sharing ideas with one another, mapping out terrains of commonality, connection, and shared concern with teaching practices."[3]

---

1 Horton, Myles, Brenda Bell, John Gaventa, and John Marshall Peters. *We Make the Road by Walking: Conversations on Education and Social Change.* Philadelphia: Temple University Press, 1990. p. xvi.

2 bell hooks, *Teaching to Transgress: Education as the Practice of Freedom* (New York: Routledge, 1994), 129-165.

3 hooks, *Teaching to Transgress,* 129-130.

In this spirit, the authors compare our structural and institutional contexts while examining how feminist pedagogy has influenced our work at the reference desk. By offering dialogue on and through the topics discussed below, we seek to explore perspectives on the diversity and strength a feminist pedagogical approach brings to the reference interaction.

Angela Pashia: I guess I'll start my introduction by taking credit for throwing in the "polyvocal" jargon term above, because it says something about the background I bring to librarianship. I earned a Masters and had started a PhD program in Anthropology, planning to become an anthropology professor, before I decided to transfer over to a library science program. This has very much influenced my approach to librarianship and reference work in a couple of ways. First, I spent years planning to become an educator, leading students to the information instead of simply providing an answer. Second, that's where I developed most of the theoretical background that informs my approach to critical librarianship.

Personally, I'm a white woman from a low income, working class background. I was a first-generation college student, as are many of the students at my university.

Jeremy McGinniss: Digging this polyvocal thing as I had not intended to become a librarian. Failing to get into a desired MA program resulted in some serious soul-searching and I decided my skills and interests would fit well with the library world. I have always been interested in teaching and learning and have been privileged to have had critical and significant teachers challenge and develop my thinking and approach. I recently began a second MA in order to broaden out my own thinking and reading as well as an attempt to locate additional teaching opportunities.

Personally, my parents were the first in their respective families to attend and finish college, so far as I know. While we were on the lower end of the income scale growing up the pursuit and interaction with ideas was a household practice, for sure.

AP: In terms of our institutional contexts, I work at a regional comprehensive state university in semi-rural Georgia. We're only about an hour away from downtown Atlanta, but that is far enough to be a distinct small town instead of part of the suburban sprawl. We have some Masters and Doctoral degree programs, but the majority of our students are undergraduates. The 2014-15 academic year was the first time we had over 12,000 students enrolled, and we had over 13,000 students enrolled in the fall semester of 2016. This growth has been good for us budgetarily, but it means consistently feeling understaffed, as there is a lag between the arrival of more new students and the allocation of funding for new positions.

My context within the university is faculty librarian in the Instructional Services department. At the time of writing, we have 9 faculty members in my department, including the department head, up from 7 when I started in 2011. We currently have 16 full time faculty positions in the library as a whole, plus a significant number of paraprofessional and administrative staff members, graduate student assistants, and undergraduate student assistants. I am on the lowest rung of the faculty hierarchy, though I do supervise three student assistants.

JM: I work at a private university, with a focus on biblical higher education, located in Northeast Pennsylvania, approximately two and a half hours west of NYC. We are a small school with a total of 1,000 students across the undergraduate, graduate and seminary populations. A growing chunk of students are online which raises interesting and complex questions for library services, particularly affecting the perception and type of reference interactions. We are tuition driven which causes the budget to be a significant point of contention.

I am the lone full time librarian and operate with the title of library director. I have two fantastic part time paraprofessionals who are invaluable to the library. The library employs 11-12 student staff, depending on the semester. In addition to library things, I also teach two undergraduate classes, Introduction to Fine Arts and World Religions and serve as the study abroad liaison.

AP: Shifting to a comparison of our reference desk models, my university uses the Brandeis model of reference. We have student research assistants (SRAs) who staff two help desks from 7am to 1am when the library is open. Librarians are available for walk-up reference help Monday through Thursday, 11am to 5pm.

Most librarians serve a single two-hour shift per week. We also offer chat reference services and appointments for research help. Our reference coordinator is continuing to experiment with other models, including a pilot project working with a few of the SRAs to provide more advanced training in the interest of developing a peer research mentor model.

Do you use a similar model, on a smaller scale, of relying on student assistants, or do your part time staff manage a lot of the reference interactions?

JM: The front desk is located at the library entrance and serves as the main point of contact for library interactions, including reference questions. Student assistants are the primary point of contact for reference transactions as they staff this front desk area. My goal is to equip the student staff to be knowledgeable and prepared for these interactions so the student staff can help patrons locate a resource, physically or online, provide some basic search term suggestions and navigate the digital interfaces. There are two catalog computers directly across from the front desk so it is easy to initiate conversations with patrons searching for information. The bulk of what would be considered traditional reference interviews originate from the graduate school and seminary, particularly the PhD students. As most graduate and seminary students are located off-campus, many of the reference questions come through email and occasionally through the IM chat. I handle the majority of these interactions.

I regularly walk through the library to see if patrons may need assistance or to check in with the student staff. I have also tried to be very intentional in our signage so a patron can locate a staff member with minimal effort if needed. My office is almost in line of sight with the front door, allowing for students to stop in my office to ask questions, so my desk/office often turns into a reference space. When students schedule sessions we typically meet in my office.

AP: This issue of signage is interesting, since that has been a challenge at my library. After a renovation that was completed in 2011, my library had woefully inadequate signage, but we were limited in how we could address that due to stipulations in the contract with the architect. Once the time limit for those ran out, a committee worked on improving signage where they could. However, in the comments on an early draft of this chapter, Maria Accardi raised an important point to consider: what about those for whom the signage is not accessible? Keeping intersectionality in mind means we need to think about how physical impairments may affect the accessibility of navigational and educational resources.

JM: One of the things I stress with my student staff and they take quite seriously is any directional questions are answered by accompanying the individual to the place/book being queried. Unless of course the staff member is "waved off" by the patron. In my opinion, signage is meant to make the library space friendlier, representing an effort on library's behalf to reach out to the patrons to show where things are. Recognizing that signage is insufficient, by its nature, is an essential part of staffing the reference desk. Expecting the signage to do the work of a person is to woefully dehumanize the library. Signage gives, in my opinion, additional weight to the staff members' directions. Not only do they know where they are going, the signage offers support on behalf of their directions. Patron direction is a multi-layered approach in which signage is just one tool in that approach. Personally, I heartily dislike asking for directions and so I rather try to follow the signs until I get so woefully lost that I'm forced to talk to somebody. I get that this is privileged in that my physical ability allows me to navigate these spaces without assistance. Signage should not be expected to replace personal interaction. The opportunity to walk with someone to a particular shelf spot is an opportunity to do pedagogical work. I find that it creates opportunity for questions like "what are you working on?" or "what else are you looking for?" Again, if the questions are waved off, then I stop asking. But the walking together can be an opportunity to build relationship/interaction with the student, faculty member, etc. Hiding behind signage greatly dehumanizes the library, depersonalizes the staff, and reduces the library to a mall of information.

AP: So, the next question we planned to discuss is: What types of interactions do we value as rewarding reference interactions?

JM: This question is particularly intriguing to me. Rewarding reference interactions come for me in two layers. The first is where a patron is

347

looking for a place to start to research a subject and I can walk with them through the process so that they are able to locate materials that fit what they are looking for. I try to practice what technology instructors call "letting them drive" so that if we're working through the library catalog, the student is doing the typing, mouse clicks, etc. The second layer are questions, typically, from faculty, graduate or seminary students who are looking for more information on how to navigate a database or utilize a citation management tool. These interactions will happen via phone or face to face. We'll sit down one-on-one and talk through what their needs are, what questions they have, and then start playing around with ideas and technologies. This allows me to begin to establish a relationship with these students, who do the vast majority of their work from off-campus, so as to put a face or voice to my email and humanize the process of asking questions and getting the resources they need. Trying not to sound cliched here but I think the most valuable reference interactions are the ones where the student/staff/faculty member comes away more confident having built up their pre-existing skill set.

I have tried to make it a practice when walking through the library or when patrons are checking out to ask them if they found, or are finding, what they were looking for. This is a question I see as being driven by a feminist pedagogy. To ask a slightly open-ended, probing question as a way of beginning a potential reference interaction because there are times when the individual is not finding what they are trying to locate. This opens up a conversation that, hopefully, expands library services for the individual or it shows me where there are unnecessary barriers or tweaks that need to be made so that other students or patrons do not encounter a similar barrier.

Since you raised the question I would like to hear how you have been thinking about and approaching this area?

AP: I see this question, particularly the "why" part, as crucial to any discussion of feminist approaches to reference, and more broadly to any discussions of what we should be doing in the role of reference librarians. Why do you find it more rewarding to discuss the research process than to direct students to the restrooms or teach them how to print (types of questions you didn't mention)? And I don't mean to put you, Jeremy, on the spot—I feel like you described the sorts of interactions that most librarians I know would describe when asked the same question. I find it more rewarding to work through the process of narrowing a research topic than to simply teach someone how to find a book in our library. Yet I find it more rewarding to teach someone how to find a book in the library than to point them in the direction of the restroom. This continuum reflects my enjoyment of participating in the research process and my satisfaction in using my expertise to teach concepts that I consider important.

In my experience at the reference desk, directional questions and questions about the equipment (printers, copiers, etc) outnumber any other type of question. The next most common questions relate to how to find a book in the library. More in depth questions about the research process are fairly rare during my desk shifts, unless I schedule appointments during that time. Published research suggests this anecdotal evidence fits a trend being reported in other academic libraries.

For example, in a study of reference transactions at Indiana University–Bloomington since 2006, Andrew Asher analyzed a sample of reported questions using the six-point Reference Effort Assessment Data (READ) scale. Using a random sample of 901 questions, he reported "a mean score of 2.3 and a standard deviation of 0.817, indicating that most of the questions in our dataset were relatively straightforward to answer and very few were difficult research questions."[4] Another recent study cited several sources that found very low percentages of recorded reference interactions actually required librarian expertise—like only seven to ten percent of interactions.[5]

So, if the majority of the questions that we get during a regular reference desk shift are not particularly rewarding, why do

---

4 Andrew Asher, "Who's Asking What? Modelling a Large Reference Interaction Dataset," *Proceedings of the 2014 Library Assessment Conference* (2015): 52-62. http://libraryassessment.org/bm-doc/proceedings-lac-2014.pdf.

5 Timothy Peters, "Taking Librarians Off the Desk: One Library Changes its Reference Desk Staffing Model," *Performance Measurement and Metrics* 16 (2015): 20. doi: 10.1108/PMM-11-2014-0038.

librarians continue to emphasize reference? One way that feminist pedagogy can be applied to this question is to focus on the ethic of care. When we value students as whole people and consider the affective dimension of the college experience, then helping them to find the restroom or alleviating their stress by helping them print their paper should be valued. So should those questions be valued as highly as the more conceptual research questions that call our expertise into service?

The counter to this, though, would shift the focus to librarians as professionals. When many librarians spend 8-12 hours a week at the reference desk, and the majority of questions do not require any specialized expertise, how does that affect the librarian as a whole person? If we apply the ethic of care to ourselves, do we need to reconsider our reference models? I consider myself fortunate that librarians at my institution only serve a single two-hour reference shift each week. Since I teach a class, I am generally able to "double-dip" by scheduling my class office hours during the same time. However, most of the more interesting/challenging questions I've helped students with have come in appointments scheduled due to referrals from faculty or from students in my class, rather than walk-ups at the desk.

So how do we balance these two concerns in a truly feminist reference model? So far, I've only raised questions about applying the ethic of care, from a feminist pedagogy perspective, to reference services. We could also examine this issue in terms of the history of our discipline, with librarianship being devalued as a feminine profession. If academic reference librarians are predominantly answering relatively simple questions when at the desk, and if those desk shifts constitute a significant portion of their work duties, what is the value of the ML(I)S degree? Is this emphasis on the ethic of care for students contributing to the devaluation of our field in the minds of those who control budgets? As a feminist in a female dominated field, should I be pushing for librarians to shift our focus away from reference and on to those parts of our jobs that more regularly employ our expertise–teaching information literacy concepts, for example?

JM: I had a recent conversation with a colleague from an area university who has been working on a pilot program to train student staff at the reference desk. He talked about how the perception of what questions were being asked and how and who was answering them seemed to be a significant contributor to professional identity, as you mention above. Perhaps since directional aka "where's the bathroom" questions can be, supposedly, answered with signage, how much training does one need to refer one to the bathroom? On the other hand, speaking from personal experience, there is no bathroom in the immediate area of my library. To access the restrooms you have to go up to up to the next floor. This works fine if one is not in a wheelchair or using a walker as the elevator is difficult to access. There was an instance this last year that enabled me to address an issue with door access that had been dragging on for at least a year so that anyone in a wheelchair or walker could access the restrooms and the library without having to travel the length of the entire building. All that to say that if the idea of an ethic of care is an underlying part of library practice then perhaps all questions are ways into conversation and relationship building? Is the reference desk or reference question an entirely separate entity or is it an integrated part of the library's pedagogical approach?

At the very least the "where's the bathroom" questions can give cause for reflection as to why they are being asked. There's a bell hooks' quote that's been challenging me in this area. hooks writes "Professors cannot empower students to embrace diversities of experience, standpoint, behavior, or style if our training has disempowered us, socialized us to cope effectively only with a single mode of interaction based on middle-class values."[6] Substituting "librarian" for professor, I challenge myself, and the library, with how to see or even develop interactions with students as ways of empowering students in diverse ways. Elmborg has asked what the role of the library is in critical literacy. Does this suggest there is not a hierarchy of questions but each question student, staff, faculty or visitors have should be answered out of a care for that individual? Or that certain questions take precedence in a particular moment of need at specific point of time for that individual? For example, the thing we are circling around in this discussion, the reference desk, was particularly in Carnegie libraries, a barrier, an imposing guardpost constructed to tower over the requester who had to

---

6 hooks, *Teaching to Transgress*, 187.

humbly approach and publicly state their request. So how do questions in the present (location, time) affect thinking not just about the present but also about the future? Angela, as you mentioned above, library practice has often framed the "where's the bathroom question" as a point of humor or exasperations (goes back to people "not properly reading" signage). The bathroom location question is a standard example of the "wrong" question which is often posed to the reference desk. To follow Drabinski's argument the idea of "where's the bathroom" as an example of a "bad" question is a truth claim which frames the questioner in a particular light. That is, this is a "useless" or "non-professional" question determined as such by the professional librarian's presence, at that moment in time at the reference desk. The concept of kairos is applicable here as "… *kairos* allows librarians an analytic alternative to grappling with the truth claims of competing frameworks…"[7] How does that jive with professional identity? Is it more important to identify as a feminist first and then a librarian?

AP: Oooh, picking apart the historical and social context of the reference desk could be a whole chapter on its own! But that idea of understanding the *kairos* of the reference desk can also lead us to question whether it should still be staffed by librarians. That made sense when answering questions required specialized knowledge. I remember hearing tales from a professor in my library science degree program about his first few times using Dialog back in the late 1960s. Though that was long after the reference desk was first introduced; in that context it seems to make sense to have specialists available to perform those searches. However, in the current context, when there is an over-abundance of information readily available online and computers available for anyone to use to get online, the specialized knowledge we bring to the table is more a matter of teaching people how to narrow their search and evaluate the quality and appropriateness of the sources they find. By the end of the semester in the credit-bearing course I teach, freshmen and sophomore undergraduate students can search the library catalog or a database for three scholarly sources on a given topic. Many of those students could

---

7 Drabinski, Emily. "Toward a Kairos of Library Instruction." *ACALIB The Journal of Academic Librarianship* 40, no. 5 (2014): 480–85. doi: 10.1016/j.acalib.2014.06.002.

effectively teach a peer how to do that as well. Given that context, does it still make sense to staff the reference desk with specialists? I'm not suggesting librarians not be available at all to help with more complex research questions, but maybe we don't need to sit at a reference desk for hours each week if only a small percentage of questions require specialist knowledge.

I wonder if this is a point where it's useful to return to intersectional identities. How does my identity as a woman and your identity as a man affect our reactions to this tension between care for students and self-care? Of course that's too simplistic, but sticking with the gender part for a bit longer, I was raised by a single working-class dad. My experience of caring meant teaching me to do something instead of just doing it for me (shows respect for my ability to do that thing) and giving me space to figure things out unless/until I ask for help. Maybe this next part is unconnected to gender, but I don't recall ever feeling like the person who directed me to a restroom really cared about me–that seems like just basic politeness I'd expect from any stranger. When I think of caring, I think of the person who went out of their way to help me with something I couldn't do on my own, whether that meant teaching me to do something or using their greater access to power to get something done. This understanding of caring affects my reaction to discussions about how directing a person to the restroom is caring for them. Spending time sitting at a desk directing people to the restroom, when there are plenty of staff and student assistants available and qualified to provide the same answer, is taking away time that could instead be spent doing something I understand as really caring for them–whether that means teaching a class or sitting in a committee to advocate for more gender neutral restrooms. Of course, now we're looping back to keeping specific contexts in mind–I would feel differently if me not being at the desk would mean that no one would be available to answer those questions. It also means we must apply this feminist pedagogical approach to all library employees, communicating with them regularly and taking their concerns seriously when they report things like problems with access to restrooms, like the example you mentioned earlier.

JM: Returning to the nurturing aspect of an ethic of care, the idea of reference transactions can overlook the fact that these questions are coming from individuals, from other human beings. And to reference your point earlier regarding teaching as a primary part of our roles, embracing an ethic of care for other people is to embrace the role of pedagogy throughout our practice. In the classroom, I am learning from engaging with the materials and my student's questions and dialogue. Can't the same thing be true at the reference desk? While the reference desk may not consistently offer a strong pedagogical platform, by being fully attentive myself, as in the classroom an "official" teaching site, to the questions that are raised, as raised by human beings in search of meaning, is a part, I think, of nurturing as part of the practice of an ethic of care.

AP: This seems like a good point at which to back up and talk about our understandings of feminist pedagogy, since that is the foundation for the debate we're getting into here!

JM: I had a conversation with Bob Schroeder in May 2015 where he said, quoting from memory here so not quite exact, even if he hadn't read anything considered feminist pedagogy he would have considered himself to be feminist. In his view, one can practice or think their way into feminist pedagogy precisely because of what you mention above, Angela, on the idea of the ethic of care. Maria Accardi writes "Feminist pedagogy seeks to transform the teacher/student relationship and disrupt traditional notions of classroom power and authority."[8] I resonate with this deeply.

While the focus of this text and this chapter is on reference, my understanding of feminist pedagogy has been significantly impacted due to working with the library's student staff and the para-professional staff. The religious tradition of my institution has historically relegated women voices, and salaries, to a secondary rank behind the dudes. I understand one of the roles that feminist pedagogy plays in the library is to equip and empower. Feminist pedagogy provides a particular way of caring about and providing opportunities to the students and staff that I work with. Feminist pedagogy challenges me to be present, to pay attention, and to value the weight of the individual's suggestion. This includes,

---

8 Maria T. Accardi, *Feminist Pedagogy for Library Instruction* (Sacramento, CA: Library Juice Press, 2013), 42.

I think, elevating and directing recognition to my staff for their ideas, contributions and input.

I do ask myself, particularly in working on this chapter, am I feminist? Feminist pedagogy offers, I think, a conceptualization or reason for doing things that I think should be done. Feminist pedagogy offers a significant and powerful counter-narrative to the dominant narrative with which I was raised. I should give credit to my staff when they come up with awesome ideas both to them and to the institution. It's the right thing to do but feminist pedagogy provides additional motivation or premise to be consistent in this practice. Identifying with or locating myself within a practice of feminist pedagogy calls me to something higher than just my own gut. Maxine Greene has written "Feminist pedagogies…demand critical examination of what lies below the surface. …they require renewed attentiveness to the construction of knowledge and the life of meaning."[9] Angela, while we've talked about this briefly, I am curious to hear more about your own development in this area.

AP: Like you, Jeremy, my understanding of feminist pedagogy did not develop in relation to the reference desk. A central part of my job is teaching, mostly in the context of a credit-bearing information literacy course.

My understanding of feminist pedagogy comes from reading bell hooks[10] and taking Maria Accardi's Feminist Pedagogy for Library Instruction class offered through the Library Juice Academy. I have identified as a feminist for as long as I can remember, but when I first started teaching, I had shamefully little training in pedagogy.

Maria Accardi highlights several themes reflected in the literature about feminist pedagogy: addressing social justice, honoring student voices, building collaborative communities, empowering students by questioning traditional power relationships, and privileging an ethic of care.[11] My current understanding of feminist

---

9 Carmen Luke and Jennifer Gore, *Feminisms and Critical Pedagogy* (New York: Routledge, 1992), x-xi.

10 hooks, *Teaching to Transgress*.

11 Maria T. Accardi, *Feminist Pedagogy for Library Instruction* (Sacramento, CA: Library Juice Press, 2013), 35-43.

pedagogy boils these down to focus primarily on authenticity and collaboration. Authenticity, to me, means being myself rather than attempting to be an objective, neutral automaton. The emphasis that feminist pedagogy places on social justice issues provides additional justification to be my authentic self and include social justice issues where I can. Authenticity also means being a whole person, not just a performer on stage, in the classroom, and interacting with students as whole persons. Collaboration in this context encompasses working together and sharing knowledge, rather than maintaining a rigid hierarchical distinction between myself and the learner.

In the context of reference, I apply feminist pedagogy by working with students without reinforcing hierarchical distinctions. Instead of using a dual monitor set-up that lets students see what I'm doing but from the other side of the desk, I invite students to come around to see my screen and "drive" the computer. Of course, the student could "drive" the computer from the other side of the desk, but where feasible, inviting the student around the desk feels less hierarchical to me–we're on the same side instead of reinforcing separation. As with most things, this can be complicated. I would advise a person to maintain that separation when needed to protect against microaggressions or harassment, for example, as a matter of caring for the librarian as a whole person.

I also take the time to discuss fundamental problems with some research topics, instead of maintaining a neutral facade. This could mean pointing out aspects of an issue that counter or complicate the information the student has found so far, such as the way racism or sexism shaped the event they are examining. Or it could mean discussing why the student is having such difficulty finding information–whether that's because the voices they're looking for have been devalued in the scholarly record or because their position is contradicted by the vast majority of scholarly research. The flip side of that is that letting go of the myth of neutrality gives me permission to get excited about research topics that empower disadvantaged groups. Even when there are few to no questions, not being neutral can mean something as simple as wearing a "Black Lives Matter" button while at the reference desk.

But, feminist pedagogy also leads me to question how many of our goals we can actually accomplish at the reference desk. How many of our reference interactions provide an opportunity to address social justice issues? As I noted above, I question whether spending so much time at the reference desk actually reinforces gendered stereotypes about a predominantly female profession. When students come to the desk wanting to learn how to do research in their major discipline, we can empower students to find the sources they need on their own without relying on an intermediary. But if students come to the desk wanting us to just give them three articles to use, can we really do much to empower them? In some cases, it may be possible to redirect the conversation and teach them how to find the sources on their own, but what if they react to this by getting annoyed that they have to do that much work? From an ethic of care standpoint, we have to recognize that this negative emotion will get in the way of effective learning and respect that we don't know enough about the student's whole lives to understand why they are reacting this way. How do we then empower the student or encourage them to be active collaborators in their education if they have this emotional response? I can honor their emotional response, but just handing them three articles that seem relevant to their topic based on how they described it to me doesn't feel very caring to me—it feels like I'm giving up on them. Not to mention the fact that I feel like I'm obstructing their education if I just select three sources for them, when the assignment was (hopefully) intended to give them practice in exploring the published research in their field.

If the format of the drop-in reference interaction makes it unlikely that we will be able to accomplish many of the goals of feminist pedagogy, should we continue to privilege reference as a significant part of our jobs? Instead of spending hours each week at the reference desk, could we do a better job of enacting feminist pedagogy by putting that energy into training student assistants to answer most questions? That arrangement ensures that someone is present to care for students who need help finding the restroom or formatting a paper, while allowing us to put our energy into empowering those student workers. While I have heard complaints about this model focusing on student workers not knowing what they don't know, so answering some complex questions poorly instead of referring them to a librarian, maybe it's worth seeing whether more in-depth training could solve this. Our reference coordinator, Naomi Stuesser, is currently piloting a project in which student reference assistants (SRAs) spend an hour each week with a librarian at the reference desk. In between answering questions, the librarian spends that hour training the SRA on information literacy and additional reference tools. It's too early to know how this will turn out, but this seems like a much more effective way of empowering students and breaking down the hierarchy than us simply being present to answer basic questions.

JM: I would love to know how that SRA/reference project turns out. That sounds awesome. I think about the social justice aspect that you mentioned earlier quite often. I've tried to move into this with our student staff by using staff meetings as discussion times for thinking about the connection of social justice to work in the library, but it has been slow going.

One thing I tell the student staff regularly is that they have access to all the tools that I do, I've just had a bit more practice using them. Thus, the student staff are just as able to answer the vast majority of questions that patrons are going to have. I try to make it a habit if a student staff member does get stuck, and they haven't tried troubleshooting (assuming the situation allows for it) that they need to go back and troubleshoot and if that fails I can step in. We will then review and discuss what happened and what to do for next time. I want my student staff to see themselves as empowered in their role and to extend that empowerment into other areas of life and learning. Can I offer strong support for the fact that a student staff member's developed ability to troubleshoot the copier effectively makes impact in their life outside of the library? Do I need to? I wrestle with this.

The social justice idea extends to the fact that students pay thousands of dollars to have access to resources that will usually be closed to them as soon as they graduate. So when I have the opportunity, students need to be exposed to tools and practices that are going to sustain them beyond the tools the library offers. This requires me to be thinking about the student as a whole person who needs something at the present and will probably need more information in the future. Also, it requires that I think of the community rather than just my own personal work satisfaction (finding a citation; providing a call number). Answering the how of this is way more difficult, in my opinion.

AP: That last piece about teaching students to find and use tools that will still be accessible after they graduate is so important!

As for your questions about how empowering it is to be trusted to troubleshoot technology, that's part of what I love about training students to answer reference questions. While we can debate how empowering it really is to fix a copier, spending that time training students to help other students with research does affect their work in other classes.

It also helps to break down hierarchies, as individual or small group training meetings gives the student workers more opportunities to get to know the librarians. A lot has been written and said about how students tend to find it less intimidating to ask other students for help. Student reference workers can help to bridge that gap when needed. Of course, I'm thinking of this in terms of my library context, where there are several librarians who work reference shifts, and can use that time to work with student workers. The logistics would work differently for a lone librarian who does not have a formal reference desk shift!

Returning again to the ways our identities affect our interactions at the reference desk, the overwhelming whiteness of librarianship has been discussed in a range of publications and conferences. The student workers at my library are notably more diverse than the faculty librarians. Brook, Ellenwood, and Lazzaro recently published an article that examines, among other topics, the "racialized dimensions of reference work."[12] This comes out in the ways we communicate and is affected by entrenched power dynamics in academia. Empowering student employees to answer reference questions, especially if we empower them to be authentic

---

12 Freeda Brook, Dave Ellenwood, and Althea Eannace Lazzaro, "In Pursuit of Antiracist Social Justice: Denaturalizing Whiteness in the Academic Library," *Library Trends* 64, no. 2 (2015): 269. doi: 10.1353/lib.2015.0048.

instead of pushing them to perform whiteness,[13] can contribute to larger social justice goals. It is clearly not the whole solution, but a way to improve the inclusivity of one aspect of library services while we work on other areas.

Moving on, the last question on our list asks how the ideological stances of one's institutional context affects how librarians pursue or build feminist pedagogical strategies.

By this point, I've written a lot of criticisms of the traditional reference desk, and both of us have talked about the way our particular settings affect the ways we can enact feminist pedagogy. Working from very different positions in very different institutions definitely constrains our options. As a member of an instructional services department in a much larger library, I get to focus a lot of my energy on pedagogy instead of administrative tasks.

JM: There is a whole discussion that would be awesome to have around the role feminist pedagogy has in administrative roles and tasks. This would take a whole other chapter to explore but the push back against power dynamics benefits from pedagogical practices at all levels.

AP: I have a lot of support in my department for using critical approaches and questioning the status quo. This support has been crucial for my ability to apply feminist pedagogy in regard to reference, in the classroom, and in working with student employees.

In our early conversations about this chapter, we each expressed some preconceived notions about the other's setting. Jeremy, you mentioned an assumption that it is much easier, in such a small library, to build "a pedagogical ethos" among your staff. I took this to be related to assumptions about how difficult it can be to change a large bureaucracy. Yet, it is precisely that bureaucracy that makes room for my department to focus primarily on pedagogy while others deal with the administration of the library. It probably also makes it easier for me to be so critical of having librarians at a reference desk, since we have student assistants and staff

---

13 See April Hathcock, "White Librarianship in Blackface: Diversity Initiatives in LIS," In the Library with the Lead Pipe (October 7, 2015). http://www.inthelibrarywiththeleadpipe.org/2015/lis-diversity/.

available and able to answer most of the questions that come in to the reference desk. On the flip side, I had assumptions about the climate at a small religious institution–that the climate would be more conservative, making it harder to implement something as revolutionary as feminist pedagogy. Jeremy, you explained the ways you use your faith to justify the need for feminist pedagogy. I feel like we've both learned a lot from the conversations that went into the proposal for this chapter!

JM: For sure. Angela, the support that you have in your institution is something largely lacking in my situation. There was a group of people engaged and interested in pedagogical methods and pursuits but they have left for various reasons. The potential benefit of a small/tiny institution becomes an issue when the size cannot sustain the individuals who suggest change or new approaches. My view of how my faith feeds into a feminist pedagogy is definitely a minority view among current colleagues. There's much that could be said here but for sake of space I hold that any pedagogical approach which emphasizes care for people in meaningful and deep ways while seeking to address issues of oppression and inequality needs to be thoughtfully considered and as possible, implemented. There's a strange division in that I have a significant autonomy in the library to implement different approaches but not a venue to talk/think through with colleagues. These kind of exchanges then take the place allowing me to think through and process "out loud." For that I'm very grateful. I really value your viewpoint and expression throughout this chapter and it has challenged me in my own practice and thinking.

While our conversation is inscribed here, Maria's voice as editor is a part of this as well which, for me, is doing its own feminist pedagogical work in challenging some of what we've written asking for clarification, further insights, and revision. Maria's largely hidden interactions with our text does or fills the place of what I think we as librarians should be doing in our contexts, regardless of type. Looking around our various institutions and asking why are we doing this? What informs our practice? What needs to change, what informs our approach to change, what needs to be strengthened?

AP: Thanks for suggesting we do this chapter, Jeremy! It has been really useful for me, too, to think through all of ground we covered in this discussion! I think the fact that we're both thinking about ways to implement feminist pedagogy in our very different contexts highlights the ways this approach can permeate all of our interactions. Though the emphasis of the chapter is on the reference desk, it's interesting that we both talked a good deal about how we enact feminist pedagogy in the context of working with student employees. You brought them up because the size of the library means you rely on them to answer most questions, and working with them is a key way you enact feminist pedagogy. And I kind of made the argument that we should do more of what it sounds like you're already doing, but from a "death to the librarian reference shift" angle!

Of course, that's only two academic contexts. None of this necessarily translates to a public library well. But, I think the key takeaway of this is that it's all connected. The signage selected by library administrators affects some of the interactions that are likely to happen at the reference desk. The library collection–both in terms of whether certain viewpoints are privileged and in terms of how accessible those materials are (considering both physical access in the library and online resources)–affects reference interactions. So even if you have no control over the way feminist pedagogy is or is not implemented by the person answering questions at the reference desk, you may still have an opportunity to create an environment more aligned with feminist pedagogical ideals for patrons... Which may loop back to affecting the reference desk, if you've reduced their need to ask for help. And if you are reading this because you want to enact feminist pedagogy at the reference desk, don't stop there.

Bibliography

Accardi, Maria T. *Feminist Pedagogy for Library Instruction* (Sacramento, CA: Library Juice Press, 2013).

Asher, Andrew. "Who's Asking What? Modelling a Large Reference Interaction Dataset," *Proceedings of the 2014 Library Assessment Conference* (2015): 52-62. http://libraryassessment.org/bm-doc/proceedings-lac-2014.pdf.

Drabinski, Emily. "Toward a Kairos of Library Instruction." *ACALIB The Journal of Academic Librarianship* 40, no. 5 (2014): 480–85. doi: 10.1016/j.acalib.2014.06.002.

Brook, Freeda, Dave Ellenwood, and Althea Eannace Lazzaro, "In Pursuit of Antiracist Social Justice: Denaturalizing Whiteness in the Academic Library," *Library Trends* 64, no. 2 (2015): 246-284. doi: 10.1353/lib.2015.0048.

Hathcock, April. "White Librarianship in Blackface: Diversity Initiatives in LIS," *In the Library with the Lead Pipe* (October 7, 2015). http://www.inthelibrarywiththeleadpipe.org/2015/lis-diversity/.

hooks, bell. *Teaching to Transgress: Education as the Practice of Freedom.* (New York: Routledge, 1994).

Horton, Myles, Brenda Bell, John Gaventa, and John Marshall Peters. *We Make the Road by Walking: Conversations on Education and Social Change.* (Philadelphia: Temple University Press, 1990).

Luke, Carmen and Jennifer Gore, *Feminisms and Critical Pedagogy* (New York: Routledge, 1992).

Peters, Timothy. "Taking Librarians Off the Desk: One Library Changes its Reference Desk Staffing Model," *Performance Measurement and Metrics* 16, no. 1 (2015): 18-27. doi:10.1108/PMM-11-2014-0038.

Postlude

The Creature Questions its Reflection: Lyrical Feminist Explorations of Reference Desk Interactions

Corinne Gilroy and Alexandrina Hanam

The *lyric scholarship* of Canadian poet-scholars such as Jan Zwicky, Anne Carson, and Kathleen McConnell provides space for literary, analytic, and artistic critique of library reference practice and interactions. Lyric scholarship is a poetic and methodological tool that is used here to interrogate the dependence-driven customer service model imbedded in women-dominated service professions, while gesturing toward alternatives that cultivate inter-dependence, independence, and equity. Significant portions of this piece are structured to evoke Zwicky's *Wisdom & Metaphor*, in which the author's own verses live on the left, mirroring and responding to quotes from other writers and thinkers on the right. The performative, call-and-response potential of lyric scholarship is used here to create dialogue across the centre margin of the page (a reflection of the reference desk itself), challenging conventional practices of library reference and instruction.

Introduction

I.

He comes up to the desk and rings the bell.
    (First warning: I forgot to hide the bell.)
I skip from my chair because it's been
    a quiet night of pointing to the toilets
    and wrong numbers.
He and his white ball cap (indoors! my mother'd die   )
    just have a little question,
    a little tiny one about where to place a period
    in a little tiny APA citation.
    (No matter how many you have,
        you probably need one more.
        Take it from me.)
That settled, keys clacked, he beams at his screen, his words, his lines,
    the last one,
    his last semester.
"Hey, is your name really *Library*?"
Grinning eyes on my chest—but not like that, right?
    (No, I forgot my regular nametag.
        No, this is not the kind of question I'm here to answer.
        No, you don't get to do this.   )
I laugh a little laugh
    a little tiny one that scoffs.
    a little tiny bull exhaling.
    The pages in the stacks hardly shiver.
    (No matter how many times,
        it will always happen again.
        Take it from me.)
And still I don't say *No* because that's a two-letter neon sign
    a two-letter four-letter word blinking in red
    at the top of a hill I refuse to die on
    (But sure, okay, a little chip of me underfoot
        To keep him here, at least
        Open, at least
        To the chance he'll have bell hooks fall on his head
        Or stub his toe on Irigaray's spine
        Even if it's his last one.   )

II.

What on earth is this, right?

Lyric scholarship
  (or at least two bookish fans'
  attempt to scrape open a
  muddy tributary with our
  hands and plastic shovels)

lyric is lithe[1]
  says Jan Zwicky, poet-
  philosopher
*It is poignant, and musical. It moves
by association of images*[2]

*it evidences a slight tang of satire on
the genre of academic writing,*[3]
  quoth poet-scholar
  Kathleen McConnell by day,
  Kathy Mac by night.

For Clare Goulet,
lyric teacher-champion, it is about
  *keeping something alive and
  whole in its context.*[4]

And maybe it's about *resisting,*[5] too,
warns Tina Northrup, her scholar's
sword plunged into the soil

  but as Anne Carson's lyric
  wisdom knows, it can be
*confusing and embarrassing to have
two mouths.*[6]

  So here we are, deep in both
  the lyric and the library.

and the feminist reference desk
  (or at least two poet-library
  workers' attempt to build up a
  seawall with our small hands
  and smaller stones)

and so is the library, lithe
  as it learns to see
  itself in the mirror,
  traces this third space sparking
  at the edges

we have to laugh a little, don't we,
  at the heavy oak chest of what we've
  been and become
  what we think we are, by day
  what we want to be, by night

for the one sitting under that curious
  sign marked Reference, it is about
  keeping the question alive,
  the bright interrogation

and yes, it's about resisting, too,
  the pink collar that appears at a
  distance, tighter on approach

never quite teacher, clerk, mother,
father, mentor
  so maybe this is just a little unclear,
    uncanny[7]

and here we are, deep in both
  the lyric and the library.

III.

We're a bit like frogs in pots, sometimes.
Heat creeping quick, quicker
toward boiled-dry space that belies
our green skin and blisters.

Then the scalding pot drops to the floor,
burnt creatures spilled on the stonework,
poison.
(Did we spill it, or were we spilled?)
Golden arches[8] at the next exit,
their impossible promise shimmering:

Shilling the consuming body, the food chain apex
mere commodities[9] to be glutted, acquired, exchanged.

> Where the highest value is placed on being
> efficient and productive: this is also
> how our interactions with students and researchers
> mutate into *transactions* with *customers*.

> How we name is how we value.

> Our nurturing, our cultivation and civic space
> That gentle coaxing toward self-efficacy.
> All of this gets
> Boiled down into dollar signs
> (glittering green snakes on skewers):
> all objects are potentially objects of exploitation.[10]

Here, we push back, step back, look.
Our faces reflected in pans and spoons.
    sharp edges
    rough margins
    empty space
—for what isn't named but still churns around in here,
before coming to rest or to boil.

The Creature at the Desk

I.

The doubling and interchangeability of the role and social status of the library worker engenders a creature in whom sex may be cancelled out by the sound of responding to an inquiry and the sound of responding to an inquiry may be cancelled out by sex.

The doubling and interchangeability of mouth engenders a creature in whom sex is cancelled out by sound and sound is cancelled out by sex.[11]

This seems a perfect answer to all the questions raised about whether this creature at the desk is necessary at all, whether her service and support are just as well performed by a machine, and whether she is herself a machine of some kind.

This seems a perfect answer to all the questions raised and dangers posed by the confusing and embarrassing continuity of female nature.[12]

And what of the dangers posed by the confusing and embarrassing continuity of the reference desk, the creep of *customer* ahead of *patron*? Can the modern patron harm her? Can she harm the modern patron?

It wasn't until yesterday afternoon around 4:30 that the library reference desk worker's subjectivity was explored sufficiently for her to gain a name for herself, and by then it was only to ask her if perhaps she would consider re-writing the rest of this paper over her lunch break; accept a salary commensurate with the softness of her skills; take on a flexible part-time schedule and an intern.

it wasn't until the Renaissance that the statue's subjectivity was explored sufficiently for her to gain a name for herself[13]

II.

> Putting a door on the mouth of women's work has been an important project of patriarchal culture from antiquity to the present day. Its chief tactic is an ideological association of female sound with monstrosity, disorder and death.

Putting a door on the female mouth has been an important project of patriarchal culture from antiquity to the present day. Its chief tactic is an ideological association of female sound with monstrosity, disorder and death.[14]

> Our apologies to Anne Carson for how little that quotation needs to be modified in order to reflect the helping professions and pink-collar work. We ask that the reader take a moment to appreciate the footnoted citation. And then another to consider again *monstrosity, disorder and death.*

Housekeeper plunges bare knuckles into a drain bloated grey with sloughed skin, hair and scum. / Mary Shelley confesses who we really are; takes the human body apart, stitches it back together. / Nurse grapples a platter of fluids the color of bricks; takes blood; folds down eyelids and pulls up bed sheets for the last time. / Sex worker grapples florid living sweating bodies, pays in empathy, gets only the margins in return.

The library is an escape into whiter collars, but there are tell-tale marks on our monstrous necks: soothe, redeem, sluice, polish, clear; carve out chunks of flesh for the public, for the love of it, for little.

III.

Is it conceivable that the exercise of hegemony, the slow creep of one body toward another, might leave the library's wilder spaces untouched?

Is it conceivable that the exercise of hegemony might leave space untouched?
[…]
Could space be nothing more than the passive locus of social relations, the milieu in which their combination takes on a body…?[15]

Even the margins have margins. The library within the institution. The reference desk within the library. The question that answers a question.
Gesture past how things are, toward struggles kept out of sight. Scratch the membrane of the status quo & a fractal polyp splits and blooms in the dark.

Though the space we take and make wild may only be the rough edge of a manicured field, it is ours.

There are loose threads on the veil of capitalism. Roots running past the property line. Shadows under the glare. This is the spot to sow something suggesting equity, ethics.

The answer must be no.[16]

Until you claw it back.

The Mirror At The Desk

I.

           Deconstruction... maintains a
           constant questioning.[18]
   Uninterrupted digging.
   Uninterrupted interruptions.

  Shovel, pick, magnifying glass;
field notes on their utility and danger.

           The acceptance of the primacy
           of rational self-interest in
           human affairs constitutes an
           institutionalization of the priority of
           certain kinds of motives over others.

           These motives are, in their essence,
           exploitative.[19]
   It's only through a fluke,
  a red stain on a glassy stone,
  that you realize the thing
   you have been cleaving,
    sampling, uprooting

  is your own displaced self,
   and another breathing
      body besides.

 This can't be just a laboratory.
Hands need to be dirty, linked,
    washed, felt. Always
 focusing on the subordinate.[17]
  And undoing, releasing.

Traluire – to become translucent
The mirror-glass stone lets go.
  (Was there ever one?)

II.

The library has come to reflect a
contemporary movement in which
professionals and staff are resisting
what seem to them to be prescriptive
and unethical programs for
scholarly, civic, and leisurely pursuit.

*the term lyric has come to signify a
contemporary movement in which
poets and scholars are resisting what
seem to them to be prescriptive
and unethical programs for
academic pursuit*[20]

The library has come to
smash the screen
smoke out the canon
pull round nails from
square corners
flense this assessment,
bleach its bones

The library has come to
rip open the box and fold it neatly
ignore the time and keep counting
on interaction, energy,
presence,
the person here and here now
with folded hands or
white knuckles
dark questions or circles
here and here now

The library has come to
this:

III.

The tenured radicals of the library are those librarians who, along with other library staff, have conducted a devastating assault on the patriarchal surveillance state and state censorship-by-proxy, deliberately and politically striving toward the egalitarian promise of the humanities via feminism, ethnic studies, and multiculturalism; and it is they who have begun to critically interrogate the contours of free speech in light of pluralism, respect, safety, and empathy —for the sake of traversing the pejorative of *political correctness.*

The tenured radicals of Kimball's book and letter [about Anne Carson] *are those scholars "who have conducted a devastating assault on the liberal arts curriculum across the country, deliberately degrading and politicizing the humanities in the name of feminism, ethnic studies and multiculturalism; and it is they who have begun to campaign against free speech and pluralism for the sake of enforcing a narrow vision of political correctness"*[21]

The Reflection in the Mirror

I.

recognition
as women, non-binary transfolk,
men; professionals and patrons;
scholars and hobbyists; Black,
of Color, White; queer and
het; refugee, immigrant, long-
settled, indigenous; neurotypical
and *a*; disabled and non; poor
and wealthy; privileged and
marginalized;

Then the third wave hove up from desire / for those same rights as women: recognition. / Equality doesn't mean homogeneity.[22]

recognition
as particular coordinates that have
to be sought, as constellations,
gravity wells and moving,
turbulent space.

we want to be recognized, to
recognize you—ships in a safe
harbour, departing, arriving,
drifting, moored;

as much of you as you want us to
see, as many facets, colors, and
angles as you are ready to reveal
with your question, your query,
your search, your curiosity;

quietly, if that's you, or at
full volume against the noise,
approaching or inviting approach;

I won't ask why you want to know,
but I will invite you to ask this
of yourself.

Compromise:
promising together.

II.

> *Brevity has been urged as the defining feature of lyric expression (Poe). But it is an economy of movement, not merely a stinginess with words, that is close to its heart: lyric is lithe.*[23]

Brevity: let's make it pejorative,
hem it in, tax the lint in its
empty pockets,
(for just a moment; for science).

And *stinginess*. It was born
petty; that helps. Small, precarious
spaces with stale air. Floor plan for a
saltine cracker wingspan.

Apply to *pink collar*, tight and
chafing. Exact and static.
Adjust in the mirror.
Pull, fruitlessly.

Dependable, yet hysterical.
That's us.
Reliable, crucial, underpaid,
expendable.
(You should want to do it for
the love of it, right? Salaries only
sully things.)

*But it is an economy of
movement*, a sharp, effective,
glinting blade, when something like
the library
will bend but not snap,
expand but not burst,
reflect but not glare.
The library is *lithe*
when we want it to be.
Space for the sweating collar to fray
into threads and inquiries.

III.

> Those in power at the reference desk, that is to say, librarians, also have responsibility to what Spivak calls "unlearning one's privilege" or to become, as we may put it, able to listen to "that other constituency," those who approach Our Reference Desk, and speak in ways that we will be taken seriously by one another and recognize that the very position we occupy can be historically powerful when we want those with whom we engage to actually be able to answer back.

Those in power also have responsibility to what Spivak calls "unlearning one's privilege" or to become "able to listen to that other constituency" and "speak in such a way that one will be taken seriously by that other constituency ... [and] recognize that the position of the speaking subject within theory can be an historically powerful position when it wants the other to actually be able to answer back"[24]

> The mouth of the library is the ear with which we listen and
> *answer back;*
> *reflect;*
> with which we listen to those who answer back.

The mouth of lyric is an ear.[25]

> The library reference desk is rooted in an integrity of response and co-response; each dimension of service and inquiry attending to the others.

Lyric is rooted in an integrity of response and co-response; each dimension attending to the others.

> The library is both mouth and ear, a speaking and a listening, an act of both observing and being observed.

Conclusion

But the lyric approach, as opposed to dissecting, taking apart for the purpose of examination, is about keeping something alive and whole in its context.[26]
It aims not just to convey an idea, but to embody it.[27]
Lyric is an attempt to comprehend the whole in a single gesture.[28]

He comes up to the desk and says hello.
I skip from my chair because it's been
    a quiet night of directions to the toilets
    and wrong numbers.
He and his white ball cap
    (*My lucky hat. My team is playing tonight.*)
    just have a little question,
    a little tiny one about where to place a period
    in a little tiny APA citation.
    (No matter how many you have,
    you probably need one more.
    And then next year maybe you won't.   )
That settled, keyboard clacked, he beams at his screen, his words, his lines,
    the last one,
    his last semester. (A small moment for small joys, just then.)
Hey, can I ask your name? (Grinning, he shares his.)
    (Well, it's not *Library*, in case you were curious.)
We laugh at the brass nameplate on my collar: *Library*.
    little tiny laughs that alight.
    little tired too-late exhalations.
    The pages in the stacks yawn along.
    (No matter how many times,
    it will always happen again:
    the late nights, the last minute.
    Work with it; not against it.)
Open is a warm neon sign at the top of a hill I'll be on for two more hours yet.
    Spreading bits of glass doors I've seen & broken through
    for traction
    (To keep him open if not here
    Even if this is his last climb.   )

Addendum: A Response to #UBCAccountable and #CanLitAccountable

Last November, they threw rocks at the neon sign on top of the hill. Warm light went all cold flickery and we haven't come down since.

(*It has been a long hill, heart. / But now the view is good.*[34])

It wasn't students with stones in hand, not young seekers testing their strength. But their teachers, mentors: Canadian Literati in defence of *process*[29] but also their power.

Winds changed and the *cloud of suspicion*,[30] the neon gas, the dust they kicked up to denounce, changed course. Some coughed, sputtered, hunkered down in the space they claimed. Others fled, abject, remorseful.

(*ignorance, old evil, is enforced / and willed, and loved... / used to manufacture madness, / ...it is the aphrodisiac / of power*[35])

But Zwicky, our *lithe*[31] lyric poet-scholar, put her voice in a valise, left her name on the stones, left the scene? We can't say, and that says what it says.

(*what will you do, / now that you / sense the path unraveling / beneath you?*[36])

Lyric is *poets and scholars... resisting... prescriptive and unethical programs for academic pursuit*,[32] and that's not what this is, what it says.

(*What will you do, / you, heart, who know the gods don't flee*[37])

The mouth of lyric is an ear[33]: and maybe an eye, and we want to, need to know if the students—the women—whose courageous backs bear the weight of this fight have yours?

(*the one sin is refusal, and refusal to keep seeking / when refused*[38])

(*You must look.*[39])

Bibliography

An Open Letter To UBC: Steven Galloway's Right To Due Process. 14 Nov 2016. http://www.ubcaccountable.com

Carson, Anne. "Gender of Sound." Chap. 5 in *Glass, Irony & God*. New York: New Directions Books, 1995.

Holberg, John E. "Relational Reference: A Challenge to the Reference Fortress." In *An Introduction to Reference Services in Academic Libraries*, edited by Sarah Connor, 39-46. New York: Haworth Information Press, 2006.

Lahey, Anita. "Academic Papers get Poetic." *University Affairs*. Last modified December 5, 2011. http://www.universityaffairs.ca/featu-res/feature-article/academic-papers-get-poetic/

Lefebvre, Henri. *The Production of Space*. Translated by Donald Nicholson-Smith. Oxford: Blackwell, 1991.

McConnell, Kathleen. *Pain, Porn, Complicity*. Hamilton, ON: Wolsak and Wynn Pub., 2012.

Northrup, Tina. "Lyric Scholarship in Controversy: Jan Zwicky and Anne Carson" *Studies in Canadian Literature / Études en littérature canadienne* 37, no. 1 (2012): 192-214. https://journals.lib.unb.ca/index.php/SCL/article/view/20036

Olson, Hope A., and Melodie J. Fox. "Gayatri Chakravorty Spivak: Deconstructionist, Marxist, Feminist, Postcolonialist." In *Critical Theory for Library and Information Science: Exploring the Social from Across the Disciplines*, edited by Gloria J. Leckie, Lisa M. Given, and John E. Buschman 295-309. Libraries Unlimited: Santa Barbara, Calif. 2010.

Quinn, Brian. "The McDonaldization of Academic Libraries?" *College & Research Libraries* 61, no. 3 (2000): 248-61.

Spivak, Gayatri Chakravorty. "Bonding in Difference: Interview with Alfred Arteaga." In *The Spivak Reader: Selected Works of Gayatri Chakravorty Spivak*, ed. Donna Landry and Gerald McLean, 15-51. New York: Routledge, 1996.

Zwicky, Jan. "Courage." *The Long Walk*, 6-7. Regina, Sask: University of Regina Press, 2016.

Zwicky, Jan. *Lyric Philosophy*. 2nd ed. Kentville: Gaspereau, 2012.

Notes

1 Jan Zwicky, *Lyric Philosophy*. 2nd ed. (Kentville: Gaspereau, 2012), L73.

2 Ibid.

3 Kathleen McConnell, *Pain, Porn, Complicity* (Hamilton, ON: Wolsak and Wynn Pub., 2012), 15-16.

4 Clare Goulet, qtd.in Anita Lahey, "Academic Papers get Poetic," *University Affairs*, last modified December 5, 2011.

5 Tina Northrup, "Lyric Scholarship in Controversy: Jan Zwicky and Anne Carson," *Studies in Canadian Literature / Études en littérature canadienne* 37, no. 1 (2012).

6 Anne Carson, "Gender of Sound," in *Glass, Irony & God*. (New York: New Directions Books, 1995), 119-137.

7 McConnell, *Pain, Porn, Complicity*, 106-107.

8 Brian Quinn, "The McDonaldization of Academic Libraries?" *College & Research Libraries* 61, no. 3 (2000): 248-61.

9 John E. Holberg, "Relational Reference: A Challenge to the Reference Fortress," in *An Introduction to Reference Services in Academic Libraries*, ed. Sarah Connor, (New York: Haworth Information Press, 2006), 45.

10 Zwicky, *Lyric Philosophy*, L52.

11 Carson, "Gender of Sound," 136.

12 Ibid.

13 McConnell, *Pain, Porn, Complicity*, 20.

14 Carson, "Gender of Sound," 121.

15 Henri Lefebvre, *The Production of Space*, trans. Donald Nicholson-Smith (Oxford. Blackwell, 1991), 11.

16 Ibid.

17 Hope A. Olson and Melodie J. Fox, "Gayatri Chakravorty Spivak: Deconstructionist, Marxist, Feminist, Postcolonialist,," in *Critical Theory for Library and Information Science: Exploring the Social from Across the Disciplines*, ed. Gloria J. Leckie, Lisa M. Given, and John E. Buschman (Santa Barbara, Calif.: Libraries Unlimited, 2010), 297.

18 Ibid.

19 Zwicky, *Lyric Philosophy*, L51.

20 Northrup, "Lyric Scholarship in Controversy."

21 Northrup, "Lyric Scholarship in Controversy."

22 McConnell, *Pain, Porn, Complicity*, 79.

23 Zwicky, *Lyric Philosophy*, L73.

24 Gayatri Chakravorty Spivak, "Bonding in Difference: Interview with Alfred Arteaga," in *The Spivak Reader: Selected Works of Gayatri Chakravorty Spivak*, ed. Donna Landry and Gerald McLean (New York: Routledge, 1996), 27.

25 Zwicky, *Lyric Philosophy*, L181.

26 Clare Goulet, qtd.in Anita Lahey, "Academic Papers get Poetic."

27 Lahey, "Academic papers get poetic."
28 Zwicky, *Lyric Philosophy*, L73.
29 An Open Letter To UBC: Steven Galloway's Right To Due Process. 14 Nov 2016.
30 Ibid.
31 Zwicky, *Lyric Philosophy*, L73.
32 Northrup, "Lyric Scholarship in Controversy."
33 Zwicky, *Lyric Philosophy*, L181.
34 Jan Zwicky. "Courage." *The Long Walk*. (Regina, Sask: University of Regina Press, 2016) Pg 6-7, lines 20-21.
35 Ibid., lines 3-5.
36 Ibid., lines 10-12.
37 Ibid., lines 16-17.
38 Ibid., lines 23-24.
39 Ibid., line 26.

Contributor Biographies

Maria T. Accardi is Librarian and Coordinator of Instruction and Reference at Indiana University Southeast, a regional campus of Indiana University located in New Albany, Indiana. Maria holds a BA in English from Northern Kentucky University, an MA in English from the University of Louisville, and an MLIS from the University of Pittsburgh. She served as a co-editor of and contributor to *Critical Library Instruction: Theories and Methods* (Library Juice Press, 2010), and is the author of *Feminist Pedagogy for Library Instruction* (Library Juice Press, 2013), for which she received the ACRL Women and Gender Studies Section Award for Significant Achievement in Women and Gender Studies Librarianship in 2014. She lives in Louisville, Kentucky.

Raina Bloom is an Academic Librarian at College Library, University of Wisconsin-Madison. She works with undergraduates, especially those who are new to academic research, and supervises and mentors graduate students. In addition to feminist praxis, her research and professional interests include the philosophy and history of librarianship, pedagogy, and library work as social justice work. She has published work in *Ada: A Journal of Gender, Media, and New Technology* and *JASIST*. She presented at the first Gender and Sexuality in Information Studies Colloquium, in addition to various LIS conferences. You can find her on Twitter @mmelibrarian.

Rose L. Chou is Budget Coordinator at the American University Library. She received her MLIS from San Jose State University and BA in Sociology from Boston College. Rose is co-editor of the forthcoming book *Pushing the Margins: Women of Color and*

Intersectionality in LIS and co-editor of Litwin Books/Library Juice Press Series on Critical Race Studies and Multiculturalism in LIS. She is a 2011 SAA Mosaic Scholar, 2013 ARL CEP Fellow, and 2014 Minnesota Institute for Early Career Librarians alumna. Her research interests include race, gender, and social justice in LIS.

Nina Clements works as a librarian in Southern California. She earned an MFA in creative writing from Sarah Lawrence College and an MLIS from the University of Pittsburgh.

Dory Cochran is a Reference & Instruction Librarian at Utah State University's Merrill-Cazier Library. Dory is originally from Kansas and holds a BA in English and Women's Studies from the University of Kansas, a MLIS from the University of Pittsburgh, and an MA in English from Kansas State University. Dory serves as the subject librarian for the English and Psychology Departments at USU and is passionate about bringing feminist pedagogy to her instruction sessions and interactions with students and faculty. She is also an active member of the Cache Valley Library Association – a local organization that brings library workers from all kinds of libraries together for library advocacy and networking.

Chloe Collins is a graduate of University of Illinois' Library and Information Science program, where she specialized in Special Collections. Her academic interests have led her to broach topics such as: how libraries can better serve patrons experiencing homelessness and/or managing mental health issues; issues of appropriation and ownership in museum contexts; Freud's philosophy on discipline, punishment, and spectacle and how his ideas transfer to librarian/patron dynamics and the organization of libraries; and how groups and individuals construct identities using dress and adornment through the creation of an exhibition proposal. A self-proclaimed dabbler, Chloe enjoys making jewelry and artists' books in her free time. She is passionate about examining the role librarians and archivists play in preserving cultural memory and shaping historical representation within cultural institutions.

Nicole A. Cooke is an Assistant Professor at the School of Information Sciences, the University of Illinois at Urbana-Champaign. She holds an M.Ed in Adult Education from Pennsylvania State University, and an MLS and a Ph.D. in Communication, Information and Library Studies from Rutgers University. Her research and teaching interests include human information behavior (particularly in an online context), critical cultural information studies, and diversity and social justice in librarianship (with an emphasis on infusing them into LIS education and pedagogy). She was named a "Mover & Shaker" by Library Journal in 2007, and was the 2016 recipient of the American Library Association's (ALA) Equality Award, and the Achievement in Library Diversity Research Award presented by ALA's Office for Diversity, Literacy & Outreach. Her latest work is *Information Services to Diverse Populations* (Libraries Unlimited, 2016). Learn more about Dr. Cooke at www.nicolecooke.info @librarynicole

Kate Crowe is the Curator for Special Collections and Archives in the University of Denver (DU) Libraries. Since 2012, Kate has overseen all special collections and archives-related physical preservation, collection development, exhibits, reference, instruction, and outreach activities for the unit. From 2008-2012, Kate was the Archives Processing Librarian and oversaw cataloging and processing for all archival materials in the DU Libraries.

Erin Elzi is the Cataloging and Metadata Librarian at the University of Denver. She spends her days trying to make both the library catalog and the world a better place, and her nights playing roller derby or snuggling with her seven pets.

Celia Emmelhainz is the anthropology and qualitative research librarian at UC Berkeley, and holds an MA in cultural anthropology from Texas A&M and an MLIS from Kent State. She has previously done ethnographic research in Mongolia, the USA, and Kazakhstan, and worked for three years as a school and academic librarian in Kazakhstan.

Corinne Gilroy is Manager of Access Services at the Mount Saint Vincent University Library in Halifax, Nova Scotia, and a graduate student in MSVU's MAEd Lifelong Learning program.

Alexandrina Hanam is an intersectional feminist, poet, and librarian from rural Nova Scotia. She earned a Diploma in Library and Information Technology from Nova Scotia Community College, a BA in Cultural Studies from Mount Saint Vincent University, and an MLIS from the University of Western Ontario. She believes that compassion and resilient curiosity will change the world.

Mellissa J. Hinton has over thirty years of experience working at the B. Davis Schwartz Memorial Library, Long Island University (LIU) Post in Brookville, New York. She has served as a Cataloging Librarian, Head of Acquisitions, Head of Technical Services, and Assistant Dean for Technical and Digital Services. Most recently, she served as Acting Dean for the LIU Libraries. She has an M.A. in English from LIU Post, an M.S. in Information Science from LIU Post, and a D.A. in English from St. John's University. Her research interests focus on the preeminent nineteenth-century American feminist, Margaret Fuller, juxtaposing Fuller's work with that of other writers of the period as well as contemporary feminist theorists.

Beth Hoppe is currently the Social Sciences Research & Instruction Librarian at Bowdoin College in Brunswick, ME. She has previously worked at Union College in Schenectady, NY and at Whitman College in Walla Walla, WA. After receiving her BA from UVM she attended Simmons Graduate School of Library and Information Science in Boston, MA. Her areas of research focus on play in the classroom as a form of critical pedagogy, feminist pedagogy and inclusive teaching, and critical librarianship.

Sara A. Howard is the Librarian for Gender & Sexuality Studies and Research Services at Princeton University. In her work, Sara focuses on the importance of self-care for librarian and researcher alike, and seeks to transform research services for traditionally underserved populations. Prior to Princeton, Sara held positions at Wesleyan University and Queens College. When outside of libraryland, Sara enjoys cooking with way too much cumin, entertaining her niece and nephew, swimming in all bodies of water, and attempting to have a green thumb. She/her/hers. @foreverhoward

Jennifer (Jen) Jacobs, is an Informational Specialist at Avon Center School, Community Consolidated School District 46. Jacobs is also an Adjunct Professor for Dominican University's School of Education. She formerly taught for Southern Illinois University (Senior Lecturer) and Northeastern Illinois University. Her specializations include Childrens/Adolescent Literature, Literacy, and Special Education. Jacobs is a 2016 MLIS graduate from the University of Illinois, Urbana Champaign. She also holds a dual BS from Western Michigan University, and a MA from Northeastern Illinois University (Learning Disabilities). Additionally, she is the proud parent of three children, Benji, Heloise, and Esther Jacobs.

Karen Jung is Coordinator of Research and Instruction Services and Music Librarian at Bowdoin College. She also serves as the instruction, research, and collections liaison to the departments of Education and Africana Studies. Prior to coming to Bowdoin, Karen was Head of Access Services and Music Librarian at Southeastern Louisiana University, where in addition to providing research support, she taught for-credit undergraduate and graduate research courses. She earned a B.M., B.M.E., M.M., and M.L.S from Indiana University, where her graduate research focused on feminist musicology. Karen has been involved in regional and national library associations as a webmaster and has chaired several committees, including serving as the RUSA representative to the ALA Intellectual Freedom Committee, and the chair of RUSA Access to Information Committee. She is passionate about providing equal and open access to research and instruction services in a caring environment that is designed around users' needs and experiences.

Sharon Ladenson is Gender and Communication Studies Librarian at Michigan State University. Her writing on feminist pedagogy and critical information literacy is included in works such as *Critical Library Instruction: Theories and Methods* (from Library Juice Press) and the *Critical Library Pedagogy Handbook* (from the Association of College and Research Libraries). She is an active member of the Women and Gender Studies Section (WGSS) of the Association of College and Research Libraries, and has presented with WGSS colleagues at the National Women's Studies Association Annual Conference.

Rebekah Loyd received her MLIS from the School of Information Sciences at the University of Illinois Urbana-Champaign, where she studied the intersection of social justice and archives. Her research interests include minority representation in archives, community archives, and identity politics. In her limited spare time, Rebekah enjoys audio books, continually learning, reorganizing her closets, and discovering Chicago's diverse food scene. Rebekah graduated in 2016 and is currently employed with Burberry Limited.

Kelly McElroy is the Student Engagement and Community Outreach Librarian at Oregon State University Libraries & Press. She received her MLIS and Master of Archival Studies from the University of British Columbia. With Nicole Pagowsky, she co-edited the *Critical Library Pedagogy Handbooks* published by ACRL Press in 2016. She enjoys organizing critical library workers at the Zine Pavilion at ALA Annual, as well as other workshops and events.

Jeremy McGinniss is Library Director at Clarks Summit University, Pennsylvania. Jeremy has published and presented on the topics of student staff development, critical pedagogy, solo librarianship, and the ACRL Framework.

Amanda Meeks is a Teaching, Learning and Research Services Librarian at Northern Arizona University with a focus in visual art and communications. Her background is in art education and interdisciplinary art making. She is an avid advocate for more diverse and inclusive libraries and classroom practices, as well as creative approaches to academic librarianship.

Melanie Meyers is the Senior Manager for Reference and Outreach at The Center for Jewish History, New York City. She is also an adjunct instructor at The Palmer School of Library and Information Science, Long Island University, where she teaches "Reference and Instruction in Special Collections." She has worked with special collections in a variety of settings, including private, non-profit, and academic institutions, and has presented at various conferences and symposia including SAA annual conference, RBMS Conference, SHARP Annual Conference, and at The Library of Congress.

Erin Pappas is currently a liaison librarian at the University of Virginia Libraries. Prior to that she was librarian for European Languages and Social Sciences at Georgetown University. She holds degrees in anthropology from Reed College and the University of Chicago, and in library science from the University of Kentucky. Her research focuses on linguistic anthropology, semiotic mediation, and textual representations of talk.

Angela Pashia is an Associate Professor and Instructional Services Librarian at the University of West Georgia. She holds a MA in Anthropology from the University of Virginia and a MA in Information Science & Learning Technologies with an emphasis in Library Science from the University of Missouri. Her current research interests focus on the application of critical pedagogies in teaching information literacy.

Annie Pho is Inquiry and Instruction Librarian for Peer-to-Peer Services and Public Programming at UCLA Libraries. She received her MLS from Indiana University-Indianapolis and BA in Art History from San Francisco State University. Her research interests are in intersectionality in LIS, critical pedagogy, and student research behavior.

Michelle Reale is an Associate Professor at Arcadia University. She is the author of *Mentoring and Managing Students in the Academic* Library (ALA Editions, 2013), *Becoming an Embedded Librarian* (ALA Editions, 2016) and *Becoming a Reflective Librarian: Strategies for Mindful Academic Practice* (ALA Editions, 2017). In addition she is the author of 4 collections of poetry, including the forthcoming The Marie Curie Sequence by Dancing Girl Press. She conducts ethnography among African refugees in Sicily and blogs about some of her experiences at www.sempresicilia.wordpress.com.

Maura Seale is currently the collections, research, and instruction librarian for African American studies, American history and studies, European history, music, and women's and gender studies at Georgetown University. She received her MA in American studies from the University of Minnesota in 2005 and her MSI from the University of Michigan in 2007. Her research interests include critical theory and librarianship, information literacy, pedagogy, and mass culture. She welcomes comments at mauraseale@gmail.com.

Katrina Spencer is the Literatures and Cultures Librarian at Middlebury College. She is an MSLIS graduate of the School of Information Science at the University of Illinois, Urbana-Champaign. She values the study of difference, particularly from linguistic, international, and diasporic perspectives and uses her role as a librarian in higher education to encourage students to broaden their horizons through traveling, reading diverse literature, and engaging with otherness. Moreover, in spite of all the controversy surrounding the word, she is a feminist. For more of her writing, search for her name in conjunction with ALA's *Intersections* blog, *Feminist Collections, Hack Library School, Glocal Notes,* and/or visit her personal website, www.katleespe.com.

Dawn Stahura is a Research and Instruction Librarian for the Social Sciences and the Zine Librarian at Simmons College. She is an adjunct instructor for the School of Library and Information Science at Simmons teaching a course on reference and information sources. Aside from research consultations and instruction sessions, she works closely with several faculty members to embed zines into their course curricula. Partnering with the Coordinator of Violence Prevention Education and Outreach at Simmons, allows Dawn to host various zine workshops throughout the academic year on a variety of social justice topics. Outside of work, she is an active zinester, tabling at several zine fests throughout the year, as well as coordinating zine workshops for several youth organizations in the Boston area. She is the author of the zine series *Everything.is.Fine.* She resides in Salem, MA with her husband, one dog, and two cats.

Brian Sullivan is the Education Librarian at James Madison University. He received his Masters of Library Science from Indiana University Bloomington.

Lauren Wallis is the First Year Experience and Student Success Librarian at the University of Delaware. She earned her MLIS and MA in English from the University of North Carolina at Greensboro. Her professional interests include critical information literacy, feminist pedagogy, and collaboration between teachers of writing and information literacy. She can be contacted at lwallis@udel.edu.

Gina Watts is a master's student in Information Studies at the University of Texas at Austin, after getting her BA from Southwestern University's Communication Studies program (Feminist Studies minor). Her academic interests focus on eliminating barriers to information through improved outreach and projects that meld traditional and digital librarianship, with a hope of someday working in a research library or archive. The ideals expressed here of accessible information being integral to change are borne in part from her previous work for Skillpoint Alliance, a non-profit dedicated to increasing access to STEM learning and workforce development in central Texas. Outside of work and school, she spends her time writing, travelling, and reading everything she gets her hands on.

Malia Willey is a Humanities Librarian, Assistant Professor at Libraries & Educational Technologies, James Madison University. She has an MA in History from the University of Maine and an MLS from Indiana University.

INDEX

access, 86-8, 91-3, 130, 161-4, 171-3, 191-3, 198, 206, 226, 306, 358
   see also universal design
   and diversity, 207, 260, 306, 314
   to information, 184, 206-7, 211, 226, 258
   to internet and technology, 128, 206
   to library resources, 167, 184, 191, 273, 294-5, 306
   open, 95, 128, 162
   subject access in catalogs, 277, 284
accessibility, 8, 169, 206, 212-3, 313-8, 347, 351, 353
   see also universal design
Association of College & Research Libraries (ACRL), 64, 167, 184, 195, 285, 286
American Library Association (ALA), 34, 40, 48, 113, 125, 206, 260, 213, 231
   Code of Ethics, 55, 88
assessment[s], 35, 37, 69, 142, 144, 146-8, 155, 283-4, 285-6, 376
   see also ARL, READ, CAT
   feminist, 143-45, 147, 259, 284, 285
   process of, 138, 143, 154
   of reference services, 143, 145
Association of Research Libraries (ARL), 144, 147
authority, 48, 139-40, 191-2, 196-7, 225, 236, 238, 274, 278, 326
   see also Framework for Information Literacy for Higher Education; NACO
   academic, 38, 190, 191, 196
   as constructed and contextual, 55, 56, 211, 286
   decentering, 106, 281
   and feminist pedagogy, 263, 329, 354
   and instructors, 190, 196, 236,
   of librarians, 40, 55, 139, 170, 193, 199, 237, 239, 264
   of the library, 49, 148
   patriarchal, 126, 131
   positive interactions with, 139, 151
   at the reference desk, 8, 112-3, 151
   scholarly, 191, 196
   of students, 191, 285

bias[es], 38, 48, 52, 91-2, 97, 130-1, 142, 173, 180, 281, 306
   children and adolescents, 169, 259

   inherent, 176, 178
   and librarians, 54, 230
   unconscious, 87, 92, 215
Black Lives Matter, 232, 304, 333, 357

cataloging, 131, 177-9, 269-88
Classroom Assessment Techniques (CAT), 145
collaboration[s], 3, 8, 63, 149, 151-3, 156, 302, 328
   and feminist principles, 147, 356
   and reference services, 66, 69
   between teachers and students, 259, 260
   between writing centers and libraries, 106, 200
critical thinking, 78, 166, 177, 179, 307

databases (library), 176, 178, 185, 191, 195-6, 283, 304, 328, 332
disability studies, 272, 316
   feminism and, 313-4, 316-18
diversity, 213, 215, 228, 231-3, 236, 293, 304
   access to college courses related to, 260, 314
   on campus, 53, 296
   and feminism and feminist pedagogy, 206, 255, 257, 259, 261, 297, 324, 344
   of ideas in libraries and among librarians, 207, 212, 227, 248
   and social justice, 253, 258, 260

education, 41, 51, 56, 58, 76, 149, 153, 162, 216, 256, 296-7, 306, 331
   see also learning
   adult, 254, 265
   banking model of, 1, 294, 307
   feminist approach to, 73, 76, 253, 300
   higher, 30, 49, 53, 55, 57-8, 78, 106, 120, 190, 273, 161-2, 294, 300, 304-5, 307-9, 324, 332, 336, 345, 357,
   of librarians, 8, 231, 266
   patriarchal, 120, 256, 300
   provision of by libraries, 206, 213
   of women, 123, 133
equity, 206, 214-5, 287, 367
ethic[s], 149, 156, 304, 374

of care, 8, 41, 73-76, 81, 110, 115, 138-9, 147, 152, 155, 180, 313, 316-18, 350-1, 354, 356-7
feminist, 61-68, 79, 106, 109, 111, 117, 316
feminist, 63, 75

Foucault, Michel, 274, 280, 326
Framework for Information Literacy for Higher Education, 55, 64, 195, 211, 285
Freire, Paulo, 270, 272, 285, 294, 323, 343

Giroux, Henry, 58, 270, 272
Google, 181, 197, 306

hierarchy[ies], 8, 116, 128, 139-40, 153, 156, 172, 185, 190, 257, 260, 295, 302, 351, 358, 359
history[ies], 172, 207-9, 209-10, 213, 216, 283, 286
family, 167, 169, 171-73
of librarianship, 87, 350
oral, 259, 262
painful parts of, 207, 210
and the role of neutrality in librarianship, 51, 53, 56
social, 172-3, 273
women's, 87, 172
hooks, bell, 124, 131, 141-2, 146, 270, 343, 351, 368
feminism defined by, 48, 206
and feminist pedagogy, 131, 133, 265, 272, 295, 355
and feminist revolution, 211, 214

identity[ies], 91, 105, 140-1, 178, 192-4, 208, 243-4, 262, 278, 316, 353
categories of, 87, 92, 269, 271-2
intersectional aspects of, 140, 228, 229, 275, 277, 353
of librarians, 87, 89, 199, 225, 238, 351-2
marginalized, 139, 270, 272, 275, 276, 281
racial and ethnic, 79, 238, 243-4
and reference service, 199, 359
and self-reflection, 229-230
ideology[ies], 52, 55, 211, 261
dominant, 49, 55, 58
information literacy, 6, 64, 106, 145, 184, 193, 208-9, 218, 258, 280, 285, 293, 295-97, 306, 318, 350, 355, 358
intersectionality, 8, 87, 206, 225, 227-8, 262, 271-2, 275-7, 347
and women of color librarians, 7, 228-9

Library of Congress Classification (LCC), 131, 177-79, 269, 274, 276, 278
Library of Congress Subject Headings (LCSH), 2, 179, 269-71, 274-78, 283
learning, 56, 66, 79, 108-9, 114, 185, 194, 211, 254, 261, 285, 294-5, 317-8, 323
see also education
active, 76-78, 106-8, 109, 117, 168, 271, 281
affective dimension of, 5, 42, 316
collaborative, 164, 173, 194, 257, 302, 308, 315, 317
and empowerment, 20, 42
equitable, 205, 207
facilitation of (at the reference desk), 21, 78, 81
feminist educational approach to, 73, 300
feminist pedagogy and, 123, 257, 261-3, 303
and LibGuides, 303, 308
lifelong, 206, 324
participatory, 166, 177
peer, 190, 192-5, 199
LibGuides, 231, 293-310
Library of Congress, 131-2, 274, 276, 284, 287
Libstats, 65, 69

microaggressions, 226-8, 235-6, 239, 247-8, 332, 356

Name Authority Cooperative Program (NACO), 274
narrative[s], 61-2, 74, 108, 166, 175-6, 178-9, 185, 195, 197, 321
dominant, 181, 183, 271, 355
oppressed, 177, 180, 182, 183
personal, 7, 303
National Alliance for Partnerships in Equity (NAPE), 215
neoliberalism, 56, 58, 317
neutrality, 47-53, 55-7, 304, 356
and feminist reference in the academic library, 47-49, 55, 56
and librarians, 37, 51, 57, 58, 207

395

oppression[s], 140, 170, 185, 206, 247-8, 304, 361
   institutional, 57, 177-8, 184
   and librarians, 207, 226
   of women and marginalized peoples, 48, 124, 178, 332

patriarchy, 37, 124, 142, 248, 372-3
pedagogy[ies], 41, 138, 279
   critical, 6, 65, 142, 186, 265, 270-72, 294, 344
   feminist, 7, 110-13, 183, 189, 269, 272-3, 309, 357
      classroom based on, 254, 256-66, 315
      and empowerment, 17, 19, 200, 256, 293
      interacting with reference, 1, 8, 20, 41, 108
      and LibGuides, 294-5, 297
      and the library profession, 105, 217, 253, 258, 334
      and Margaret Fuller, 120, 123-26, 128-30, 133
      principles of, 177, 255, 285, 297, 302
      and PRN's, 190, 192, 194, 199-201
      and the reference desk, 321, 323-4, 329, 343, 344, 348, 350, 354-57, 360-62
      strategies of, 5, 216
   and the reference desk, 170, 175
   and special collections reference, 161, 164, 166, 168-9, 173
play (as learning), 107-9, 117
policy[ies], 49, 77, 163, 170, 173, 208-9, 216, 235, 246, 263, 302
   egalitarian, 161, 171
   and student workers, 323, 327-8, 336-7
   public, 77-8, 338
politics, 47, 80, 124,178, 206
privilege, 55, 57, 92, 127, 140, 142, 184, 262-4, 266, 272, 277, 379-80
Peer Research Navigators (PRN), 189-90, 192, 194-5, 197-201

racism, 57, 115, 131, 123, 226, 228, 234, 244-5, 247-8, 356
Race, Gender, and Sexuality (RGS), 253-55, 258-60, 262-3
Reference Effort Assessment Data (READ), 144, 349
Reference & User Services Association (RUSA), 28, 33, 34, 48-50, 53, 54, 167, 191-93
Guidelines for Behavioral Performance of Reference and Information Service Providers, 28, 48
reference interviews, 50, 53-6, 61-2, 117, 132, 141, 150, 193, 196-7, 243, 329-30
   and ALA guidelines, 34, 37
   and archives, 162, 166
   and feminist pedagogical values, 112, 115
   need for empathy, compassion, and ethic of care, 50, 80, 81, 109
   traditional, 149, 346

social justice, 9-10, 52, 116, 127-8
   and feminist pedagogy, 123, 128
   library's role in, 52-3, 56
source[s], 49, 54, 78-81, 106, 141, 149, 172, 176-7, 191, 196, 270, 283, 299, 304, 349
   archival, 280-82
   evaluation of, 176, 332
   librarians as guides to, 199, 294, 328, 352, 357
   and library search tools, 198, 294
   primary, 2, 164, 177, 186, 270, 272, 273, 281, 282
   scholarly, 197, 201, 353
   secondary, 270, 272, 277, 283
status quo, 57-8, 66, 173, 181, 185, 200, 296, 360, 373
student reference assistants, 325-6, 331-5, 338-9
Strengths, Weaknesses, Opportunities, Threats (SWOT) analysis, 147, 154
survey[s], 146, 148, 229, 235

universal design, 313-5
user experience (UX), 167-8, 173, 274

value[s], 63, 75, 86, 112-3, 116-7, 140, 147, 205-6, 242, 248, 261, 313-4, 351

Wikipedia, 47, 181

www.ingramcontent.com/pod-product-compliance
Lightning Source LLC
Chambersburg PA
CBHW070805300426
44111CB00014B/2431